All About the Details:
Room by Room

A Collection of LEGO® Mini-builds   By Chris Schroeder

All About the Details:
Room by Room
A Collection of LEGO® Mini-builds
Copyright © 2025

Hand-drawn arrow collection "Designed by alicia_mb / Freepik.com". Hand-drawn speech bubble doodles, water splashes, soap bubbles - "Designed by www.Freepik.com". "Everyone is Awesome" (Set 40516) minifigure conga line image - ©LEGO.com. Xtras sticker sheet image - ©2019 The LEGO Group. Exploded views and instructions were generated with the Stud.io program available at Bricklink.com. Some custom printed imagery from www.CitizenBrick.com, Firestartoys.com, OneMoreBrick.com.

Published by Chris Schroeder
Edited by Chris Schroeder, Jesse Byrd
Cover Art by Chris Schroeder

ISBN: 979-8-9927235-0-2 (paperback)
ISBN: 979-8-9927235-1-9 (eBook)
ISBN: 979-8-9927235-2-6 (hardcover)

Library of Congress Control Number: 2025904540

TABLE OF CONTENTS

Acknowledgments

To Jesse, the main designer, thank you for your brilliant mind. Without your unique design style and willingness to partner together, this book would not have been made.

To my friends and family who encouraged me to pursue this idea to fruition, thank you. Especially, Joey Lewis, my local used LEGO® store owner for your support. Visit "Madhouse of Bricks" in Jeffersonville, IN!

Thank you to Nick Playforth and Matt Amos for all your critical reviews and invaluable non-AFOL feedback.

Finally, thank you to my wife, Kristi, who allows me to pursue this intensive, time-consuming, and expensive hobby.

Preface from the Author

Have you ever gotten "builder's block" (kind-of like "writer's block") while designing a MOC? Maybe you just finished a building, but it's empty. What are you going to fill the space with? Maybe you've expended all your thoughts and energy in the architecture, the layout, and design of the MOC and now you just need some neccessary detail to bring the whole thing to life.

Wouldn't it be great if someone collected a bunch of small builds together so you could see all the different ways designers have built simple, everyday things - like couches, beds, refrigerators, tables, and chairs?

That was my inspiration behind this book.

This book is all about the details...and we're going room by room to provide you with a plethora of pretty designs! The original idea behind this book was an ambitious effort to catalog every single mini build within official LEGO® sets along with community designs. In the end, the book would've wound up an endless encyclopedia. Instead, I found a couple of very talented designers. I collated and organized their designs into this visual catalog brochure and inspirational reference guide.

Most current LEGO® books target a young audience. They are overly simple and geared for all ages. This book is aimed at AFOLs and does not include step-by-step building instructions in the back of the book. Instead, I take a unque, exploded-view technique and leave it up to you, the AFOL (or TFOL), to piece it together. I also omit instructions for very simple builds where you can just look at them and tell how they are built. I hope you welcome the new compact format and appreciate the intellectual challenge.

After all, great design often thinks outside the brick!

HOW TO USE THE
FRONT HALF OF THIS BOOK

Browse the <u>Visual Catalog</u> of designs in each household room by chapter for inspiration. Keep an open mind. Several designs can work in multiple or different rooms.

DESIGNS ARE IN THIS FORMAL FONT.

TABLE LAMPS

CARROT LAMP (PAGE ███)

ACORN LAMP (PAGE ███)

SMALL LAMPS (PAGE ███)

Is that a Carrot?! <u>Yes, it is.</u> See how these things are made starting on page ███.

LAVA LAMP

DESK LAMPS

(Page #) points to the parts list and instructions in the back.

No (Page #) indicates that the simple design can be built visually from here.

(PAGE ███)   (PAGE ███)   (PAGE ███)   (PAGE ███)

Just two pieces, but BRILLIANT design!

The same chapter colors in the front half match the back half.

PAGE ██

INDOOR LIGHTING

There are various icons found throughout this book. Here is the legend.

⚠ Warning <u>"Illegal" technique</u>! If you are a stickler for rules, look away. This design uses non-conventional building methods, which may or may not bother you.

🔍 Design uses <u>hard to find</u> piece(s).

Check out this <u>official</u> <u>LEGO® set</u> for <u>more design</u> <u>references</u>.

Look at this cool scene for <u>inspiration</u>. No how-to provided, but isn't it awesome?

HOW TO USE THE
BACK HALF OF THIS BOOK

Flip to the back for select <u>Instructions and Parts Lists</u>. Back here you will find more detailed views and clues on how to build some designs.

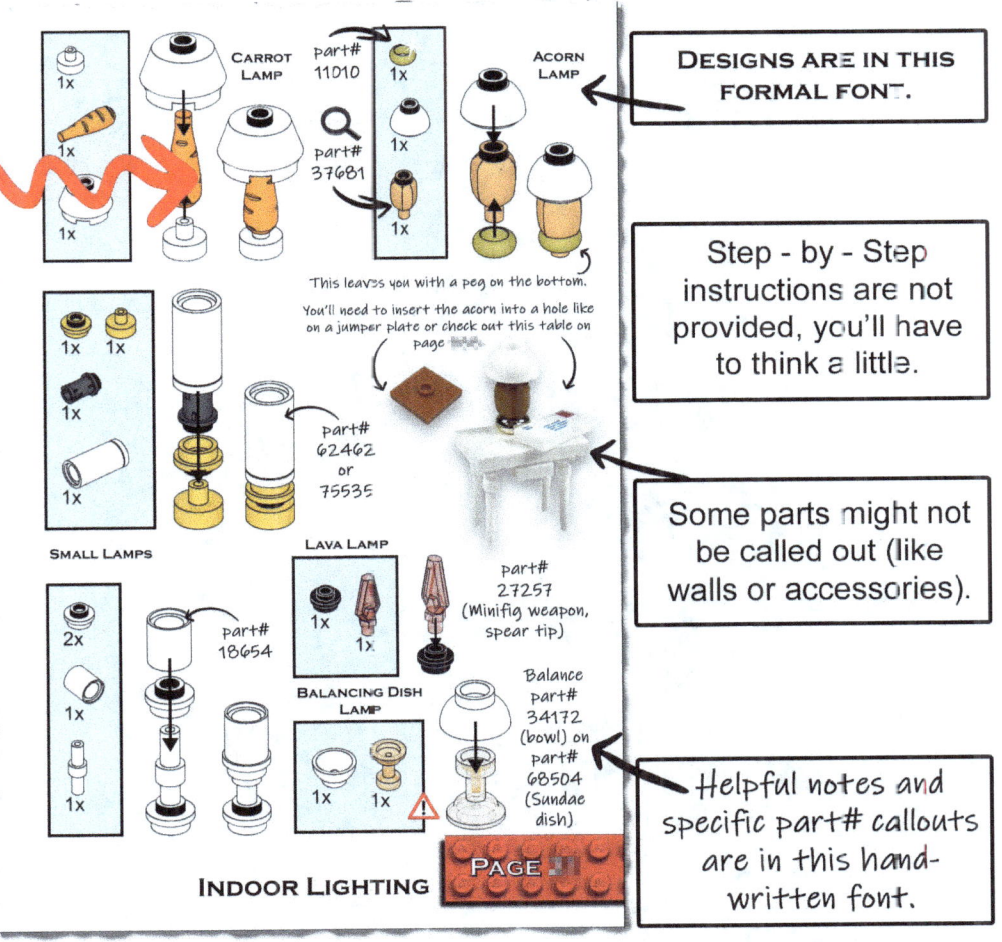

CARROT LAMP — part# 11010 — 1x

ACORN LAMP — part# 37681 — 1x

This leaves you with a peg on the bottom.
You'll need to insert the acorn into a hole like on a jumper plate or check out this table on page [xx].

part# 62462 or 75535

SMALL LAMPS

LAVA LAMP — part# 18654

part# 27257 (Minifig weapon, spear tip)

BALANCING DISH LAMP

Balance part# 34172 (bowl) on part# 68504 (Sundae dish)

INDOOR LIGHTING   PAGE [1]

DESIGNS ARE IN THIS FORMAL FONT.

Step - by - Step instructions are not provided, you'll have to think a little.

Some parts might not be called out (like walls or accessories).

Helpful notes and specific part# callouts are in this hand-written font.

Remember, more designs exist in the front half. Don't spend too much time flipping through the back thinking that's all there is! On y complex designs are back here. Simple designs in the front can be effective too.

Also, don't let names or chapter placement stifle your creativity. Imagine these designs in different rooms in your MOC.

Lastly, be creative. Don't just copy these designs. Swap colors, sub-stitute parts for what you have, and add accessories for more detail. After all, it's <u>**All About the Details!**</u>

1. Indoor Lighting

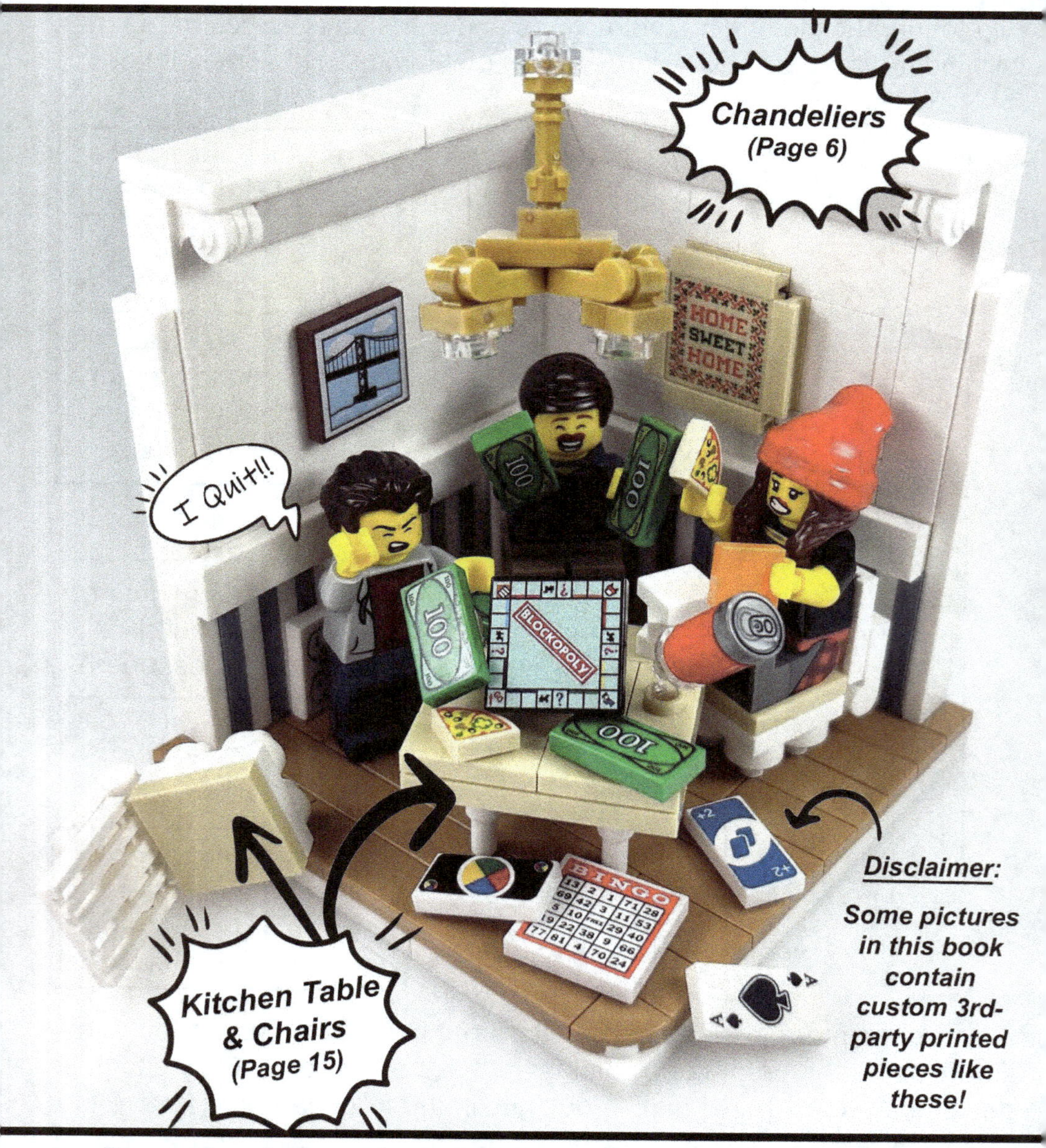

Chandeliers (Page 6)
HOME SWEET HOME
I Quit!!
BLOCKOPOLY
100
BINGO
Kitchen Table & Chairs (Page 15)
Disclaimer:
Some pictures in this book contain custom 3rd-party printed pieces like these!

From simple two piece desk lamps to complex chandeliers, lighting is a necessity for every home that is instantly recognizable in LEGO®. Minimal, yet effective, the following designs can be used in any room or added to any scene.

FANCY TABLE LAMPS

(PAGE 83)

(PAGE 83)

SPYGLASS LAMPS

Imperial Guard Shako hat from Eldorado Fortress (LEGO® set #6276), first seen in 1989.

BOTTLE LAMPS

(PAGE 83)

LAMPS USING UTENSILS

SALT LAMP

INDOOR LIGHTING

PAGE 2

TABLE LAMPS

Is that a Carrot?! *Yes, it is.* See how these things are made starting on page 83.

CARROT LAMP (PAGE 84)

ACORN LAMP (PAGE 84)

SMALL LAMPS (PAGE 84)

LAVA LAMP

DESK LAMPS

(PAGE 85) (PAGE 85) (PAGE 85) (PAGE 85)

Just two pieces, but BRILLIANT design!

PAGE 3

INDOOR LIGHTING

FUTURISTIC LAMPS
(PAGE 85)

(PAGE 86)

ADJUSTABLE LAMPS

(PAGE 86)

TALL FLOOR LAMPS
(PAGE 86)

(PAGE 86)

UNIQUE FLOOR LAMPS

(PAGES 86 - 87)

PAGE 4

INDOOR LIGHTING

Diamond Gems

WALL SCONCES

BATHROOM VANITIES

Outdoor?
(Page 77)

TRACK LIGHTING

**BUILT-IN WALL
LIGHTS
(PAGE 87)**

INDOOR LIGHTING

2. WINDOW DRESSINGS

Opposite
Page

→

Naked windows, oh no! Your building may look nice from the outside, but what about the view for the poor minifigures inside? Dressing up the windows elevates the level of detail inside each room. It's all about the details. They bring your creation to life!

WINDOW DRESSINGS

um, meow.

BLINDS & SHADES
(PAGE 88)

These pulled up shades can be adapted into a window AC unit by using grey bricks, removing the stick, and flipping it to the bottom.

These vertical blinds are created by dangling long tiles snapped into clips at the top.

Green Grocer (set #10185) has a luxurious red curtain window dressing.

VERTICAL BLINDS
(PAGE 89)

WINDOW DRESSINGS

CURTAINS
(PAGE 89)

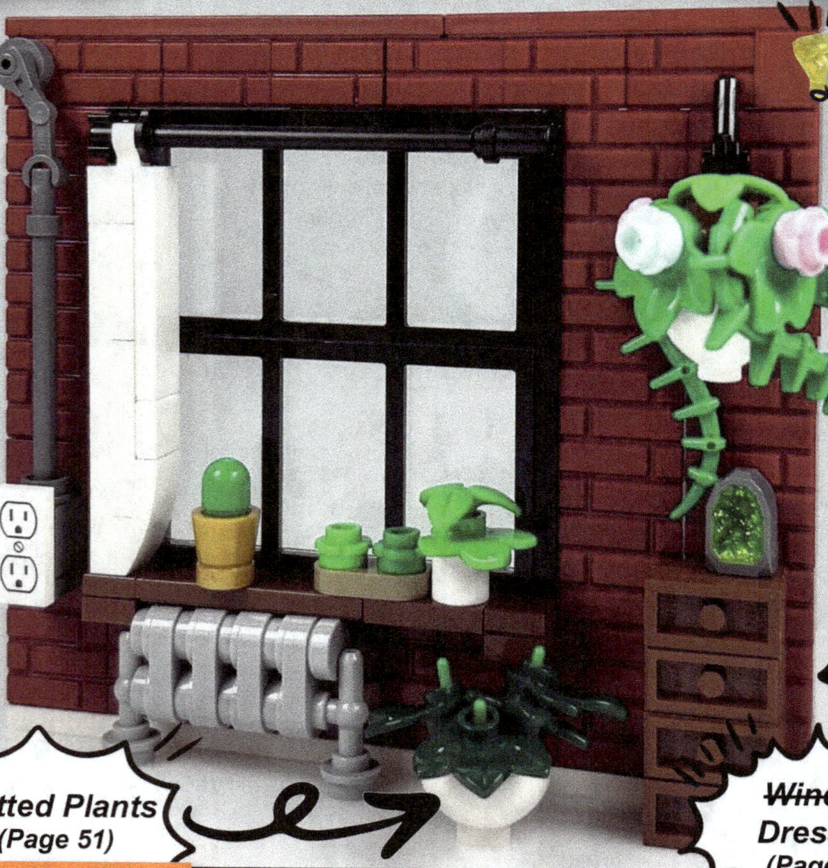

Potted Plants
(Page 51)

~~*Window*~~
Dressers
(Page 35)

WINDOW DRESSINGS

3. THE FOYER

"Foyer", "Mudroom", "Entryway" - Whatever you call it, this is the first thing you see when you enter your humble cammode.
Hang your hat, drop your keys, and toss your mail down.
Unwind and relax.
Welcome home.

THE FOYER

ENTRYWAY BENCH AND COAT RACK (PAGE 90)

CONSOLE DESK AND TABLE (PAGE 90)

This Lamp (Page 84)

HAT RACKS

NEWSPAPER RACK

THE LEGO NEWS

My hands!

PAGE 11

THE FOYER

4. KITCHEN & DINING

The heart and soul of every house - The Kitchen.

In this chapter you'll find everything pictured above _including_ the kitchen sink.

(Look in Bathrooms on _page 23_ for more sinks!) Additionally, you can check The Living Room chapter on _page 39_ for other furniture that could also work in the kitchen.

CABINETS AND COUNTERTOPS

Panels make great shelves & cubbies.

Try these parts:

Windows can be re-purposed as cabinets or as supports underneath countertops.

They add depth and interest!

KITCHEN & DINING

KITCHEN SINKS
(PAGE 91)

Part# 99563 "gold bar" ingot in sand blue.

KITCHEN ISLAND
(PAGE 92)

SMALL TABLE AND CHAIR
(PAGE 92)

This Fridge
(Page 103)

This crate (part#30150) is placed on it's side and a 2x3 tile is attached loosely on one side to give the appearance of a hinged cabinet.

Appliances
(In this chapter)

LOWER CABINETS
(PAGE 91)

KITCHEN & DINING

ROUND TABLE & HORNY CHAIRS
(PAGE 92)

WOODEN TABLE & RECLINED CHAIRS (PAGE 93)

INDUSTRIAL TABLE & CHAIRS (PAGE 93)

TAN TABLE & CHAIRS

FANCY CHAIR (PAGE 92)

part#87580pr0001

KITCHEN & DINING

**TAN TABLE &
SLIDING CHAIRS**
(PAGE 93)

**ISLAND BAR &
BAR STOOLS**
(PAGE 93)

⚠ Round 1x2
plates friction
fit under chair

**WOOD SLAB TABLE &
SNOWSHOE CHAIRS**
(PAGE 94)

**BOOMERANG TABLE &
TALL FANCY CHAIRS**
(PAGE 94)

⚠

**FARMHOUSE TABLE
& CHAIRS
WITH BENCH**
(PAGES 94 - 95)

Look close. How is that done?
(Page 95)

KITCHEN & DINING

**TAN CHINA
DISPLAY
CABINET
(PAGE 96)**

**MID-CENTURY
MODERN HUTCH
(PAGE 95)**

**FANCY TEA
DISPLAY CABINET
(PAGES 97 - 98)**

**FARMHOUSE
STYLE PANTRY
(PAGE 100)**

**ANTIQUE
HUTCH
(PAGES 98 - 99)**

KITCHEN & DINING

**FRIDGES WITH
ICE DISPENSERS
(PAGES 100 - 101)**

**SINGLE DOOR
REFRIGERATOR
(PAGE 101)**

**FRENCH DOORS
& BOTTOM
FREEZERS
(PAGES 101 - 102)**

**GLASS CHILLER
(PAGE 102)**

**RETRO FRIDGES
(PAGE 103)**

**MODERN FRIDGE
(PAGE 103)**

KITCHEN & DINING

ELECTRIC RANGES
(PAGE 104)

Part#98138pb088
1x1 round tile with egg
pattern

OVENS
(PAGE 104)

DOUBLE COOKTOP
(PAGE 105)

GAS STOVES
(PAGES 105 - 106)

KITCHEN & DINING

KEURIG BREWER
(PAGE 106)

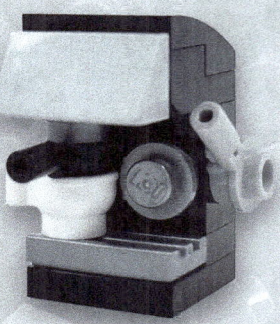

ESPRESSO MACHINE
(PAGE 106)

(PAGE 106)

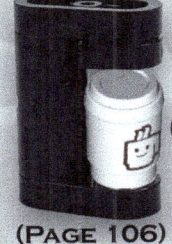

(PAGE 106)

COFFEE

COFFEE MAKERS

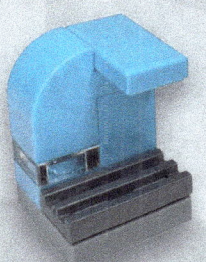

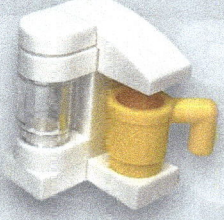

(PAGE 106)

DWIGHT, SAM

Do NOT drink
the coffee

FUTURE DWIGHT

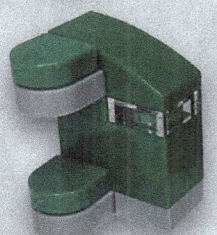

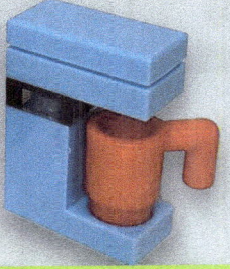

PAGE 20

KITCHEN & DINING

BLENDERS

Part #4274 (Technic pin) & #18654 (Technic round spacer) stuck together.

TOASTER (PAGE 107)

*www.FirestarToys.com

POPCORN MACHINE

MICROWAVES (PAGE 107)

Part #65700

BIRTHDAY CAKE

MIXER

ROLLING PIN

Neat kitchen in set# 10243 (Parisian Restaurant)

Part #60208

KITCHEN & DINING

5. BATHROOMS

Showers and Bathtubs (Pages 24-25)

Toilets (Page 26)

Sinks and Vanities (Page 23)

"Shut the door, some privacy please!"

Every house has to have one - That's why it's called the "Necessary Room".
Space is usually constrained for the bathroom, so designs can get tight.
Get those white pieces ready and don't forget the chocolate icing. :D

BATHROOMS

SINGLE
VANITY SINKS
(PAGE 108)

All Monsters
MUST Wash
Hands!

FANCY
PEDESTAL
SINK
(PAGE 108)

PEDESTAL SINK
(PAGE 108)

BATHROOMS

WALK-IN
SHOWERS
(PAGES 109-111)

Space-saving
Corner design!

Nice "ugly"
color!

BUILT-IN TUB SHOWER
(PAGE 111)

BATHROOMS

PAGE 24

BUILT-IN SHOWER (PAGE 112)

LARGE JACUZZI TUB (PAGE 113)

PINK SHOWER/TUB COMBO (PAGE 113)

Optional Accessory to this tub!

SOAKING TUBS (PAGE 115)

SINGLE BATHTUB (PAGE 114)

BATHROOMS

TOILETS
(PAGES 115-117)

Part# 3822 (car door) turned on it's side makes TP coming off the roll.

FLUSH HANDLE TOILETS
(PAGE 116)

Part# 64847 (cattle horn)

Bucket handles are handy holders!

PLUNGERS & PAPER ROLLS

KIDDIE POTTIES

OLD GREEN TOILET
(PAGE 116)

Ninjago® City Markets (set# 71799) has a working 'flushable' toilet!

STORM POOPER
(PAGE 116)

NEWSPAPER RACK

THE LEGO NEWS

TOILET & ROLL HOLDERS
(PAGE 116)

"I can't cram any more crap on this page!"

BATHROOMS

6. BEDROOMS

Bookshelves are found
in Ch.8 - The Study
(Page 62)

Dressers
(Page 35)

All kinds of Beds!
(Kids, Bunk, Single,
Double, Four-Post)
(Kids start on next Page)

Nightstands
(Page 34)

Closets and
Storage
(Page 38)

Boomerang + Hook
= clothes hanger

Even one simple piece in
the right setting can
represent something!

This is your personal space.
Aside from sleeping half of your life away in this room, this is
your minifigure's personal canvas. Decorate it with plenty of
accessories. Check out Ch.8 - The Study (p.56) for more furniture.

BEDROOMS

HIS & HERS TODDLER BUNK
(PAGE 117)

LEGO® Juniors or Duplo® parts can make builds interesting

KIDS RACE CAR BED *

Part# 27925pb001 (rainbow tile)

KIDS RAINBOW BED WITH STORAGE (PAGE 118)

KIDS BED (PAGE 118)

Pillows are "loose"

DAY BED (PAGE 119)

* Available at www.brickdesigned.com

BEDROOMS

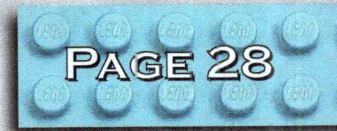

PAGE 28

TWIN BUNK
BEDS
(PAGES 119-120)

PIPE IRON BUNK BED
(PAGE 121)

LOFT WITH
PLAYSPACE
UNDERNEATH
(PAGE 121)

WOODEN
BUNK BED
(PAGE 122)

PRISON BUNK

PAGE 29

BEDROOMS

Door Head-board Bed (Page 123)

Single Panel Beds (Pages 123 - 124)

Metal Iron Single Bed (Page 124)

Try different colors!

Checker Bed With Storage (Page 125)

Single Beds (Pages 125 - 126)

12:00

Bedrooms

TRADITIONAL DOUBLE BED (PAGE 126)

CLASSIC PINE RAIL BED (PAGE 127)

KING-SIZED WATER BED (PAGE 127)

MODERN LARGE BED (PAGE 128)

JAIL DOOR BED (PAGE 129)

⚠ This headboard connection is "fragile"

BRIGHT COTTAGE DOUBLE QUEEN (PAGES 129 - 130)

OPEN-FRAME SLAT BED (PAGE 130)

BEDROOMS

MID-CENTURY
MODERN BED
(PAGE 131)

LARGE & COMFY
CABIN BED
(PAGE 132)

CONTEMPORARY
CURVED BED
(PAGE 132)

Pillows are
"loose"

WROUGHT
IRON BED
(PAGE 133)

Try making an
"unmade" bed.

OPEN-ENDED
PLATFORM BED
(PAGE 134)

MISSION-STYLE
KING BED
(PAGES 134 - 136)

BEDROOMS

4-POST CANOPY (PAGE 139)

ORNATE WOODEN 4-POST (PAGE 136)

Scrooge would love it!

EXOTIC 4-POST BED (PAGE 140)

MURPHY BED *

* Available at www.brickdesigned.com

BEDROOMS

NIGHT STANDS

NIGHT STANDS

NIGHT STANDS

(PAGE 141)

Goes great with the Kids Race Car Bed!

NIGHT STANDS

(PAGE 141)

(PAGE 141)

NIGHT STANDS

(PAGE 141)

(PAGE 141)

NIGHT STANDS

Check out End Tables (Page 44) for more ideas.

NIGHT STANDS

PAGE 34

BEDROOMS

ARMOIRES /
WARDROBES
(PAGE 142)

VANITY DRESSER
(PAGE 143)

END OF BED
OTTOMAN

⚠ Ice
skates!

ELEGANT
DRESSER
(PAGE 143)

BEDROOMS

LOW DRESSERS
(PAGE 144)

PLUSH BED BENCH
(PAGE 144)

Adding details like
accessories & clutter to
the tops of dressers
help bring them to life.

HIGH DRESSERS
(PAGES 144-145)

GREEN DRESSER
(PAGE 145)

LOW DRESSER CABINET
(PAGE 145)

BEDROOMS

FASHION
VANITY
(PAGE 146)

KIDS DRESSER
(PAGE 146)

DREAM
RIG

BLUE DRESSER SET
(PAGE 147)

Works for
Adults

Works for
Kids

TALL DRESSER
DRAWERS
(PAGE 148)

DRAWERS WITH
"HANDLES"
(PAGE 147)

STANDING
MIRROR

BEDROOMS

Bucket handles
friction fit inside
1x2 bricks

CLOSET SHELVING

SLIDING MIRROR DOOR CLOSET *

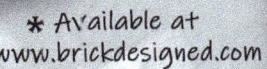

Torsos make great hanging shirts!

* Available at
www.brickdesigned.com

CLOSET STORAGE (PAGE 148)

SHOE DISPLAY (PAGE 149)

BEDROOMS

7. LIVING ROOM

Entertainment Centers (Page 47)

Couches, Loveseats, Chaises, & Armchairs (Pages 40 - 43)

Fireplaces (Pages 54 - 55)

Clocks (Page 50)

Potted Plants (Pages 51 - 53)

Coffee & End Tables (Pages 44 - 46)

TVs and Radios (Pages 48 - 50)

The Living Room...a place to...live?
Whether entertaining guests, opening Christmas gifts, napping in front of the boob tube, or just reading a good novel - it all takes place in this central hub for any home. How are your minifigs going to use it?

LIVING ROOM

**PULL OUT SOFA
(PAGE 149)**

Slides in

**MID-CENTURY
LOVE SEAT
(PAGE 150)**

⚠️

**CHESTERFIELD
SOFA
(PAGE 150)**

**DEEP CURVY
LEATHER SOFA
(PAGE 151)**

⚠️

**RED TUXEDO SOFA
(PAGE 151)**

This footstool
can also act as a
throw pillow!

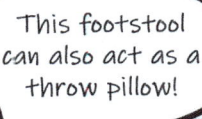

**ENGLISH ROLL ARM
(PAGE 152)**

**LEATHER
TUXEDO SOFA
(PAGE 152)**

LIVING ROOM

POP ART
LIPS COUCH
(PAGE 153)

⚠
Throw pillows
are loose.

🔍 *

* www.CitizenBrick.com

MID-CENTURY
MODERN COUCH
(PAGE 154)

WINGBACK
BRIDGEWATER SOFA
(PAGE 154)

SWOOP ARM
VELVET SOFA
(PAGE 155)

CHANNEL BACK
LAWSON COUCH
(PAGE 156)

CONTEMPORARY
LOVESEAT
(PAGE 155)

DAY BED /
CHAISE LOUNGE
(PAGE 156)

PAGE 41

LIVING ROOM

TIGHT BACK SOFAS WITH
CHAISE LOUNGES
(PAGE 157)

SECTIONAL SOFA
WITH RECLINER
(PAGE 158)

CORNER
SECTIONAL
(PAGE 159)

RECLINED VELVET
WINGBACK
ARM CHAIR
(PAGE 160)

MID-CENTURY
WINGBACK
ARM CHAIR
(PAGE 160)

WORKING
RECLINER
(PAGE 161)

LIVING ROOM

BUCKET ARM CHAIR
(PAGE 161)

ART DECO
SWIVEL CHAIR
(PAGE 162)

MODERN EASY CHAIR
(PAGE 162)

CAPTAIN'S
WINGBACK
ARM CHAIR
(PAGE 163)

ROLLED ARM
ACCENT CHAIR
(PAGE 163)

CHESTERFIELD
TUFTED
ARM CHAIR
(PAGE 162)

CLUB ARM CHAIR
(PAGE 164)

ANTIQUE SITTING CHAIR
(PAGE 164)

BARREL CHAIR
(PAGE 164)

LIVING ROOM

END TABLES
WITH LAMPS

These Lamps (Page 2)

END TABLES

Part# 80677

Jerry! You know the Night Stands on Page 34 could also be End Tables? Fascinating!

Part# 51283 Satin Trans-clear

(PAGE 165)

Potted Plants (Page 51) look nice on End Tables.

(PAGE 165)

THE COFFEE TABLE BOOK
COFFEE TABLES

⚠

END TABLES
WITH PLANTS

ELEGANT END TABLE
(PAGE 165)

(PAGE 165)

LIVING ROOM

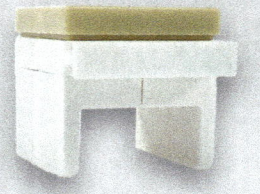

COFFEE TABLES

(PAGE 165)

(PAGE 165)

This chess board is a custom tile, but could easily be from a race flag sticker!

⚠️

⚠️

⚠️

⚠️

COFFEE TABLES

⚠️

(PAGE 165)

COFFEE TABLES

(PAGE 166)

⚠️

⚠️

ROUNDED LEG COFFEE TABLE

FOLDING TABLE

PAGE 45

LIVING ROOM

THICK WOODEN COFFEE TABLE (PAGE 166)

Free Pro TIP: A sure fire way to turn your accent table or ottoman into a coffee table is to add some ... "coffee" to it!

CHESTER TRUNK COFFEE TABLE

SOFA TABLE (PAGE 166)

Part# 61287 (2x2 cylinder)

MID-CENTURY COFFEE TABLE (PAGE 166)

COFFEE TABLES

(The sticker is from a LEGO® Xtras sticker sheet from 2019.)

Part# 2586 (Ovoid shield) These white & yellow parts are both found in set# 40747 (Daffodils).

CHIC COFFEE TABLES

Surf's up!

LIVING ROOM

(PAGE 167)

(PAGE 167)

ENTERTAINMENT CENTERS

(PAGE 167)

(PAGE 168)

ENTERTAINMENT CENTERS

(PAGE 168)

(PAGE 168)

ENTERTAINMENT CENTERS

(PAGE 169)

(PAGE 169)

ENTERTAINMENT CENTERS

(PAGE 169)

LIVING ROOM

TELEVISIONS

TELLIES

BOOB TUBES

IDIOT BOXES

PLASMAS & LCDS

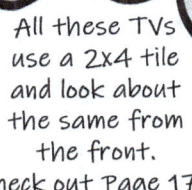

CORNER TV STAND*

LARGE MEDIA CENTERS (PAGES 170-171)

All these TVs use a 2x4 tile and look about the same from the front. Check out Page 172 to see all the neat ways they are connected in the back.

BIG SCREEN (3x6) TV (PAGE 172)

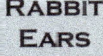

RABBIT EARS

SMALL (2x3) TV (PAGE 172)

*Available at www.OneMoreBrick.com

LIVING ROOM

Custom tile*

Part# 3070pb118

BUILT-IN STEREO CONSOLE

1950'S TV SET (PAGE 173)

CRT (TUBE) TELEVISION (PAGE 173)

Part# 3069pb0399

RECORD PLAYER (PAGE 174)

There are several options for vinyl records

PORTABLE RECORD PLAYER WITH RECORDS (PAGE 174)

Part# 26603pb185

AUDIO RACK WITH SPEAKERS (PAGE 175)

HAND CRANK PHONOGRAPH

LIVING ROOM

*Available at www.OneMoreBrick.com

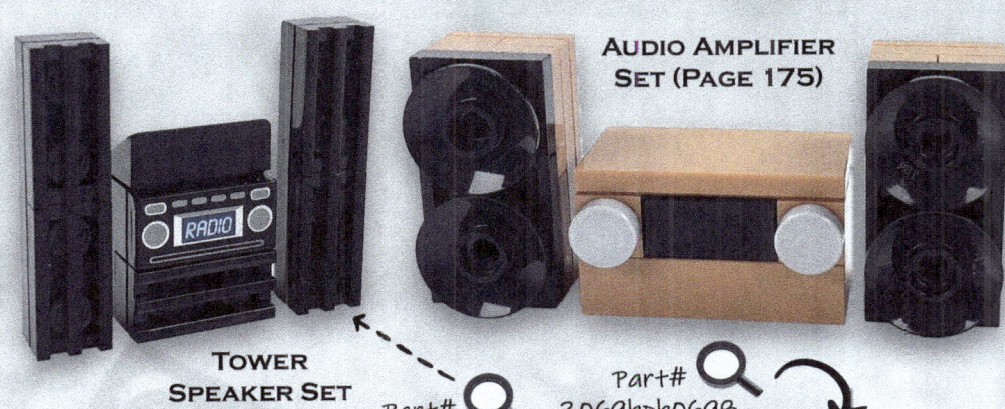

AUDIO AMPLIFIER SET (PAGE 175)

TOWER SPEAKER SET

Part# 3069pb0348

Part# 3069bpb0698

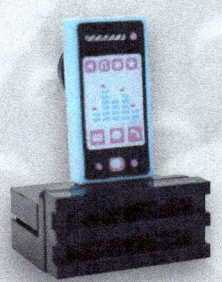

BLUETOOTH SPEAKER (PAGE 176)

MODERN RADIO

PHONE DOCK (PAGE 176)

MANTEL TIMEPIECE (PAGE 176)

GRAND GREAT-GRANDFATHER CLOCK (PAGE 177)

GRANDFATHER CLOCK (PAGE 177)

CLASSIC CAT CLOCK (PAGE 176)

GREAT-GRAND-FATHER CLOCK (PAGE 177)

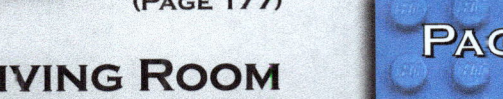

LIVING ROOM

SHINY PLANTER

🔍 Naboo Star-
fighter cone
(2002)

**BIG & TALL
PLANTERS
(PAGE 178)**

🔍 Part# 35709
(from Series 18)
Flowerpot
Girl

**HELMET
PLANTER
(PAGE 178)**

Whoops...
Dead!

**POTTED
PLANT STANDS
(PAGE 179)**

**LARGE PLANTER
(PAGE 179)**

WATERING CANS

**BUSHY BARREL
(PAGE 179)**

PAGE 51

LIVING ROOM

SMALL STARTER PLANTS

Egg

Helmet

SMALL PLANT POTS

FLOWER VASES (PAGE 180)

Green hands!

Part# 51283 (Satin trans-clear fishbowl)

BONSAI TREE

LITTLE PLANTER

Got a broken bamboo leaf? Don't throw them away!

Look at these creative ways to reuse those broken pieces.

BROKEN BAMBOO IDEAS

LIVING ROOM

Is that a Chia head?!

INDOOR PLANT DISPLAY SHELVES (PAGE 180)

HANGING PLANTS (PAGE 181)

LARGE POTTED PLANTS (PAGE 181)

MEDIUM POTTED PLANTS (PAGE 182)

PLANTER BENCHES (PAGE 182)

CORNER PLANT SHELF

LIVING ROOM

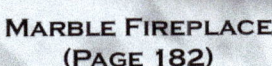

It's all about the details...
These small parts can be picture frames!

MARBLE FIREPLACE
(PAGE 182)

Flames sit loosely
inside window
frames.

ELEGANT MODERN
GAS FIREPLACE
(PAGE 183)

RADIATOR
(PAGE 183)

SPACE
HEATERS
(PAGE 184)

STONE FIREPLACE

LIVING ROOM

FREE-STANDING
WOOD STOVE
(PAGE 185)

STUCCO
FIREPLACE
(PAGES
186-187)

CLASSIC FIREPLACE
(PAGES 185-186)

STONE
FIREPLACE
WITH WOOD
MANTEL
(PAGES
188-189)

Notice here how plates and tiles are used to simulate the texture of stone.

Placement of tile seams can be an important detail.

DOUBLE-SIDED
FIREPLACE
(PAGES 187-188)

LIVING ROOM

8. THE STUDY

Antiques
(Page 63)

Bookshelves
(Page 62)

Bars &
Credenzas
(Page 60)

Computers,
Desks, & Chairs
(Pages 57 - 59)

Curio Cabinets
(Page 61)

"I have several leather-bound books that smell of..rich mahogany."
Anyway, that's not important. What I'm trying to say is, this chap-
ter is all about the Study. A gentlemanly space for curiosities,
knowledge, stuff, scotch, and
(maybe a home office).

IKEA DESKS
(PAGES 189-190)

ANTIQUE
WRITING DESK
(PAGE 189)

EXECUTIVE DESK
(PAGE 191)

SLEEK BLACK DESK
(PAGE 190)

SMALL DESK
(PAGE 191)

DRAFTING DESKS
(PAGE 192)

Dragon
tile (Part#
26603pb006)

Spaceship
tile (Part#
26603pb076)

PAGE 57

THE STUDY

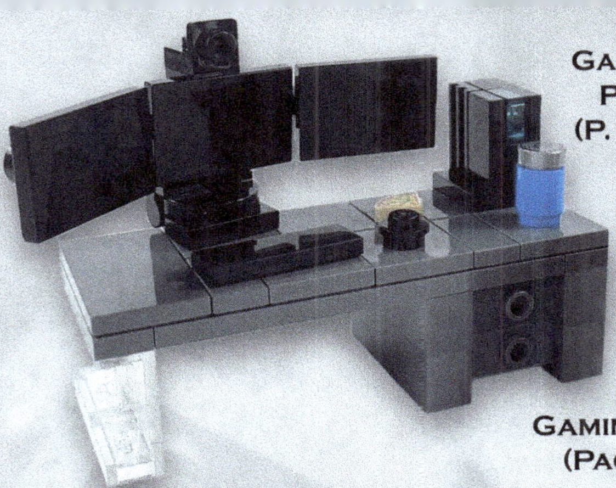

GAMING PCs (P. 192)

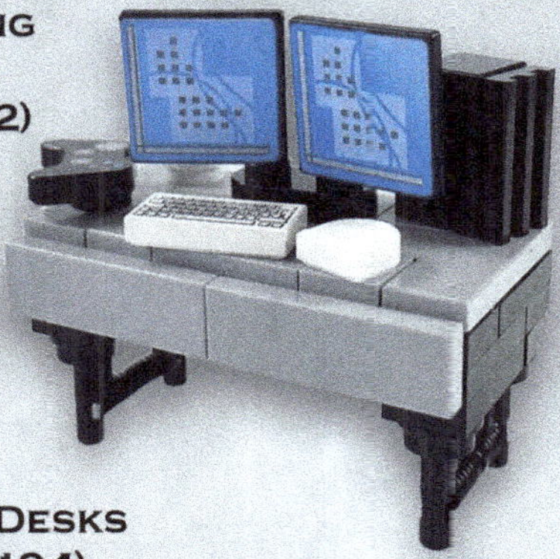

GAMING DESKS (PAGE 194)

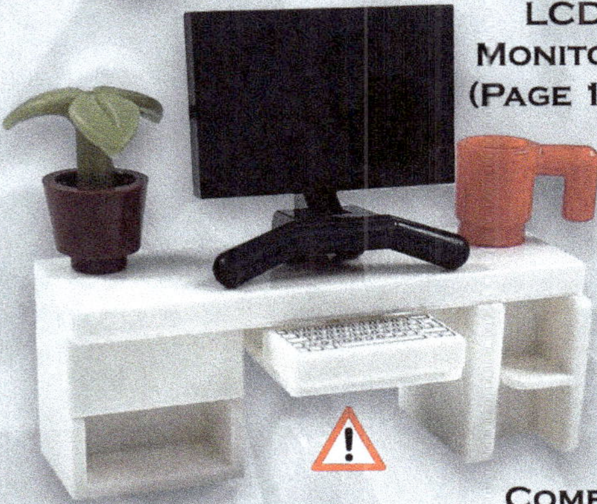

LCD MONITORS (PAGE 172)

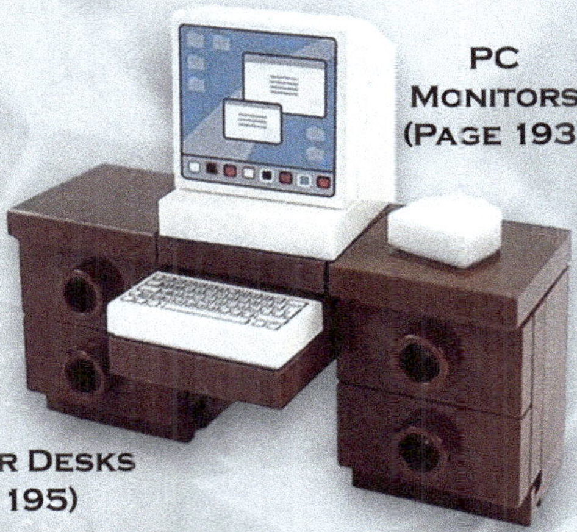

PC MONITORS (PAGE 193)

COMPUTER DESKS (PAGE 195)

MODERN COMPUTER

Keyboard tile (Part# 3069pb0030)

THE STUDY

PILOT'S CHAIR
(PAGE 195)

CAPTAIN'S CHAIR
(PAGE 196)

ANTIQUE
3-LEG CHAIR
(PAGE 196)

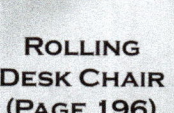

ROLLING
DESK CHAIR
(PAGE 196)

SWIVEL
DESK CHAIR
(PAGE 198)

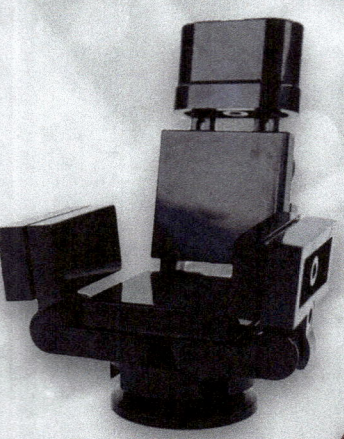

EXECUTIVE
DESK CHAIR
(PAGE 198)

GAMING CHAIR I
(PAGE 197)

GAMING CHAIR II
(PAGE 197)

THE STUDY

DRY BAR
(PAGE 199)

BEVERAGE CART
(PAGE 199)

SIDEBOARD / BUFFET
(PAGE 200)

MCM CREDENZA
(PAGE 200)

A Personal Full
Wet Bar!

THE STUDY

Part# 26603pb095

LOW CURIO CABINET
(PAGE 201)

KNICK KNACK CABINET
(PAGE 201)

Part#
49656pb01
(Geode)

CURIO CABINET
(PAGE 202)

Part#
98138pb025
(Fossil)

THE
COLLECTOR'S BOOKCASE
(PAGES 202-203)

DISPLAY CASE

DISPLAY SHELVES
(PAGE 203)

THE STUDY

Radio tile
(Part#
3069pb0348)

**WHITE
BOOKSHELVES
(PAGES 204
- 205)**

NASA statue
(Part#
90398pb008)

"Books" are
made with 1x2 tiles
shoved together or 1x2
"door rail" plates to make
the book stick out.

**KIDS
BOOK
SHELF**

There's two
interesting methods to
reverse stud direction
in this mode!

**REGAL
BOOKSHELF
(PAGES 205-206)**

**STATELY
BOOKSHELF
(PAGES
207-208)**

THE STUDY

Part# 4346px5 (Safe door)

ANTIQUE SAFE (PAGE 208)

OLD TRUNK (PAGE 208)

ANTIQUE SEWING MACHINE (PAGE 209)

Speed Champions Wheel Rim Part# 18978b

DESK FAN

DESK FAN

Part# 61287c01pb03 (Globe)

ANTIQUE GLOBES (PAGE 209)

PLASTER BUST

Globes may be loose.

PAGE 63

THE STUDY

9. LAUNDRY & UTILITIES

Washers and Dryers (Page 65)

Vacuums (Page 66)

LOST DOG

LOVE IS LOVE

OPEN

AWESOME

Ironing Board (Page 66)

Roombas (Page 66)

Wash later. Dry tomorrow. Fold next week. Vacuuming sucks. You want to add some realism to your scenes? - make them dirty! (not that way ;) Real life is a mess. Place some dirty clothes, dishes, clutter around your house. Lego looks too clean by default.

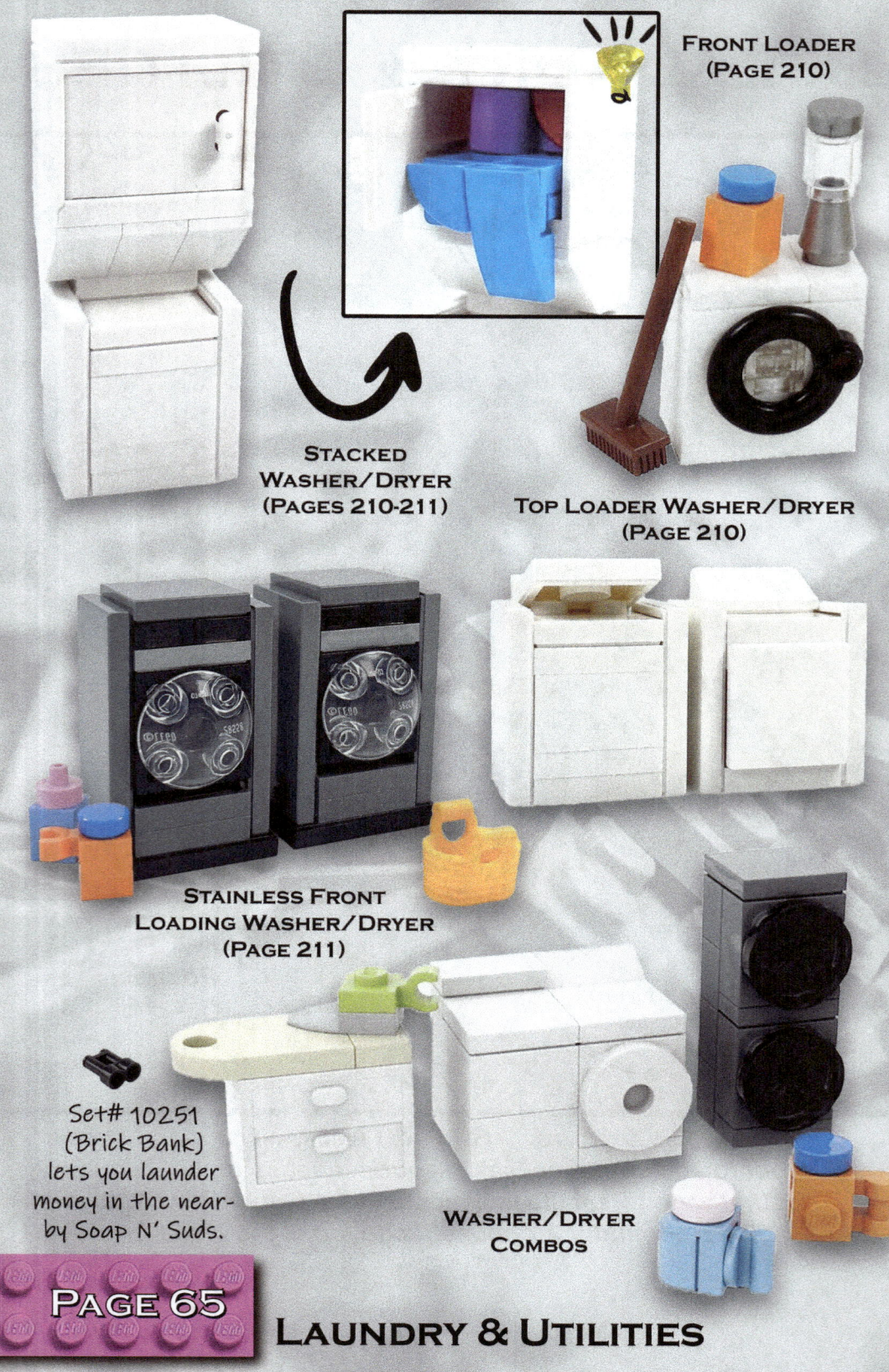

FRONT LOADER
(PAGE 210)

STACKED
WASHER/DRYER
(PAGES 210-211)

TOP LOADER WASHER/DRYER
(PAGE 210)

STAINLESS FRONT
LOADING WASHER/DRYER
(PAGE 211)

Set# 10251
(Brick Bank)
lets you launder
money in the near-
by Soap N' Suds.

WASHER/DRYER
COMBOS

PAGE 65

LAUNDRY & UTILITIES

IRONING BOARD
(PAGE 211)

VACUUMS
(PAGE 212)

VACUUMS
(PAGE 212)

ROOMBAS

Part#
X1608
(Tommy gun)

Roman crest
headpiece from
2013 (Part#
12886pb01)

LAUNDRY & UTILITIES

10. The Basement

Water Heater
(Page 69)

The Man Cave
(This Chapter)

Pool Tables
(Page 68)

Junk and Stuff
(Page 69)

Ping Pong &
Foosball
(Page 68)

You either love it or you're afraid of it - The Basement!
If you're lucky enough to own one, they can be a great, cool place
to store stuff, hang out, tuck away utilities, or escape a storm.
Finished basements can be super-rad, while unfinished ones end
up in horror movies.

THE BASEMENT

POOL TABLES

All three of these are built very differently. (Check it out in the back!)

TAN/RED POOL TABLE (PAGE 214)

BLACK/BLUE POOL TABLE (PAGE 213)

(A little cheat for this photo): "That's a cake sprinkle!"

BROWN/GREEN POOL TABLE (PAGE 215)

PING PONG TABLE (PAGE 216)

FOOSBALL TABLE (PAGE 216)

THE BASEMENT

PAGE 68

WATER HEATER
(PAGE 217)

1. 98374pb03
2. 32474pb009
3. 93220pb01
4. 1621pb01
5. 3069pb0718
6. Series 20 Athlete
7. 57753-pb01

There are a lot of rare minifigure accessories in these pics, but substitute your own clutter for your build!

www.FirestarToys.com

Stickers

Part# 14769-pb024

www.CitizenBrick.com

TROPHY CASE
(PAGE 217)

THE BASEMENT

11. THE GARAGE

Shop Tools
(Pages 71 - 72)

Workbenches
(Page 71)

Sports &
Storage
(Page 72)

Trash Bins
(Page 72)

Mowers &
Tractors
(Page 73)

So much more than just an enclosed structure to store your motor vehicle, for many, the garage creates an extension to your dwelling. A place to store big stuff, seasonal items, bicycles, sporting goods, recreation, camping, hobbies, tools...How do your minifigs use this space?

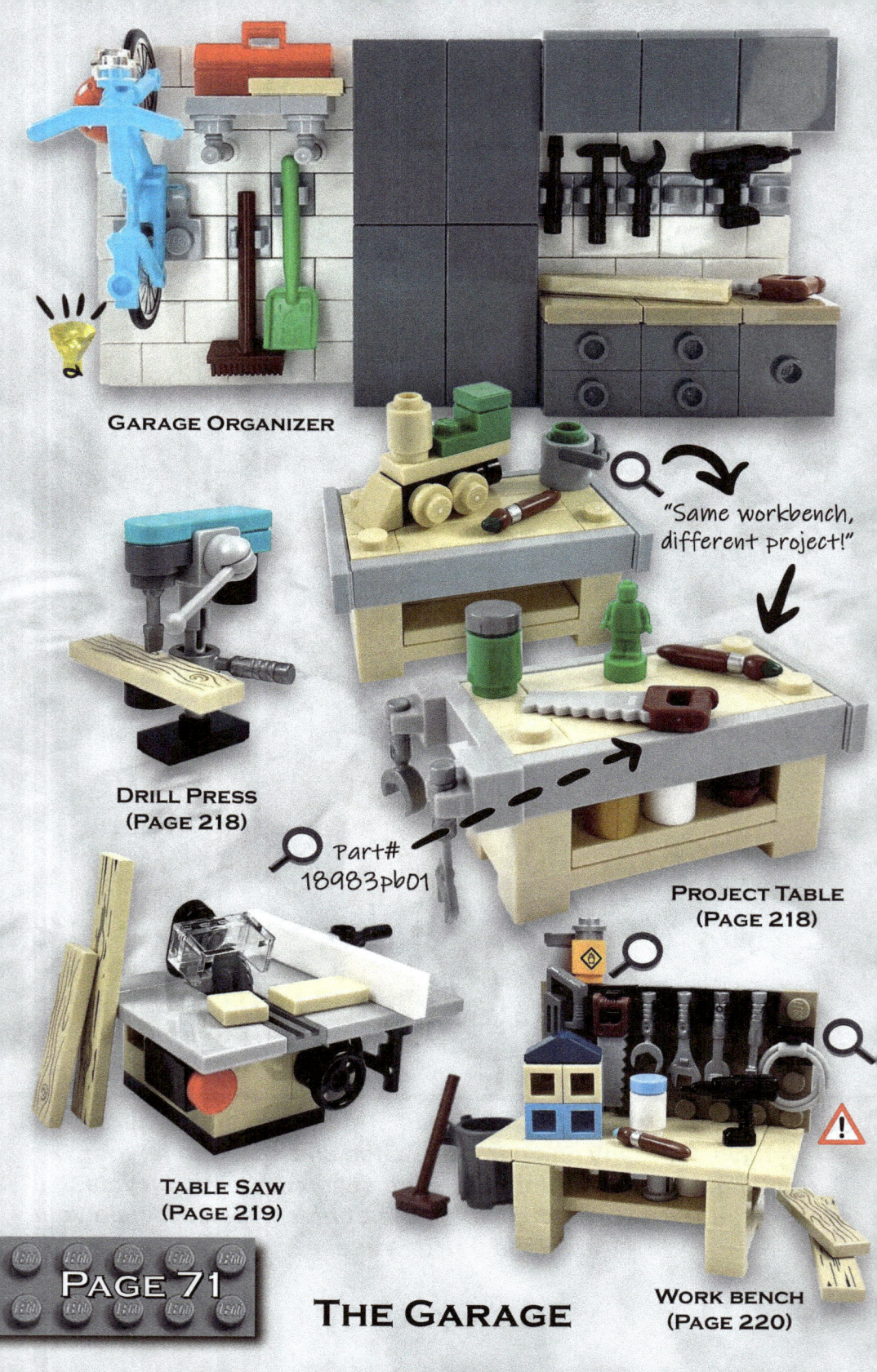

GARAGE ORGANIZER

"Same workbench, different project!"

DRILL PRESS
(PAGE 218)

Part# 18983pb01

PROJECT TABLE
(PAGE 218)

TABLE SAW
(PAGE 219)

THE GARAGE

WORK BENCH
(PAGE 220)

www.Citizen
Brick.com

Part#
45730
(Golf Club)

BASKETBALL
GOAL
(PAGE 221)

Part#
57753pb01
(Rugby)

SPORTS STORAGE
(PAGE 221)

SHOP VAC

TOOL
CHEST
(PAGE 223)

CAR JACK
(PAGE 222)

RECYCLE BIN
(PAGE 222)

Sticker from 2019
LEGO® Xtras set

PRESSURE
WASHER

TRASH
BINS
(PAGE 224)

PAGE 72

THE GARAGE

WALK-BEHIND
PUSH MOWER
(PAGE 224)

ECO ELECTRIC
PUSH MOWER
(PAGE 225)

SELF-PRO-
PELLED MOWER
(PAGE 225)

Speed
Champions
wheel cover

RIDING LAWN
MOWER
(PAGE 225)

ROBOTIC MOWER
(PAGE 227)

J.D. HYDROSTATIC
LAWN MOWER
(PAGE 226)

J.D. TRACTOR

THE GARAGE

12. THE BACKYARD

While not technically a part of the house, your outside environment and surroundings are very much a part of your life. Urban living may not grant a large area, so how can you maximize your minifig's greenspace? Create some interesting detail with that exterior potential!

ADRIONDACK
ROCKING CHAIRS
(PAGE 228)

PATIO CHAIR
(PAGE 228)

Fire pits
(Page 77)

Gardening
(Page 79)

ROCKING CHAIR
(PAGE 228)

PATIO
CHAISE
(PAGE 229)

OUTDOOR
TABLE & CHAIR
(PAGES 229 - 230)

"Grab a
cold one!"

OUTSIDE SEATING
(PAGE 230)

PAGE 75

THE BACKYARD

OUTDOOR SOFA
(PAGE 231)

OUTDOOR LOVESEAT
(PAGE 231)

PATIO UMBRELLA

PORCH SWING
WITH STAND
(PAGE 232)

"Grab a seat!"

PATIO FURNITURE
(PAGES 233 - 234)

THE BACKYARD

MARKET LIGHTS

"Poles for lights"

Hands holding part# 20482

OUTDOOR LIGHTS

PATHWAY LIGHTS

More wall sconces (Page 5)

SECURITY LIGHTS (PAGE 234)

Speed Champions wheel rim

FIRE PITS (PAGE 234)

OUTDOOR HEATER (PAGE 235)

BIG GREEN EGG SMOKER (PAGE 235)

THE BACKYARD

BBQ GRILL
(PAGE 235)

OUTDOOR KITCHEN
(PAGE 236)

BUILT-IN GRILL
(PAGE 236)

BIRD
FEEDERS
(PAGES 238
- 239)

BIRD HOUSES
(PAGE 237)

BIRD
BATH
(PAGE 239)

BIRD
HOUSE
POST
(PAGE 238)

BIRD
FEEDERS
(PAGES 238
- 239)

PAGE 78

THE BACKYARD

GARDEN SHED

GREENHOUSE
(PAGES 242
- 244)

Removable roof

RAISED GARDEN BED
(PAGE 240)

SUNFLOWERS
(PAGE 241)

WATERING CANS

GARDEN CART
(PAGE 241)

Bring the indoor
Potted Plants
(Page 51) outside!

PAGE 79

THE BACKYARD

Instructions
&
Parts Lists

HOW TO USE THE FRONT HALF OF THIS BOOK

Browse the <u>Visual Catalog</u> of designs in each household room by chapter for inspiration. Keep an open mind. Several designs can work in multiple or different rooms.

DESIGNS ARE IN THIS FORMAL FONT.

TABLE LAMPS

CARROT LAMP (PAGE ▮▮▮)

ACORN LAMP (PAGE ▮▮▮)

SMALL LAMPS (PAGE ▮▮▮)

Is that a Carrot?! Yes, it is. See how these things are made starting on page ▮▮▮.

LAVA LAMP ⚠

DESK LAMPS

(Page #) points to the parts list and instructions in the back.

No (Page #) indicates that the simple design can be built visually from here.

(PAGE ▮▮▮) (PAGE ▮▮▮) (PAGE ▮▮▮) (PAGE ▮▮▮)

Just two pieces, but BRILLIANT design!

The same chapter colors in the front half match the back half.

PAGE ▮▮

INDOOR LIGHTING

There are various icons found throughout this book. Here is the legend.

⚠ Warning <u>"Illegal" technique!</u> If you are a stickler for rules, look away. This design uses non-conventional building methods, which may or may not bother you.

🔍 Design uses <u>hard to find</u> piece(s).

Check out this <u>official</u> <u>LEGO® set</u> for <u>more design references</u>.

Look at this cool scene for <u>inspiration</u>. No how-to provided, but isn't it awesome?

HOW TO USE THE
BACK HALF OF THIS BOOK

Flip to the back for select <u>Instructions and Parts Lists</u>. Back here you will find more detailed views and clues on how to build some designs.

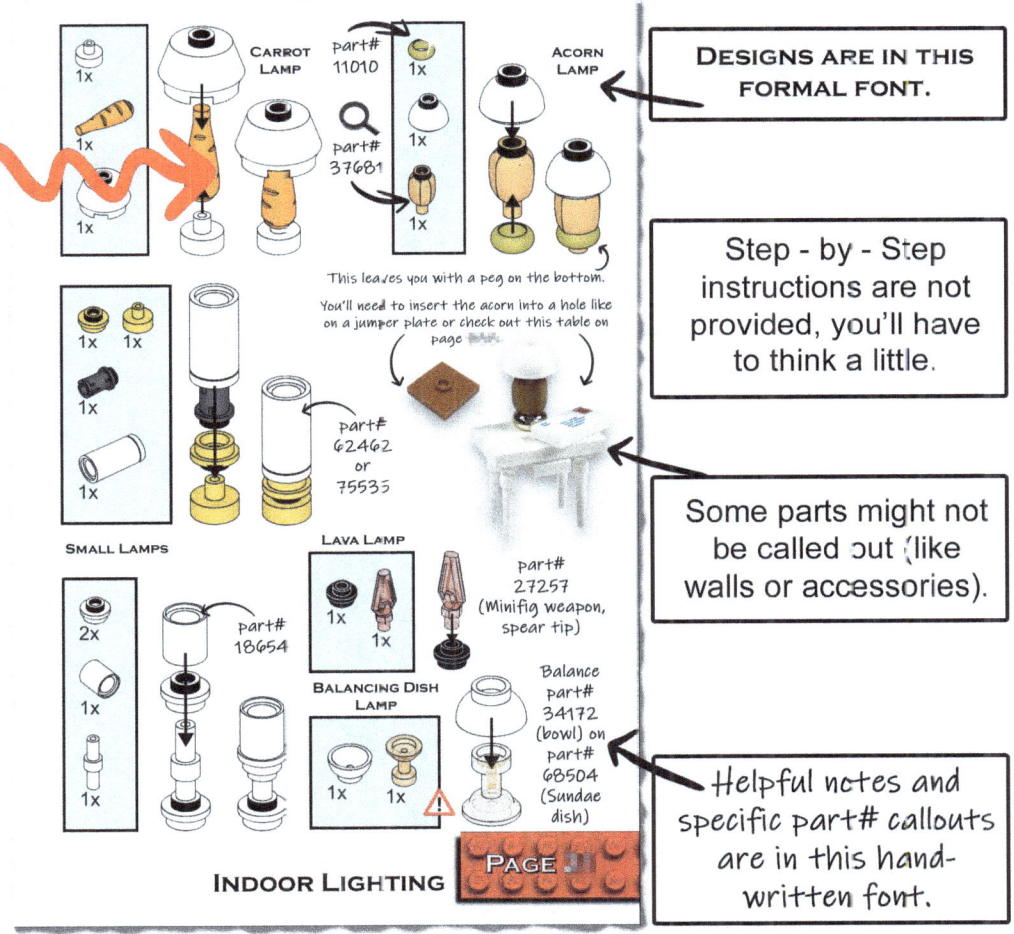

DESIGNS ARE IN THIS FORMAL FONT.

Step - by - Step instructions are not provided, you'll have to think a little.

Some parts might not be called out (like walls or accessories).

Helpful notes and specific part# callouts are in this hand-written font.

Remember, more designs exist in the front half. Don't spend too much time flipping through the back thinking that's all there is! Only complex designs are back here. Simple designs in the front can be effective too.

Also, don't let names or chapter placement stifle your creativity. Imagine these designs in different rooms in your MOC.

Lastly, be creative. Don't just copy these designs. Swap colors, sub-stitute parts for what you have, and add accessories for more detail. After all, it's <u>**All About the Details!**</u>

FANCY TABLE LAMPS

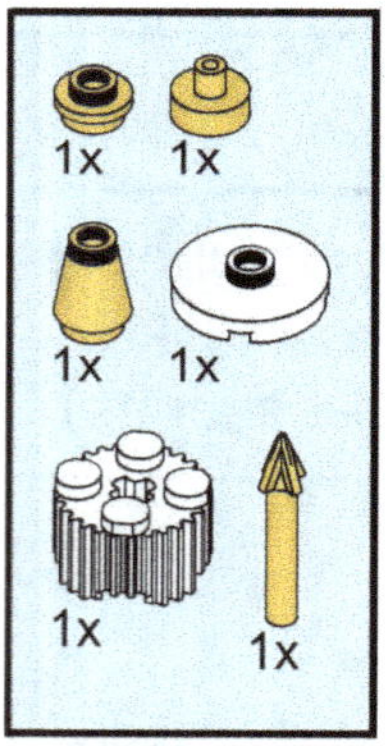

3x **2x**

1x **1x**

1x

1x

Slip rings over the center peg

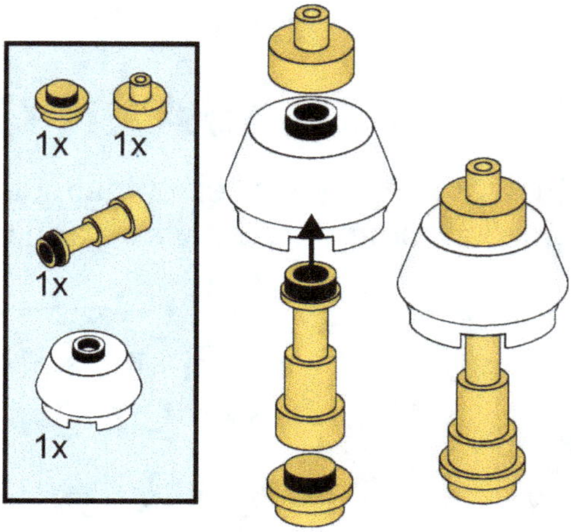

FANCY TABLE LAMPS

1x **1x**

1x

1x

FANCY TABLE LAMPS

1x **1x**

1x **1x**

1x **1x**

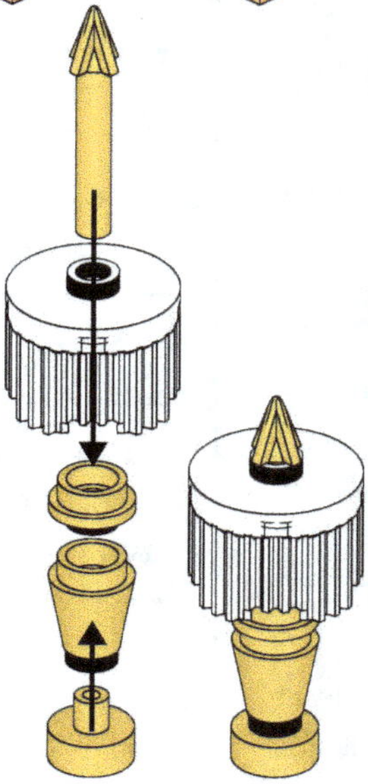

FANCY TABLE LAMPS

1x **1x**

1x

1x 3L

1x

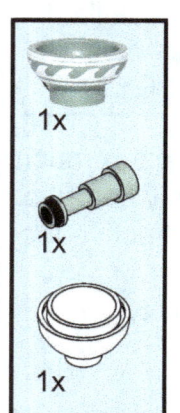

1x

1x

1x

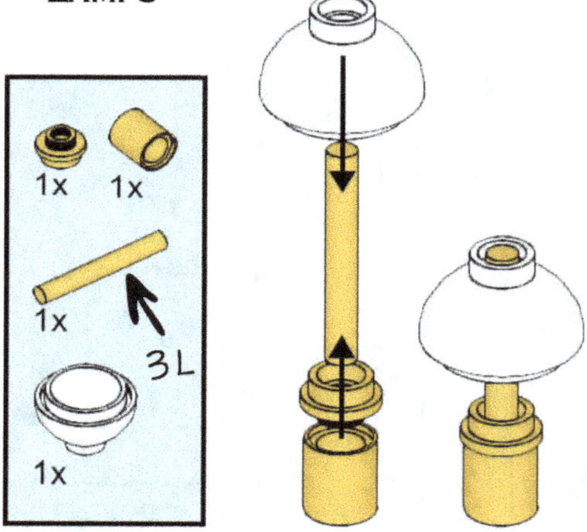

This bowl (part# 34172) only shows up in a few sets from 2017 (Ninjago Movie minifigs) in a decorated form, but feel free to substitute a plain bowl (which is more common) in it's place.

INDOOR LIGHTING

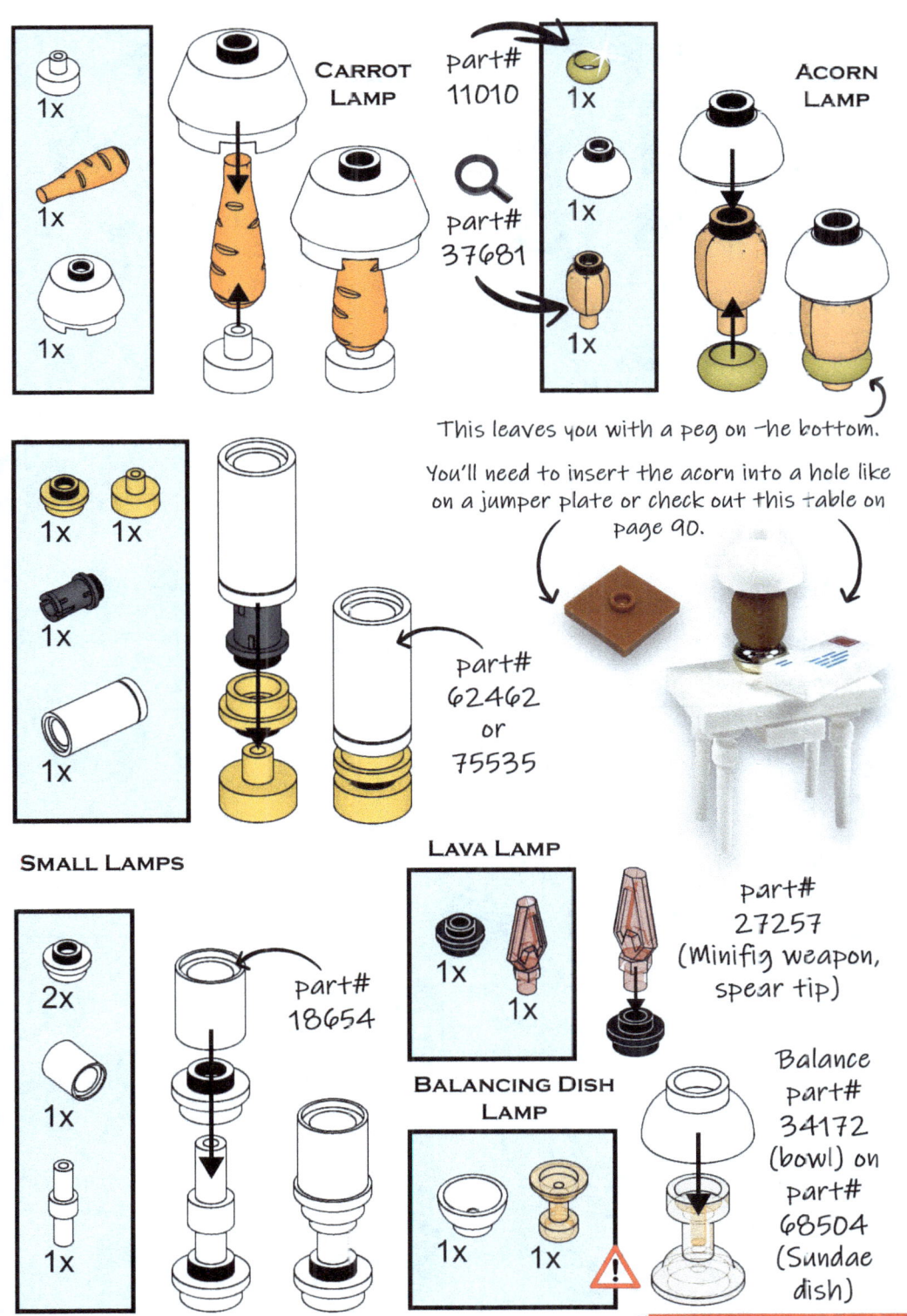

CARROT LAMP

1x

1x

1x

part# 11010

1x

part# 37681

1x

1x

ACORN LAMP

This leaves you with a peg on the bottom.

You'll need to insert the acorn into a hole like on a jumper plate or check out this table on page 90.

part# 62462 or 75535

1x 1x

1x

1x

SMALL LAMPS

part# 18654

2x

1x

1x

LAVA LAMP

1x

1x

part# 27257 (Minifig weapon, spear tip)

BALANCING DISH LAMP

1x 1x ⚠

Balance part# 34172 (bowl) on part# 68504 (Sundae dish)

INDOOR LIGHTING

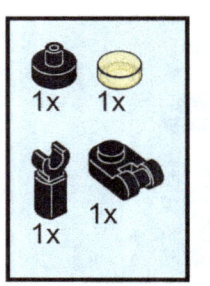

DESK LAMPS

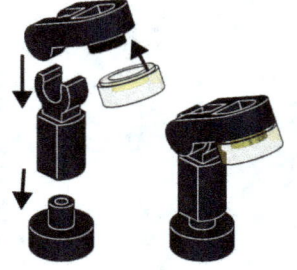

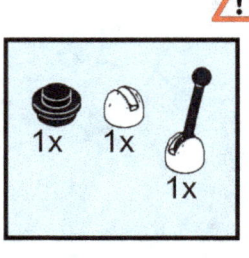

DESK LAMPS

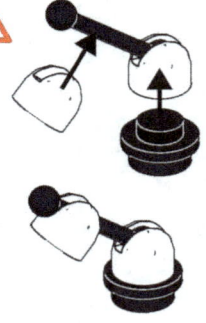

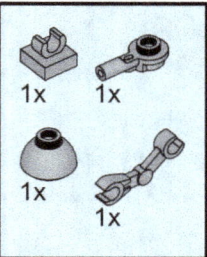

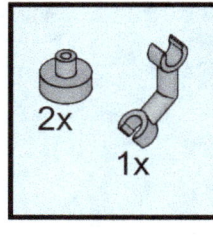

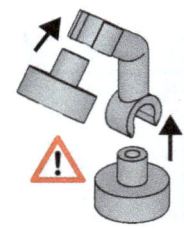

part#3626cpb2957 only comes in one set from 2022, but here are some alternates ==>

part# 3626bpb0005, 3626bpb0034, 3626cpb1025

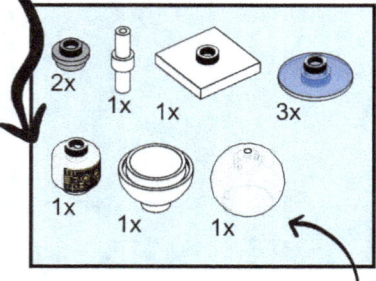

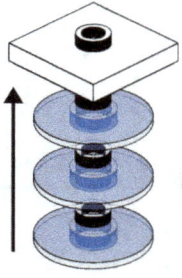

part# 51283

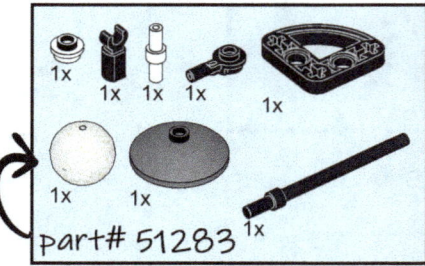

(Satin Trans-clear Fishbowl)

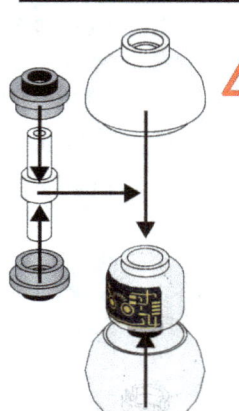

Fishbowl rests on jumper plate

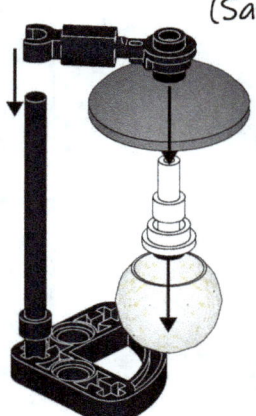

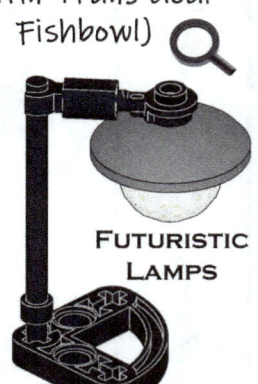

FUTURISTIC LAMPS

INDOOR LIGHTING

ADJUSTABLE LAMPS

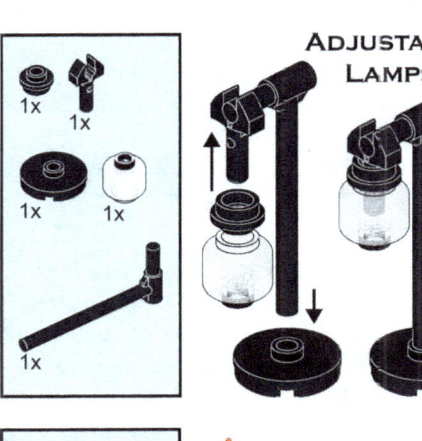

1x 1x
1x 1x
1x

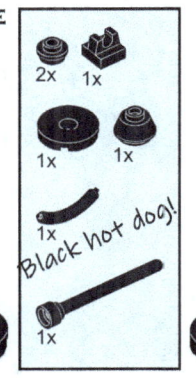

2x 1x
1x 1x

1x Black hot dog!
1x

part# 33492

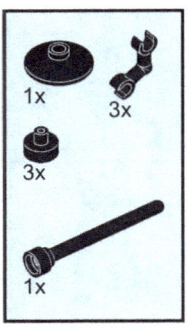

1x 3x
3x
1x

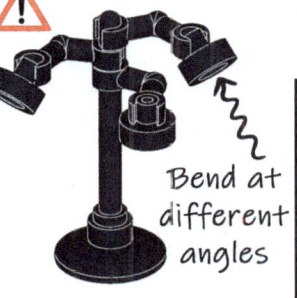

⚠️ Bend at different angles

TALL FLOOR LAMPS

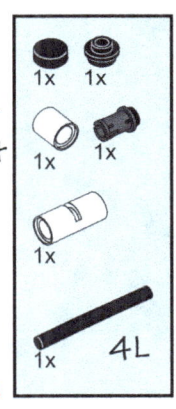

1x 1x
1x 1x
1x
1x 4L

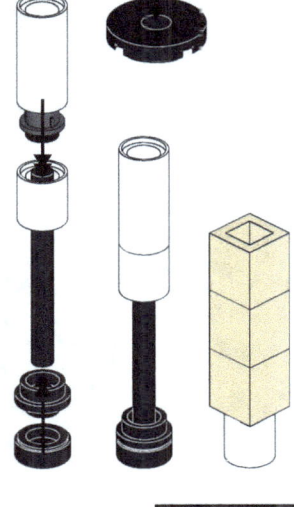

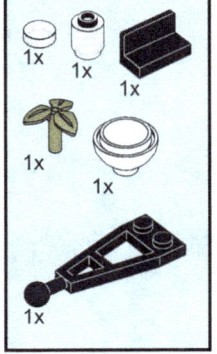

1x 1x
1x
1x 1x
1x

⚠️ The dome just rests on the ball hitch.
<== part# 2508

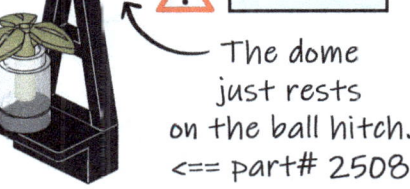

1x 3x

UNIQUE FLOOR LAMPS

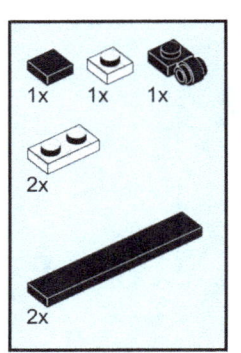

1x 1x 1x
2x
2x

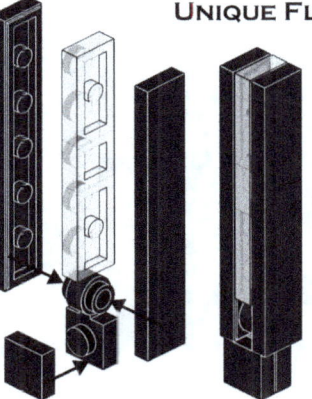

1x
1x 3L
2x

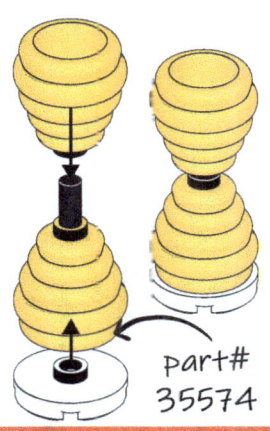

part# 35574

INDOOR LIGHTING

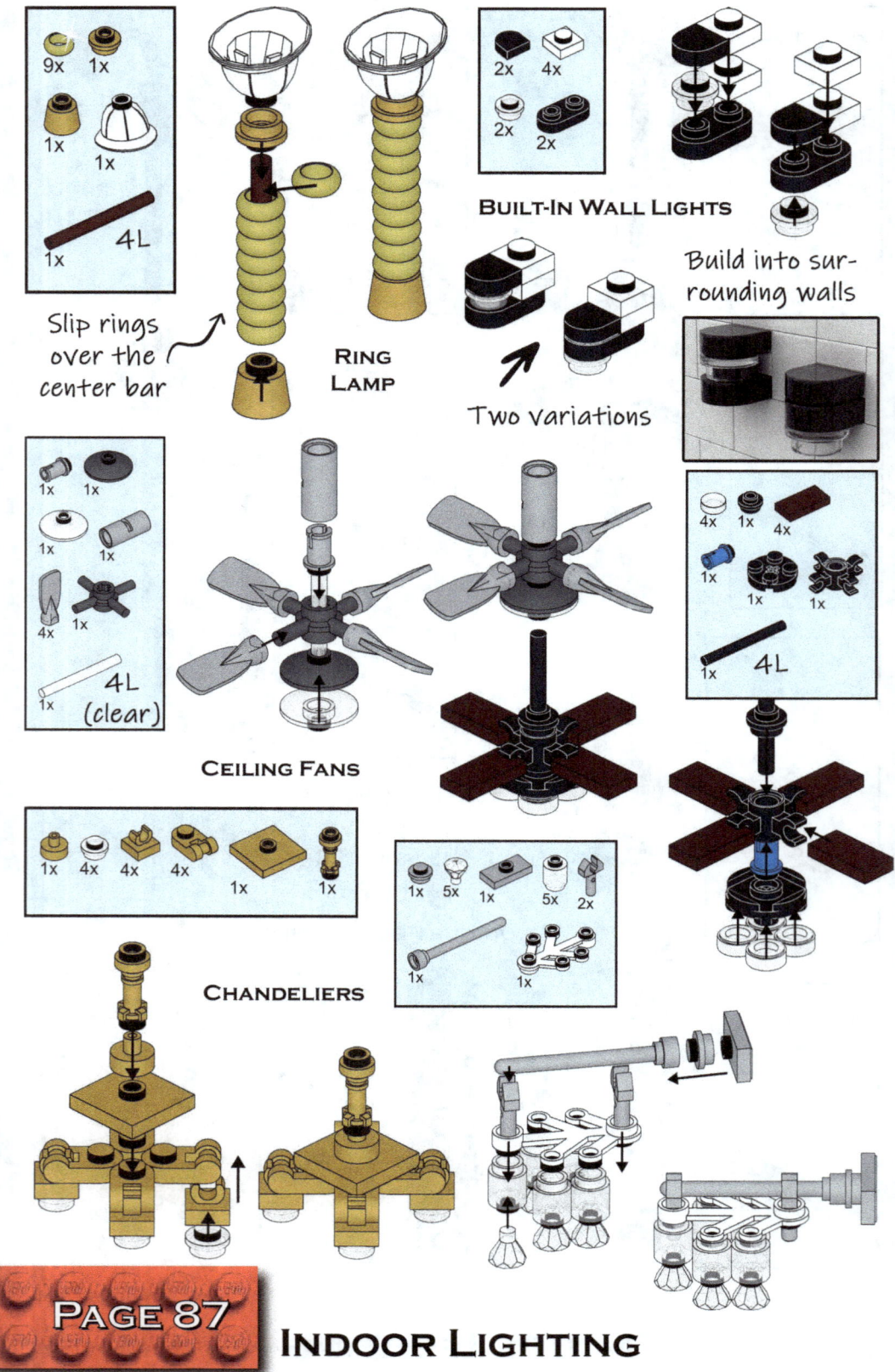

Slip rings over the center bar

RING LAMP

BUILT-IN WALL LIGHTS

Two variations

Build into surrounding walls

CEILING FANS

CHANDELIERS

4L (clear)

4L

INDOOR LIGHTING

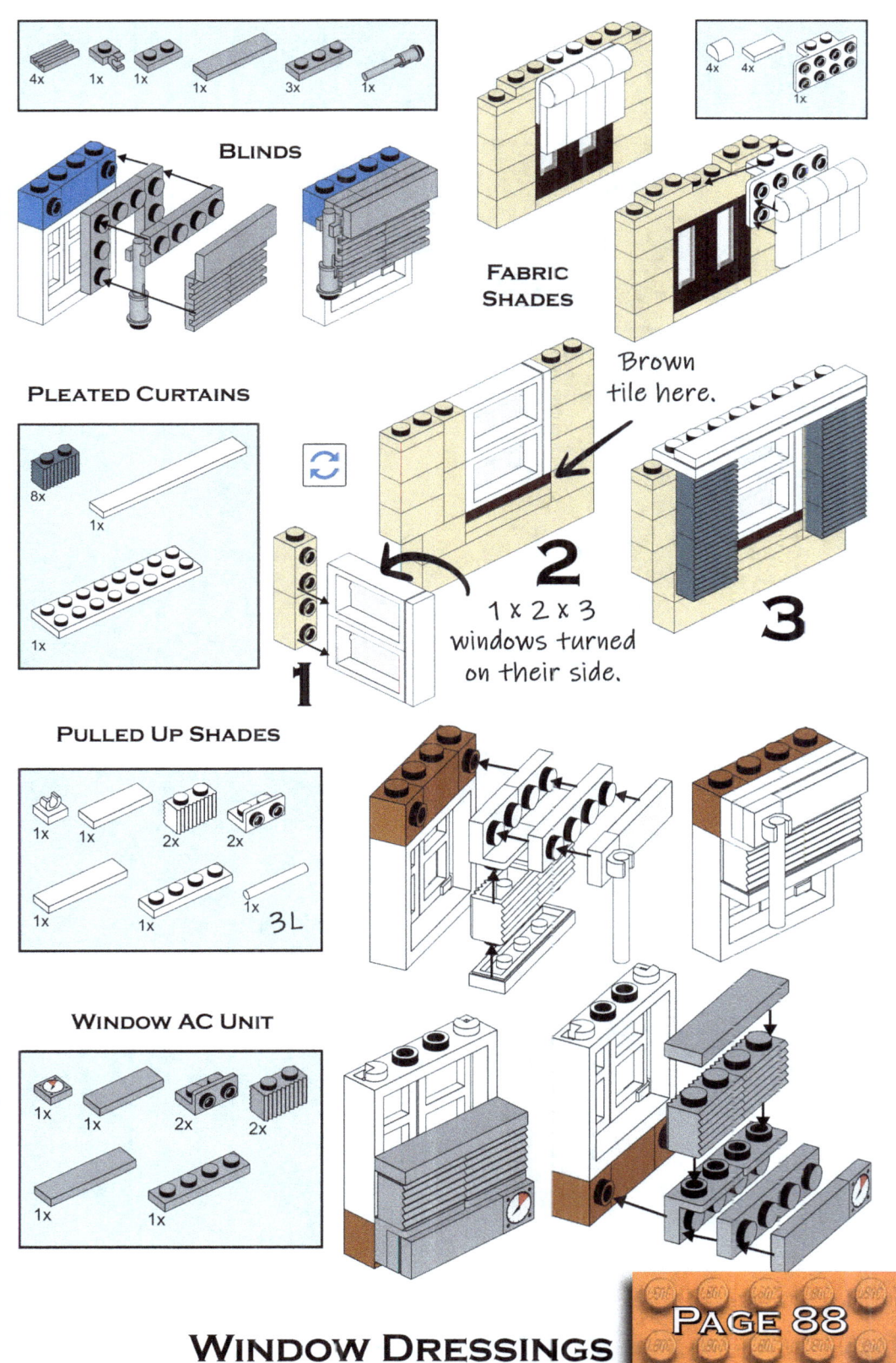

BLINDS

FABRIC SHADES

PLEATED CURTAINS

Brown tile here.

2

1 x 2 x 3 windows turned on their side.

1

3

PULLED UP SHADES

WINDOW AC UNIT

WINDOW DRESSINGS

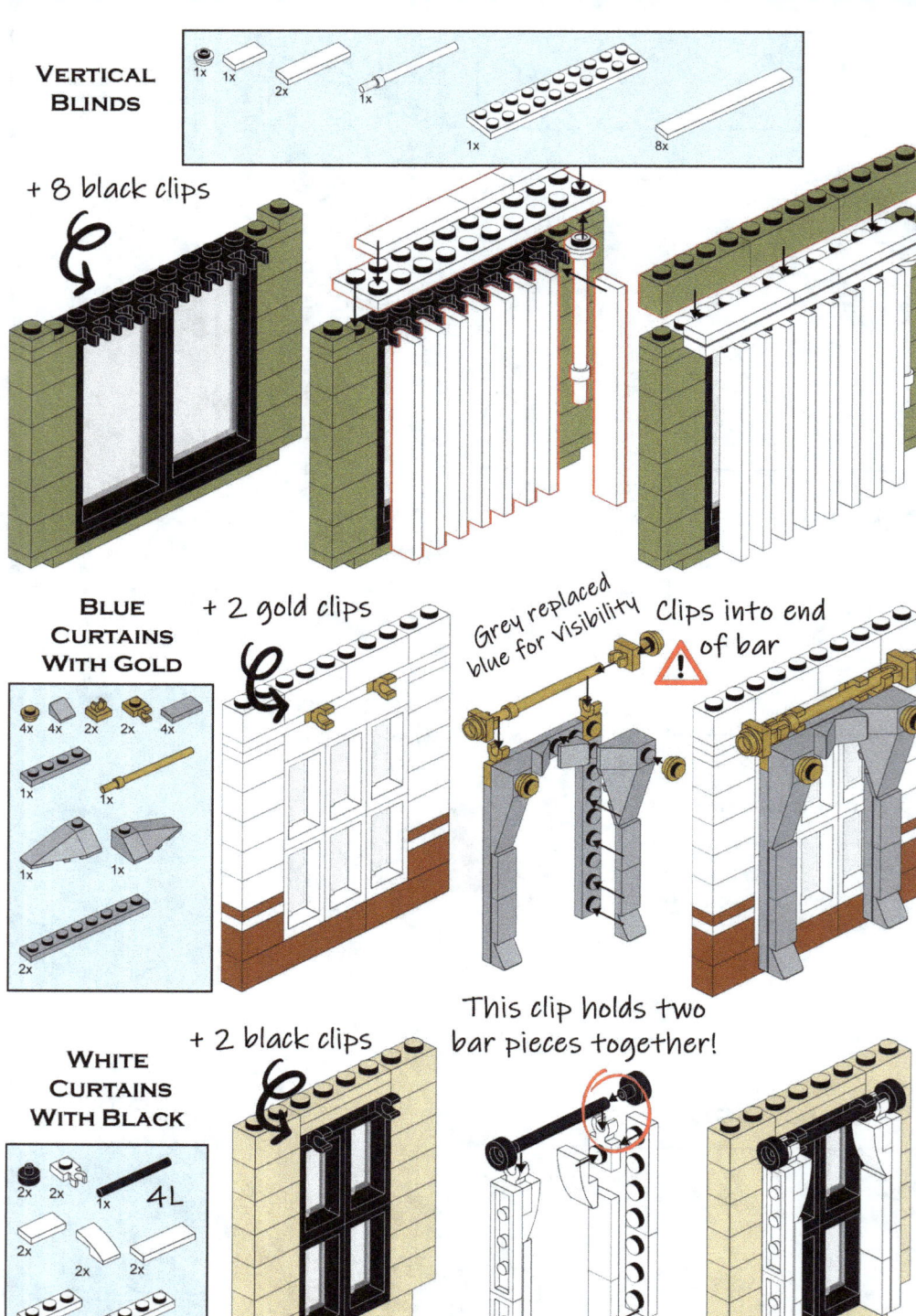

VERTICAL BLINDS

1x 1x 2x 1x 1x 8x

+ 8 black clips

BLUE CURTAINS WITH GOLD

4x 4x 2x 2x 4x
1x 1x
1x 1x
2x

+ 2 gold clips

Grey replaced blue for visibility

Clips into end of bar

⚠

This clip holds two bar pieces together!

WHITE CURTAINS WITH BLACK

2x 2x 1x 4L
2x
2x 2x
2x 2x

+ 2 black clips

WINDOW DRESSINGS

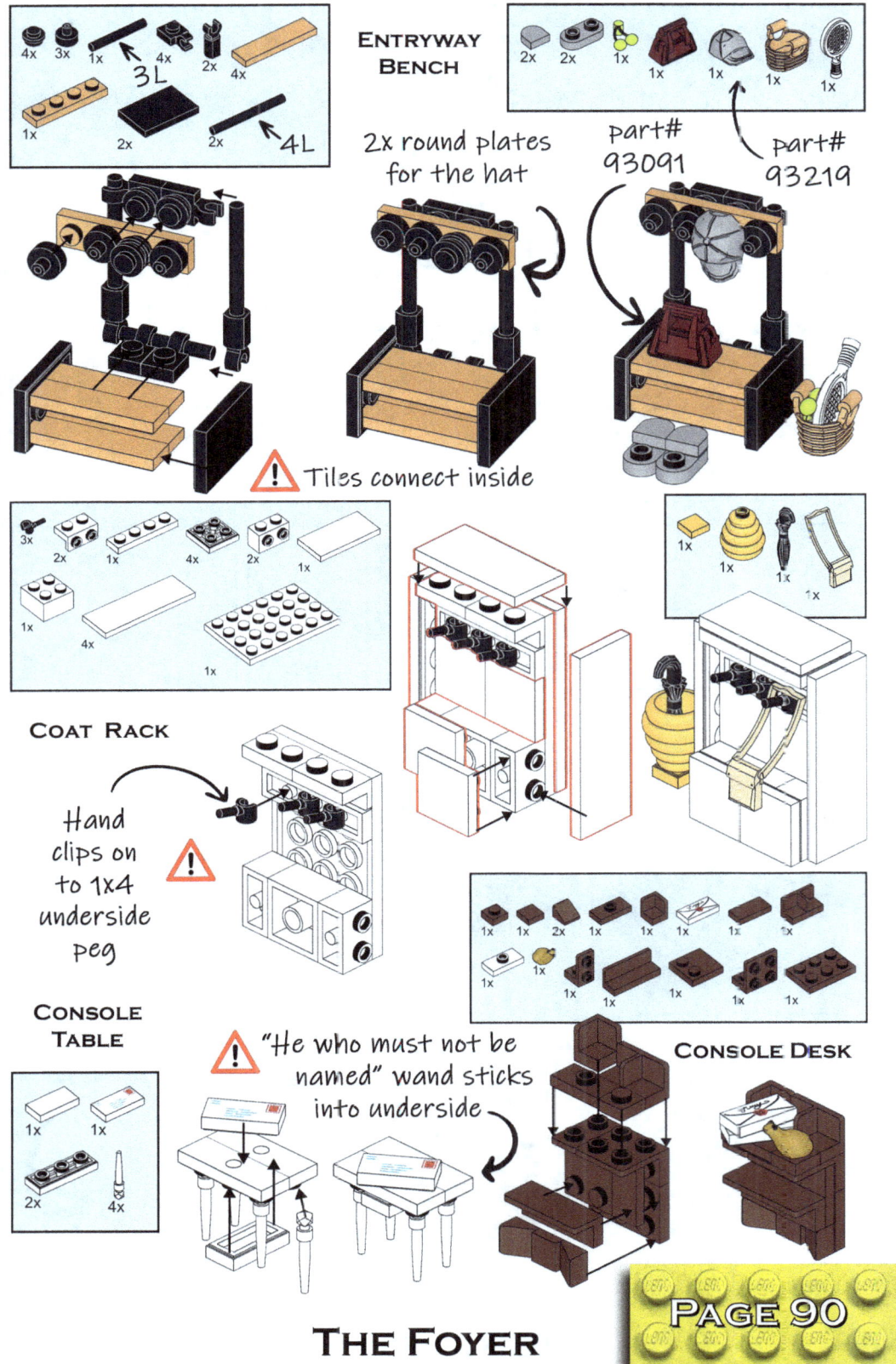

ENTRYWAY BENCH

4x 3x 1x 4x 2x 4x
3L

1x 2x 2x 4L

2x 2x 1x 1x 1x 1x

2x round plates
for the hat

part#
93091

part#
93219

⚠ Tiles connect inside

3x 2x 1x 4x 2x 1x

1x 4x 1x

1x 1x 1x 1x

COAT RACK

Hand
clips on
to 1x4
underside
peg ⚠

1x 1x 2x 1x 1x 1x 1x 1x

1x 1x 1x 1x 1x 1x

CONSOLE TABLE

1x 1x

2x 4x

⚠ "He who must not be
named" wand sticks
into underside

CONSOLE DESK

THE FOYER

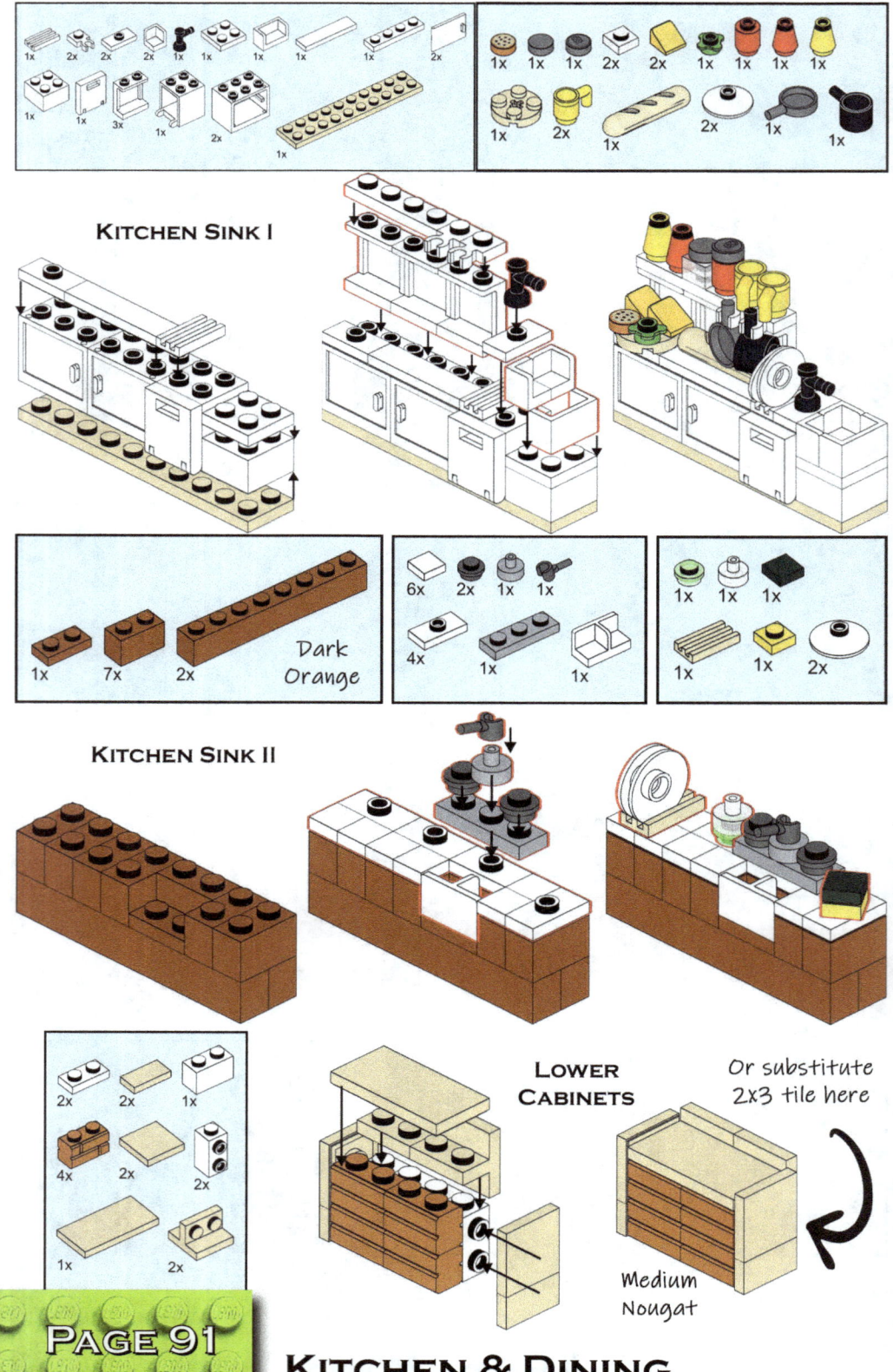

KITCHEN SINK I

Dark Orange

1x 7x 2x

6x 2x 1x 1x
4x 1x 1x

1x 1x 1x
1x 1x 2x

KITCHEN SINK II

2x 2x 1x
4x 2x 2x
1x 2x

LOWER CABINETS

Or substitute 2x3 tile here

Medium Nougat

KITCHEN & DINING

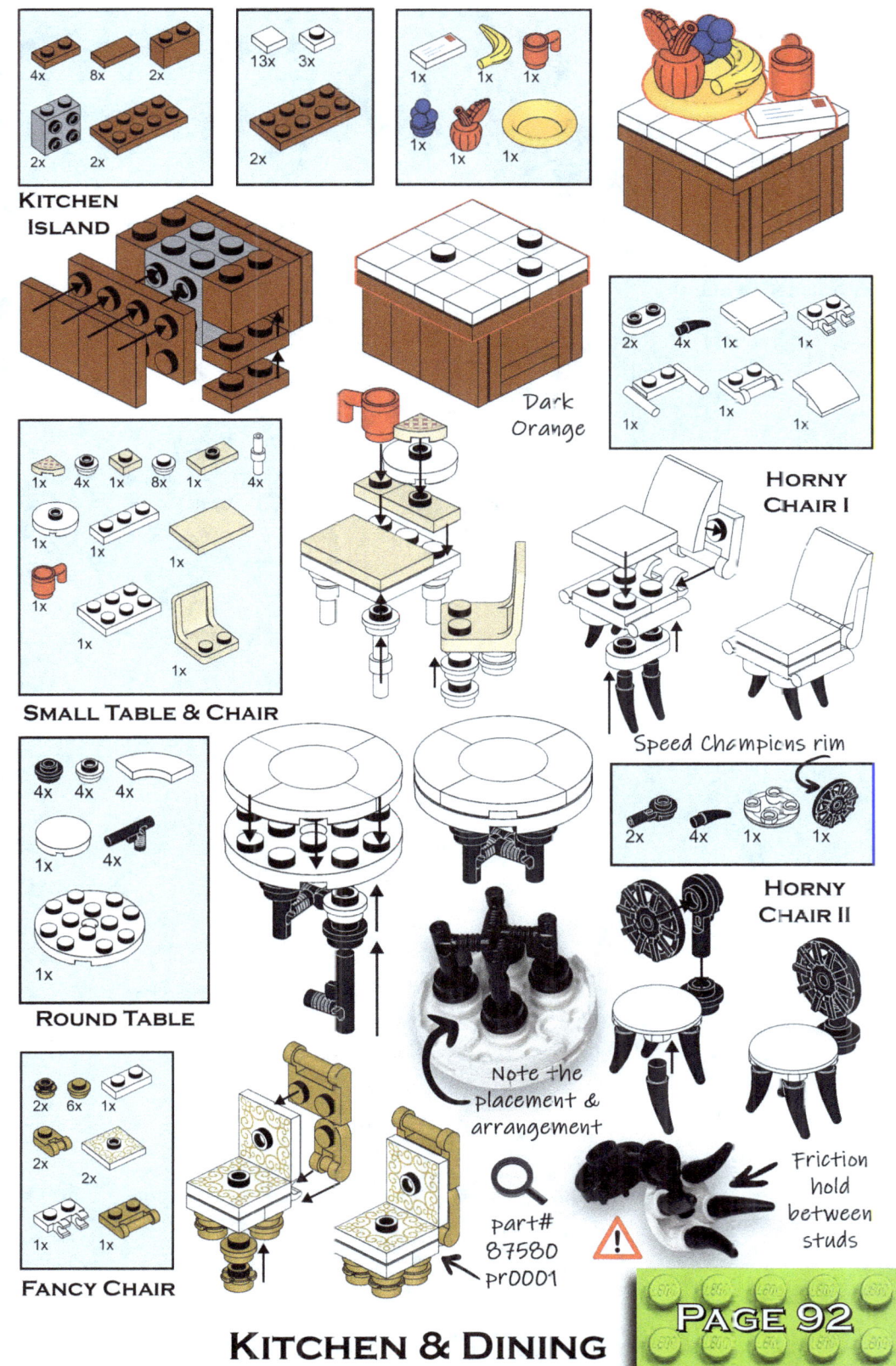

KITCHEN ISLAND

4x 8x 2x
2x 2x

13x 3x
2x

1x 1x 1x
1x 1x 1x

Dark Orange

HORNY CHAIR I

2x 4x 1x 1x
1x 1x 1x

SMALL TABLE & CHAIR

1x 4x 1x 8x 1x 4x
1x 1x 1x
1x 1x 1x

Speed Champions rim

2x 4x 1x 1x

HORNY CHAIR II

ROUND TABLE

4x 4x 4x
1x 4x
1x

Note the placement & arrangement

part# 87580 pr0001

Friction hold between studs

FANCY CHAIR

2x 6x 1x
2x 2x
1x 1x

KITCHEN & DINING

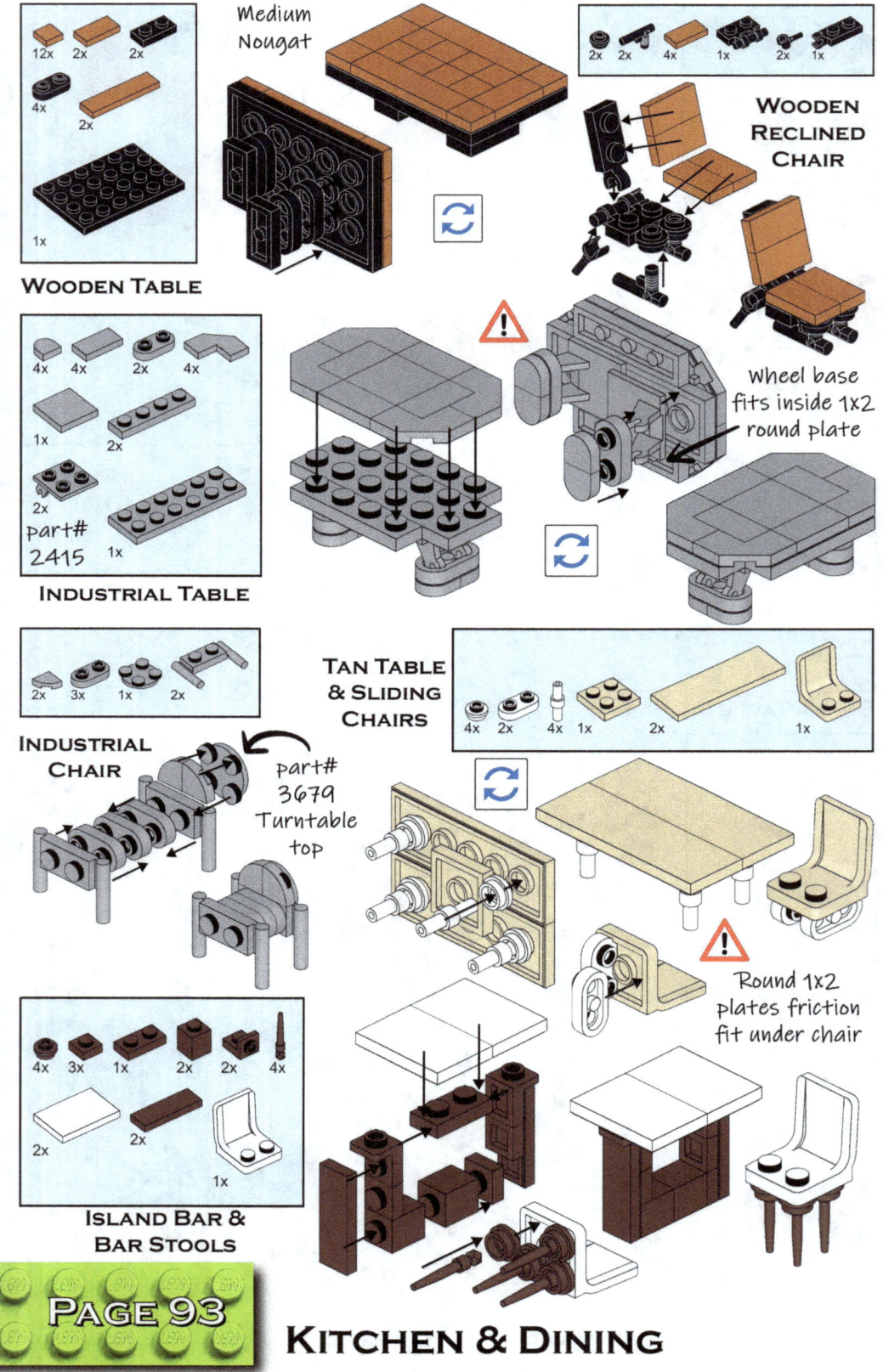

Medium Nougat

12x 2x 2x

4x

2x

1x

WOODEN TABLE

WOODEN RECLINED CHAIR

2x 2x 4x 1x 2x 1x

4x 4x 2x 4x

1x

2x

2x
part# 2415 1x

INDUSTRIAL TABLE

wheel base fits inside 1x2 round plate

TAN TABLE & SLIDING CHAIRS

4x 2x 4x 1x 2x 1x

2x 3x 1x 2x

INDUSTRIAL CHAIR

part# 3679 Turntable top

Round 1x2 plates friction fit under chair

4x 3x 1x 2x 2x 4x

2x 2x

1x

ISLAND BAR & BAR STOOLS

KITCHEN & DINING

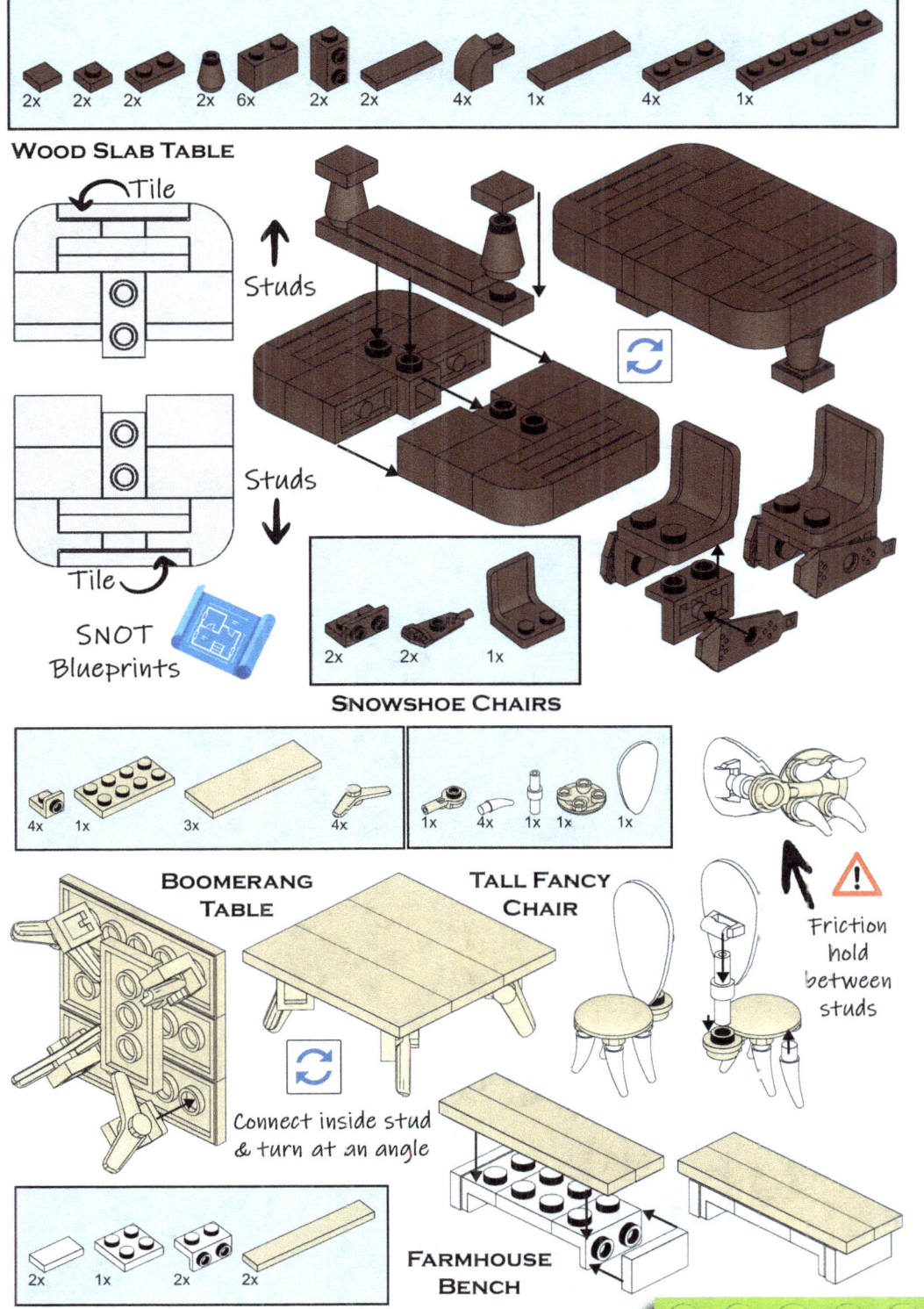

WOOD SLAB TABLE

Tile

Studs

Studs

Tile

SNOT Blueprints

SNOWSHOE CHAIRS

2x 2x 1x

BOOMERANG TABLE

TALL FANCY CHAIR

Friction hold between studs

Connect inside stud & turn at an angle

FARMHOUSE BENCH

2x 1x 2x 2x

KITCHEN & DINING

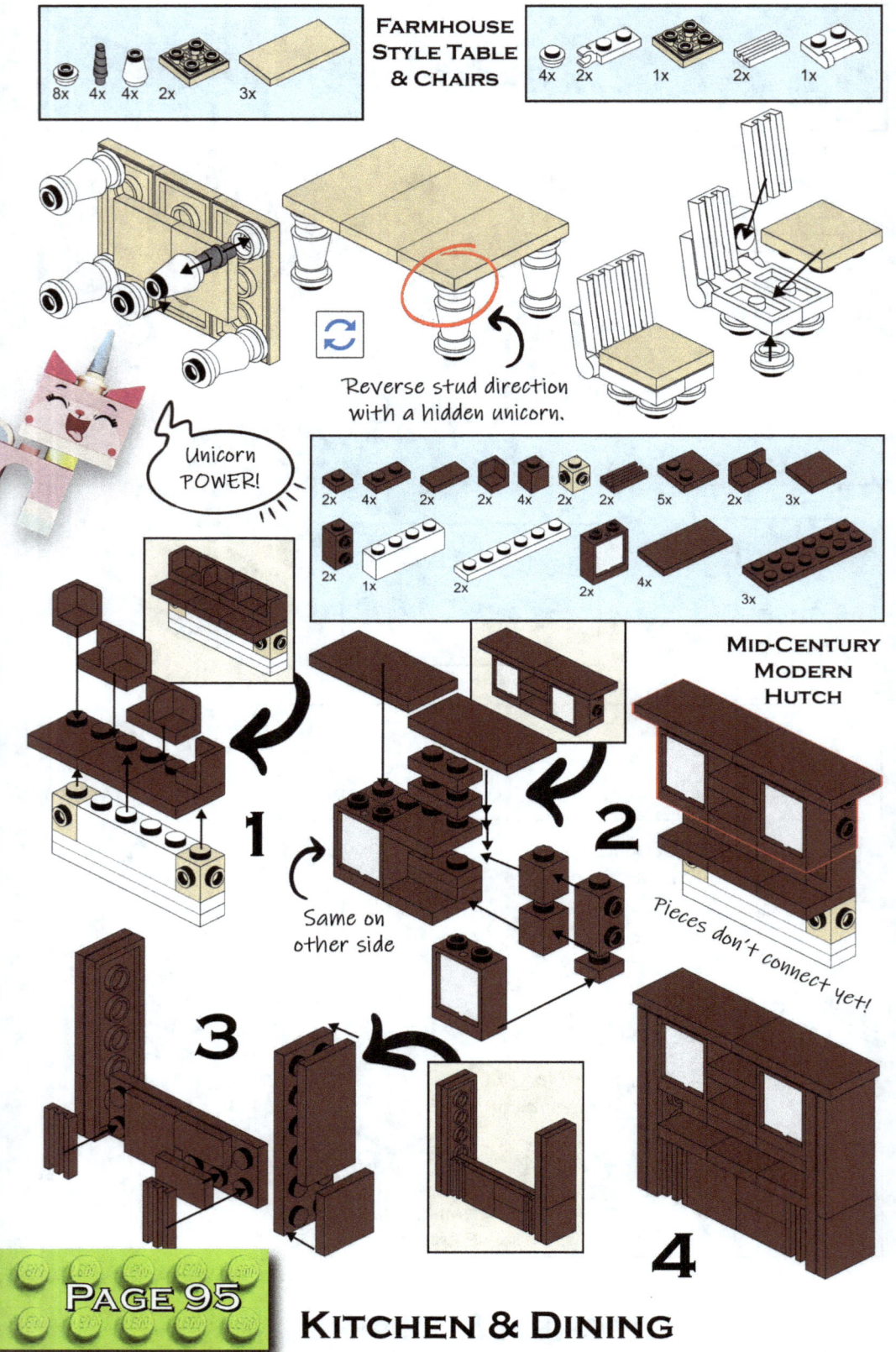

FARMHOUSE STYLE TABLE & CHAIRS

8x 4x 4x 2x 3x

4x 2x 1x 2x 1x

Reverse stud direction with a hidden unicorn.

Unicorn POWER!

2x 4x 2x 2x 4x 2x 2x 5x 2x 3x

2x 1x 2x 2x 4x 3x

MID-CENTURY MODERN HUTCH

1

Same on other side

2

Pieces don't connect yet!

3

4

KITCHEN & DINING

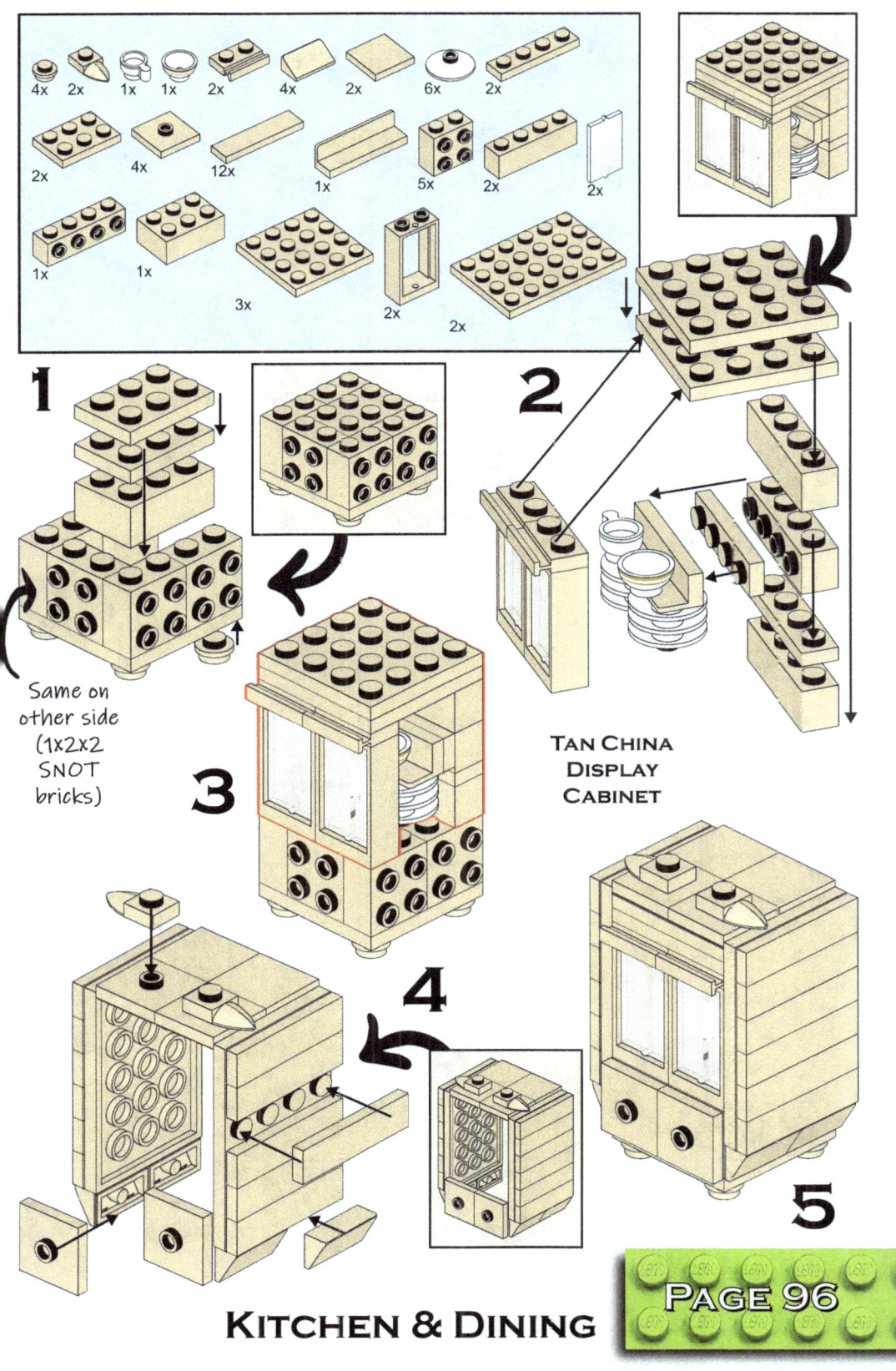

1

Same on other side (1x2x2 SNOT bricks)

2

3

TAN CHINA DISPLAY CABINET

4

5

KITCHEN & DINING

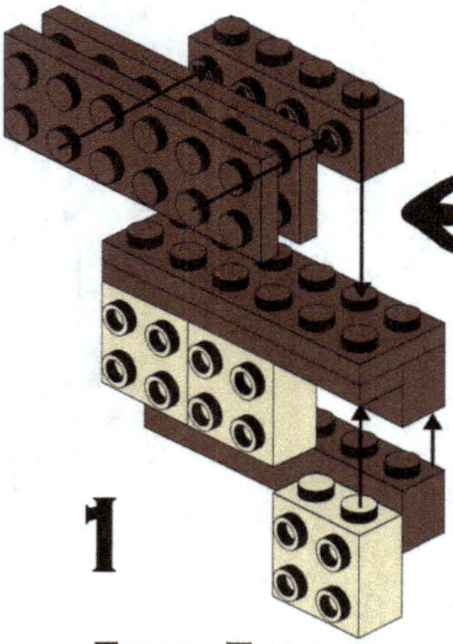

1

**FANCY TEA
DISPLAY CABINET**

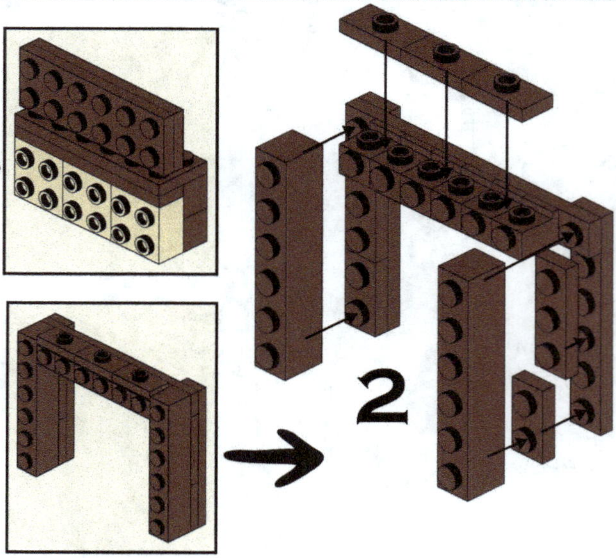

*Build these four
components
separately first*

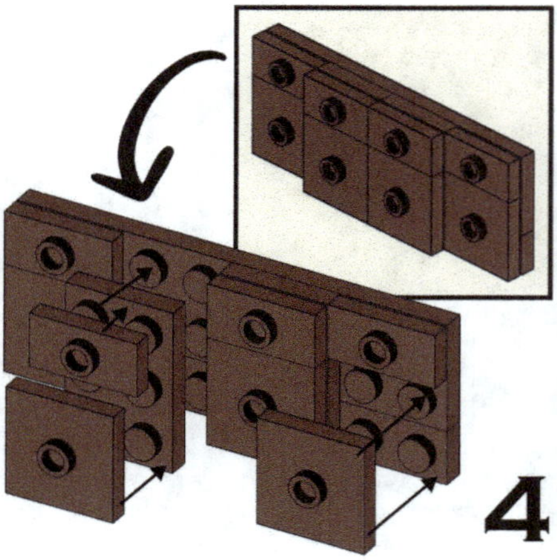

2

3

4

KITCHEN & DINING

5

Components
are loose!

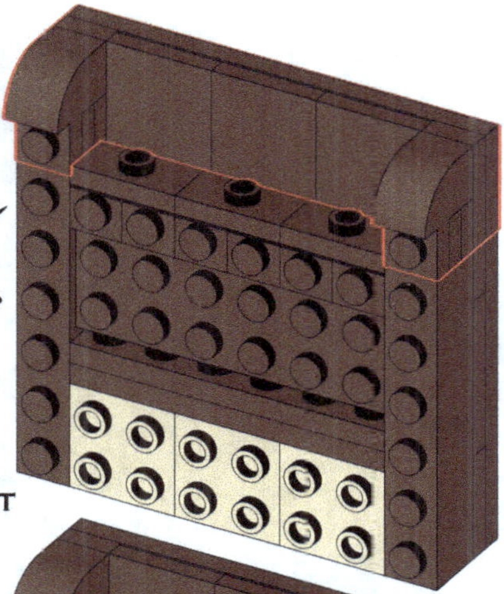

FANCY TEA
DISPLAY CABINET

6

Locked
together!

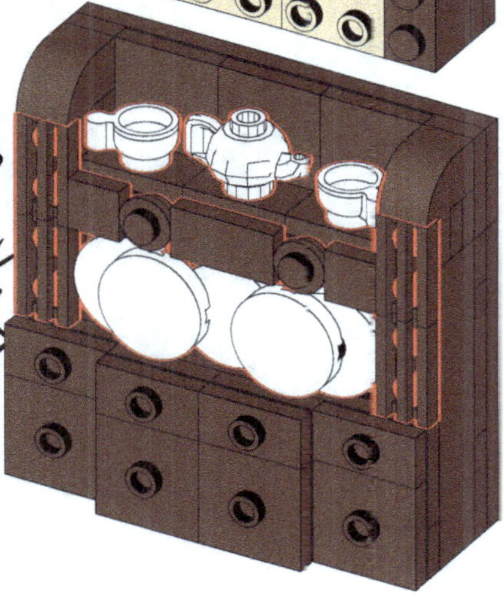

ANTIQUE HUTCH

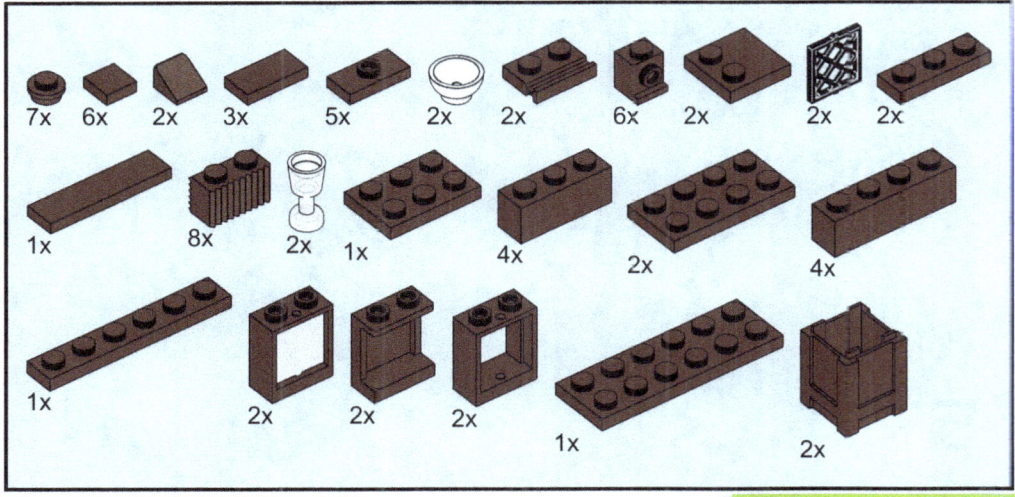

7x   6x   2x   3x   5x   2x   2x   6x   2x   2x   2x

1x   8x   2x   1x   4x   2x   4x

1x   2x   2x   2x   1x   2x

KITCHEN & DINING

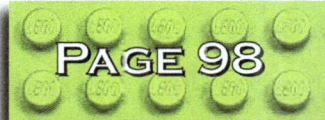

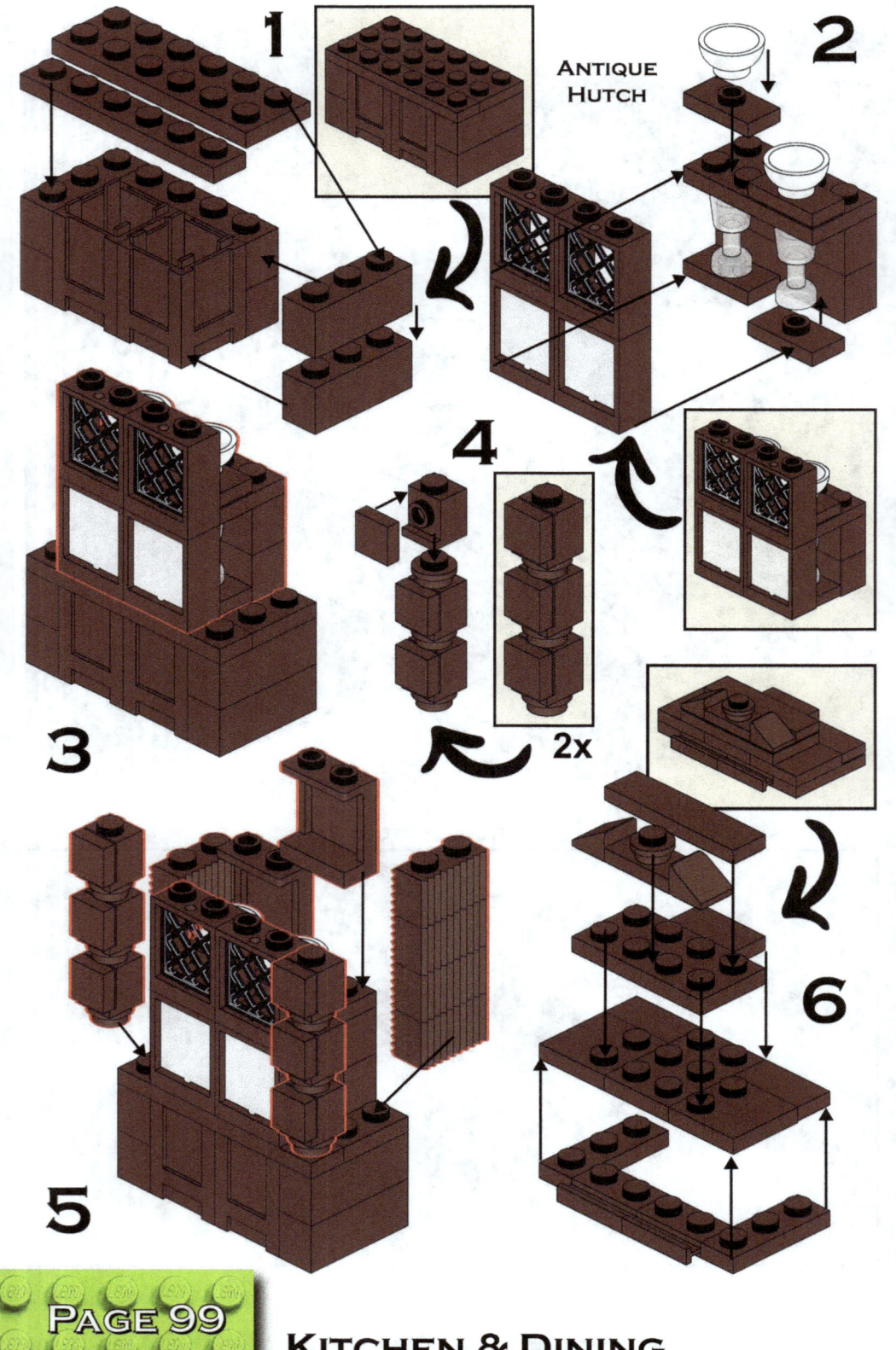

ANTIQUE HUTCH

1

2

4

2x

3

6

5

KITCHEN & DINING

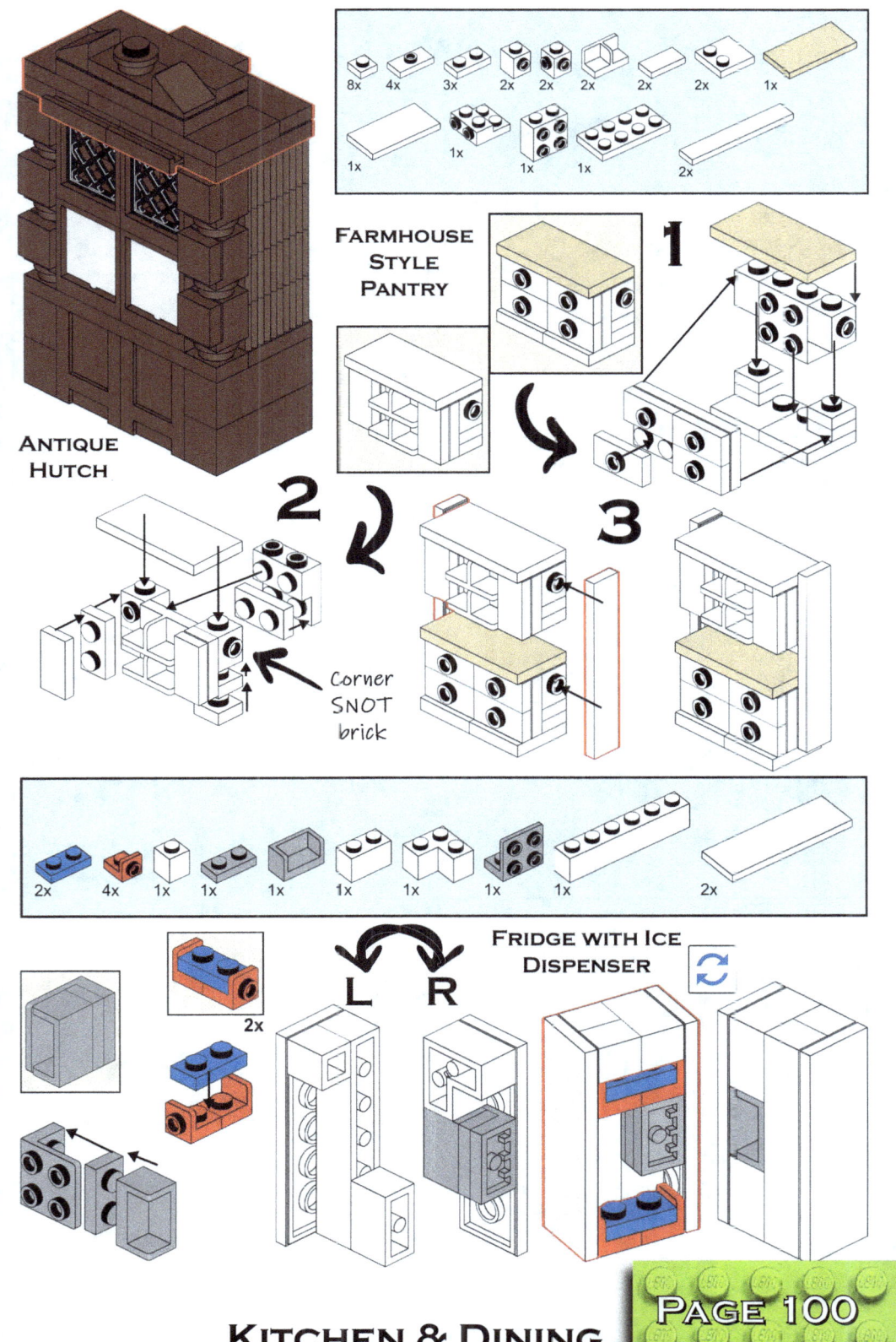

ANTIQUE HUTCH

FARMHOUSE STYLE PANTRY

1

2

3

Corner SNOT brick

FRIDGE WITH ICE DISPENSER

L R

2x

KITCHEN & DINING

WITH ICE DISPENSER

Two SNOT bricks down here!

Part# 3070pb093 & Part# 3069bpb0989

SINGLE DOOR REFRIDGE-RATOR

FRENCH DOOR WITH BOTTOM FREEZER I

KITCHEN & DINING

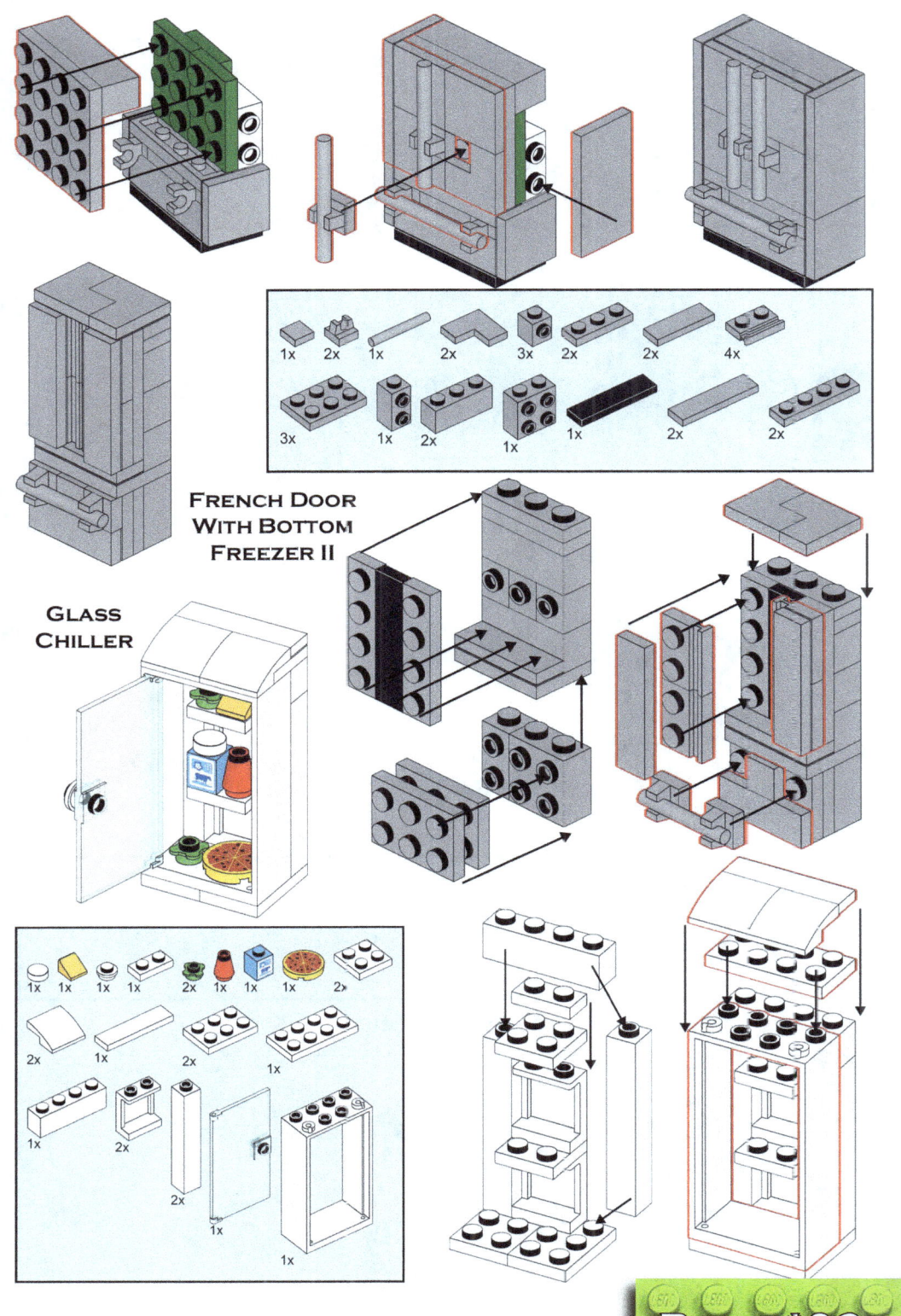

FRENCH DOOR WITH BOTTOM FREEZER II

GLASS CHILLER

1x 2x 1x 2x 3x 2x 2x 4x

3x 1x 2x 1x 2x 2x

1x 1x 1x 1x 2x 1x 1x 1x 2x

2x 1x 2x 1x

1x 2x 2x 1x

1x

KITCHEN & DINING

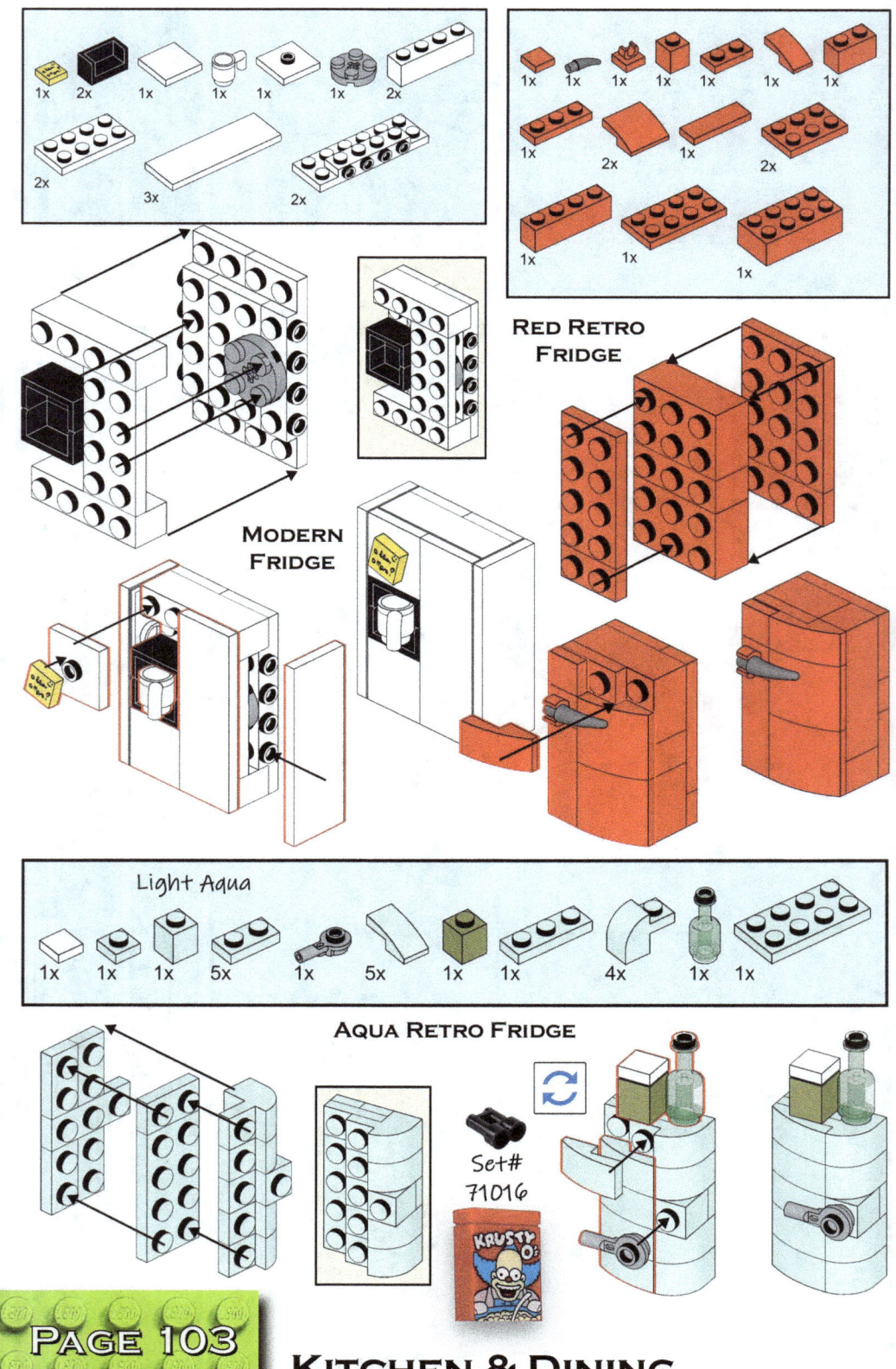

RED RETRO FRIDGE

MODERN FRIDGE

Light Aqua

1x 1x 1x 5x 1x 5x 1x 1x 4x 1x 1x

AQUA RETRO FRIDGE

Set# 71016

KRUSTY O's

KITCHEN & DINING

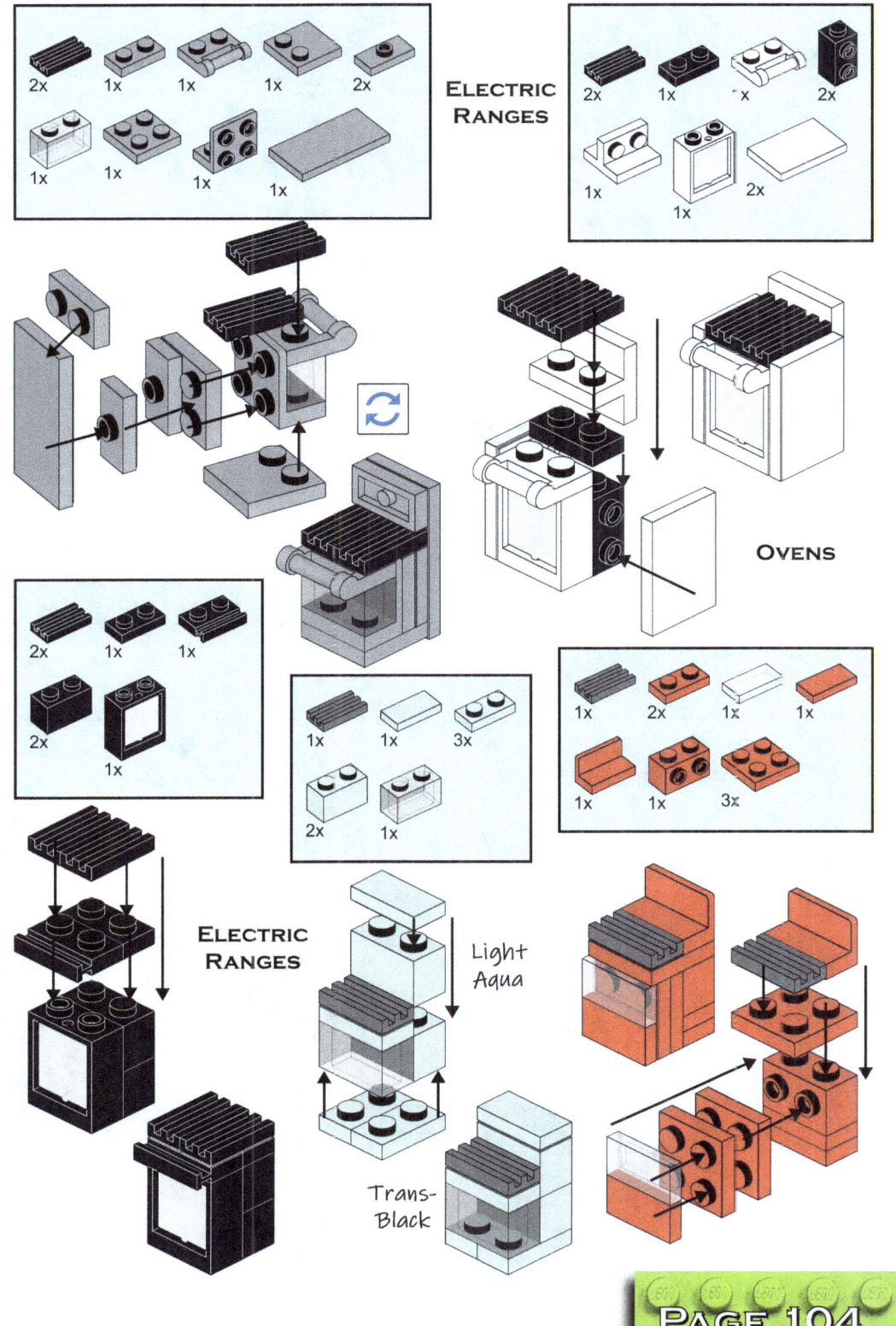

ELECTRIC RANGES

OVENS

ELECTRIC RANGES

Light Aqua

Trans-Black

KITCHEN & DINING

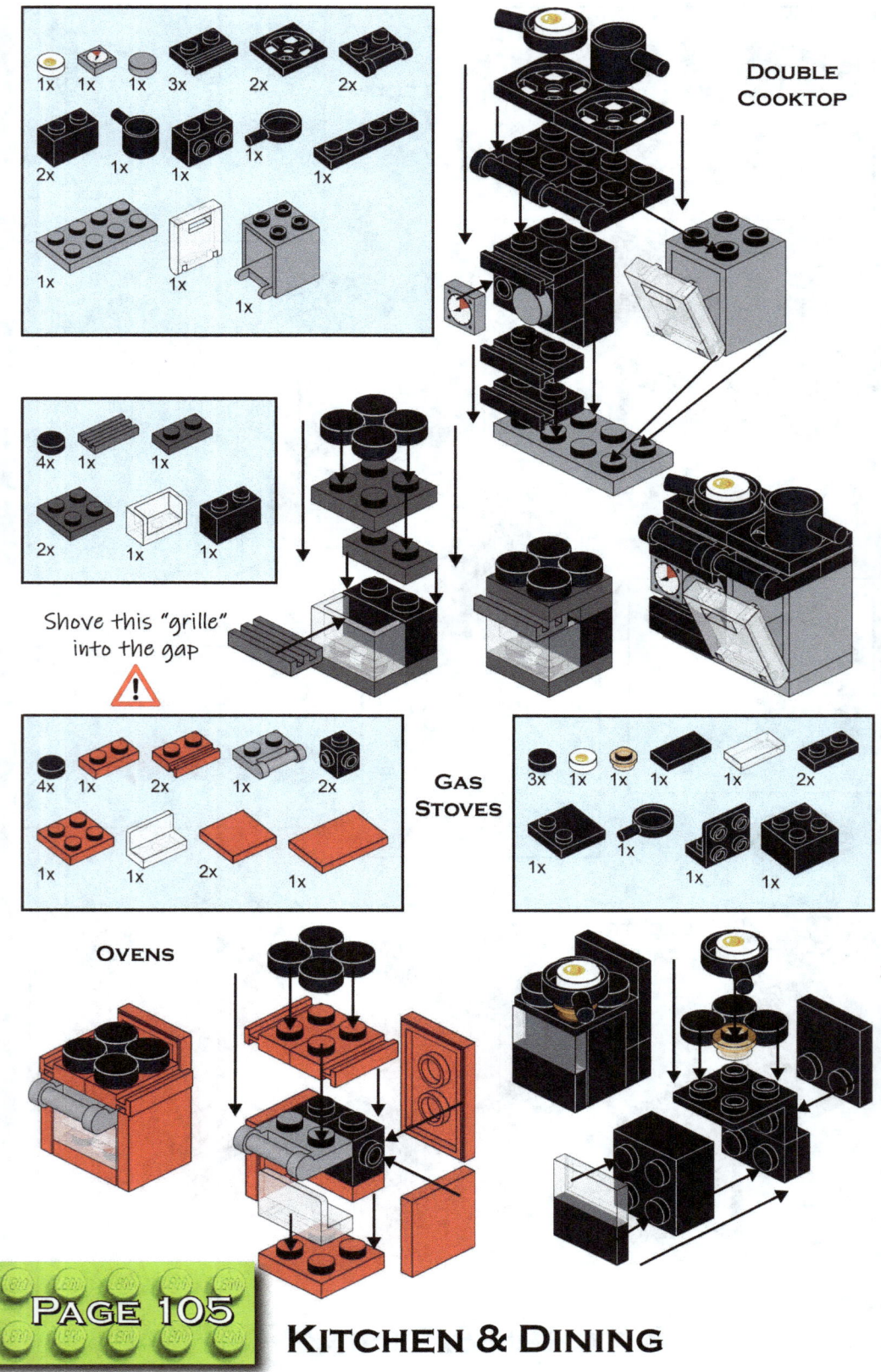

DOUBLE COOKTOP

Shove this "grille" into the gap ⚠️

GAS STOVES

OVENS

KITCHEN & DINING

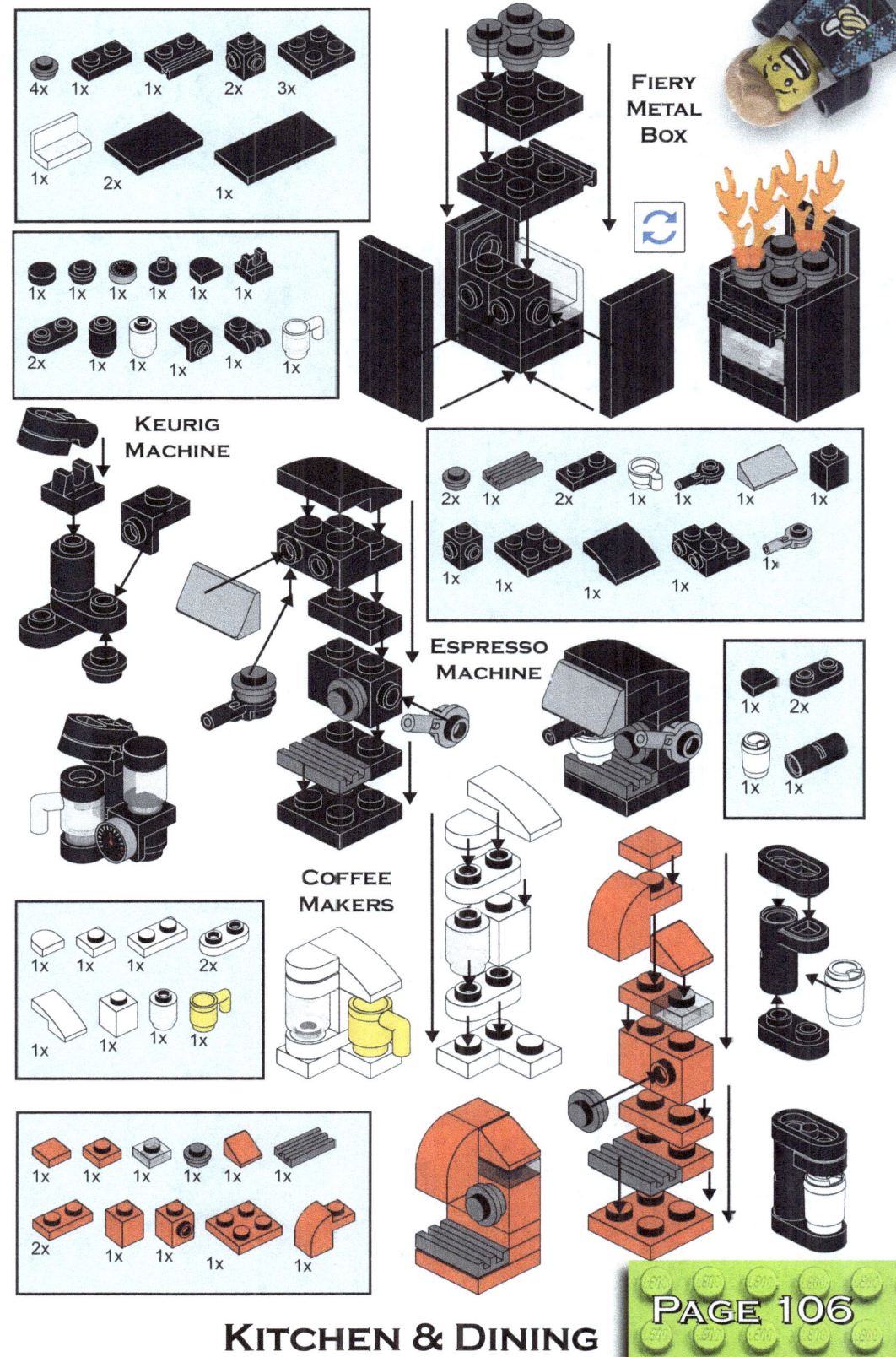

FIERY METAL BOX

KEURIG MACHINE

ESPRESSO MACHINE

COFFEE MAKERS

KITCHEN & DINING

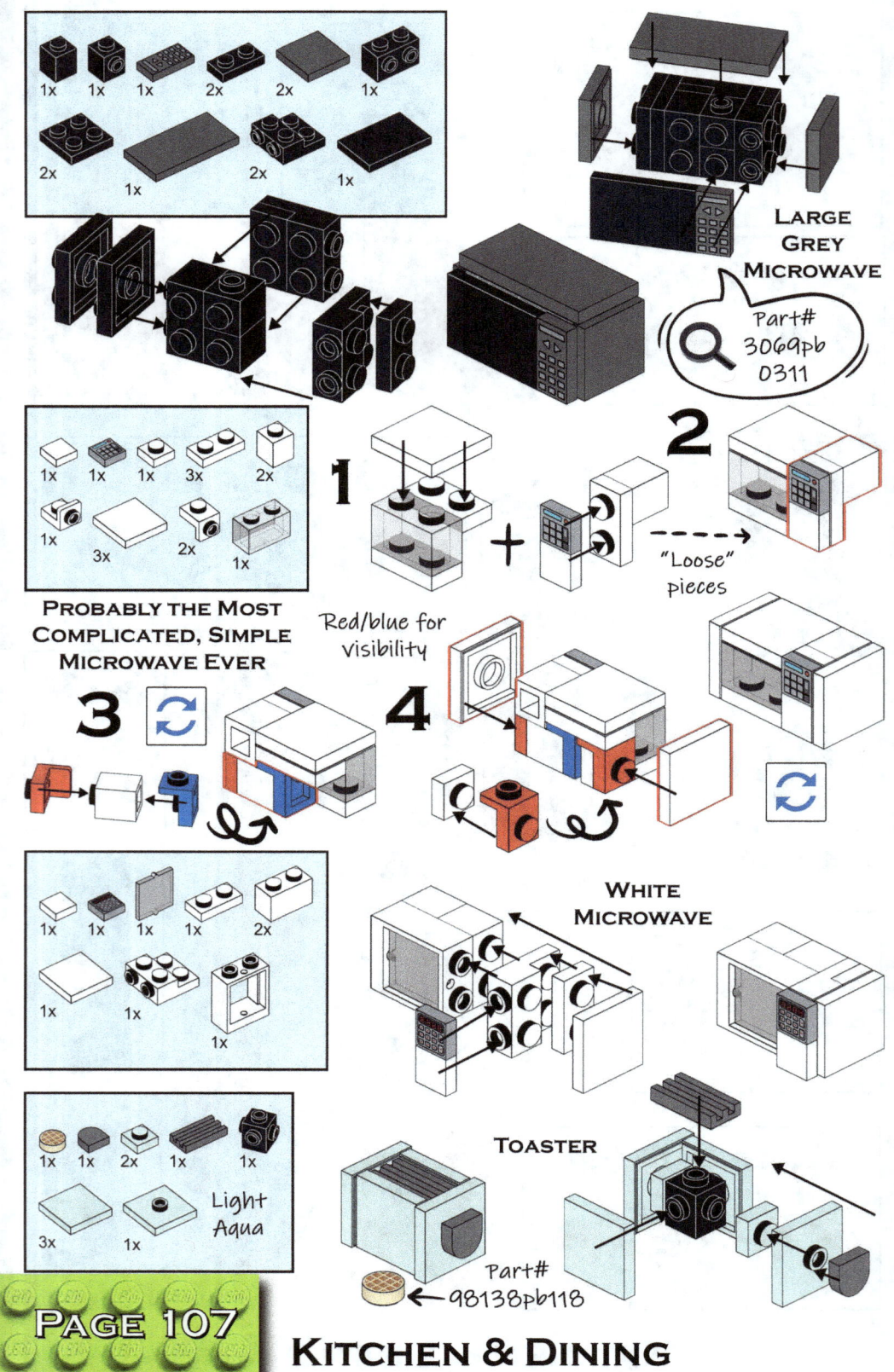

1x 1x 1x 2x 2x 1x

2x 1x 2x 1x

LARGE GREY MICROWAVE

Part# 3069pb 0311

1x 1x 1x 3x 2x

1x 3x 2x 1x

PROBABLY THE MOST COMPLICATED, SIMPLE MICROWAVE EVER

1

+

2

"Loose" pieces

3

Red/blue for visibility

4

1x 1x 1x 1x 2x

1x 1x

1x

WHITE MICROWAVE

1x 1x 2x 1x 1x

3x 1x

Light Aqua

TOASTER

Part# 98138pb118

KITCHEN & DINING

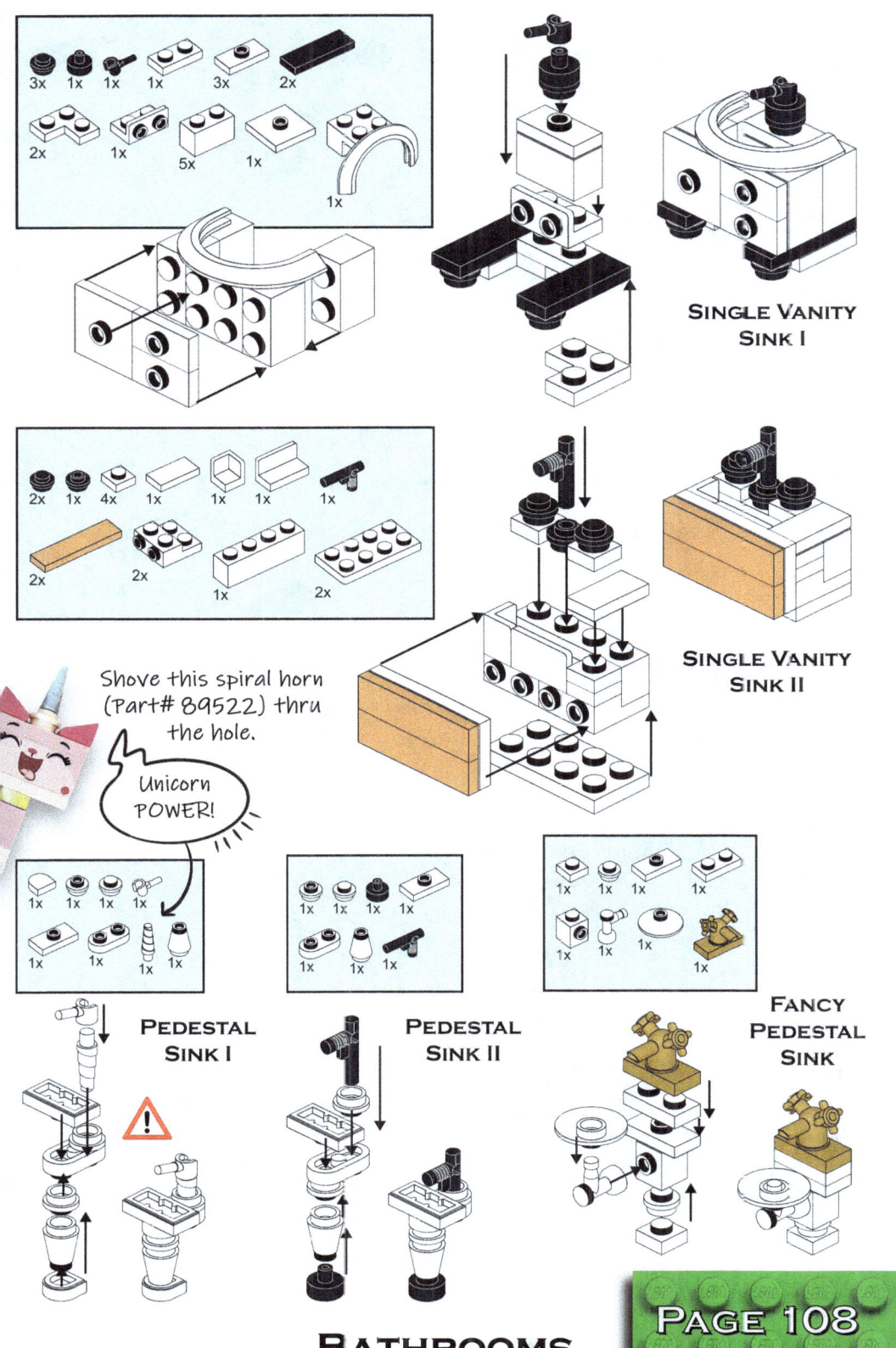

3x 1x 1x 1x 3x 2x

2x 1x 5x 1x 1x

SINGLE VANITY SINK I

2x 1x 4x 1x 1x 1x 1x

2x 2x 1x 2x

Shove this spiral horn (Part# 89522) thru the hole.

Unicorn POWER!

SINGLE VANITY SINK II

1x 1x 1x 1x

1x 1x 1x 1x

PEDESTAL SINK I

1x 1x 1x 1x

1x 1x 1x

PEDESTAL SINK II

1x 1x 1x 1x

1x 1x 1x

1x

FANCY PEDESTAL SINK

BATHROOMS

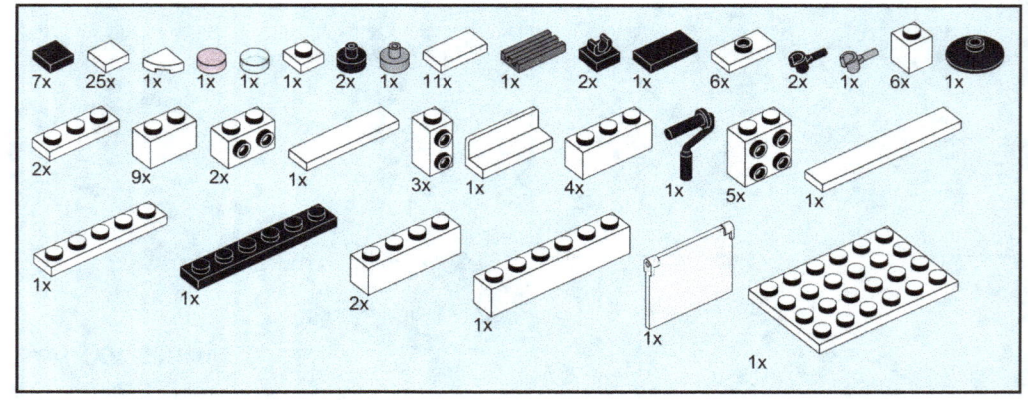

WALK-IN SHOWER I

The stud base is 7x5. Fill in with any plates you have available.

1

2

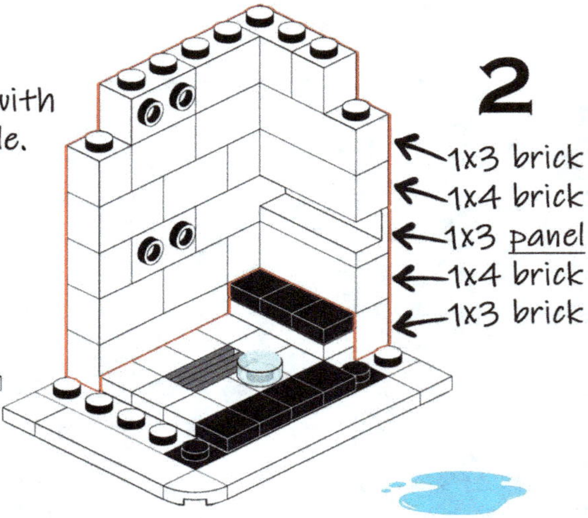

←1x3 brick
←1x4 brick
←1x3 <u>panel</u>
←1x4 brick
←1x3 brick

3

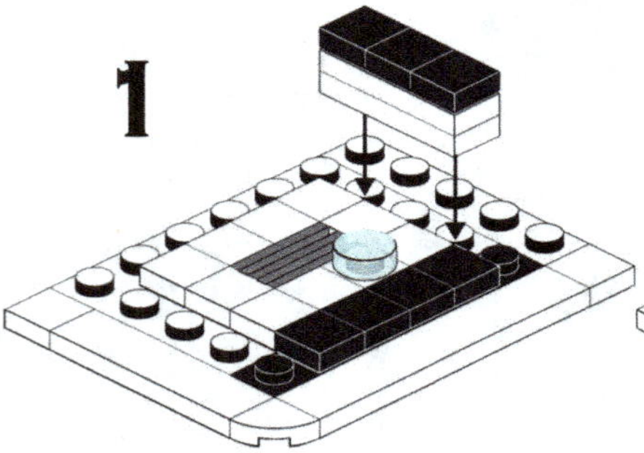

Try to stagger the wall bricks to create overlapping subway tile grout lines.

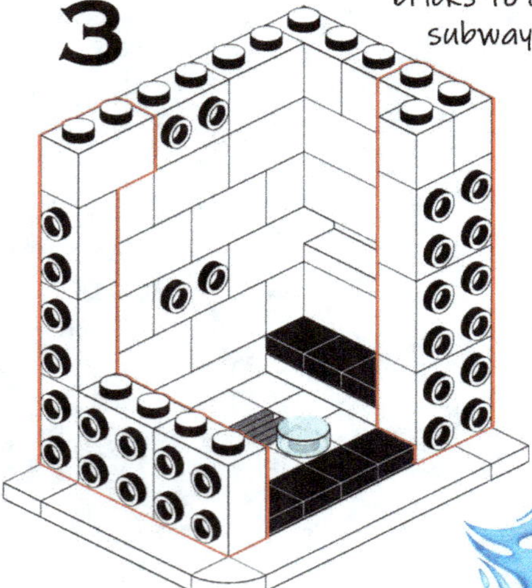

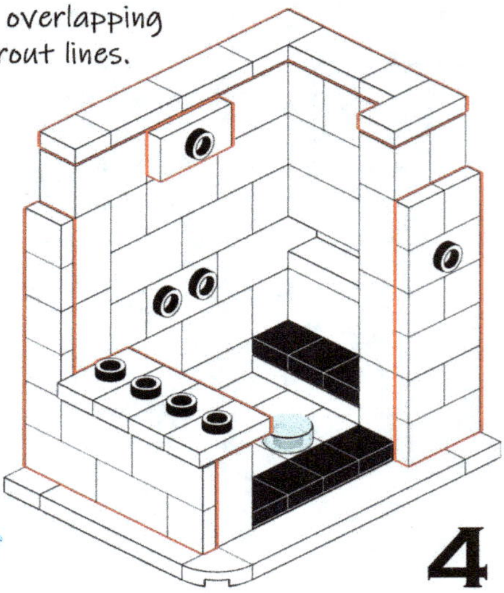

4

BATHROOMS

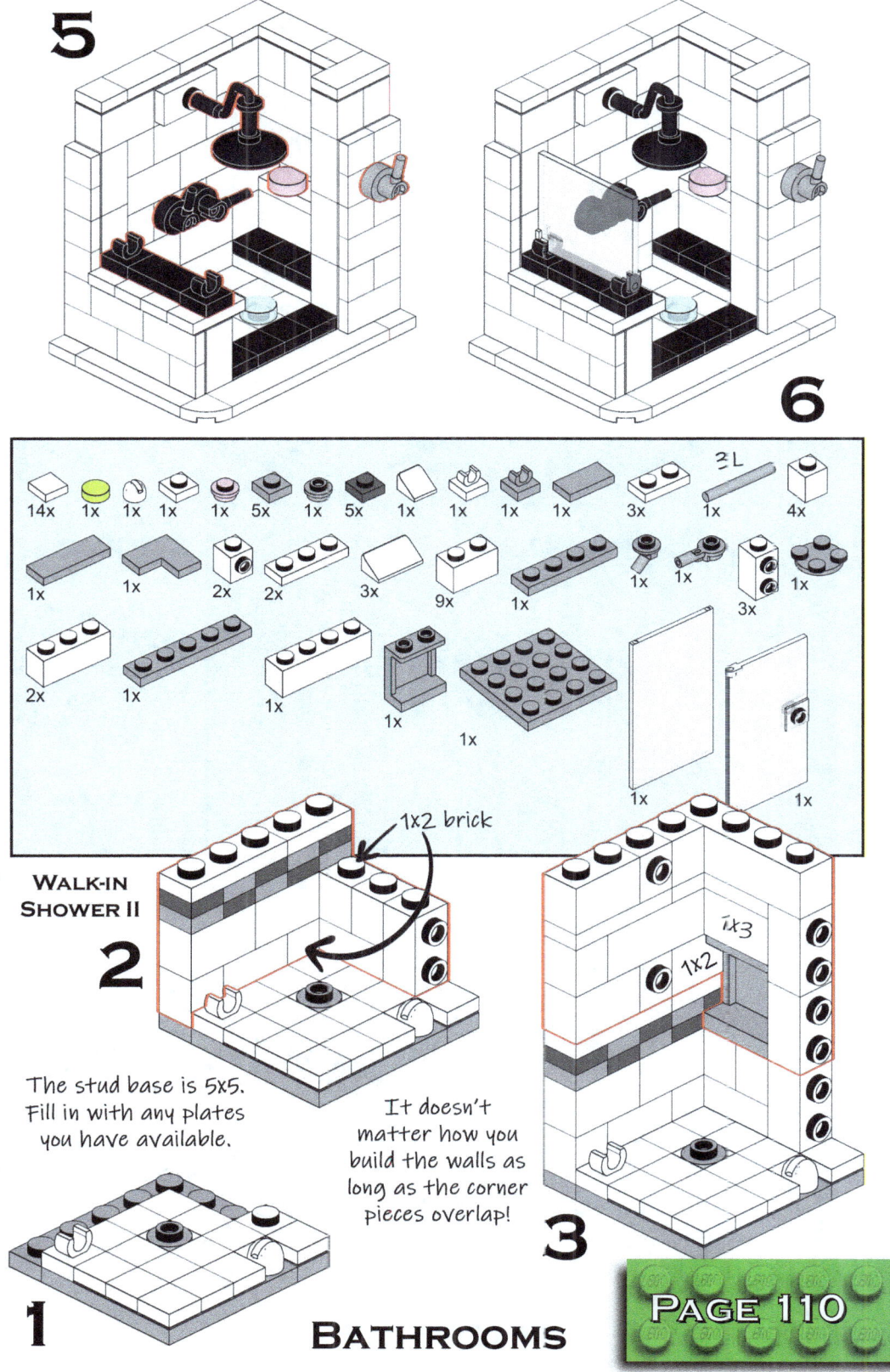

5

6

3L

**WALK-IN
SHOWER II**

1x2 brick

2

The stud base is 5x5.
Fill in with any plates
you have available.

1x3

1x2

It doesn't
matter how you
build the walls as
long as the corner
pieces overlap!

3

1

BATHROOMS

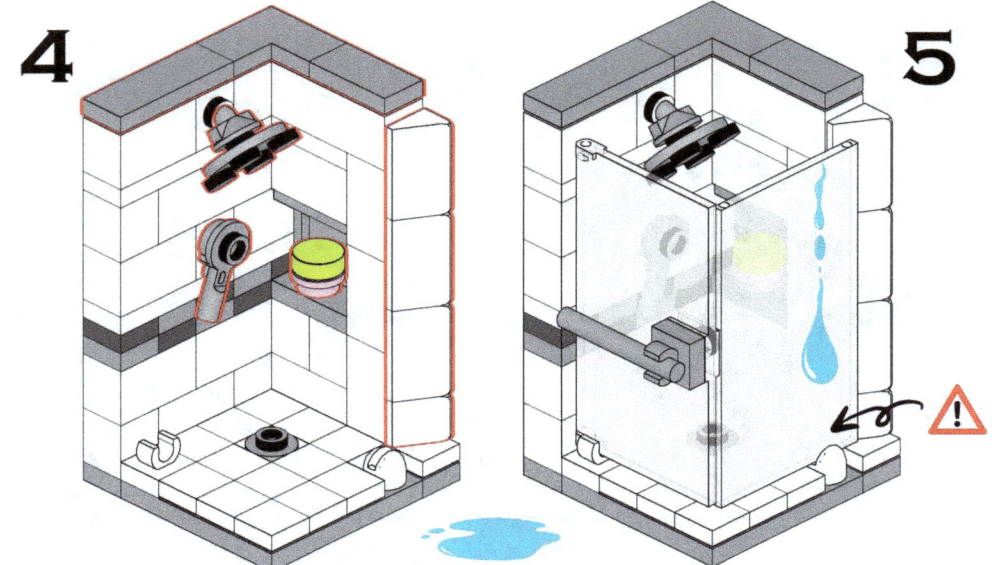

BUILT-IN TUB SHOWER

In this model, 1x2 bricks are purposely stacked to create grout lines that line up.

The stud base is 9x5. Fill in with any plates you have available.

4

5

⚠

4x
1x
1x
1x
1x
1x
1x
1x
2x
1x
3x
4x
1x
1x
2x

9x
2x
3x
2x
3x
1x
1x
2x
2x
4x

29x
1x
4x
1x
1x
4x
3x
1x

1x
~7L cut rigid hose

2x
1x
1x

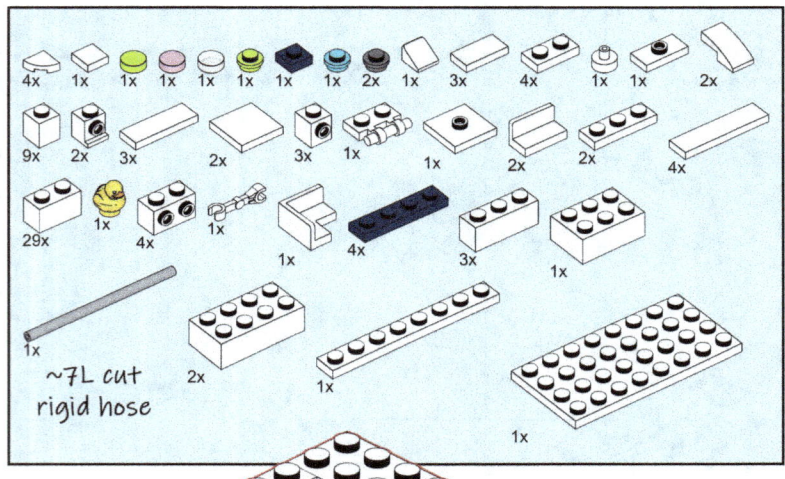

2

1x2
1x3

1

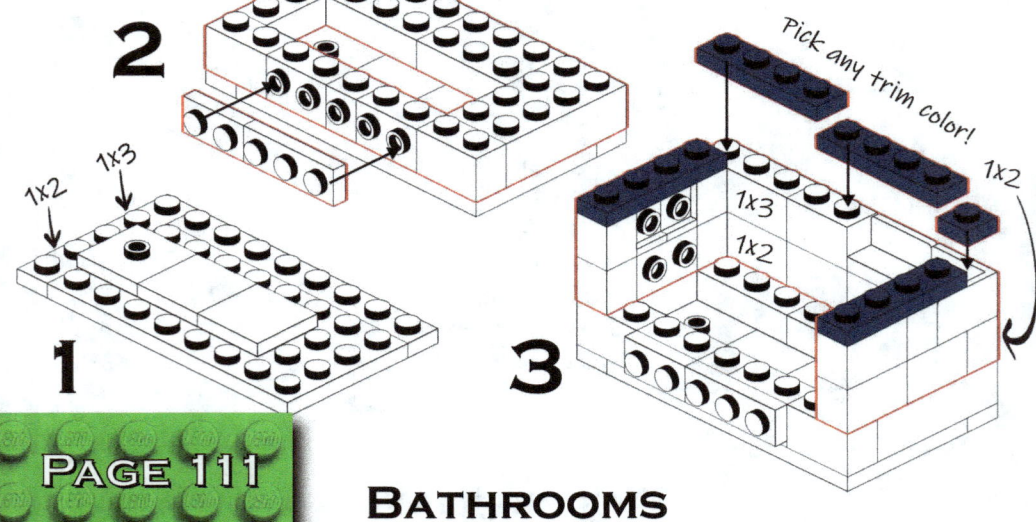

3

Pick any trim color!

1x3
1x2
1x2

BATHROOMS

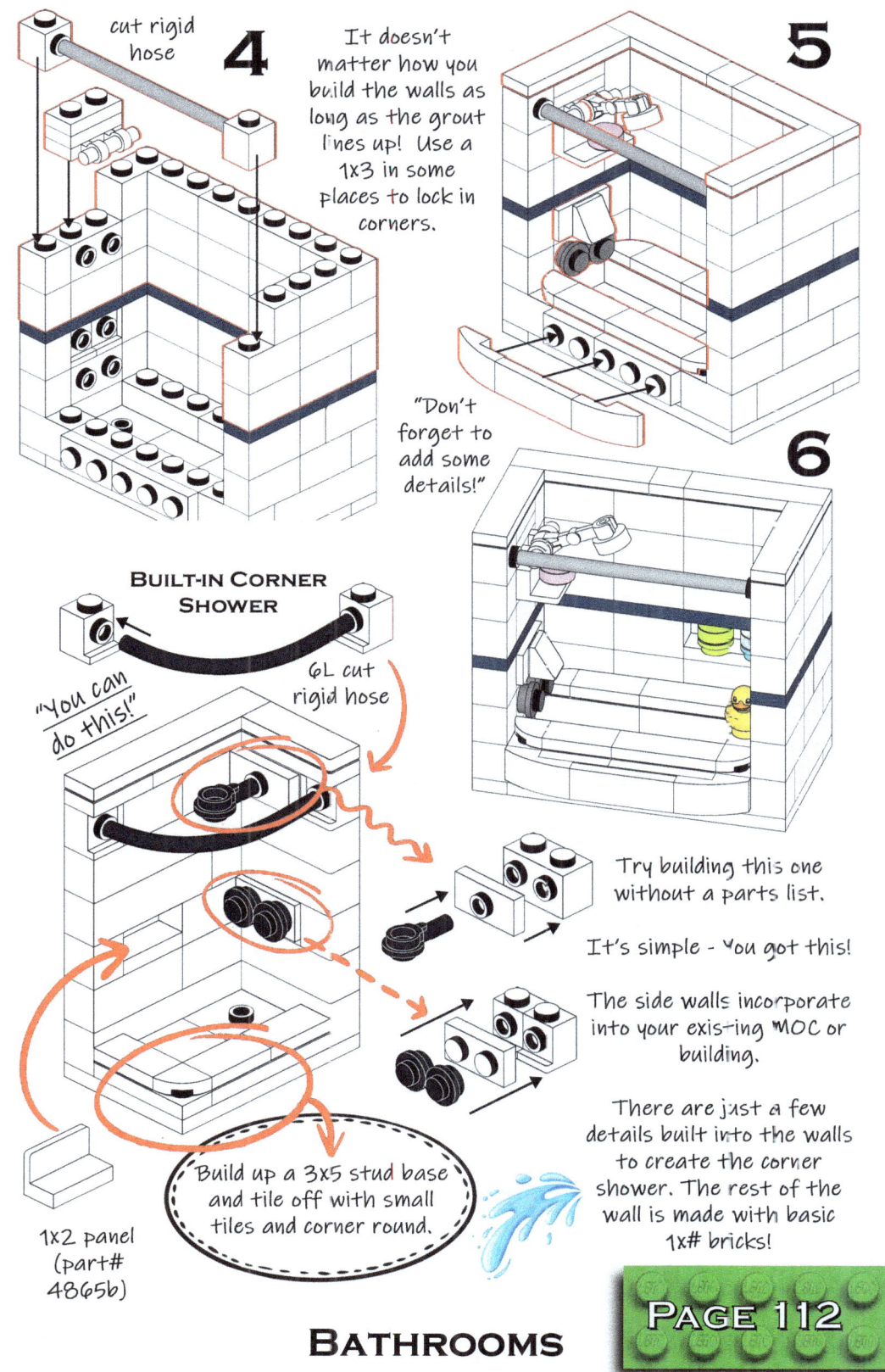

cut rigid hose

4

It doesn't matter how you build the walls as long as the grout lines up! Use a 1x3 in some places to lock in corners.

5

"Don't forget to add some details!"

6

BUILT-IN CORNER SHOWER

"You can do this!"

6L cut rigid hose

Try building this one without a parts list.

It's simple - You got this!

The side walls incorporate into your existing MOC or building.

There are just a few details built into the walls to create the corner shower. The rest of the wall is made with basic 1x# bricks!

Build up a 3x5 stud base and tile off with small tiles and corner round.

1x2 panel (part# 4865b)

BATHROOMS

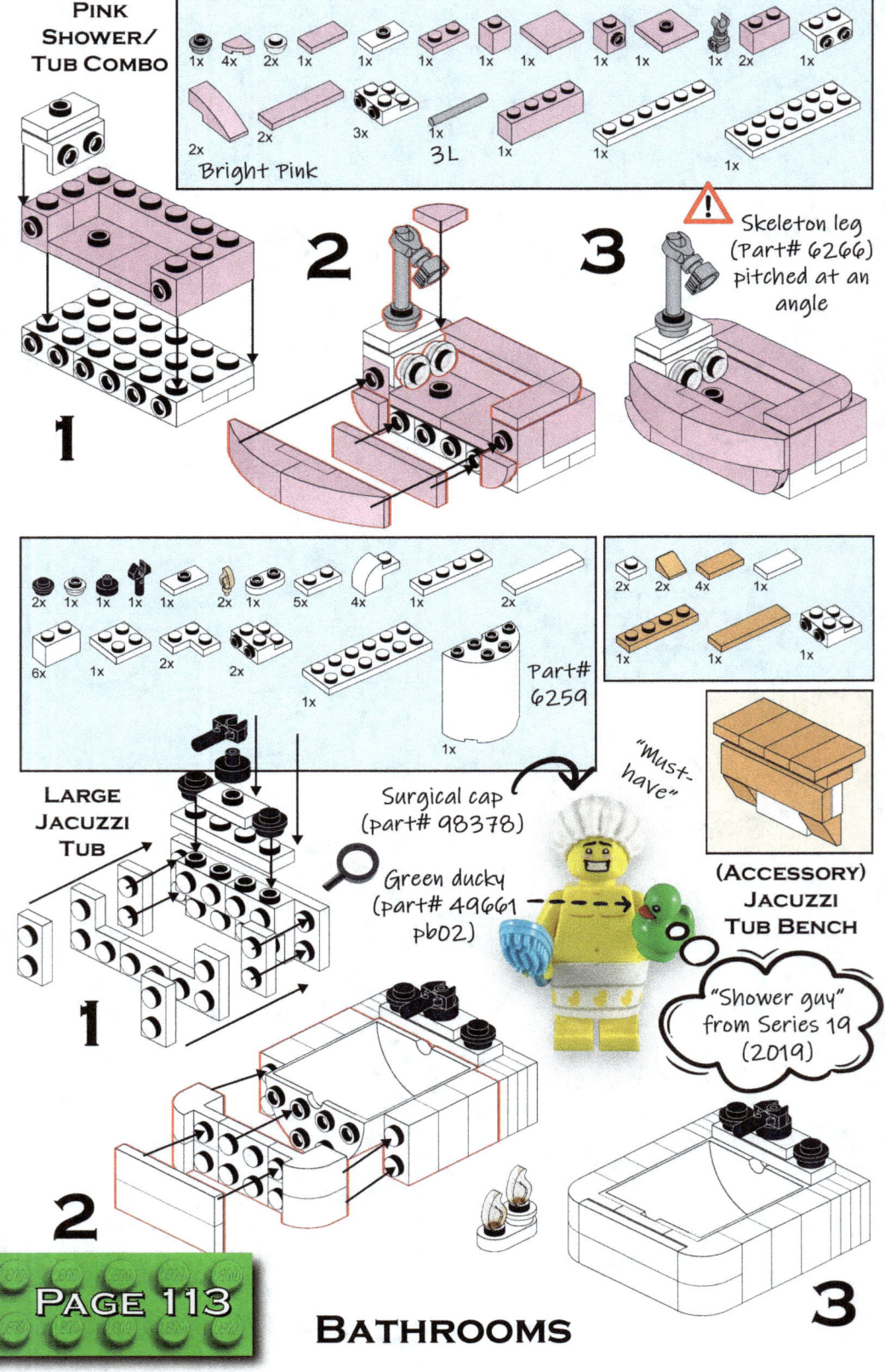

PINK SHOWER/ TUB COMBO

1x 4x 2x 1x 1x 1x 1x 1x 1x 1x 1x 2x 1x

2x 2x 3x 3L 1x 1x 1x

Bright Pink

1

2

3

⚠️ Skeleton leg (Part# 6266) pitched at an angle

2x 1x 1x 1x 1x 2x 1x 5x 4x 1x 2x

6x 1x 2x 2x 1x

1x Part# 6259

1x

2x 2x 4x 1x

1x 1x 1x

LARGE JACUZZI TUB

1

Surgical cap (part# 98378)

"Must-have"

Green ducky (part# 49661 pb02)

(ACCESSORY) JACUZZI TUB BENCH

"Shower guy" from Series 19 (2019)

2

3

BATHROOMS

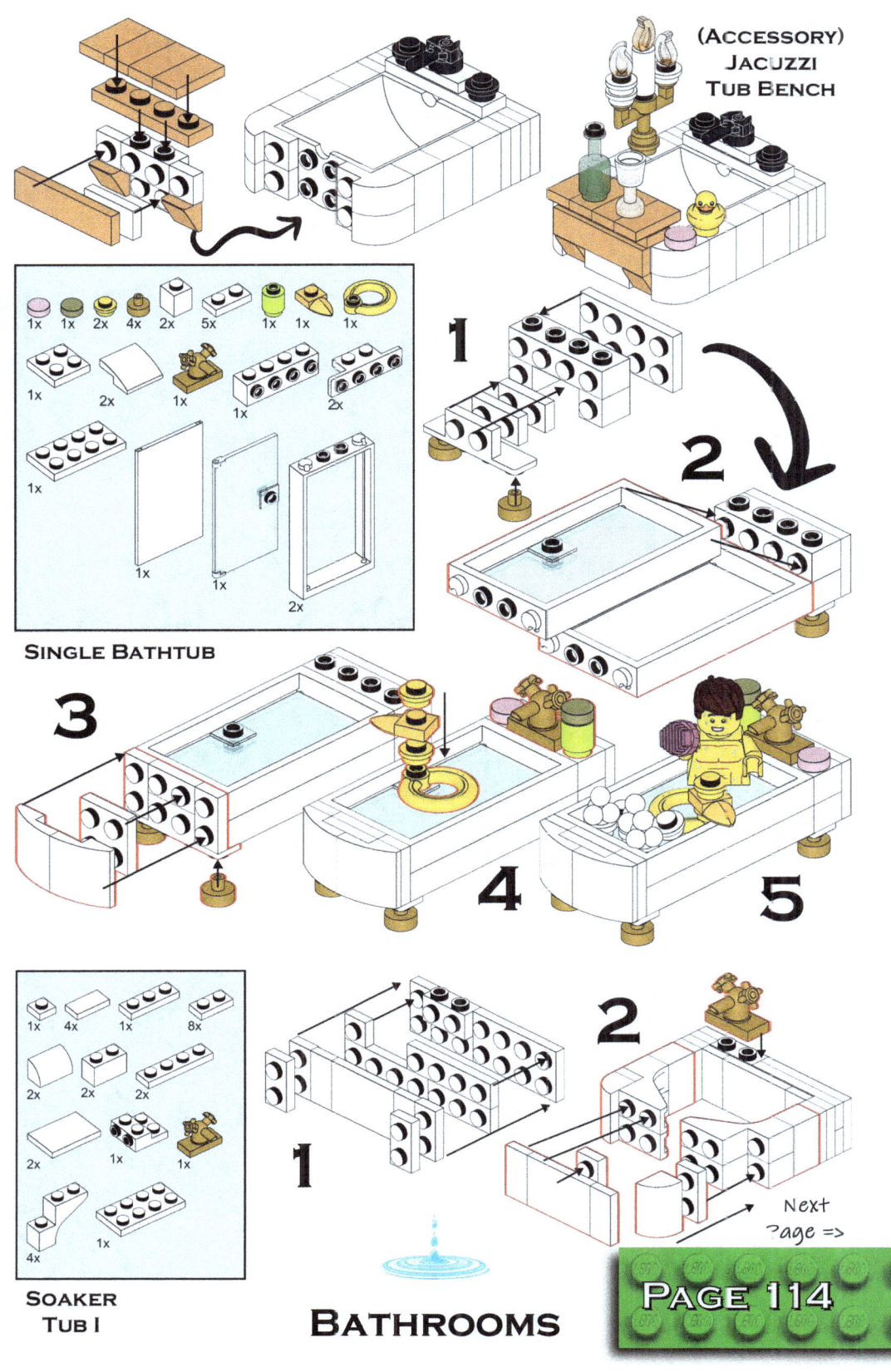

(ACCESSORY)
JACUZZI
TUB BENCH

SINGLE BATHTUB

1

2

3

4

5

**SOAKER
TUB I**

1

2

Next
?age =>

BATHROOMS

3

We need a base. Try a tiled white 7x6 floor. Embellish it with some edge tile.

"your wall"

upside-down part# 99563 "gold bar" ingot

The tub bottom is missing and the SNOT method left it smooth!

Use part# 32952 to hold the tub in place.

part# 58176 "bionicle" eye (bulb)

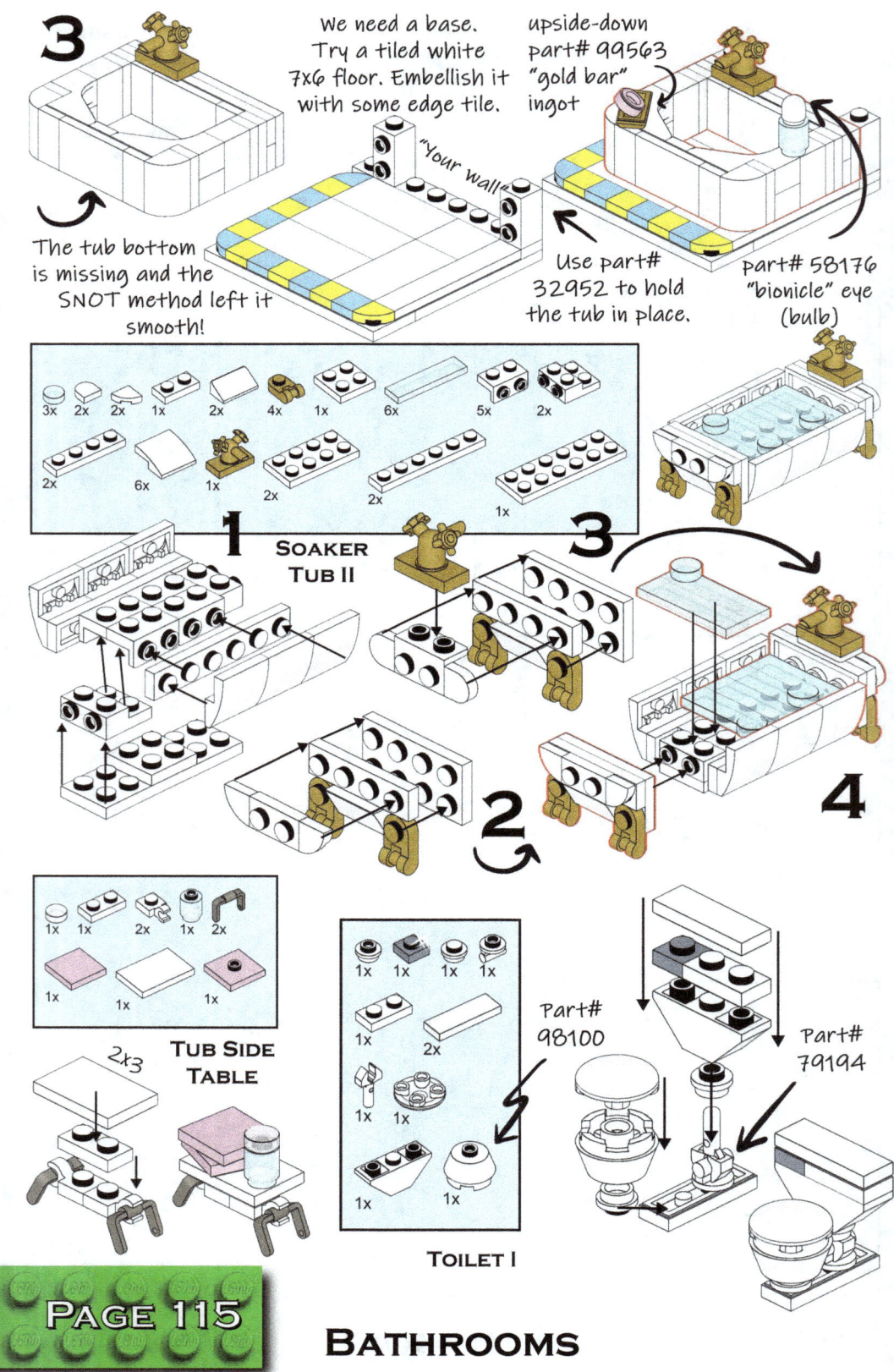

1 SOAKER TUB II

3x 2x 2x 1x 2x 4x 1x 6x 5x 2x

2x 6x 1x 2x 2x 1x

2

3

4

TUB SIDE TABLE

1x 1x 2x 1x 2x

1x 1x 1x

2x3

TOILET I

1x 1x 1x 1x

1x 1x 2x

1x

1x 1x

1x 1x

Part# 98100

Part# 79194

BATHROOMS

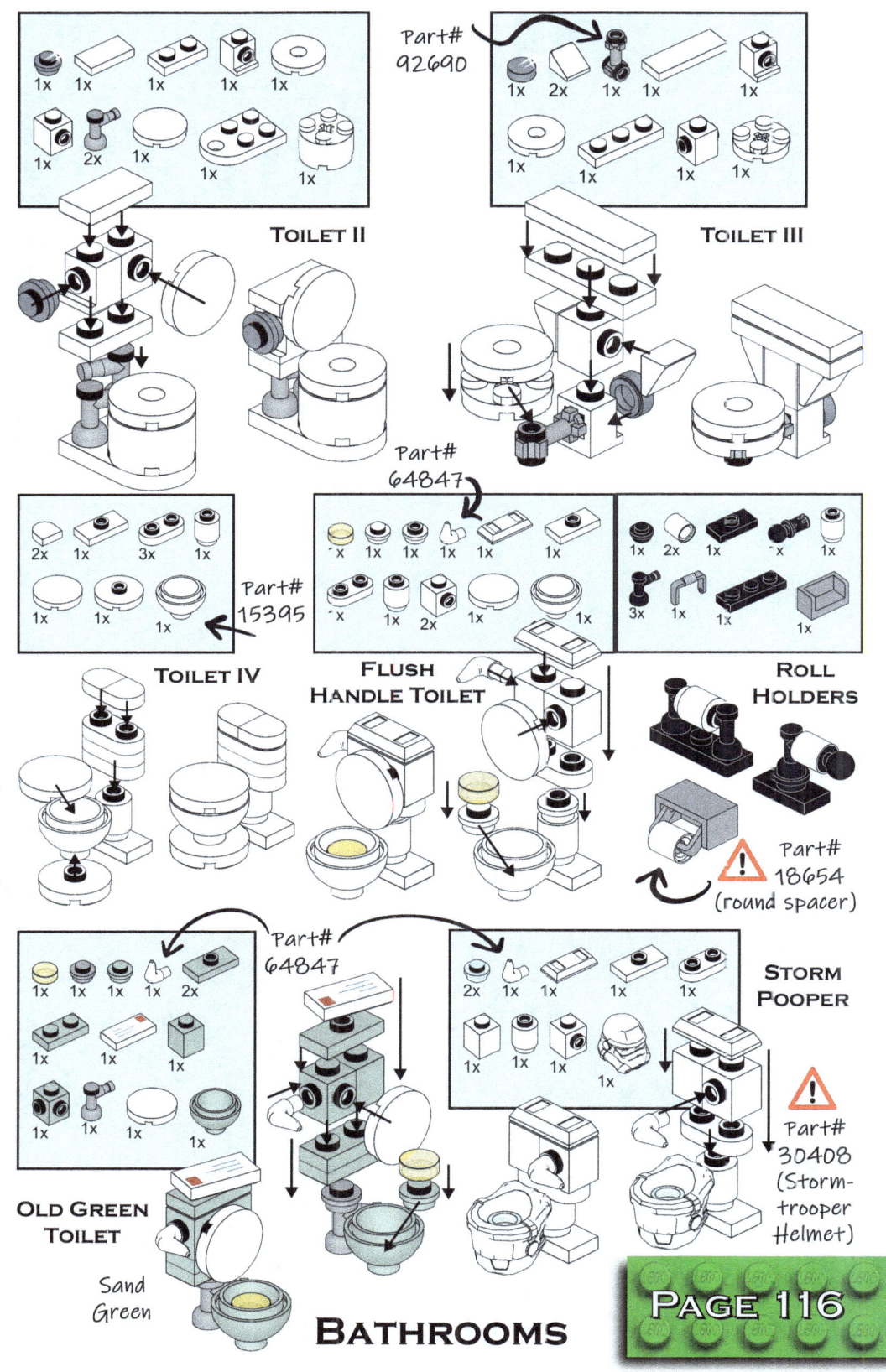

Part# 92690

TOILET II

TOILET III

Part# 15395

Part# 64847

TOILET IV

FLUSH HANDLE TOILET

ROLL HOLDERS

Part# 18654 (round spacer)

Part# 64847

STORM POOPER

Part# 30408 (Stormtrooper Helmet)

OLD GREEN TOILET

Sand Green

BATHROOMS

PAGE 116

FLUSH HANDLE TOILET II

1x 2x 1x 1x 1x 2x 1x
1x 1x 1x 1x

Part# 18654 (round spacer)

3L

Part# 4589
Part# 33492
Part# 85975
Part# 20952

PLUNGERS

2x 8x 8x 1x 2x 1x 3x 1x 1x 1x 1x 2x
12x 3x 2x 2x 1x 1x 4x

Make 2x of these.

HIS & HERS TODDLER BUNK BEDS

Part# 3070pb141 (cat tiles) or Choose your own design! Lego® Dots are a good source.

Make one with this clip.

Make one with a 1x2 plate.

Part# 6179pb009

BEDROOMS

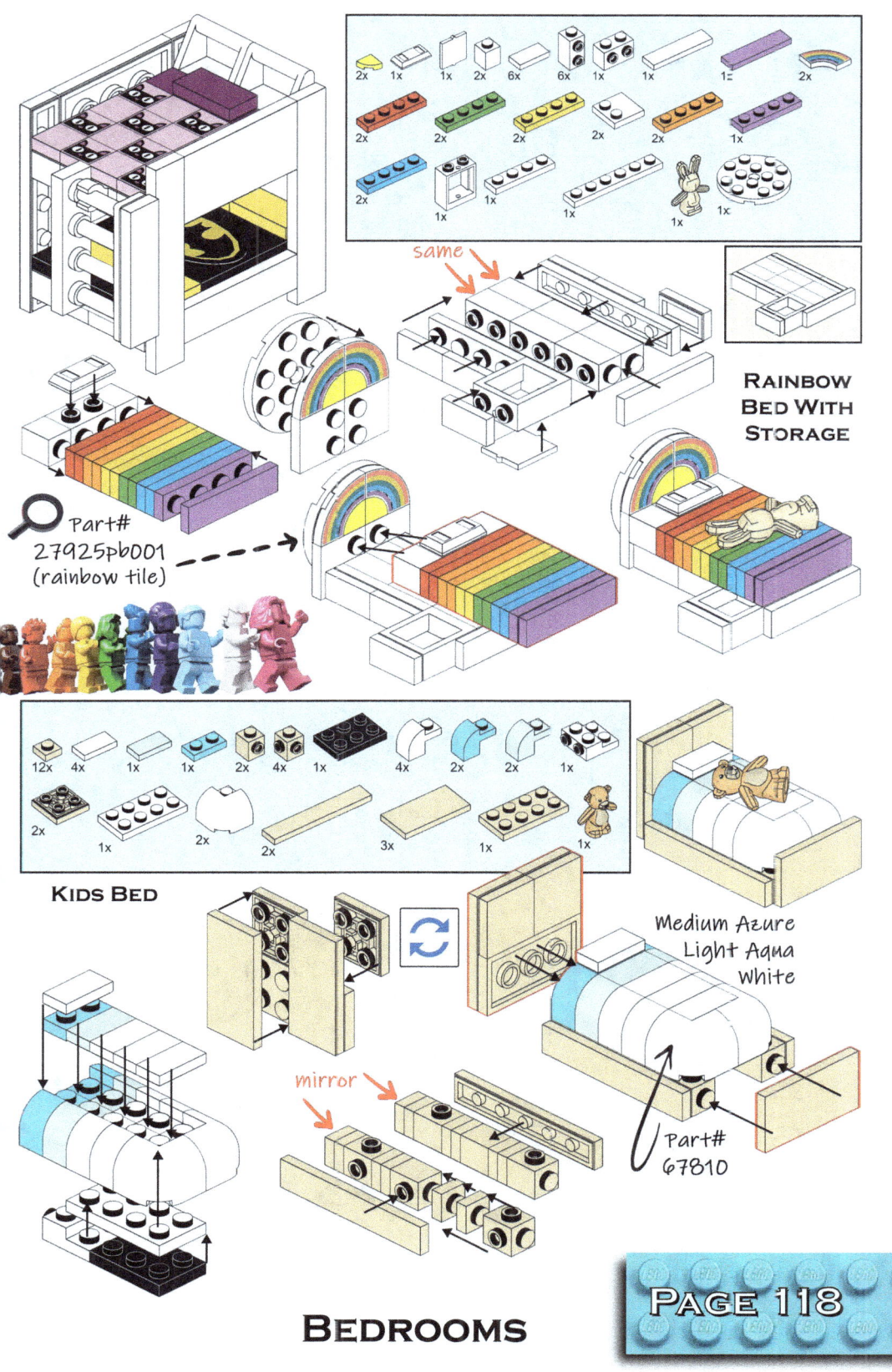

Part# 27925pb001 (rainbow tile)

RAINBOW BED WITH STORAGE

same

KIDS BED

Medium Azure
Light Aqua
White

mirror

Part# 67810

BEDROOMS

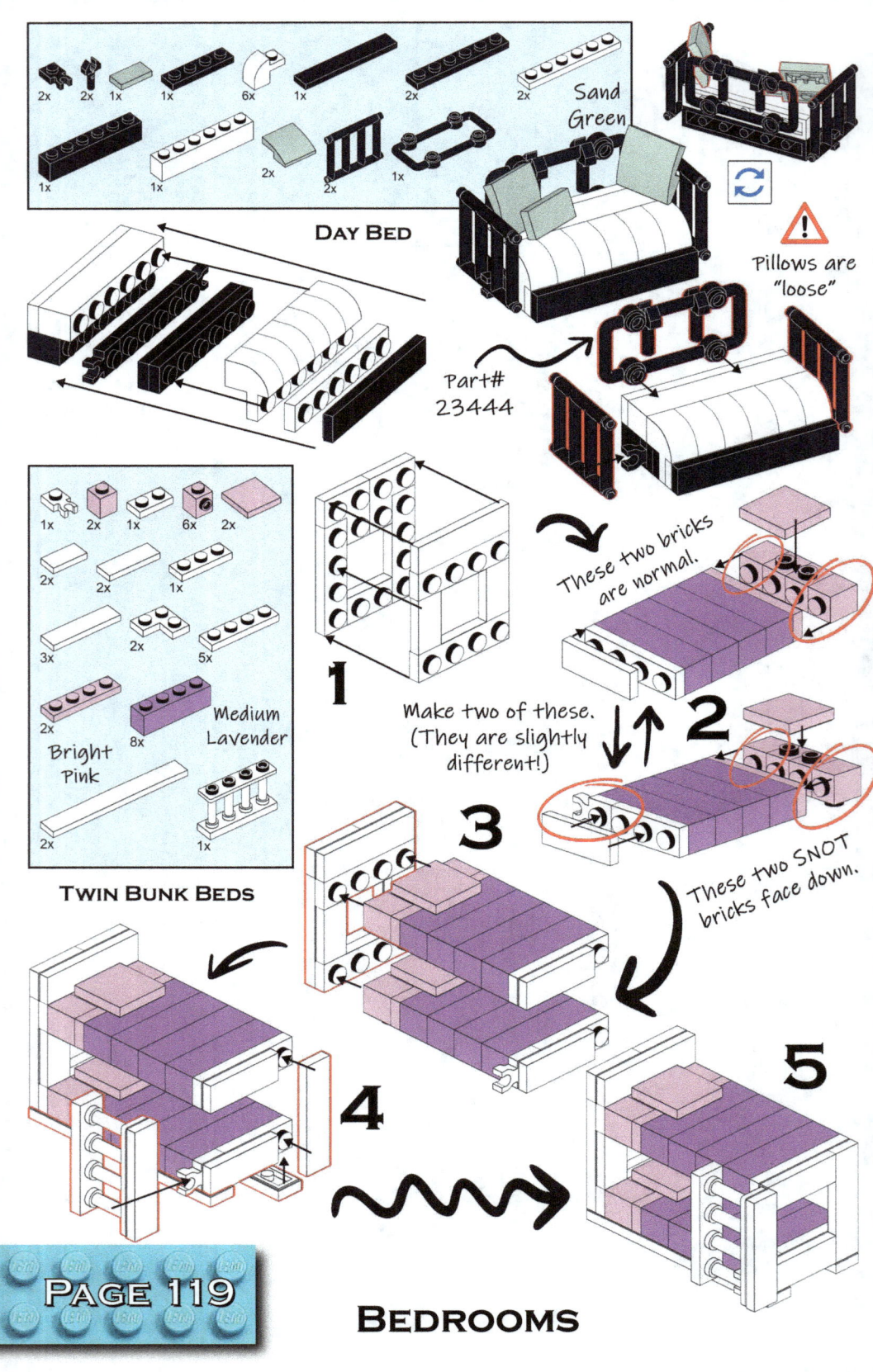

DAY BED

Sand Green

Pillows are "loose"

Part# 23444

TWIN BUNK BEDS

Bright Pink

Medium Lavender

1

These two bricks are normal.

Make two of these. (They are slightly different!)

2

These two SNOT bricks face down.

3

4

5

BEDROOMS

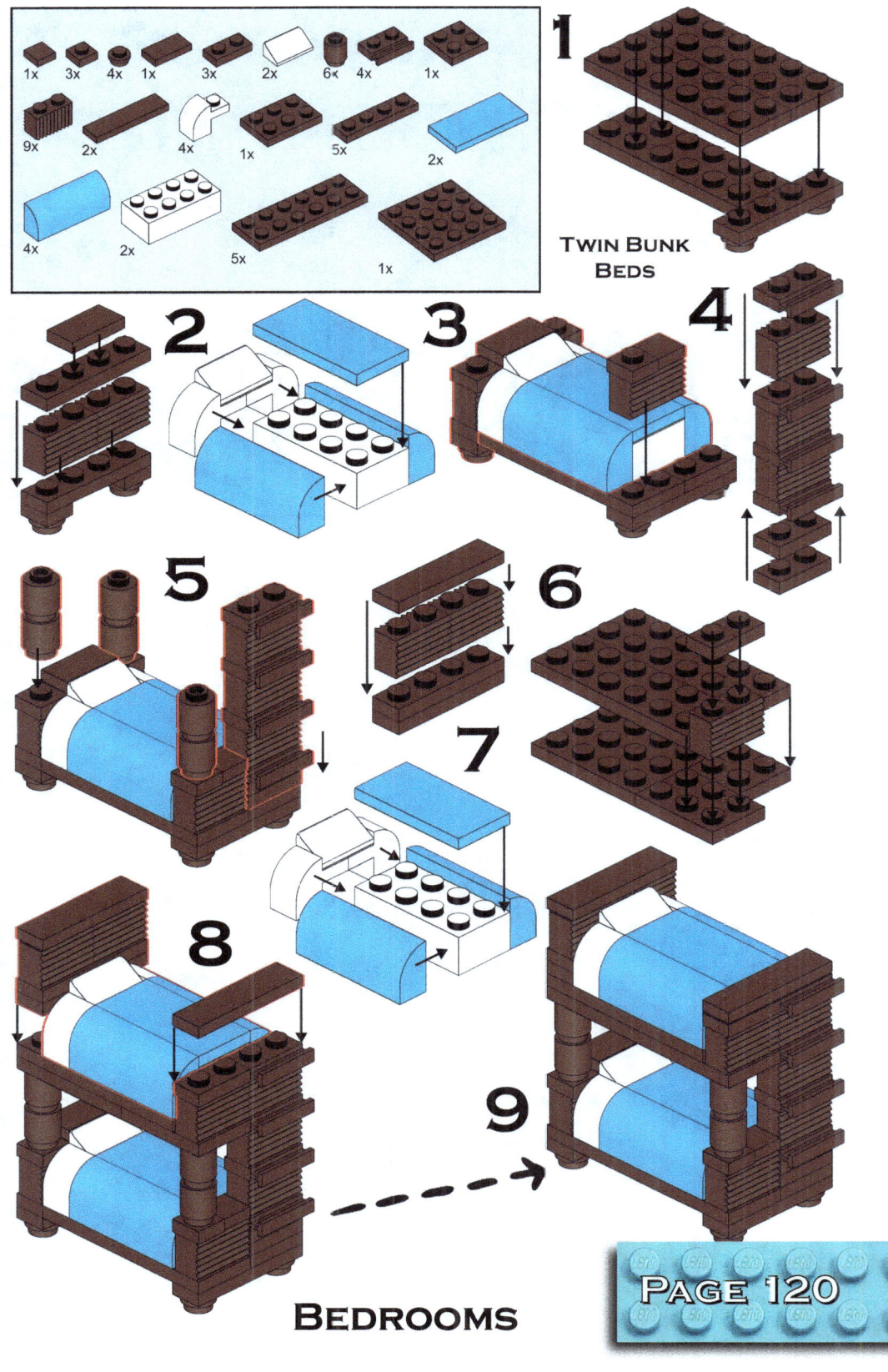

1

TWIN BUNK BEDS

2

3

4

5

6

7

8

9

BEDROOMS

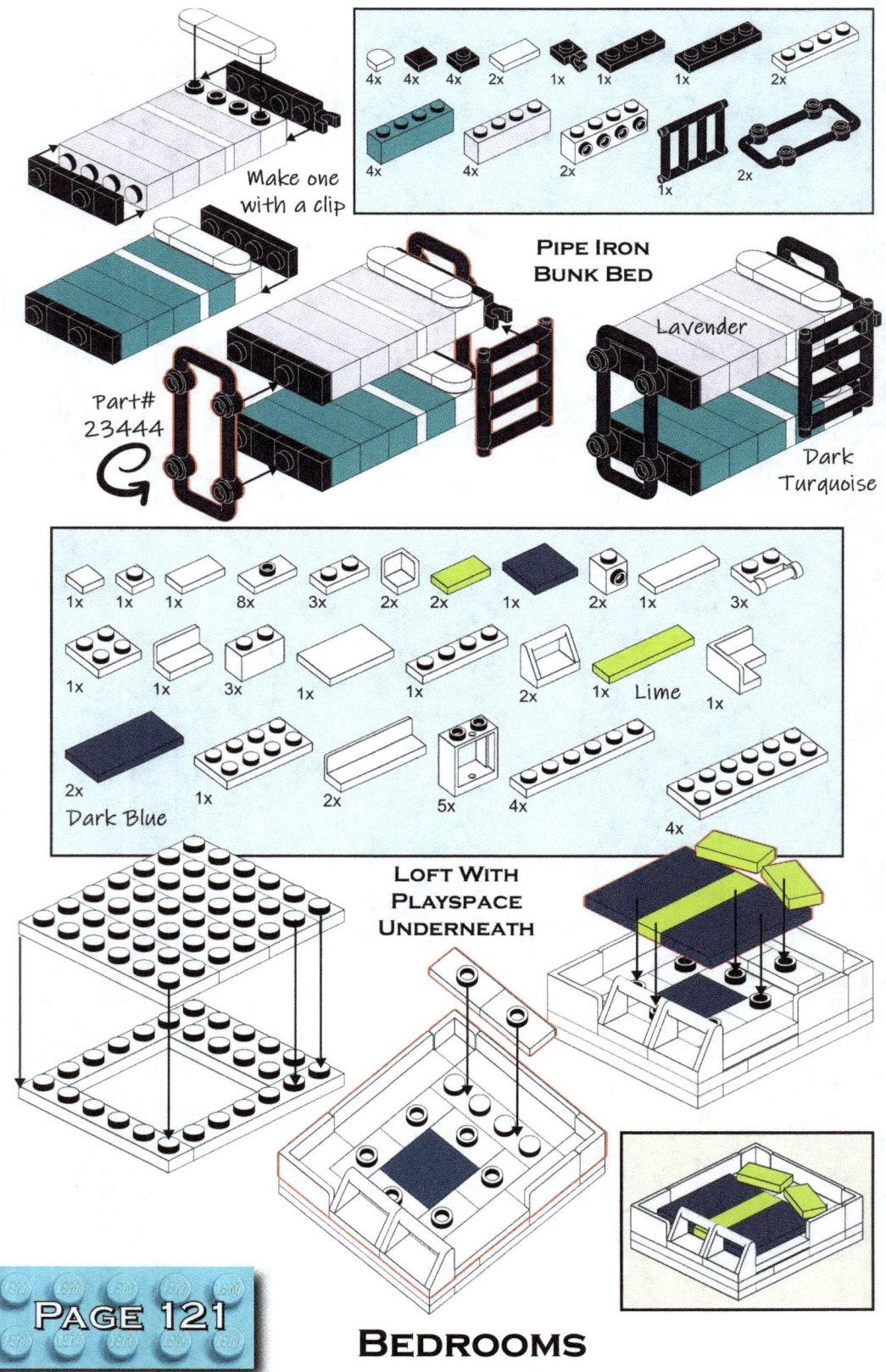

Make one with a clip

PIPE IRON BUNK BED

Lavender

Part# 23444

Dark Turquoise

Dark Blue

Lime

LOFT WITH PLAYSPACE UNDERNEATH

BEDROOMS

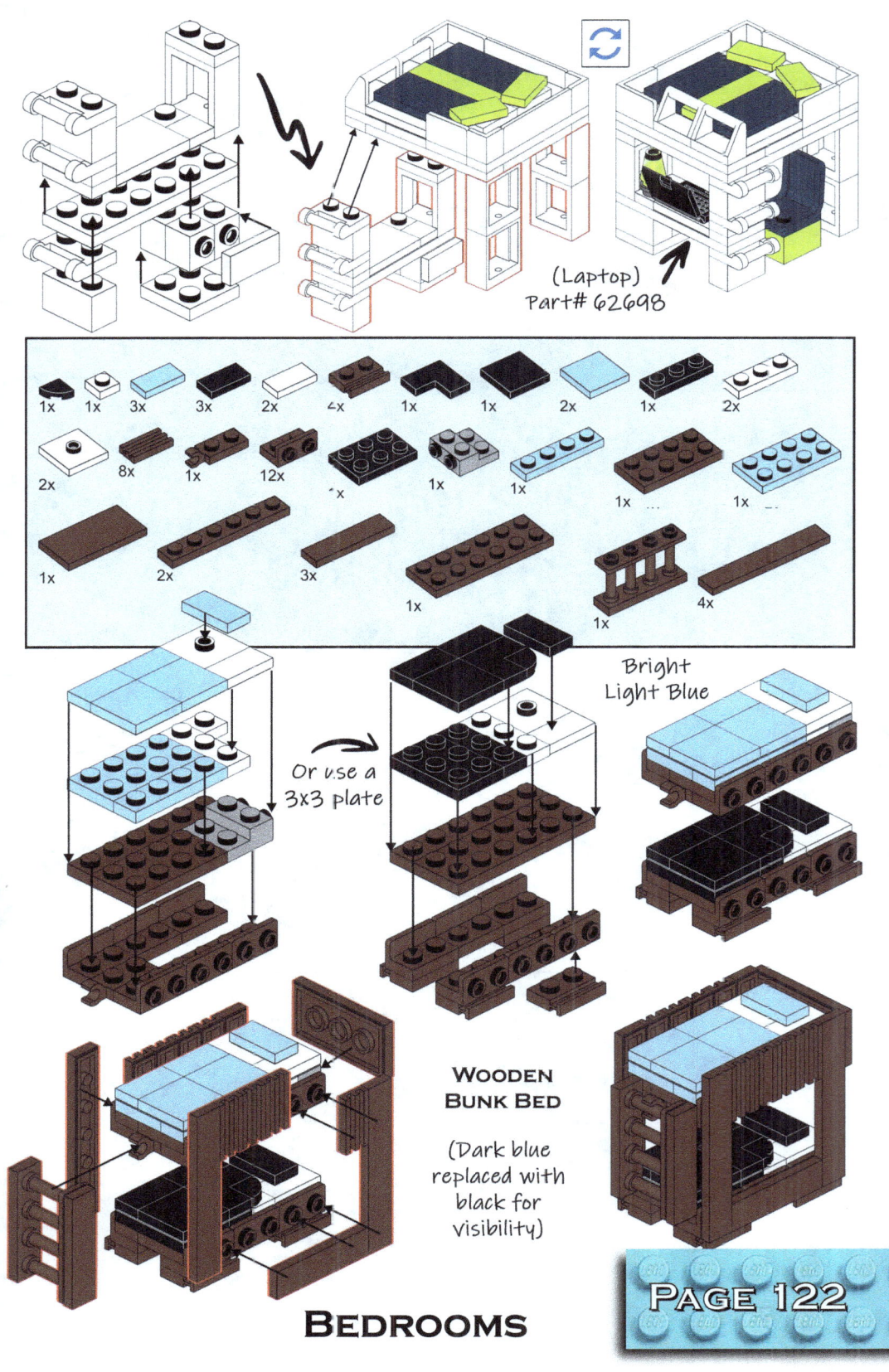

(Laptop)
Part# 62698

Bright
Light Blue

Or use a
3x3 plate

**WOODEN
BUNK BED**

(Dark blue
replaced with
black for
visibility)

BEDROOMS

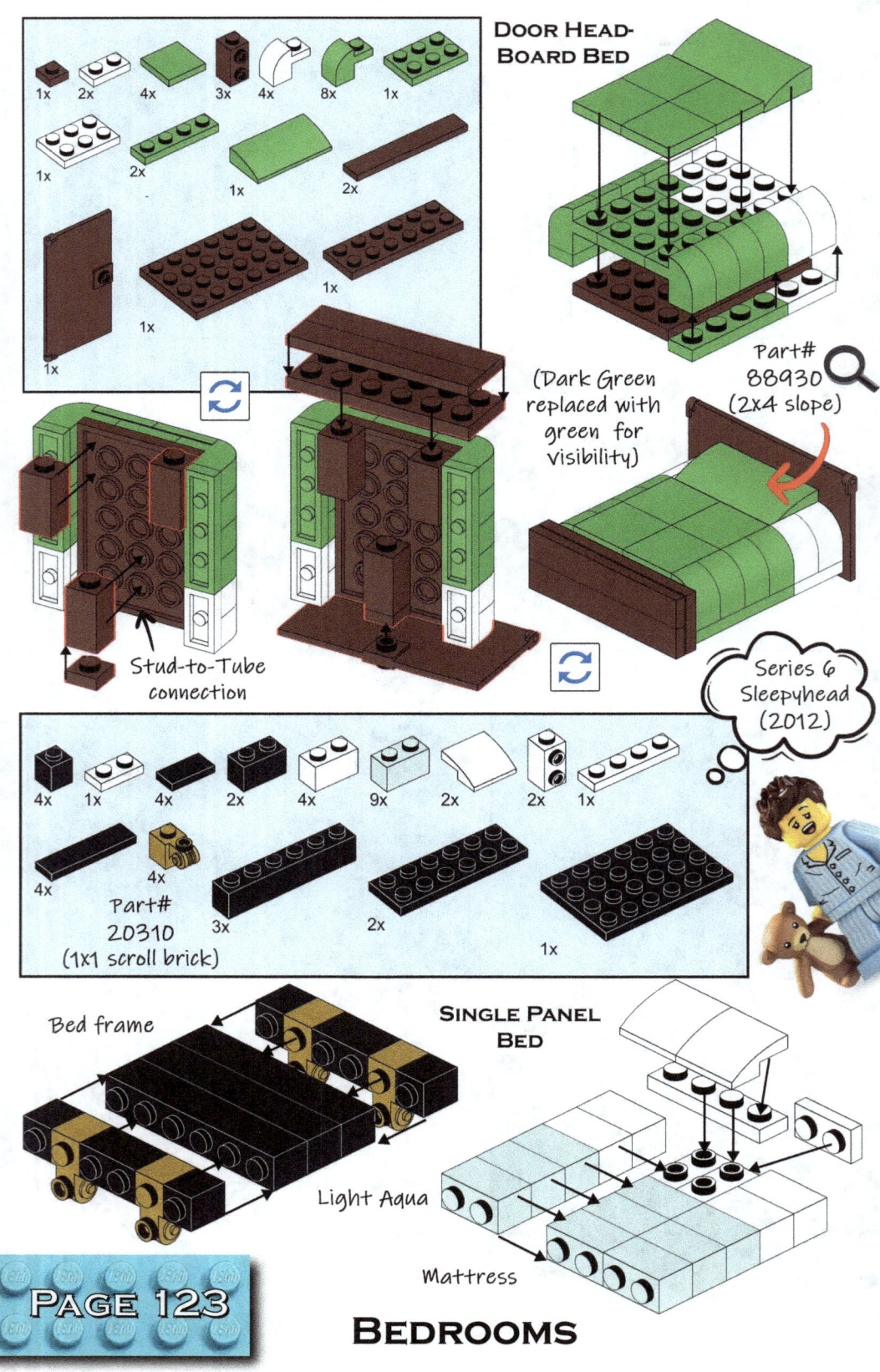

DOOR HEAD-BOARD BED

1x 2x 4x 3x 4x 8x 1x

1x 2x 1x 2x

1x 1x 1x 1x

Part# 88930 (2x4 slope)

(Dark Green replaced with green for visibility)

Stud-to-Tube connection

Series 6 Sleepyhead (2012)

4x 1x 4x 2x 4x 9x 2x 2x 1x

4x 4x Part# 20310 (1x1 scroll brick) 3x 2x 1x

Bed frame

SINGLE PANEL BED

Light Aqua

Mattress

BEDROOMS

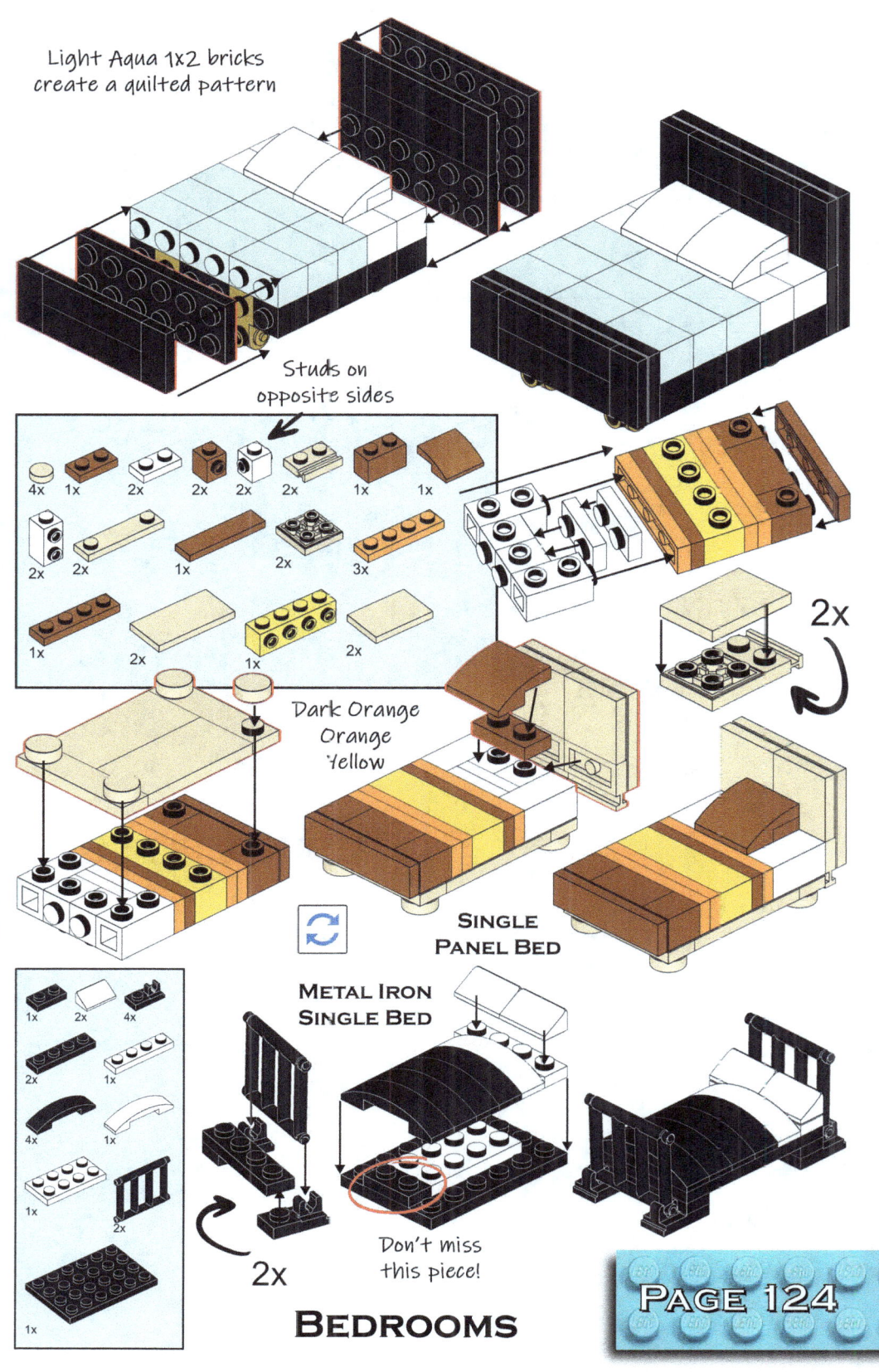

Light Aqua 1x2 bricks create a quilted pattern

Studs on opposite sides

Dark Orange
Orange
Yellow

SINGLE PANEL BED

METAL IRON SINGLE BED

Don't miss this piece!

2x

BEDROOMS

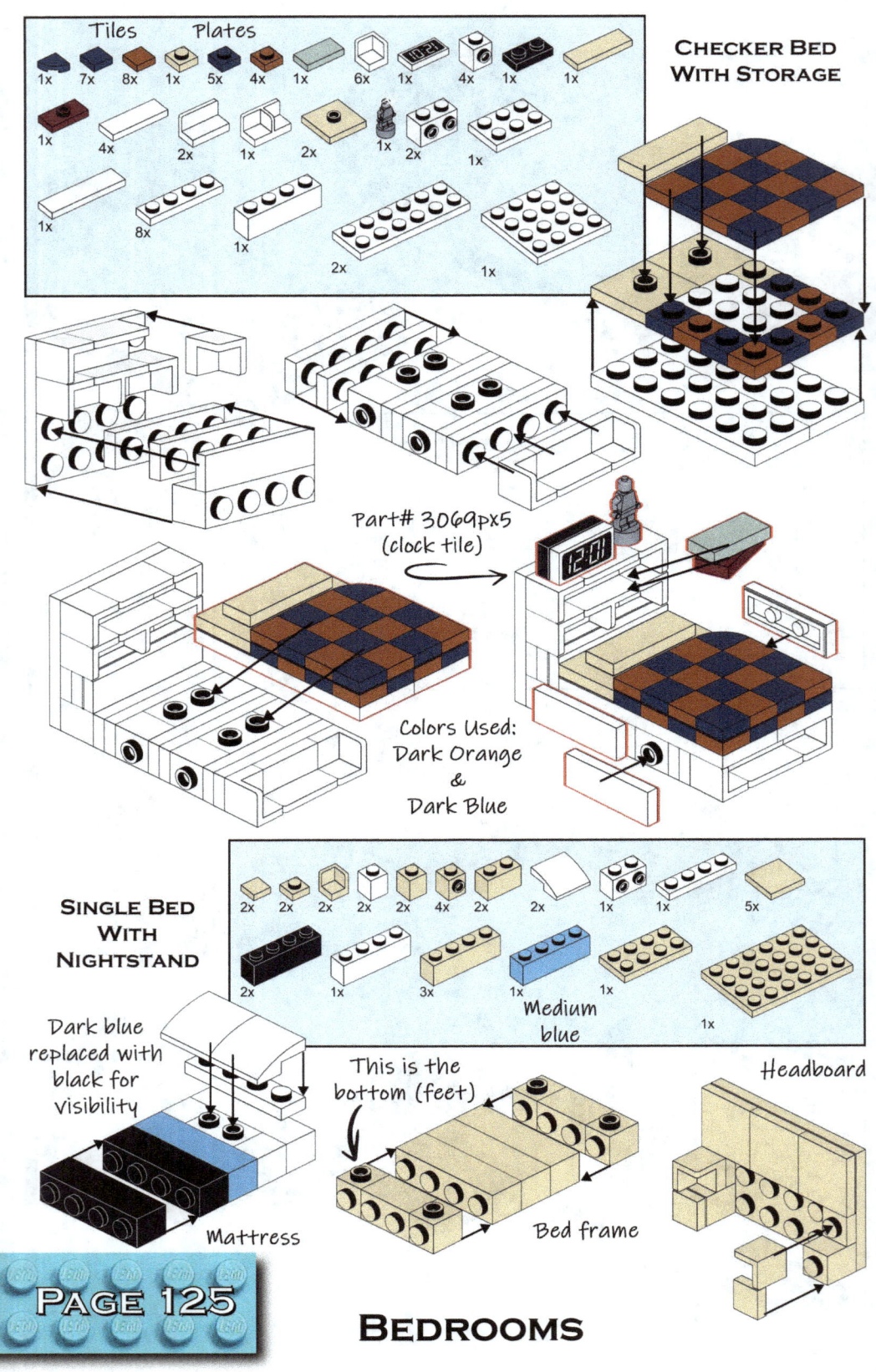

Tiles   Plates

1x 7x 8x 1x 5x 4x 1x 6x 1x 4x 1x 1x

1x 4x 2x 1x 2x 1x 2x 1x

1x 8x 1x 2x 1x

CHECKER BED WITH STORAGE

Part# 3069px5
(clock tile)

Colors Used:
Dark Orange
&
Dark Blue

SINGLE BED WITH NIGHTSTAND

2x 2x 2x 2x 2x 4x 2x 2x 1x 1x 5x

2x 1x 3x 1x 1x 1x

Medium blue

Dark blue replaced with black for visibility

This is the bottom (feet)

Headboard

Mattress

Bed frame

BEDROOMS

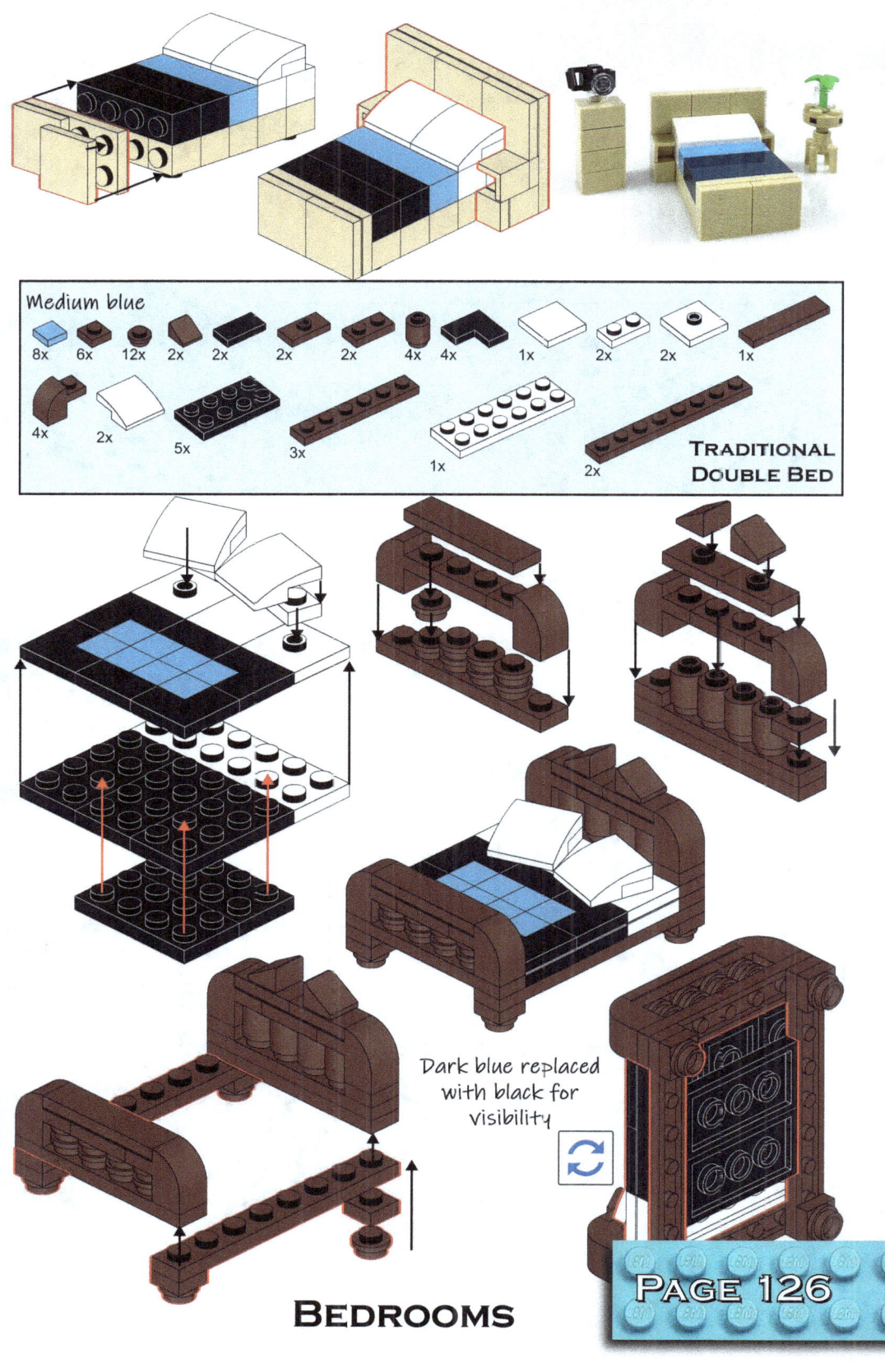

Medium blue

8x 6x 12x 2x 2x 2x 2x 4x 4x 1x 2x 2x 1x

4x 2x 5x 3x 1x 2x

TRADITIONAL DOUBLE BED

Dark blue replaced with black for visibility

BEDROOMS

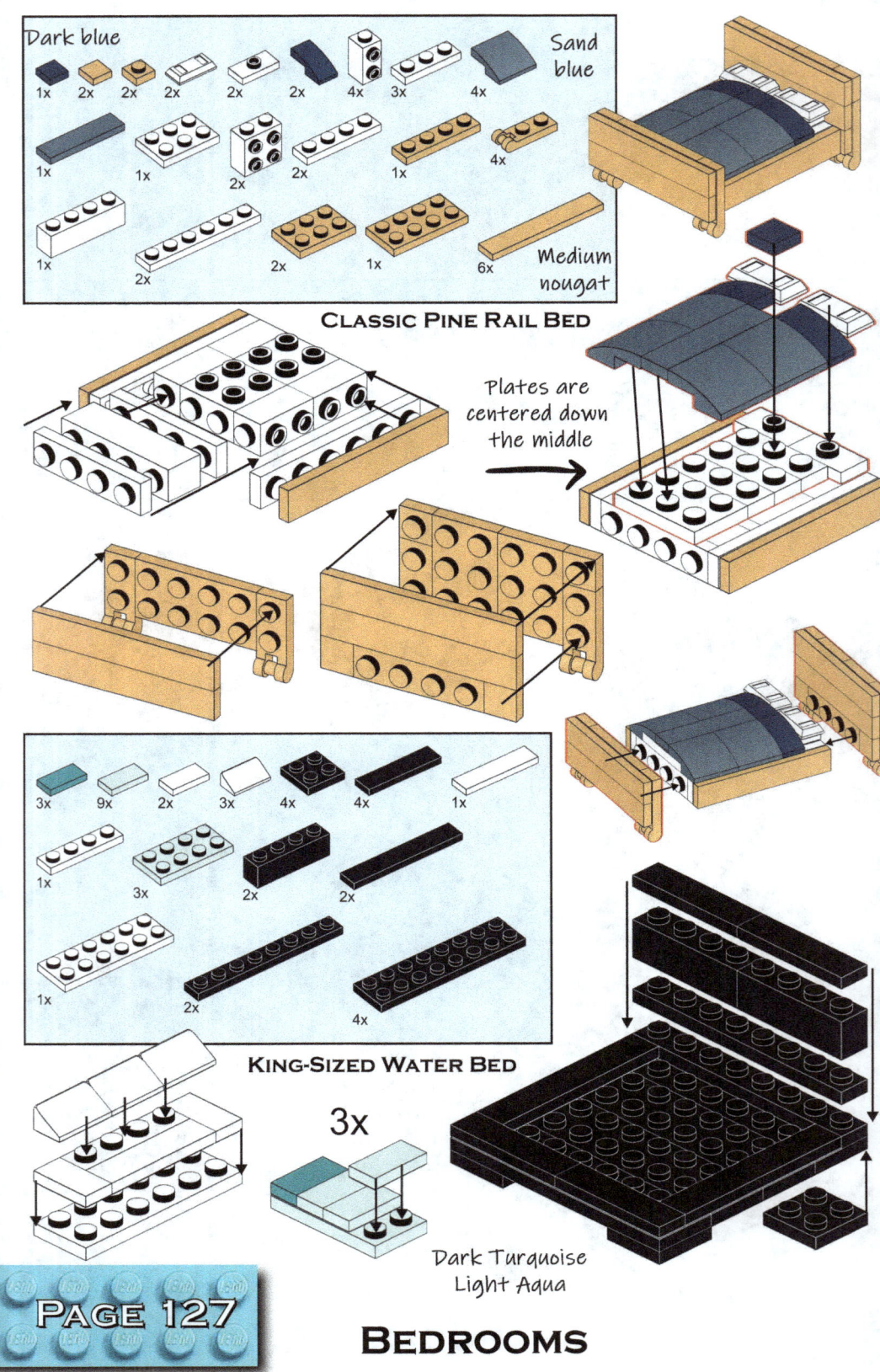

Dark blue

1x 2x 2x 2x 2x 2x 4x 3x 4x Sand blue

1x 1x 2x 2x 1x 4x

1x 2x 2x 1x 6x Medium nougat

CLASSIC PINE RAIL BED

Plates are centered down the middle

Dark blue

3x 9x 2x 3x 4x 4x 1x

1x 3x 2x 2x

1x 2x 4x

KING-SIZED WATER BED

3x

Dark Turquoise
Light Aqua

BEDROOMS

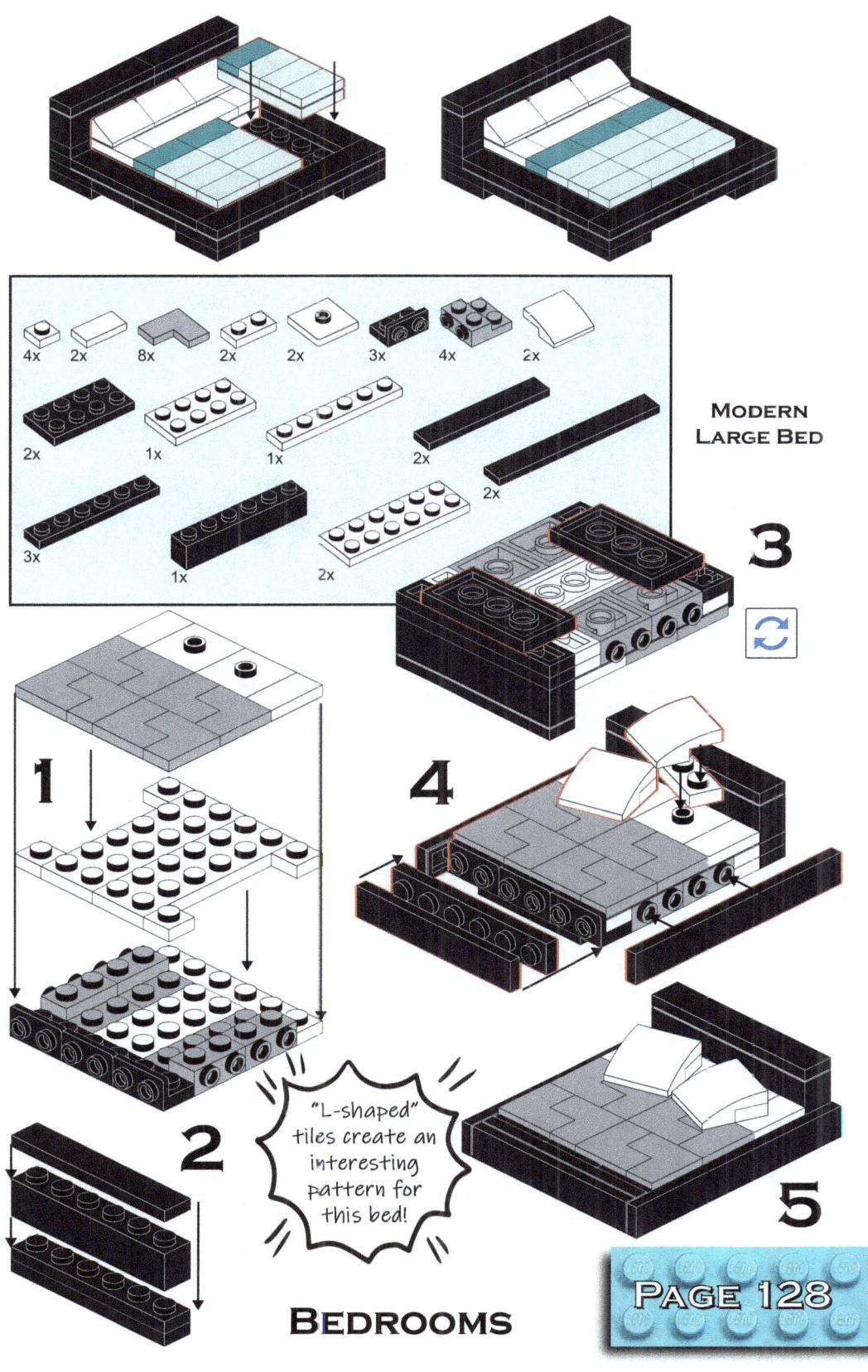

MODERN
LARGE BED

"L-shaped" tiles create an interesting pattern for this bed!

BEDROOMS

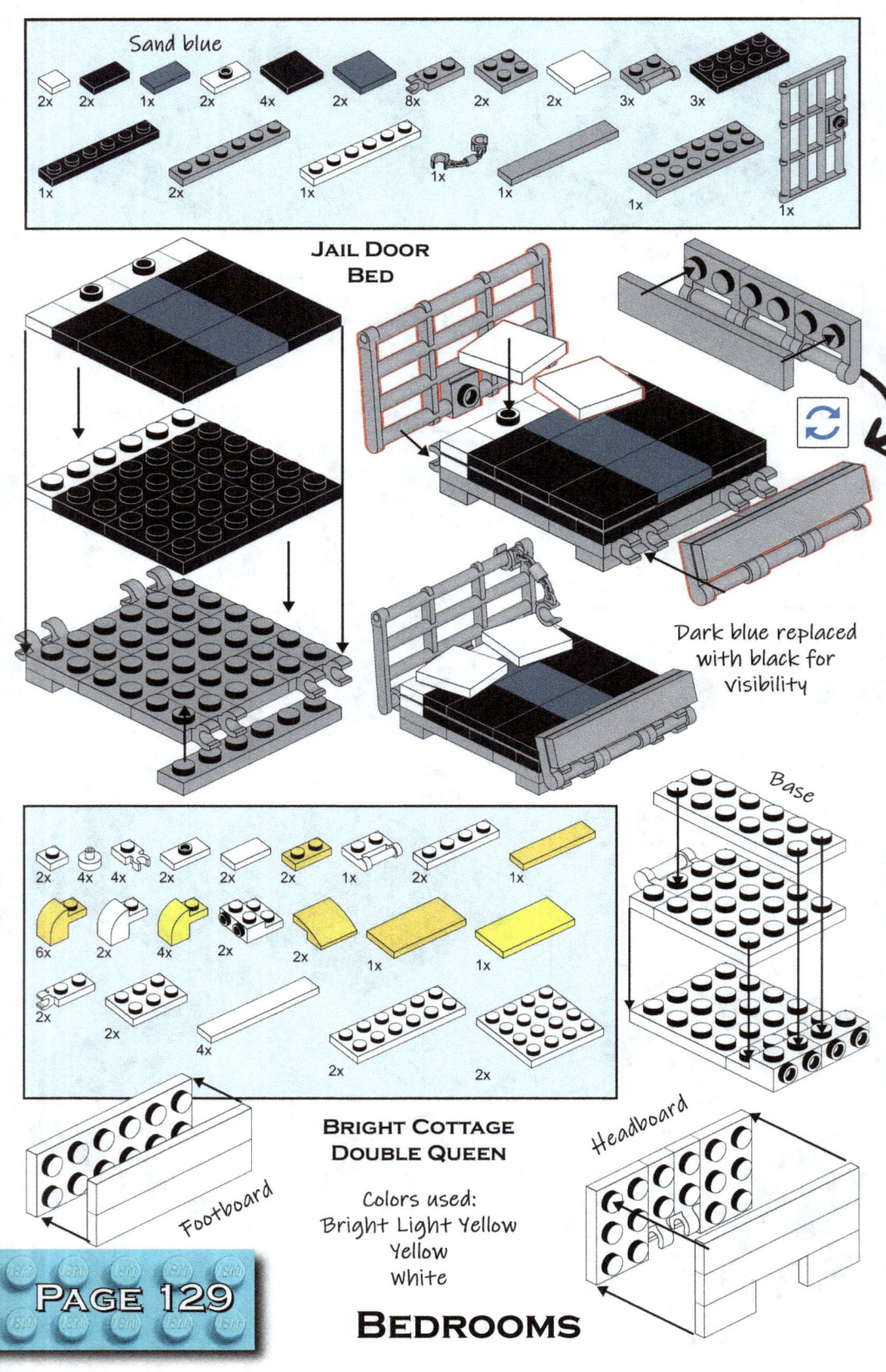

Sand blue

JAIL DOOR
BED

Dark blue replaced
with black for
visibility

Base

BRIGHT COTTAGE
DOUBLE QUEEN

Colors used:
Bright Light Yellow
Yellow
White

Footboard

Headboard

PAGE 129

BEDROOMS

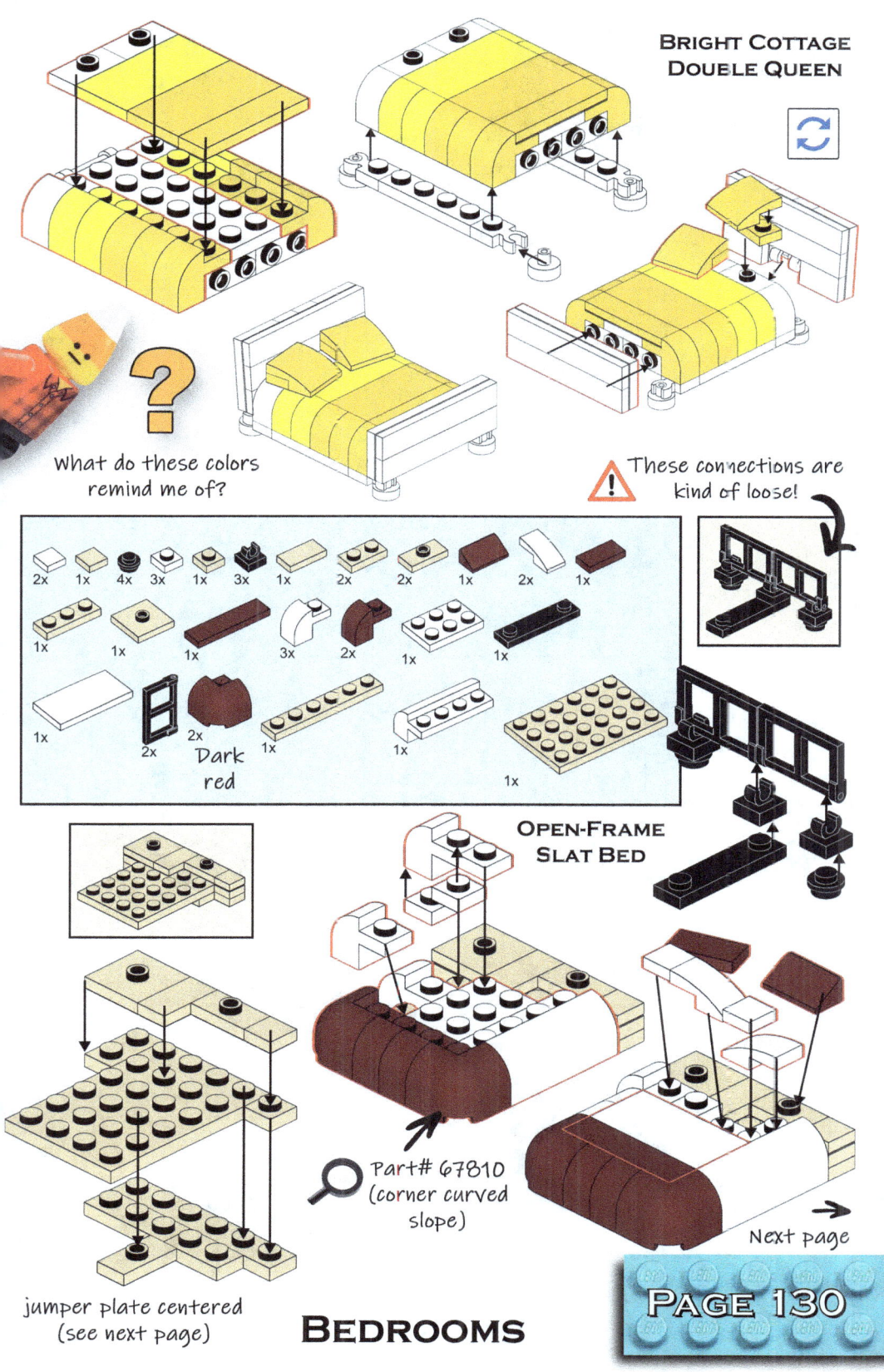

BRIGHT COTTAGE DOUBLE QUEEN

What do these colors remind me of?

⚠ These connections are kind of loose!

Dark red

OPEN-FRAME SLAT BED

Part# 67810 (corner curved slope)

jumper plate centered (see next page)

Next page →

BEDROOMS

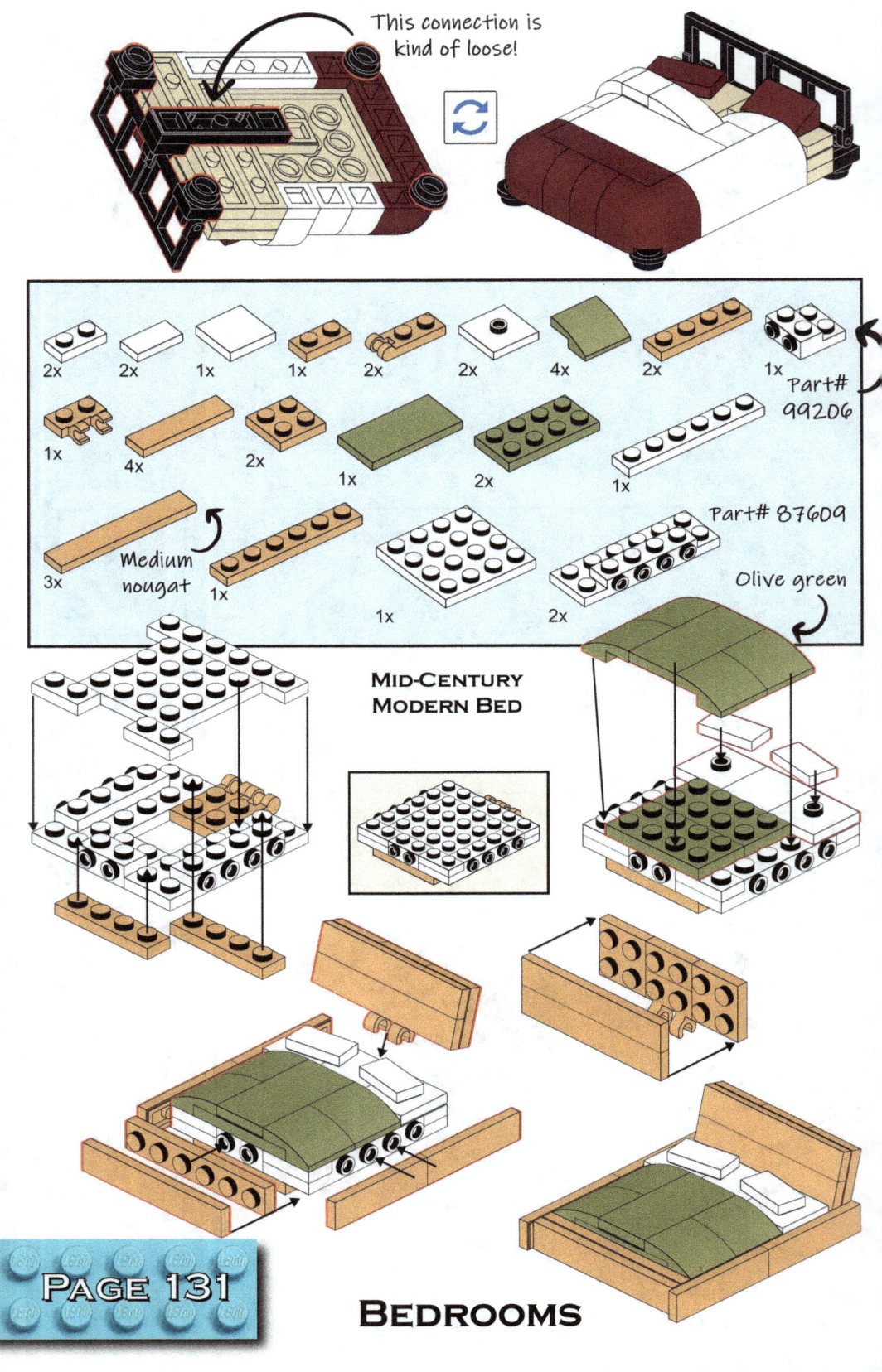

This connection is kind of loose!

2x 2x 1x 1x 2x 2x 4x 2x 1x Part# 99206

1x 4x 2x 1x 2x 1x

Part# 87609

3x Medium nougat 1x 1x 2x Olive green

MID-CENTURY MODERN BED

BEDROOMS

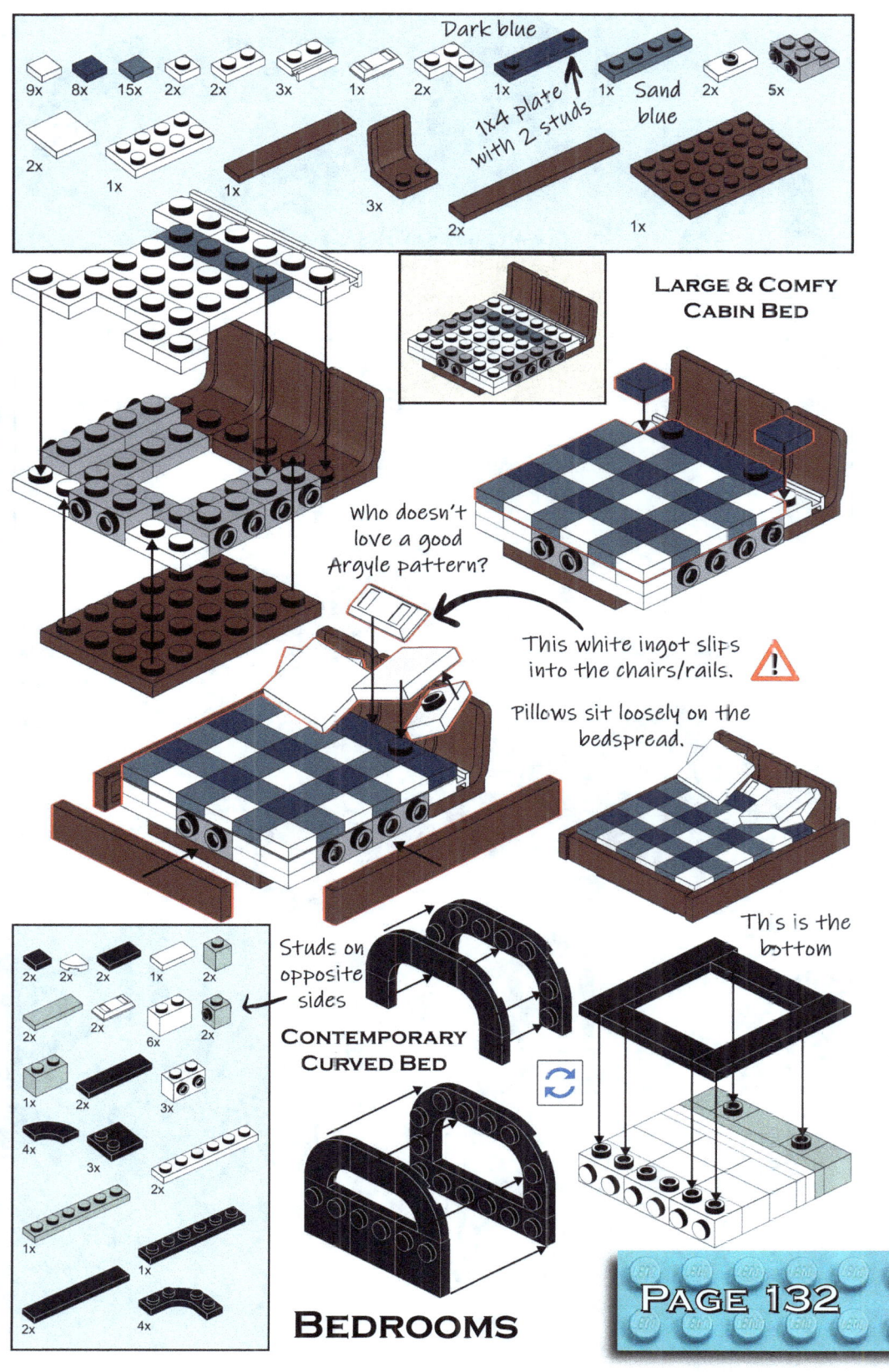

9x 8x 15x 2x 2x 3x 1x 2x

Dark blue

1x4 plate with 2 studs

Sand blue

1x 2x 5x

2x 1x 1x 3x 2x 1x

LARGE & COMFY CABIN BED

Who doesn't love a good Argyle pattern?

This white ingot slips into the chairs/rails. ⚠

Pillows sit loosely on the bedspread.

2x 2x 2x 1x 2x

2x 2x 6x 2x

Studs on opposite sides

1x 2x 3x

CONTEMPORARY CURVED BED

🔄

This is the bottom

4x 3x

1x

2x

2x 1x

2x 4x

BEDROOMS

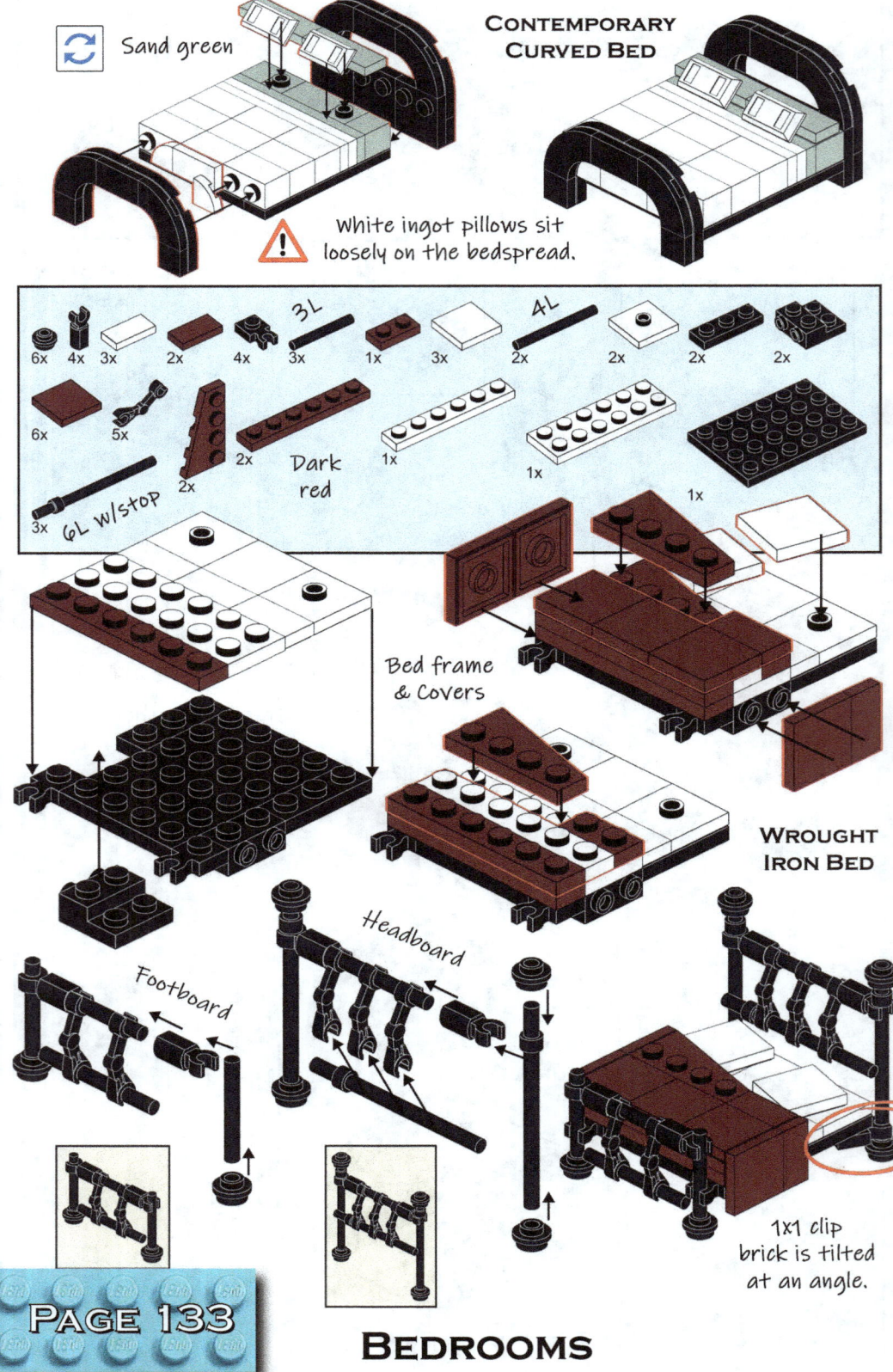

CONTEMPORARY CURVED BED

Sand green

White ingot pillows sit loosely on the bedspread.

3L

4L

Dark red

6L w/stop

Bed frame & Covers

WROUGHT IRON BED

Headboard

Footboard

1x1 clip brick is tilted at an angle.

BEDROOMS

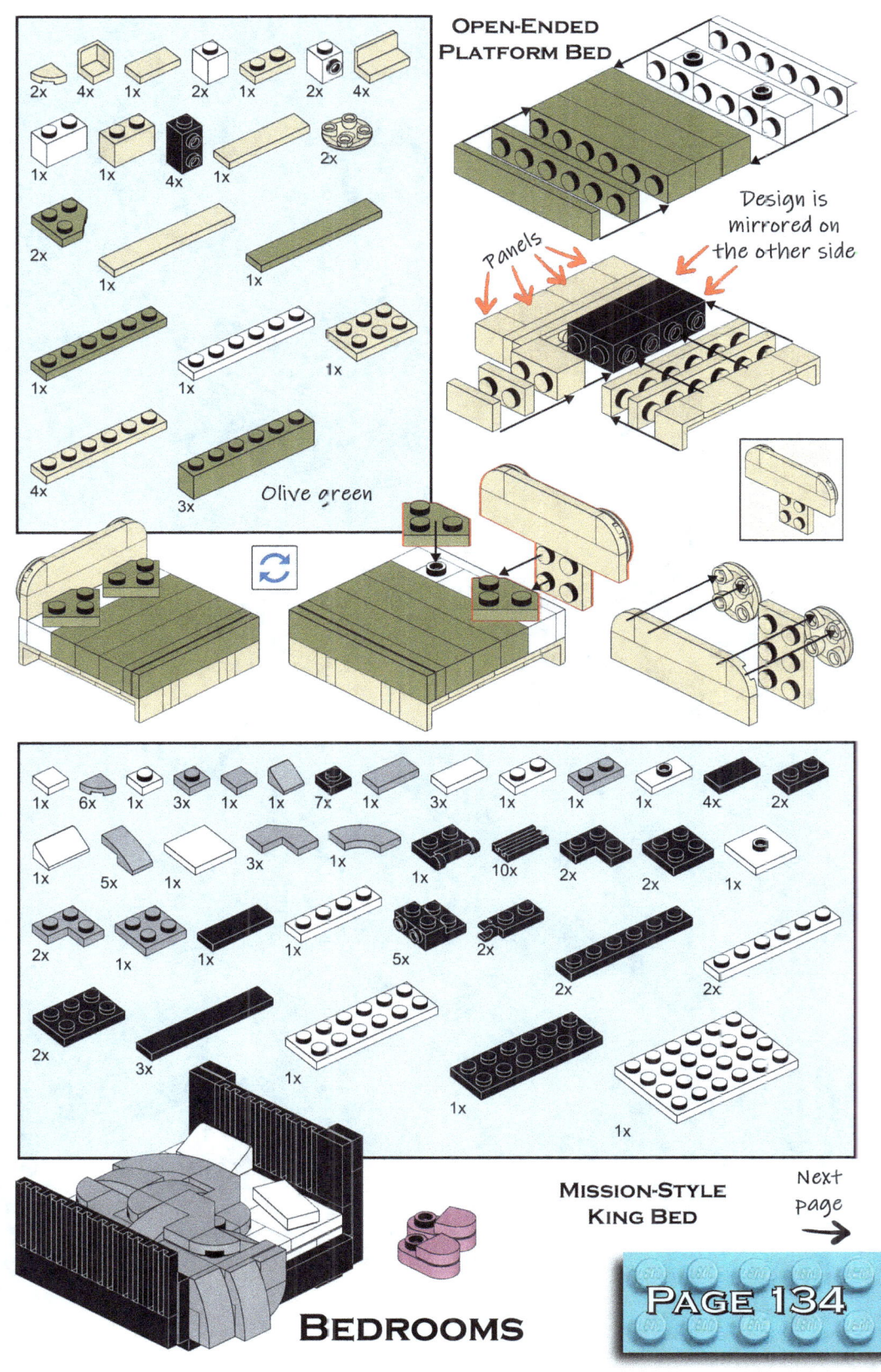

OPEN-ENDED PLATFORM BED

Panels

Design is mirrored on the other side

2x
4x
1x
2x
1x
2x
4x

1x
1x
4x
1x
2x

2x
1x
1x

1x
1x
1x

4x
3x
Olive green

1x
6x
1x
3x
1x
1x
7x
1x
3x
1x
1x
1x
4x
2x

1x
5x
1x
3x
1x
1x
10x
2x
2x
1x

2x
1x
1x
1x
5x
2x
2x
2x

2x
3x
1x
1x
1x

MISSION-STYLE KING BED

Next page →

BEDROOMS

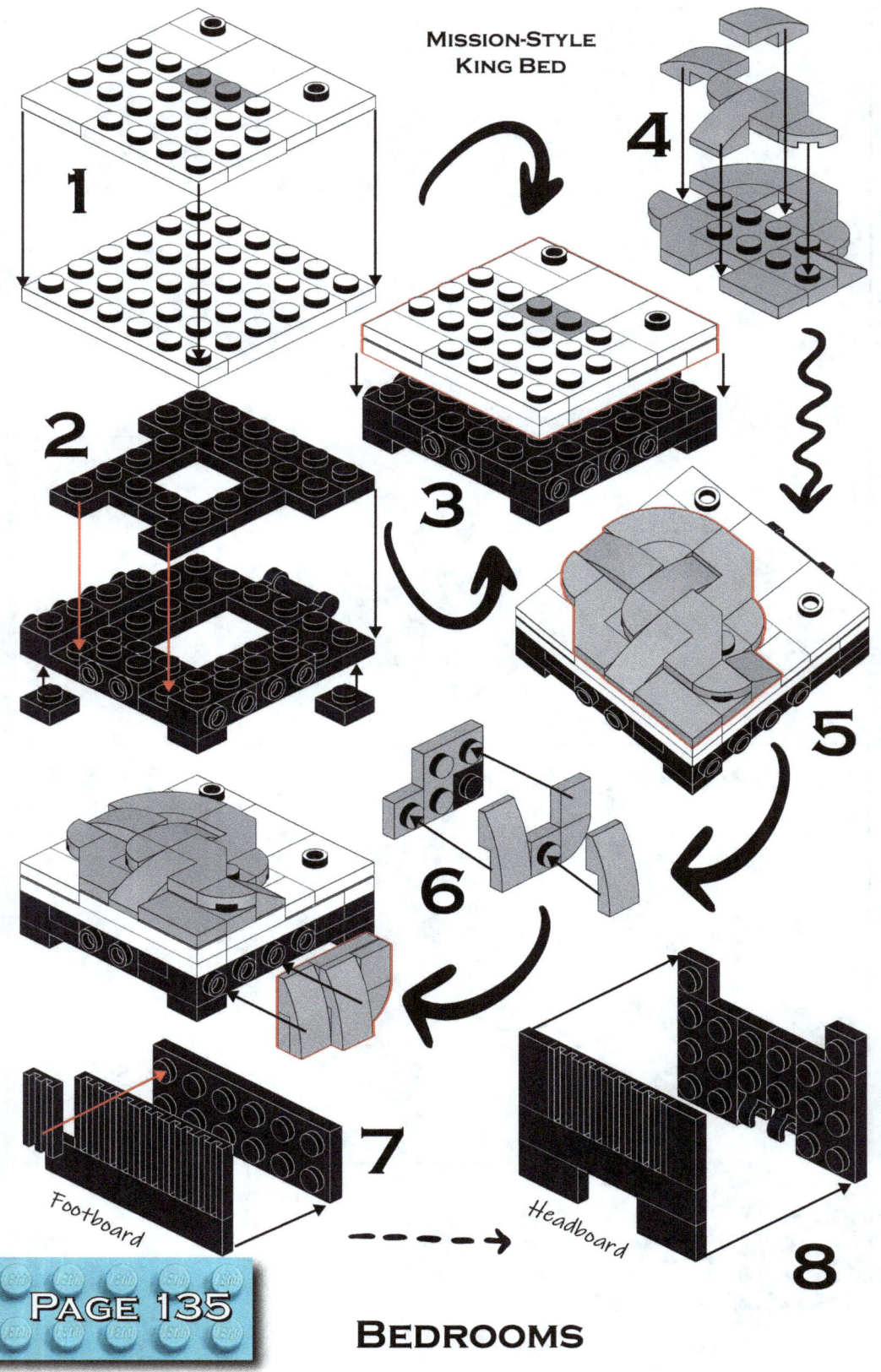

MISSION-STYLE KING BED

1

2

3

4

5

6

7

Footboard

Headboard

8

BEDROOMS

9

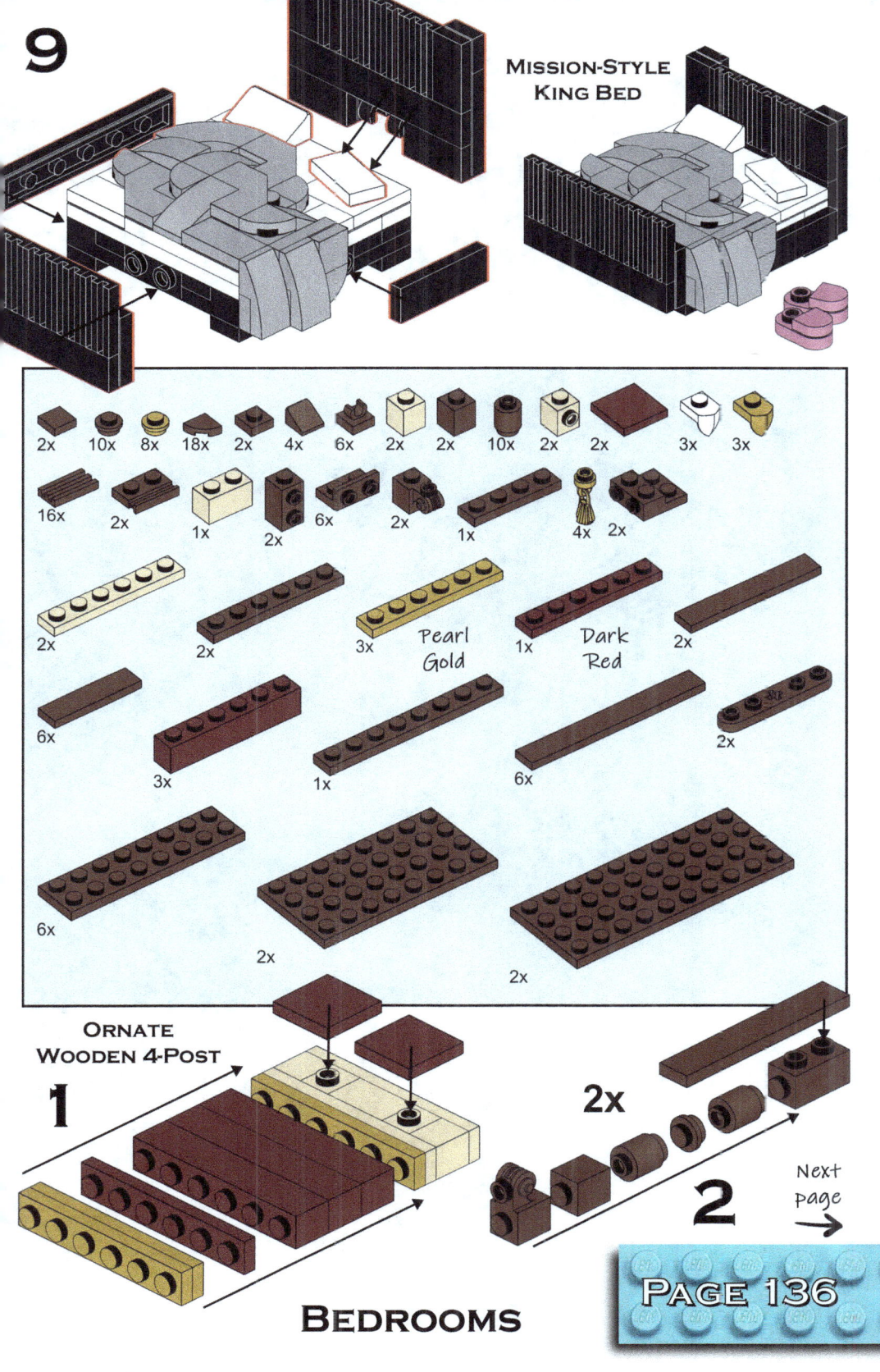

MISSION-STYLE KING BED

2x · 10x · 8x · 18x · 2x · 4x · 6x · 2x · 2x · 10x · 2x · 2x · 3x · 3x

16x · 2x · 1x · 2x · 6x · 2x · 1x · 4x · 2x

2x · 2x · 3x · **Pearl Gold** · 1x · **Dark Red** · 2x

6x · 3x · 1x · 6x · 2x

6x · 2x · 2x

ORNATE WOODEN 4-POST

1

2x

2

Next page →

BEDROOMS

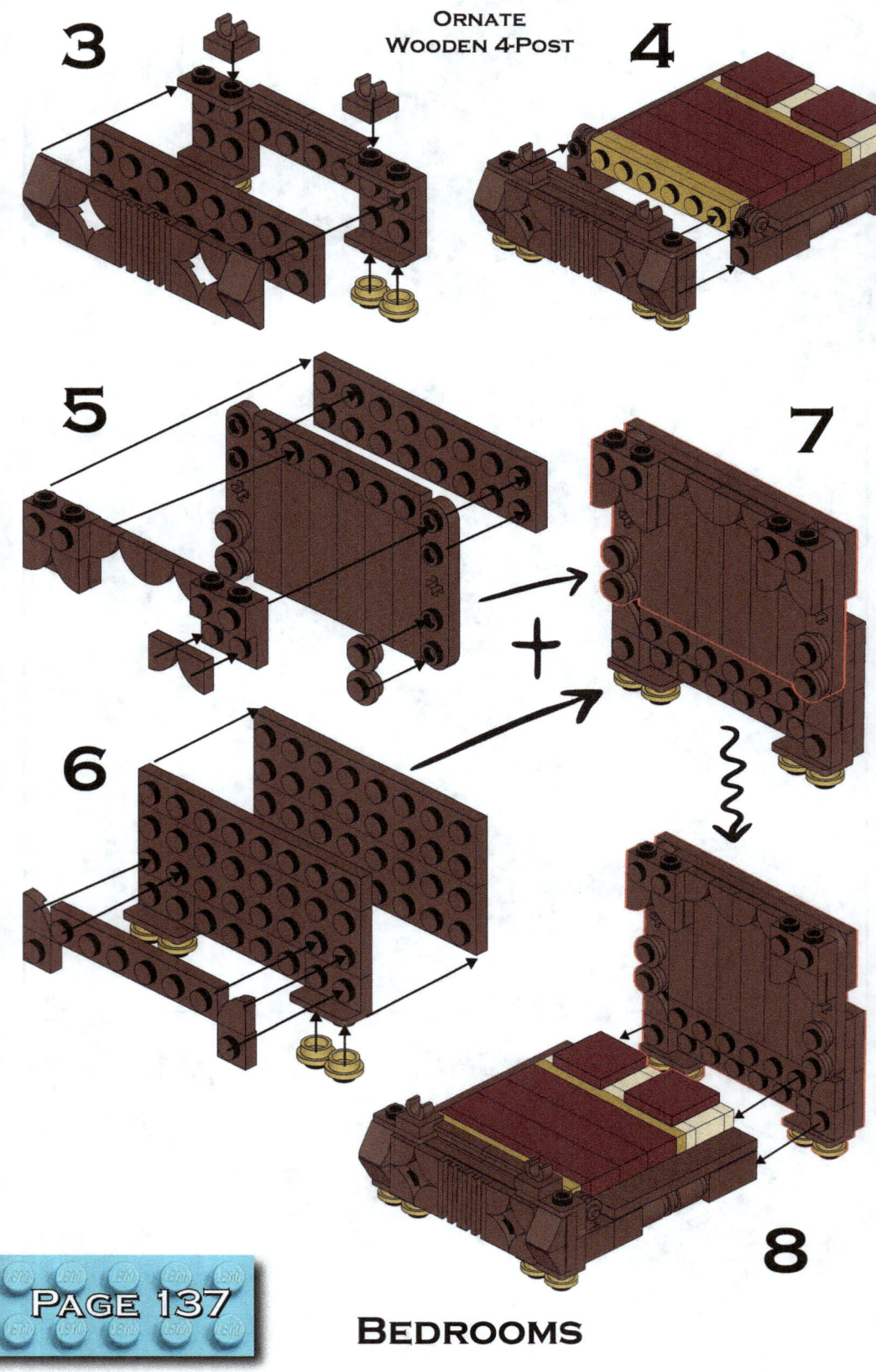

ORNATE WOODEN 4-POST

3

4

5

6

+

7

8

BEDROOMS

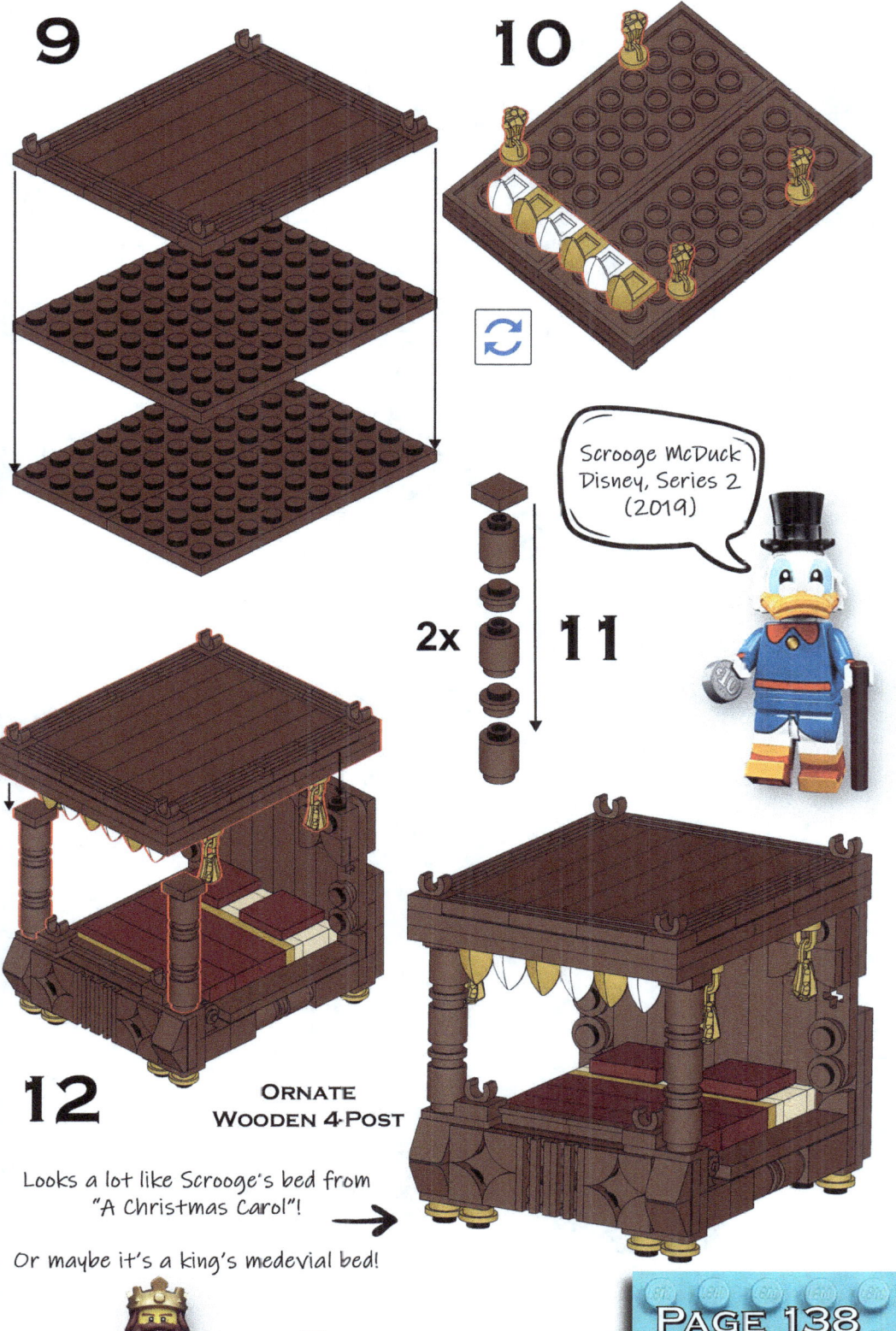

9

10

11 2x

Scrooge McDuck
Disney, Series 2
(2019)

12

ORNATE
WOODEN 4-POST

Looks a lot like Scrooge's bed from
"A Christmas Carol"! →

Or maybe it's a king's medevial bed!

BEDROOMS

Olive green

14x **2x** **8x** **4x** **16x**

4x **2x** **8x** **1x** **2x**

9x **2x** **3x** **1x**

Dark Orange

2x **1x**

4x **6x** **4x**

4-POST CANOPY

These 4 slopes hold the bed and headboard together.

SNOT stud

SNOT stud

You could drape some superhero capes on each post to create fabric curtains!

BEDROOMS

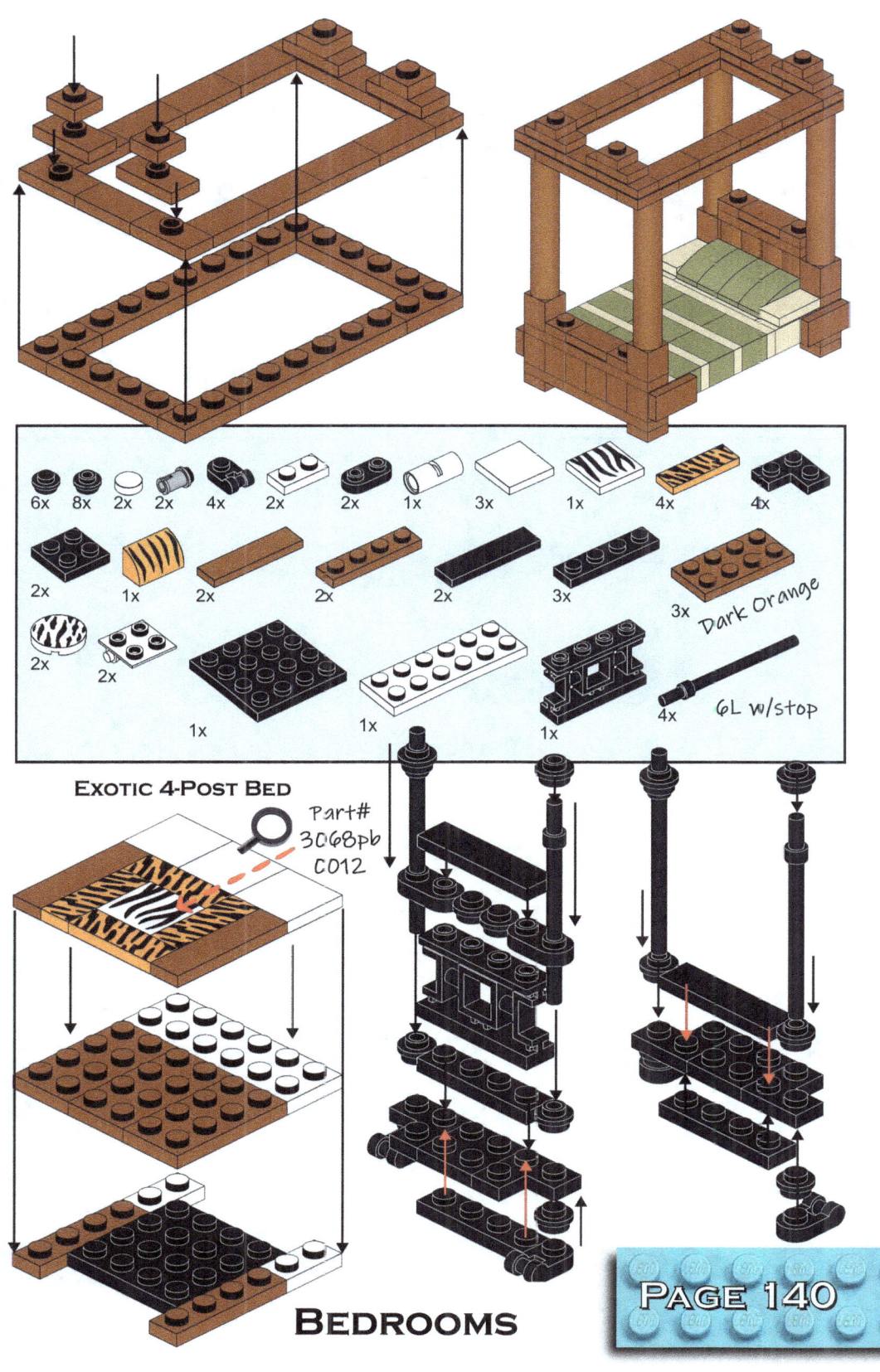

EXOTIC 4-POST BED

Part#
3068pb
C012

BEDROOMS

6x 8x 2x 2x 4x 2x 2x 1x 3x 1x 4x 4x

2x 1x 2x 2x 2x 3x 3x Dark Orange

2x 2x 1x 1x 1x 4x 6L w/stop

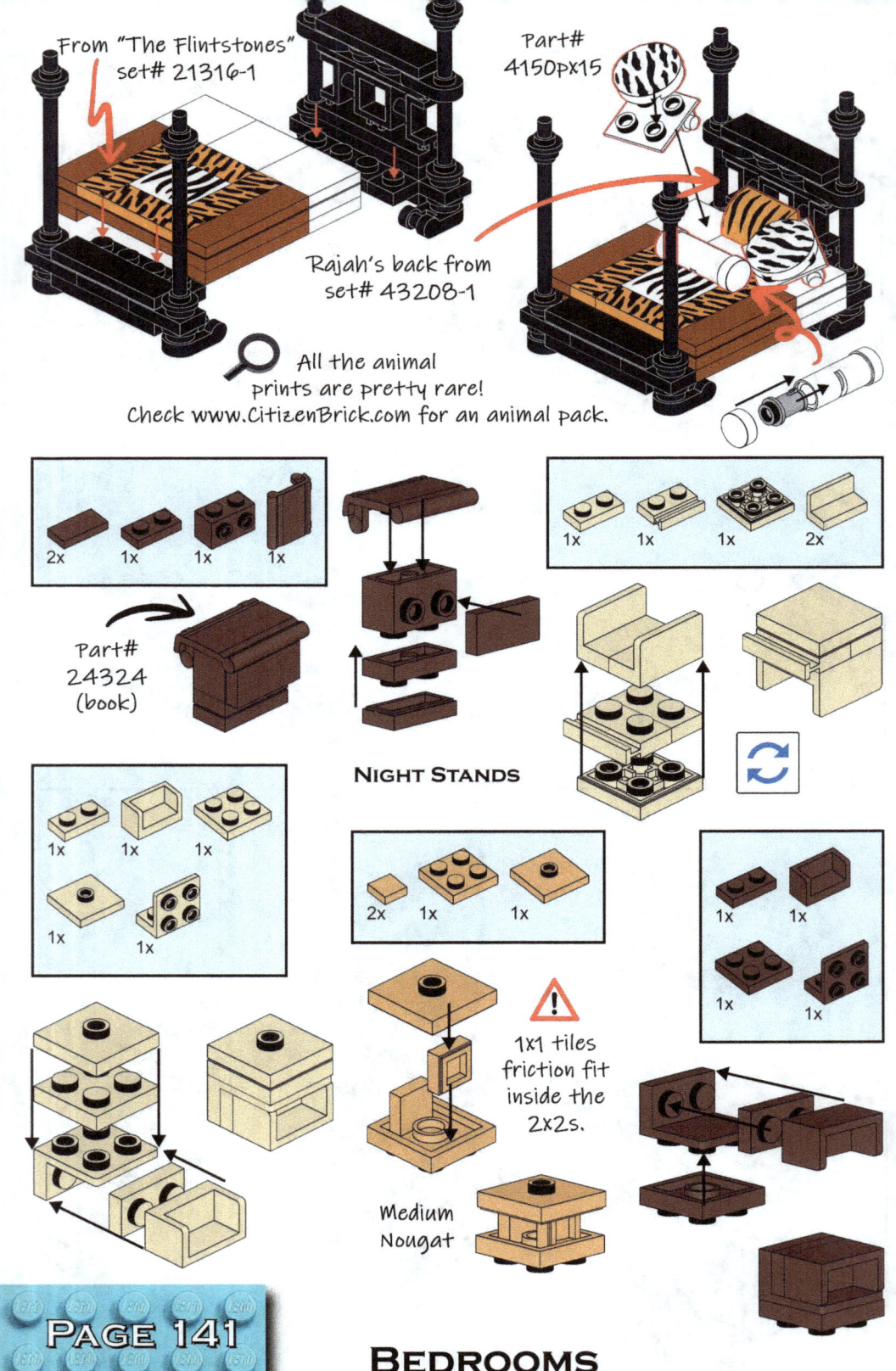

From "The Flintstones"
set# 21316-1

Part#
4150px15

Rajah's back from
set# 43208-1

All the animal
prints are pretty rare!
Check www.CitizenBrick.com for an animal pack.

2x   1x   1x   1x

1x   1x   1x   2x

Part#
24324
(book)

NIGHT STANDS

1x   1x   1x

1x   1x

2x   1x   1x

1x   1x

1x   1x

⚠️ 1x1 tiles
friction fit
inside the
2x2s.

Medium
Nougat

BEDROOMS

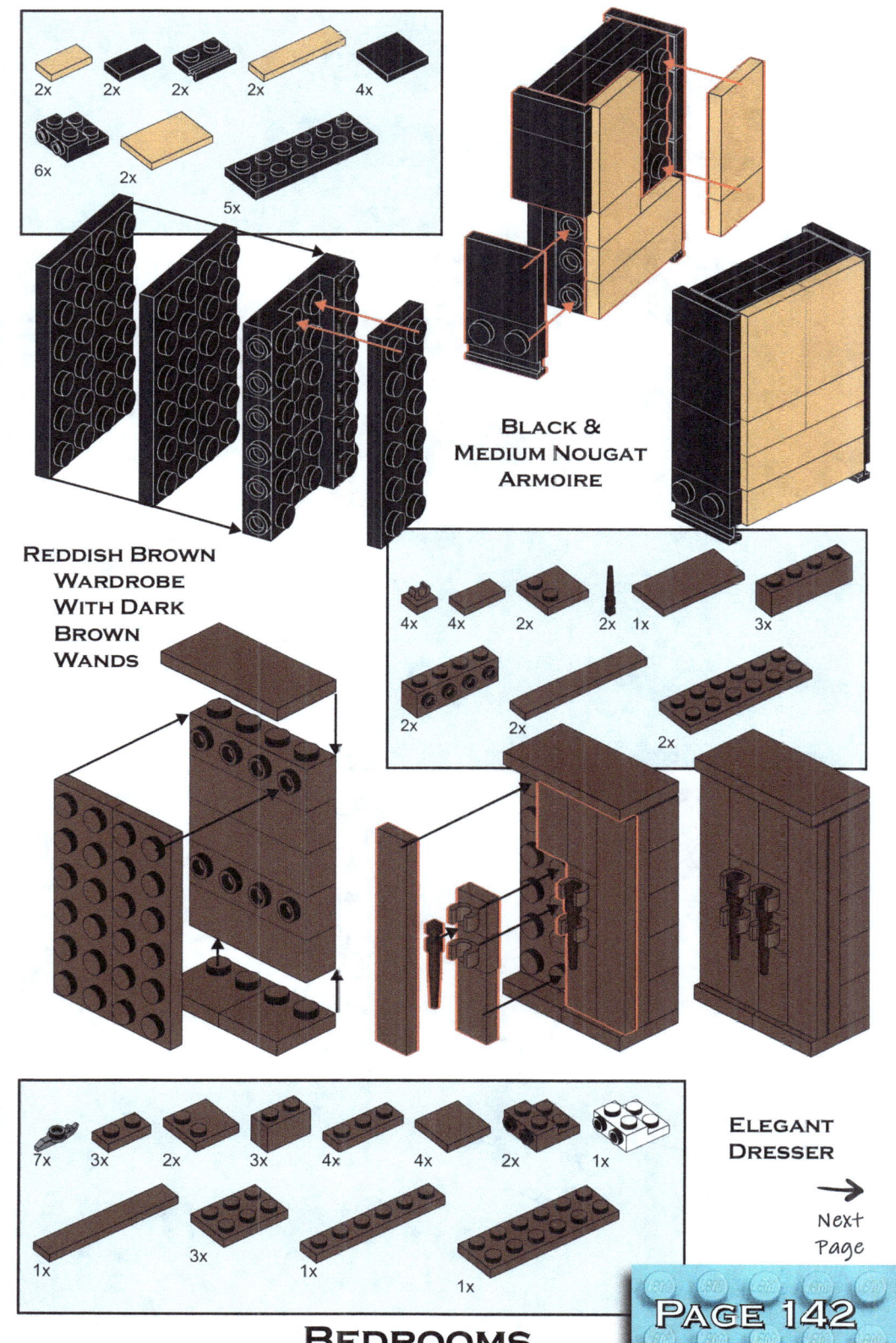

2x 2x 2x 2x 4x

6x 2x

5x

BLACK & MEDIUM NOUGAT ARMOIRE

REDDISH BROWN WARDROBE WITH DARK BROWN WANDS

4x 4x 2x 2x 1x 3x

2x 2x 2x

7x 3x 2x 3x 4x 4x 2x 1x

ELEGANT DRESSER

→

Next Page

1x 3x 1x 1x

BEDROOMS

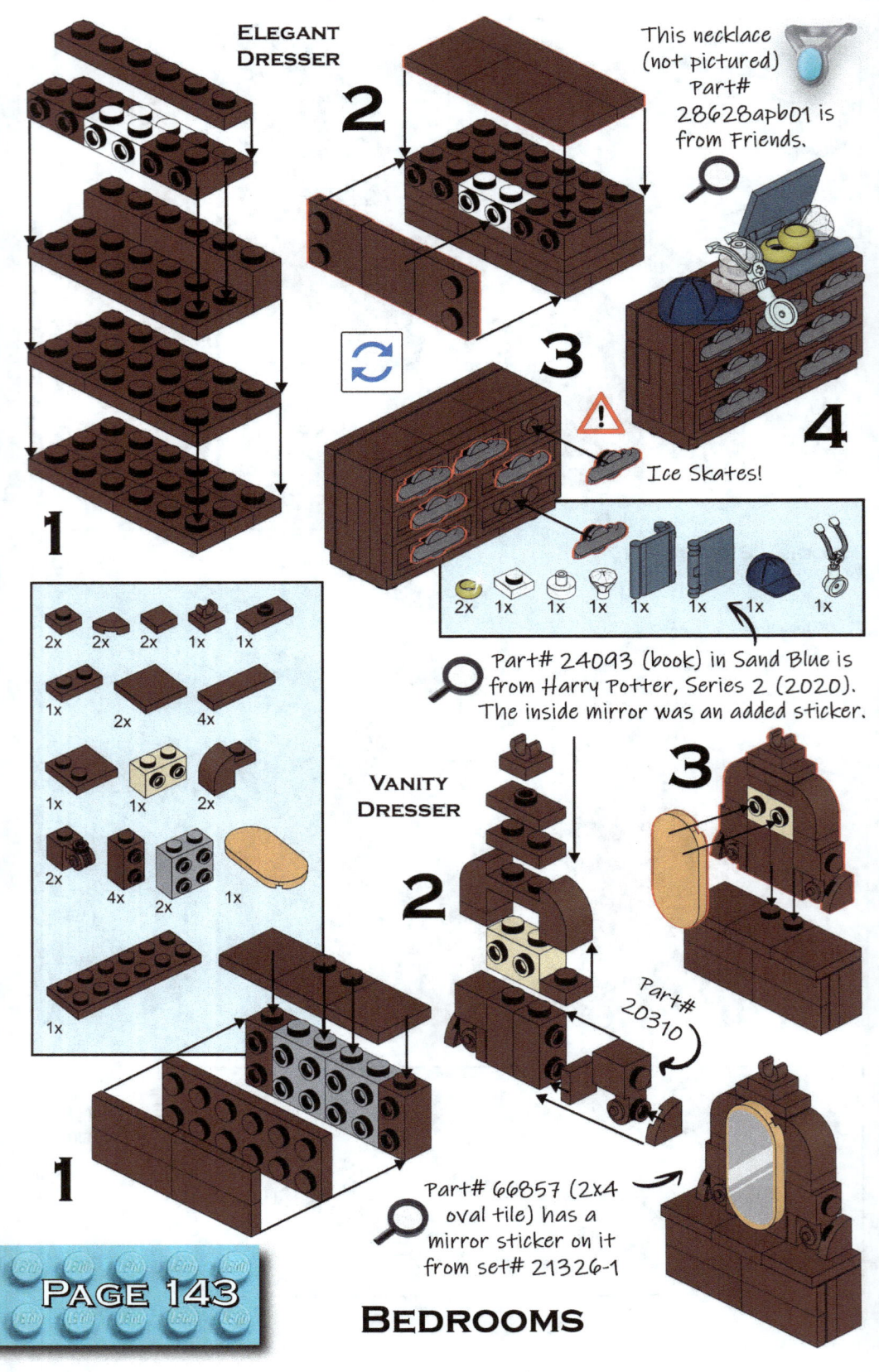

ELEGANT DRESSER

1

2

3

4

This necklace (not pictured) Part# 28628apb01 is from Friends.

⚠ Ice Skates!

2x 1x 1x 1x 1x 1x 1x 1x

Part# 24093 (book) in Sand Blue is from Harry Potter, Series 2 (2020). The inside mirror was an added sticker.

VANITY DRESSER

1

2x 2x 2x 1x 1x

1x 2x 4x

1x 1x 2x

2x 4x 2x 1x

1x

2

3

Part# 20310

Part# 66857 (2x4 oval tile) has a mirror sticker on it from set# 21326-1

BEDROOMS

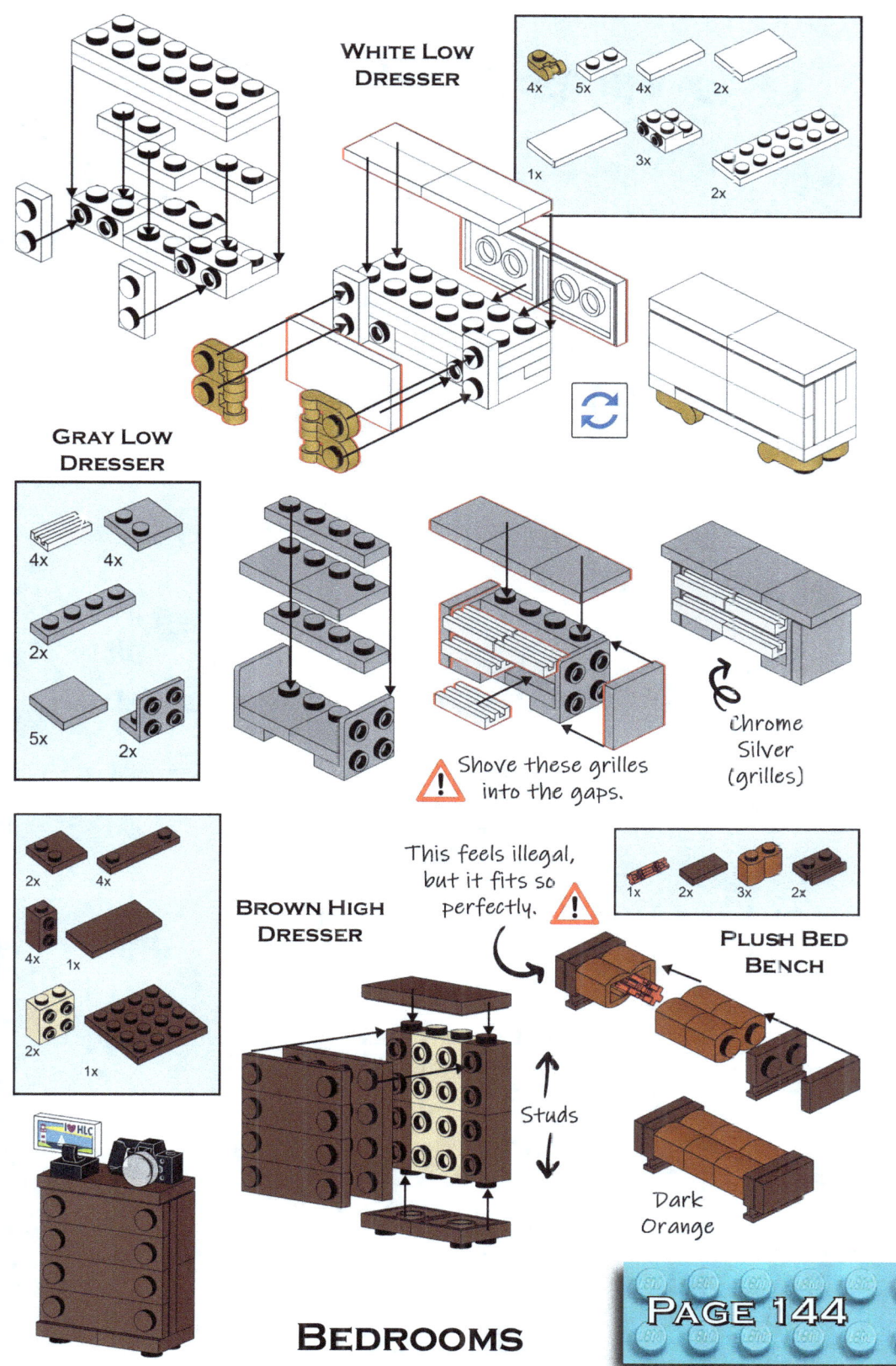

WHITE LOW DRESSER

4x · 5x · 4x · 2x
1x · 3x · 2x

GRAY LOW DRESSER

4x · 4x
2x
5x · 2x

⚠ Shove these grilles into the gaps.

Chrome Silver (grilles)

2x · 4x
4x · 1x
2x · 1x

BROWN HIGH DRESSER

This feels illegal, but it fits so perfectly. ⚠

Studs

PLUSH BED BENCH

1x · 2x · 3x · 2x

Dark Orange

I ♥ HLC

BEDROOMS

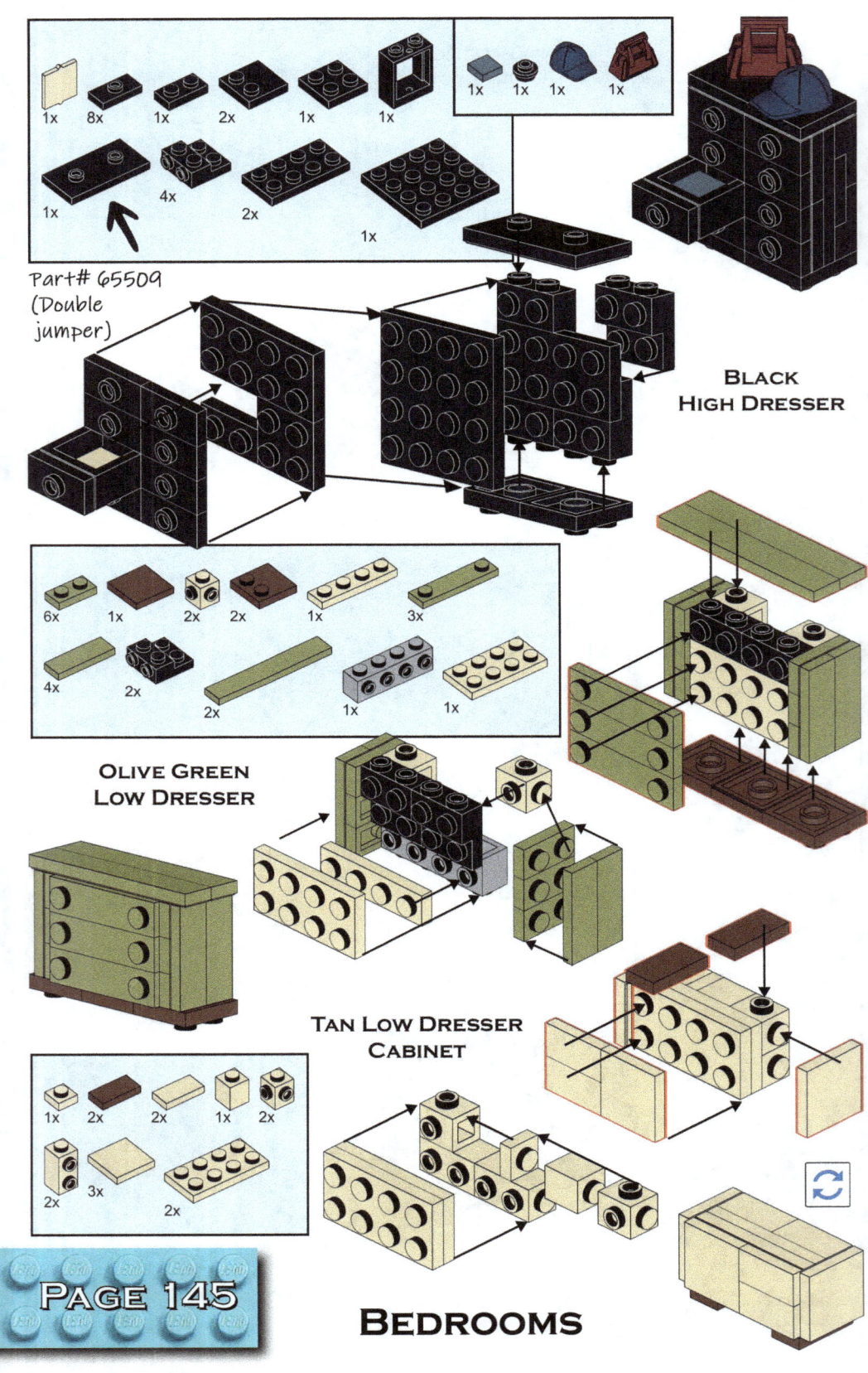

Part# 65509
(Double jumper)

BLACK HIGH DRESSER

OLIVE GREEN LOW DRESSER

TAN LOW DRESSER CABINET

BEDROOMS

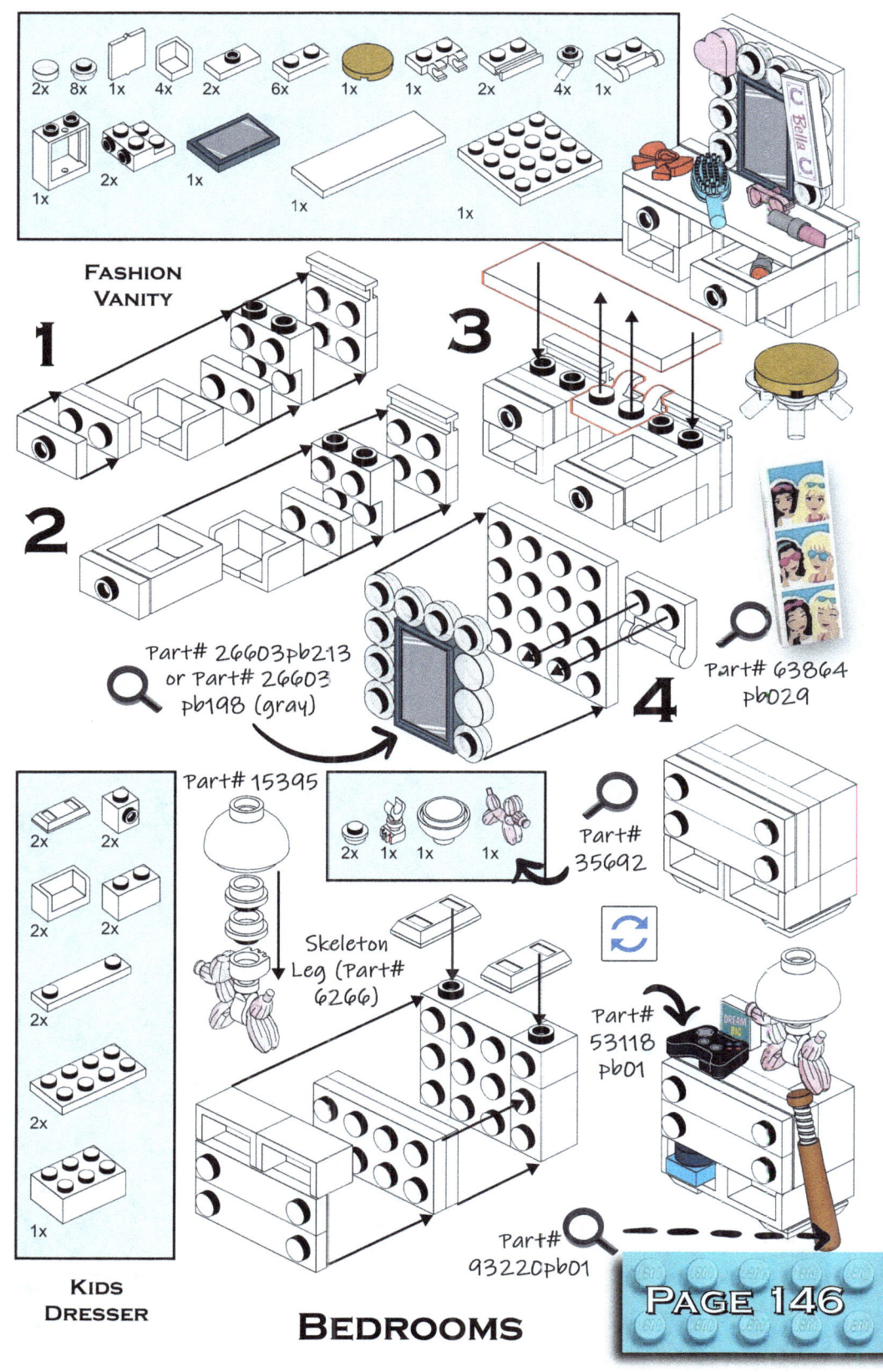

1

2

3

Part# 26603pb213
or Part# 26603
pb198 (gray)

4

Part# 63864
pb029

Part# 15395

Part#
35692

Skeleton
Leg (Part#
6266)

Part#
53118
pb01

DREAM BIG

Part#
93220pb01

BEDROOMS

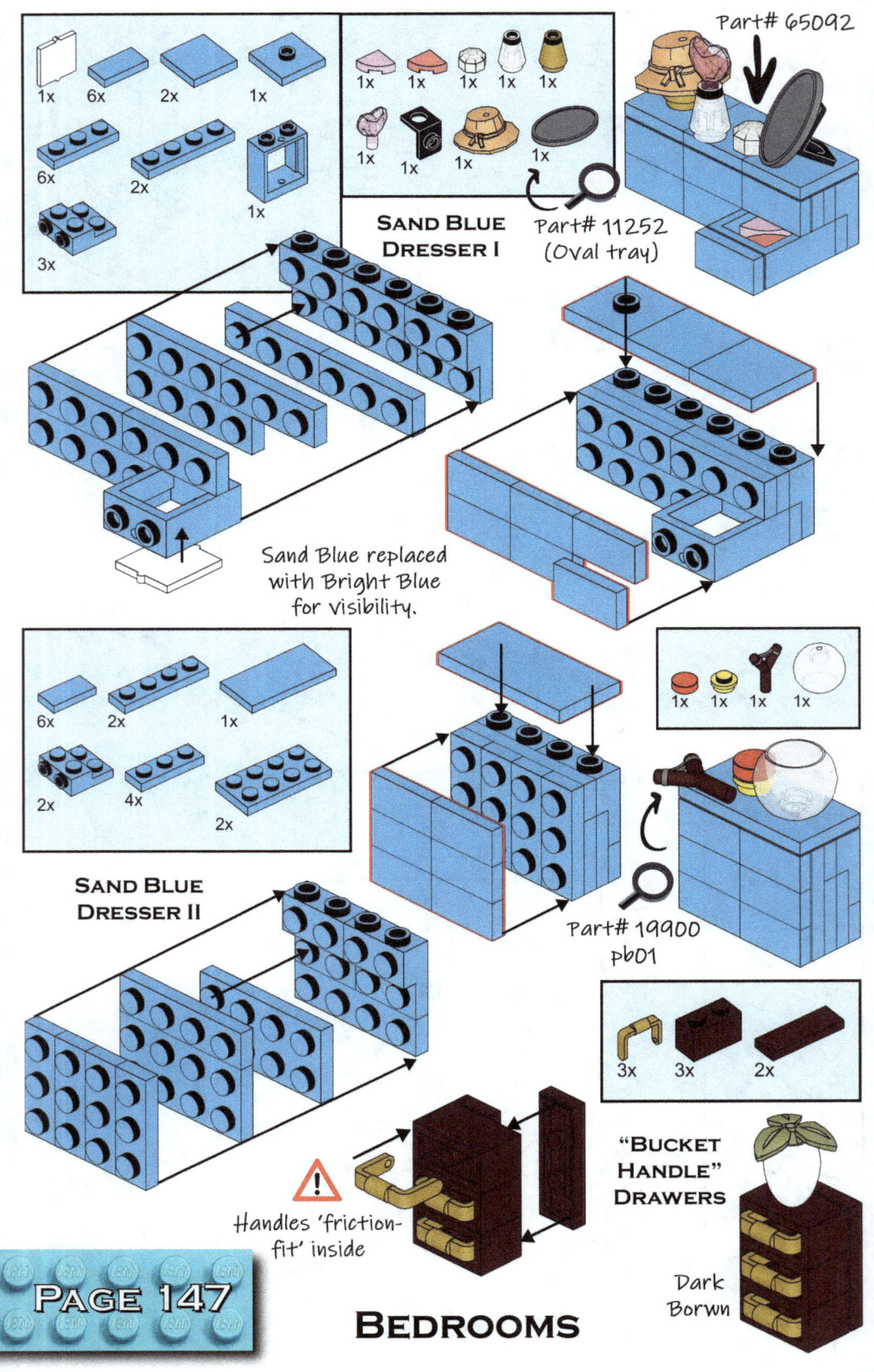

Part# 65092

1x 6x 2x 1x
1x 1x 1x 1x 1x
6x 2x 1x
1x 1x 1x 1x
3x

SAND BLUE DRESSER I

Part# 11252
(Oval tray)

Sand Blue replaced
with Bright Blue
for visibility.

1x 1x 1x 1x

6x 2x 1x
2x 4x
2x

SAND BLUE DRESSER II

Part# 19900 pb01

3x 3x 2x

Handles 'friction-
fit' inside

"BUCKET HANDLE" DRAWERS

Dark Borwn

BEDROOMS

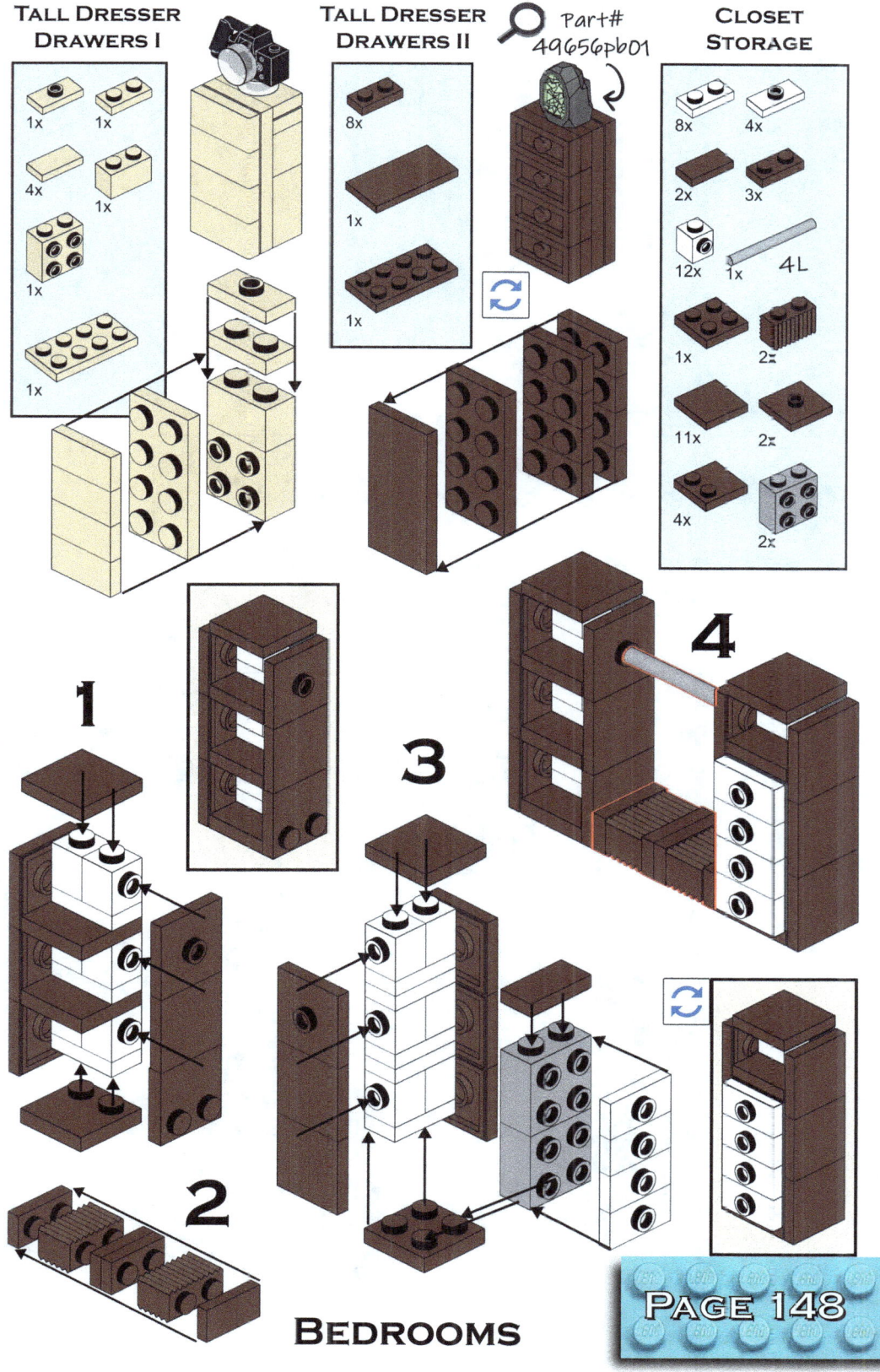

TALL DRESSER DRAWERS I

1x
1x
4x
1x
1x
1x

TALL DRESSER DRAWERS II

8x
1x
1x

Part#
49656pb01

CLOSET STORAGE

8x
4x
2x
3x
12x
1x 4L
1x
2x
11x
2x
4x
2x

1

2

3

4

BEDROOMS

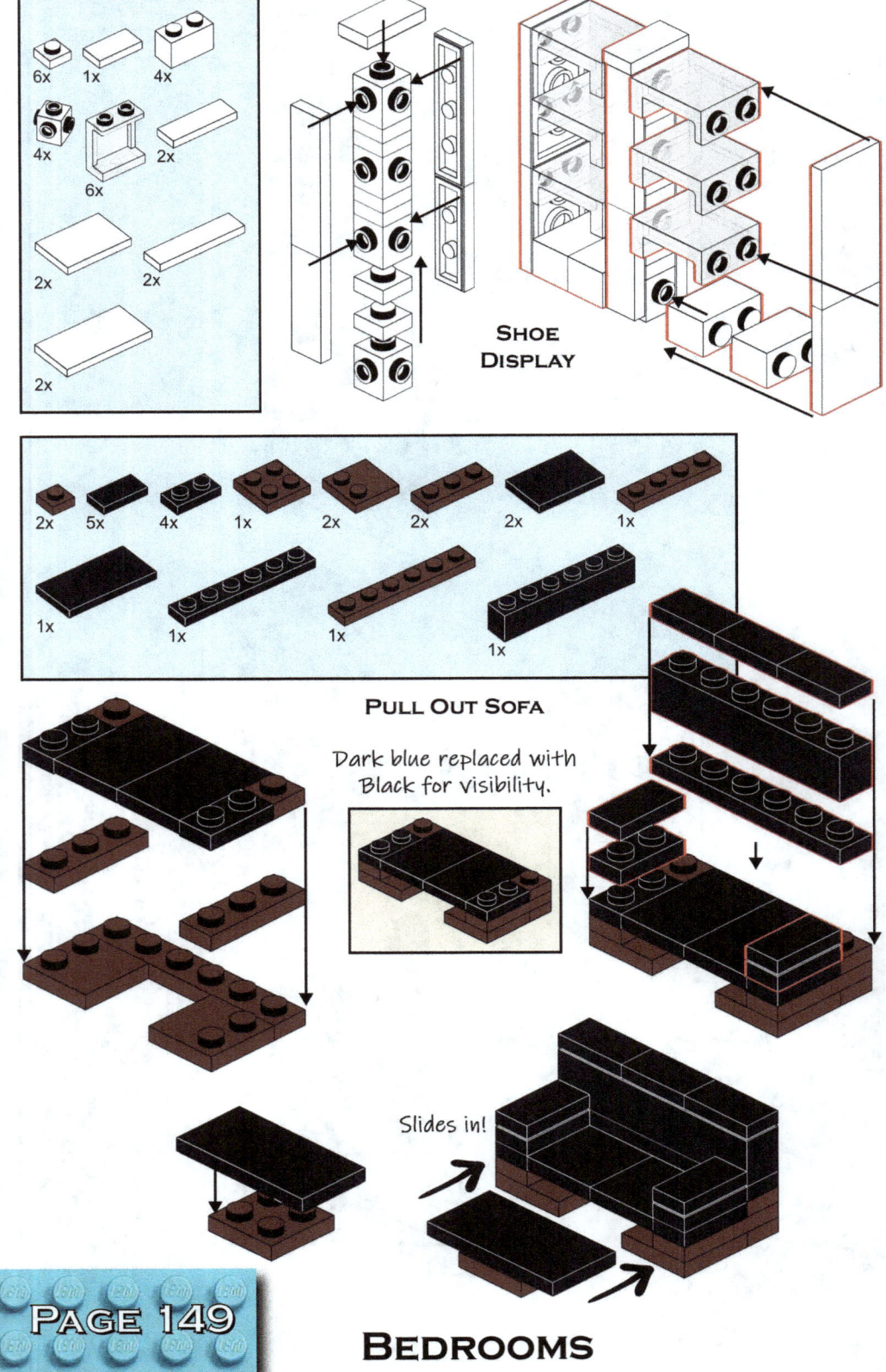

SHOE DISPLAY

PULL OUT SOFA

Dark blue replaced with Black for visibility.

Slides in!

BEDROOMS

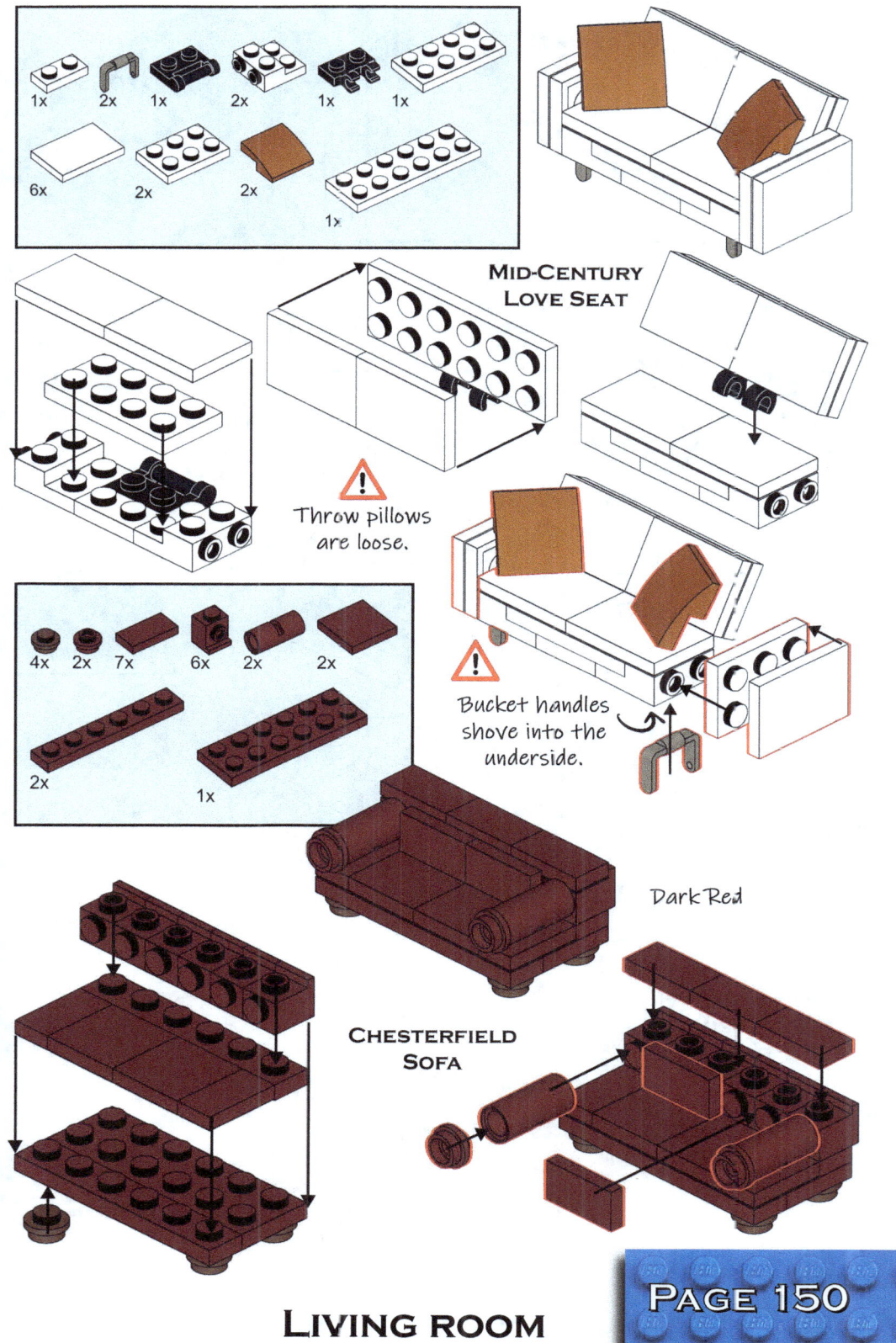

1x	2x	1x	2x	1x	1x
6x	2x	2x			

1x

MID-CENTURY LOVE SEAT

⚠ Throw pillows are loose.

⚠ Bucket handles shove into the underside.

4x	2x	7x	6x	2x	2x

2x

1x

Dark Red

CHESTERFIELD SOFA

LIVING ROOM

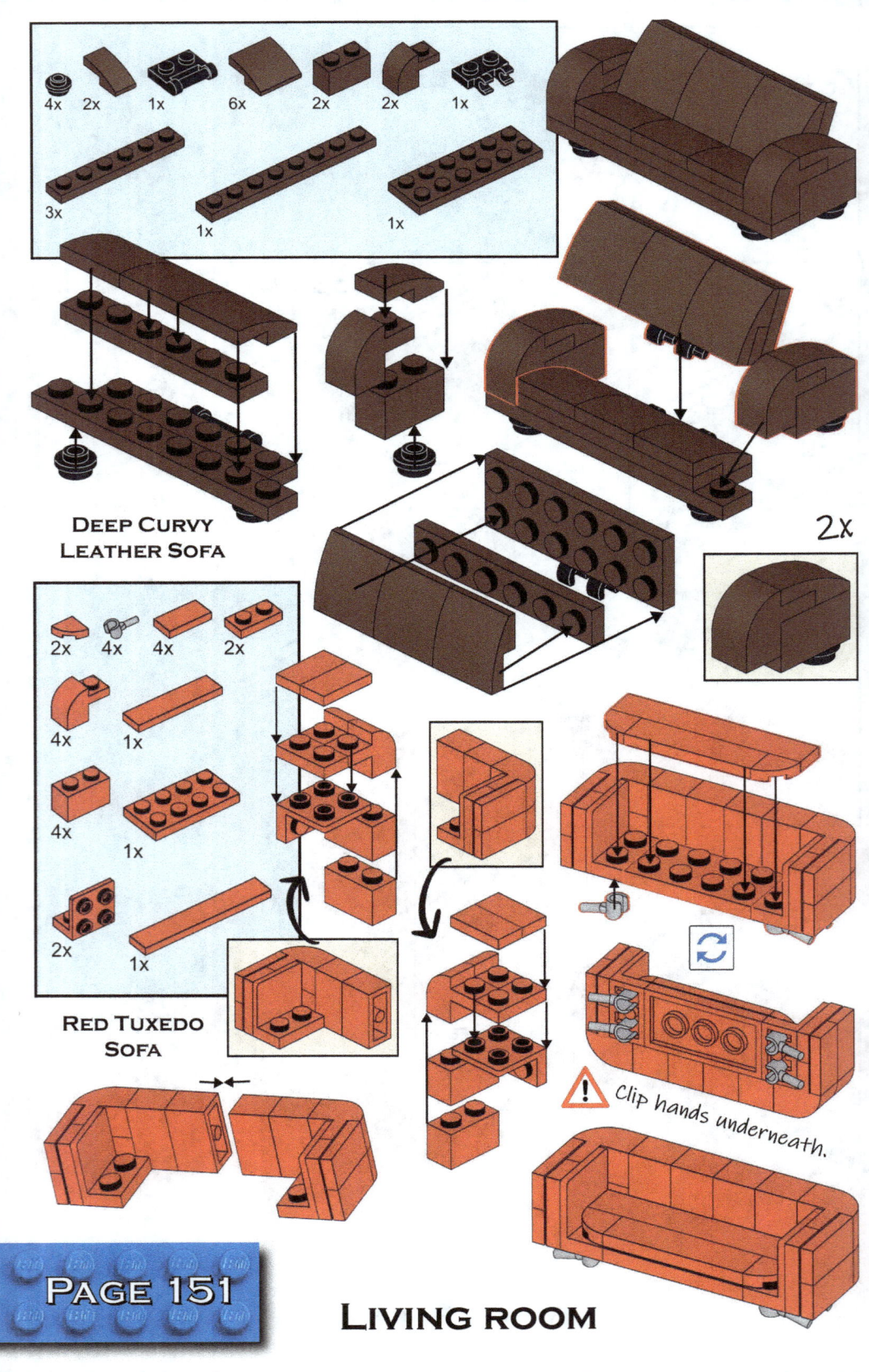

DEEP CURVY LEATHER SOFA

4x 2x 1x 6x 2x 2x 1x

3x

1x

1x

2x

RED TUXEDO SOFA

2x 4x 4x 2x

4x 1x

4x 1x

2x 1x

⚠️ Clip hands underneath.

LIVING ROOM

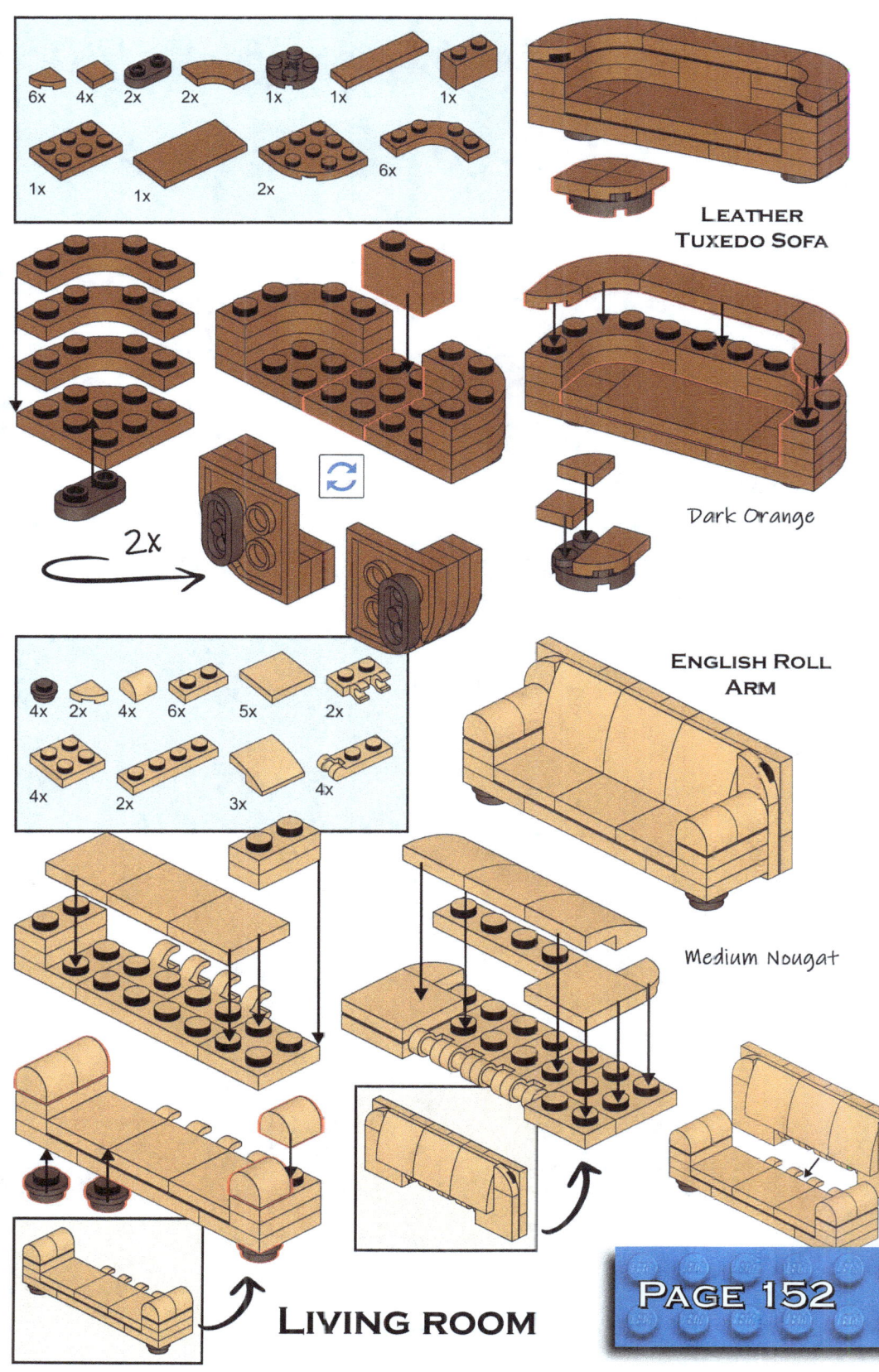

LEATHER
TUXEDO SOFA

Dark Orange

2x

ENGLISH ROLL
ARM

Medium Nougat

LIVING ROOM

PAGE 152

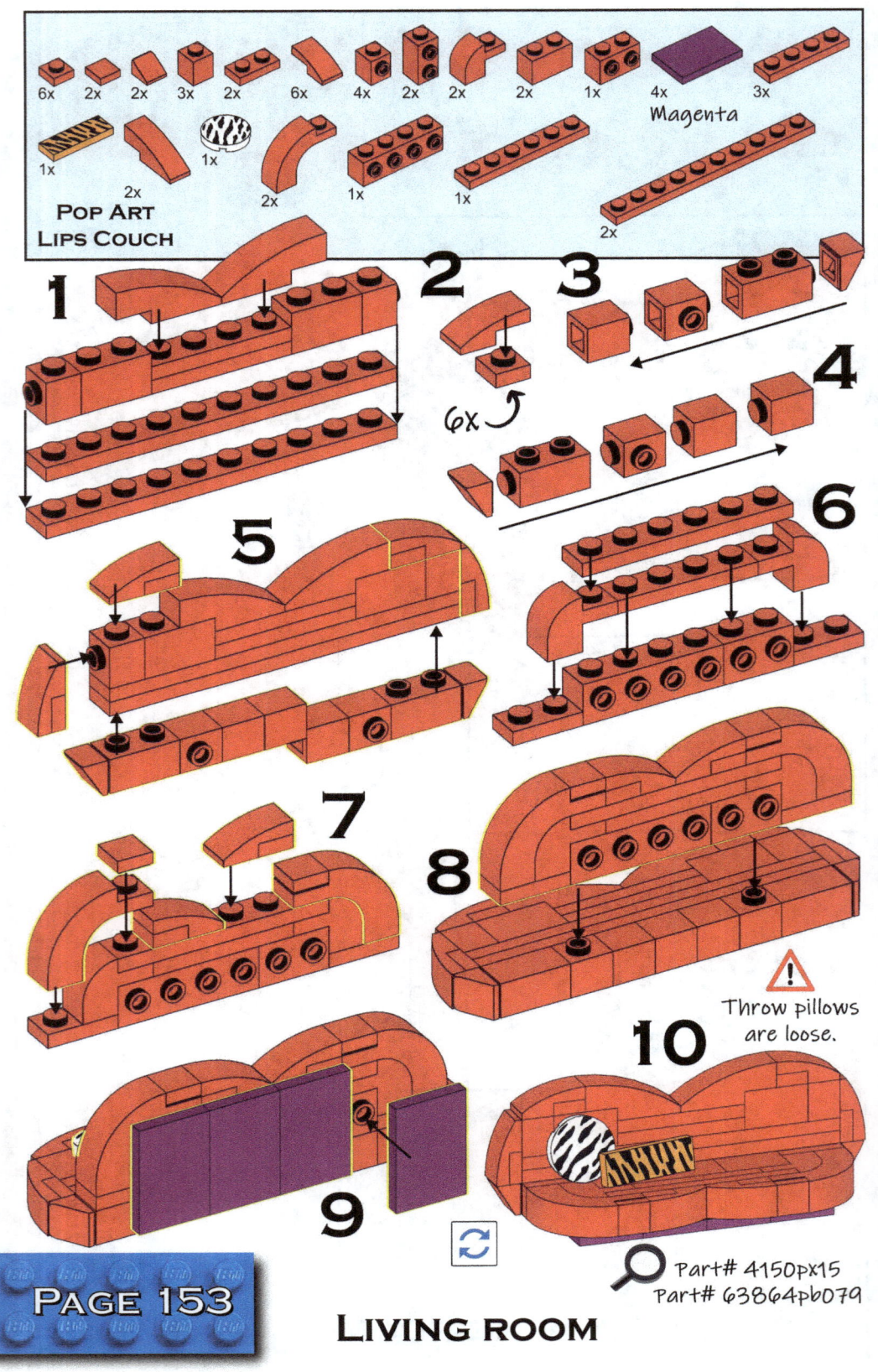

POP ART
LIPS COUCH

Magenta

1 2 3 4 5 6 7 8 9 10

6x ↺

⚠ Throw pillows are loose.

PAGE 153

LIVING ROOM

🔍 Part# 4150px15
Part# 63864pb079

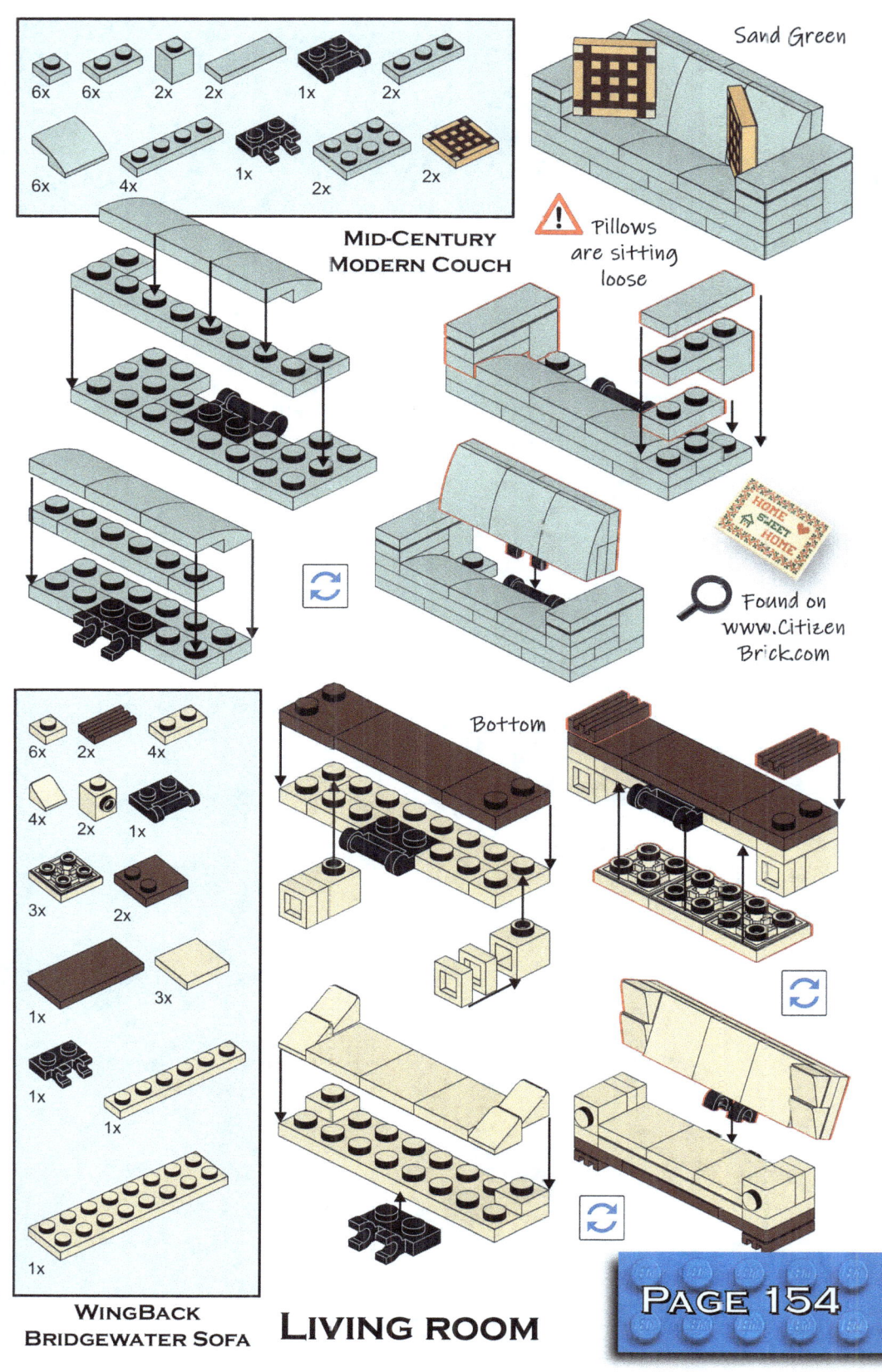

Sand Green

MID-CENTURY
MODERN COUCH

⚠ Pillows
are sitting
loose

HOME
SWEET
HOME

🔍 Found on
www.Citizen
Brick.com

Bottom

WINGBACK
BRIDGEWATER SOFA

LIVING ROOM

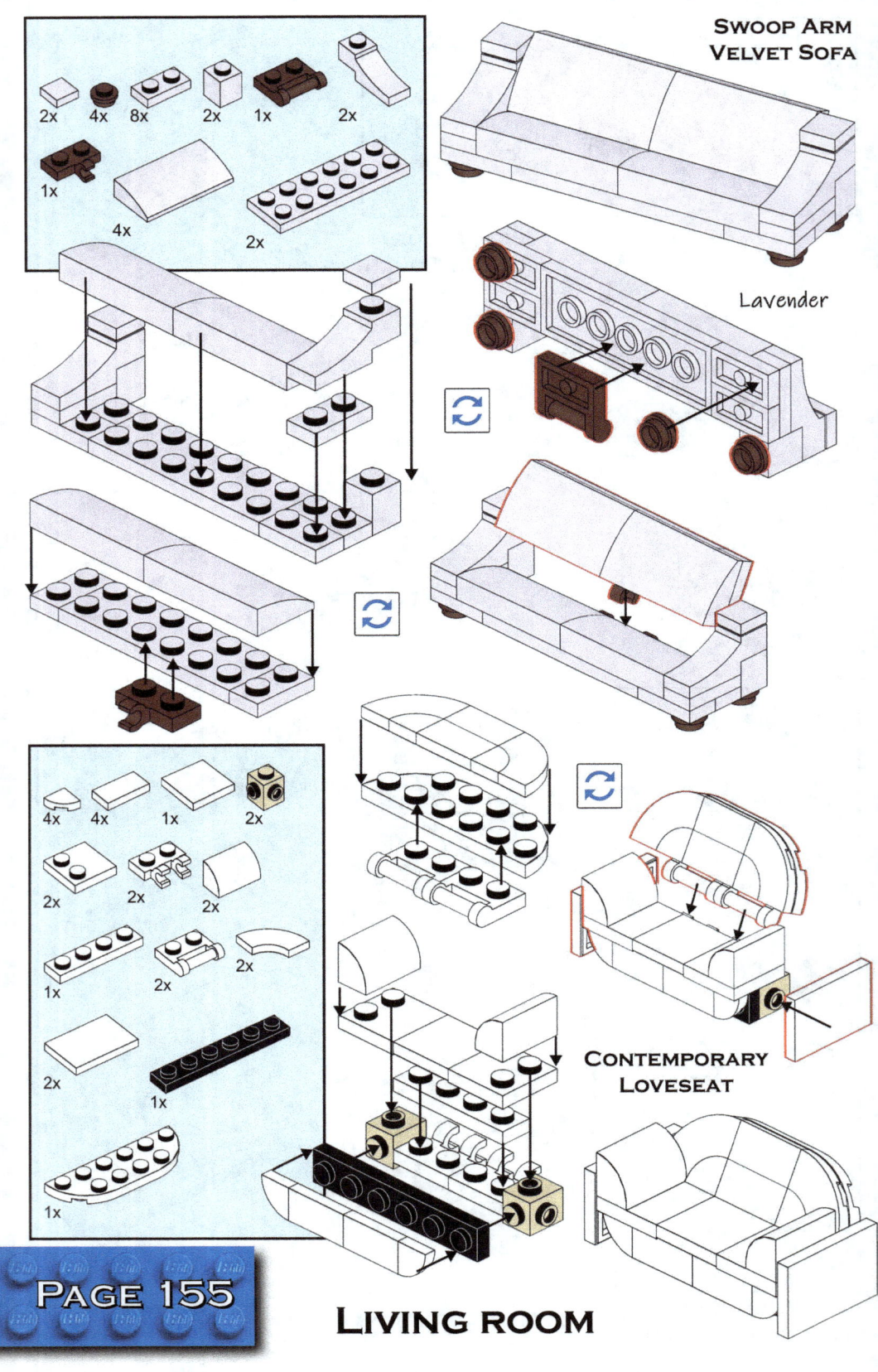

SWOOP ARM
VELVET SOFA

Lavender

CONTEMPORARY
LOVESEAT

LIVING ROOM

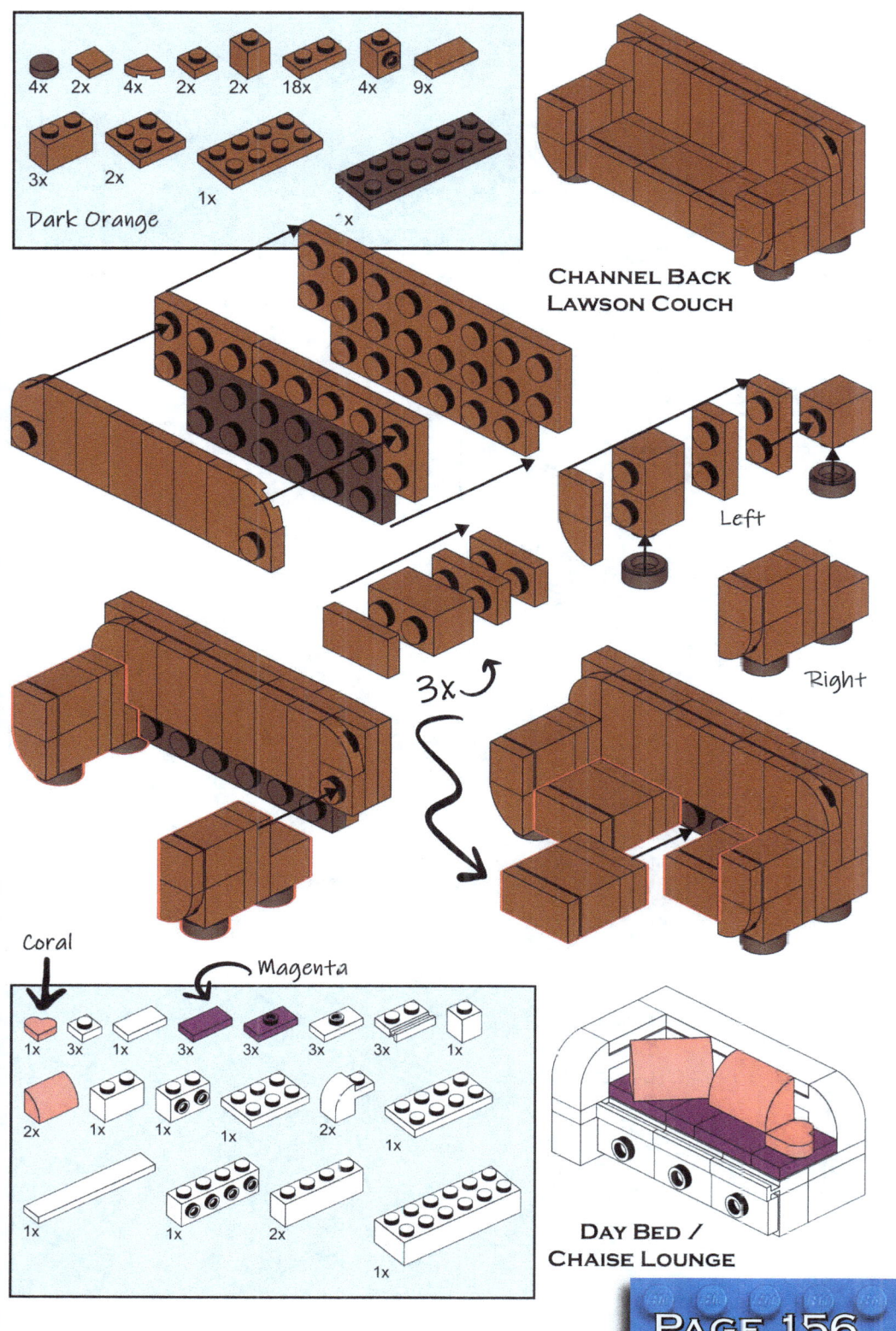

4x 2x 4x 2x 2x 18x 4x 9x

3x 2x 1x

Dark Orange

**CHANNEL BACK
LAWSON COUCH**

Left

Right

3x

Coral

Magenta

1x 3x 1x 3x 3x 3x 3x 1x

2x 1x 1x 1x 2x 1x

1x 1x 2x

1x

**DAY BED /
CHAISE LOUNGE**

LIVING ROOM

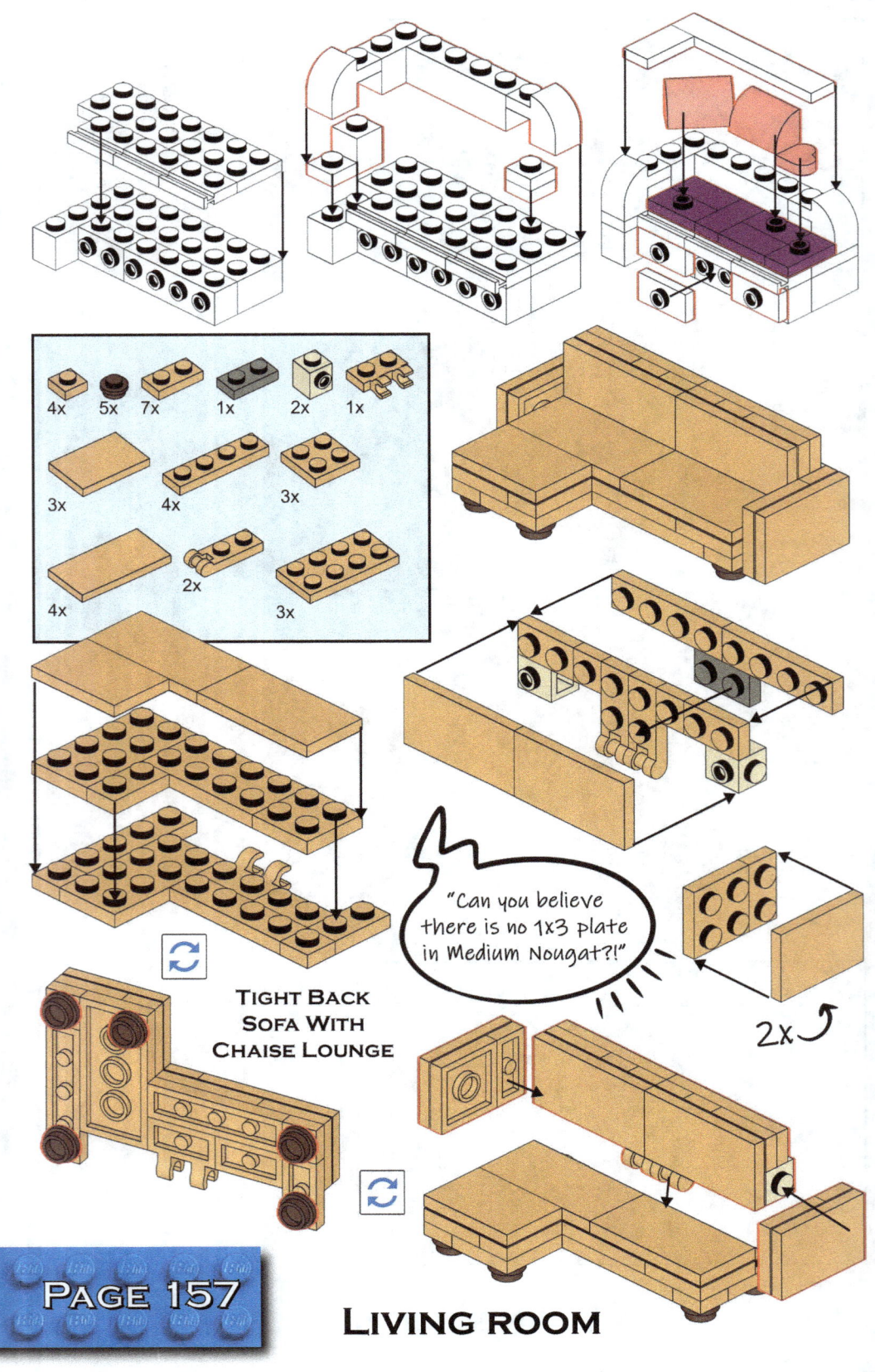

"Can you believe there is no 1x3 plate in Medium Nougat?!"

TIGHT BACK SOFA WITH CHAISE LOUNGE

2x

LIVING ROOM

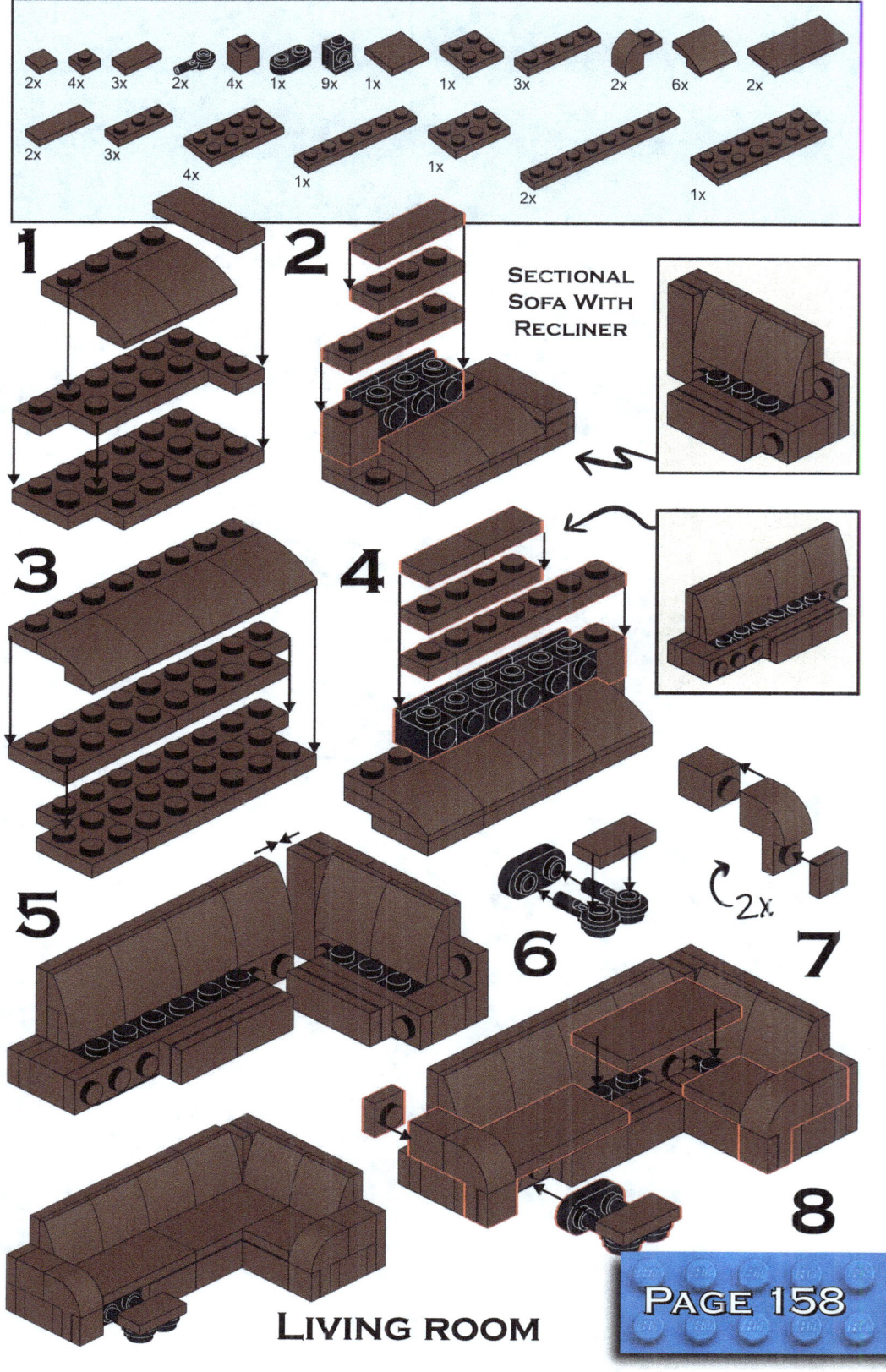

SECTIONAL SOFA WITH RECLINER

1

2

3

4

5

6

7

2x

8

LIVING ROOM

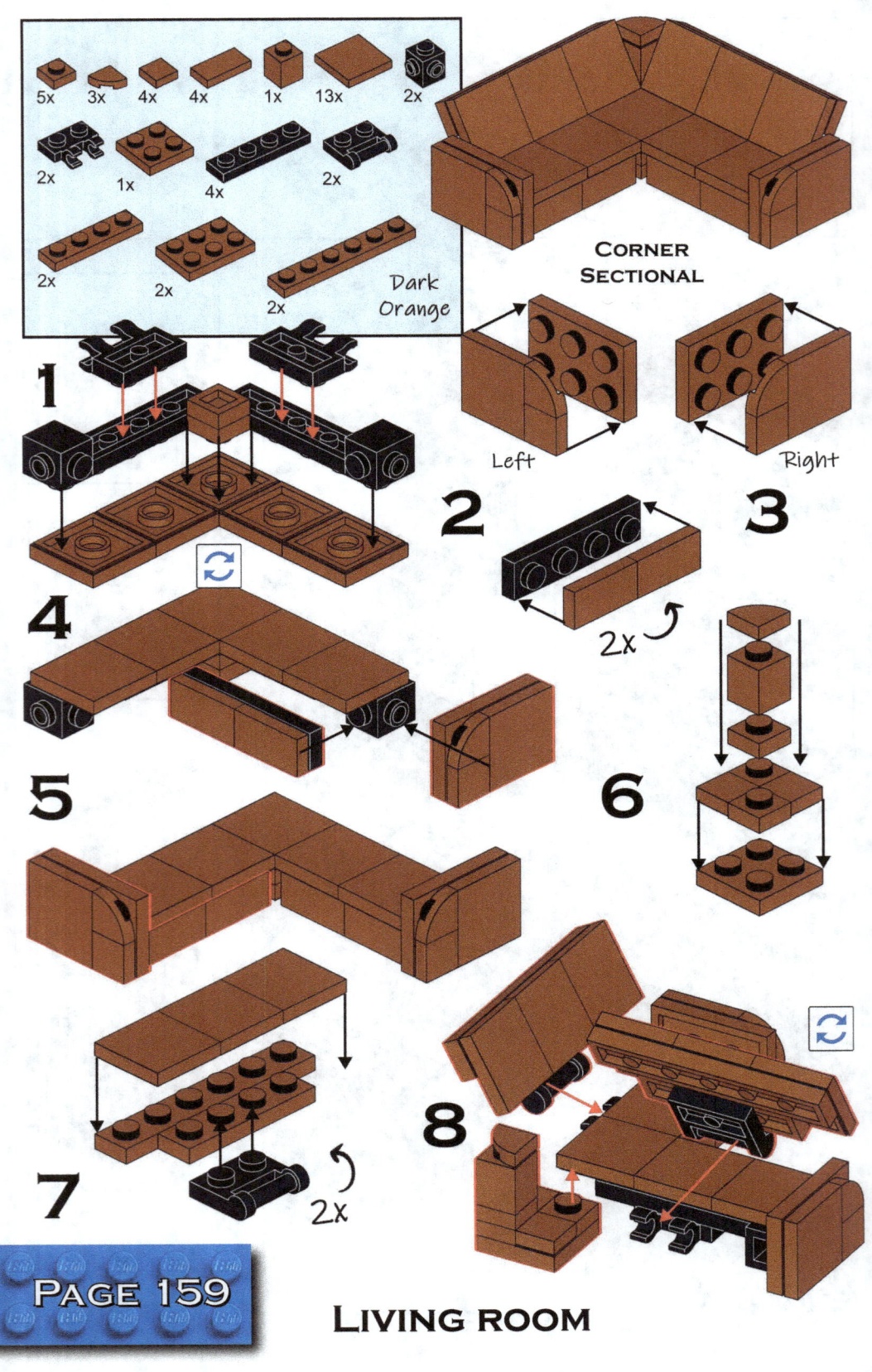

CORNER SECTIONAL

Left

Right

Dark Orange

5x 3x 4x 4x 1x 13x 2x

2x 1x 4x 2x

2x 2x 2x

1

2 2x

3

4

5

6

7 2x

8

LIVING ROOM

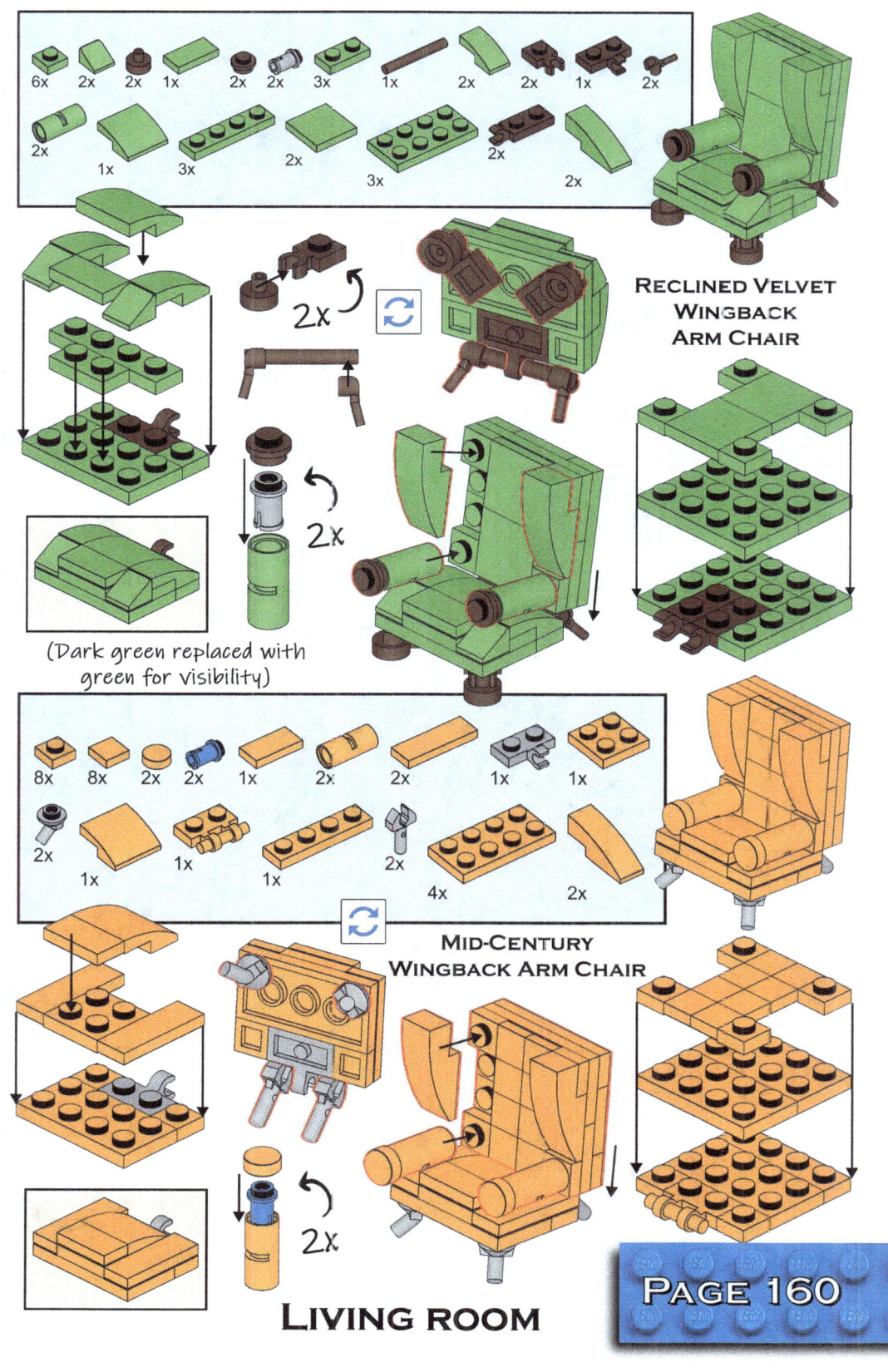

6x 2x 2x 1x 2x 2x 3x 1x 2x 2x 1x 2x

2x 1x 3x 2x 3x 2x 2x

2x

RECLINED VELVET
WINGBACK
ARM CHAIR

(Dark green replaced with
green for visibility)

8x 8x 2x 2x 1x 2x 2x 1x 1x

2x 1x 1x 1x 2x 4x 2x

MID-CENTURY
WINGBACK ARM CHAIR

LIVING ROOM

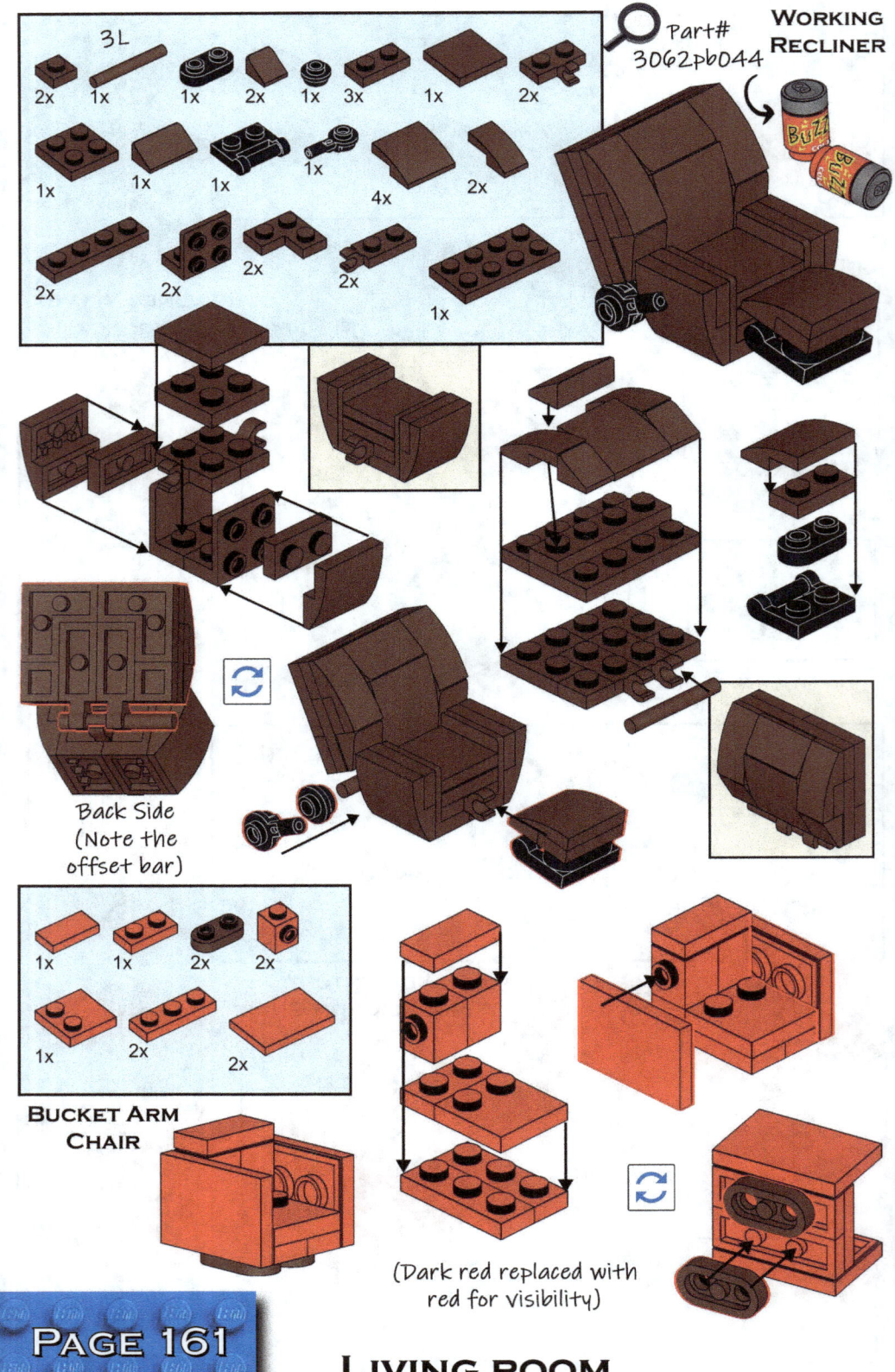

3L

2x 1x 1x 2x 1x 3x 1x 2x

1x 1x 1x 1x 4x 2x

2x 2x 2x 2x

1x

WORKING RECLINER

Part# 3062pb044

BUZZ

Back Side
(Note the
offset bar)

BUCKET ARM CHAIR

1x 1x 2x 2x

1x 2x 2x

(Dark red replaced with
red for visibility)

LIVING ROOM

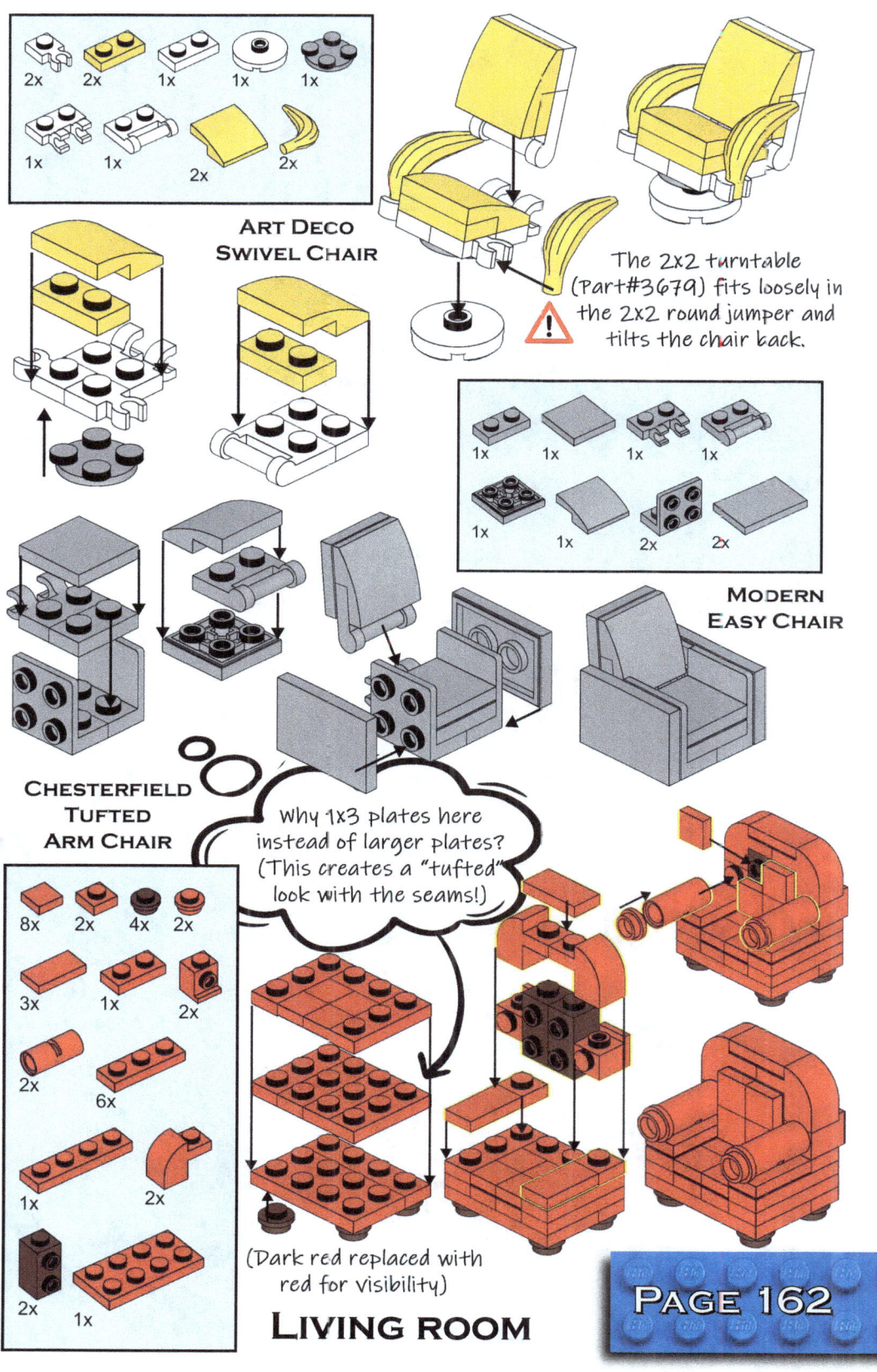

ART DECO
SWIVEL CHAIR

The 2x2 turntable (Part#3679) fits loosely in the 2x2 round jumper and tilts the chair back.

2x 2x 1x 1x 1x
1x 1x 2x 2x

MODERN
EASY CHAIR

1x 1x 1x 1x
1x 1x 2x 2x

CHESTERFIELD
TUFTED
ARM CHAIR

Why 1x3 plates here instead of larger plates? (This creates a "tufted" look with the seams!)

8x 2x 4x 2x
3x 1x 2x
2x 6x
1x 2x
2x 1x

(Dark red replaced with red for visibility)

LIVING ROOM

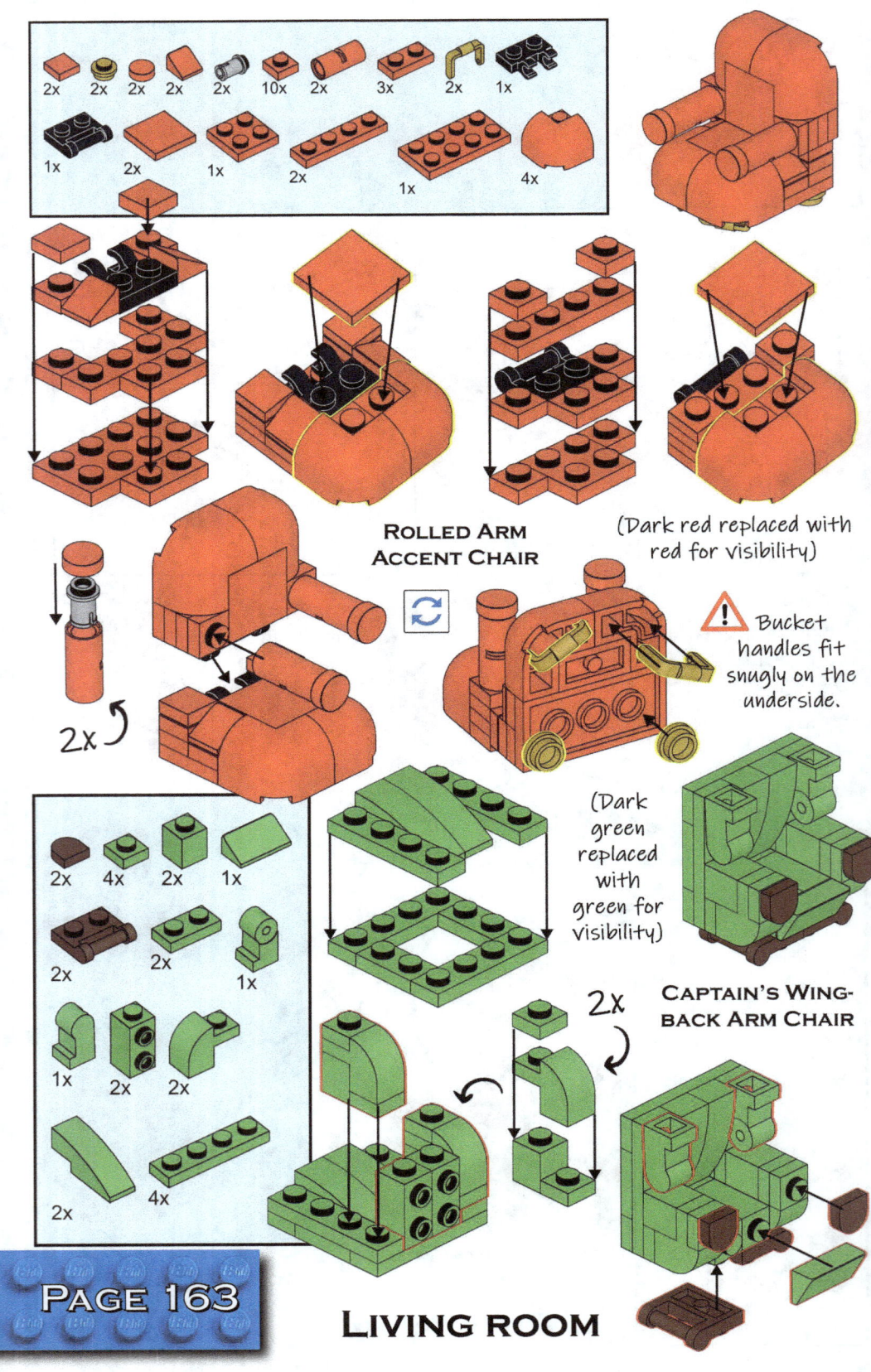

ROLLED ARM ACCENT CHAIR

(Dark red replaced with red for visibility)

⚠ Bucket handles fit snugly on the underside.

(Dark green replaced with green for visibility)

2x

CAPTAIN'S WING-BACK ARM CHAIR

LIVING ROOM

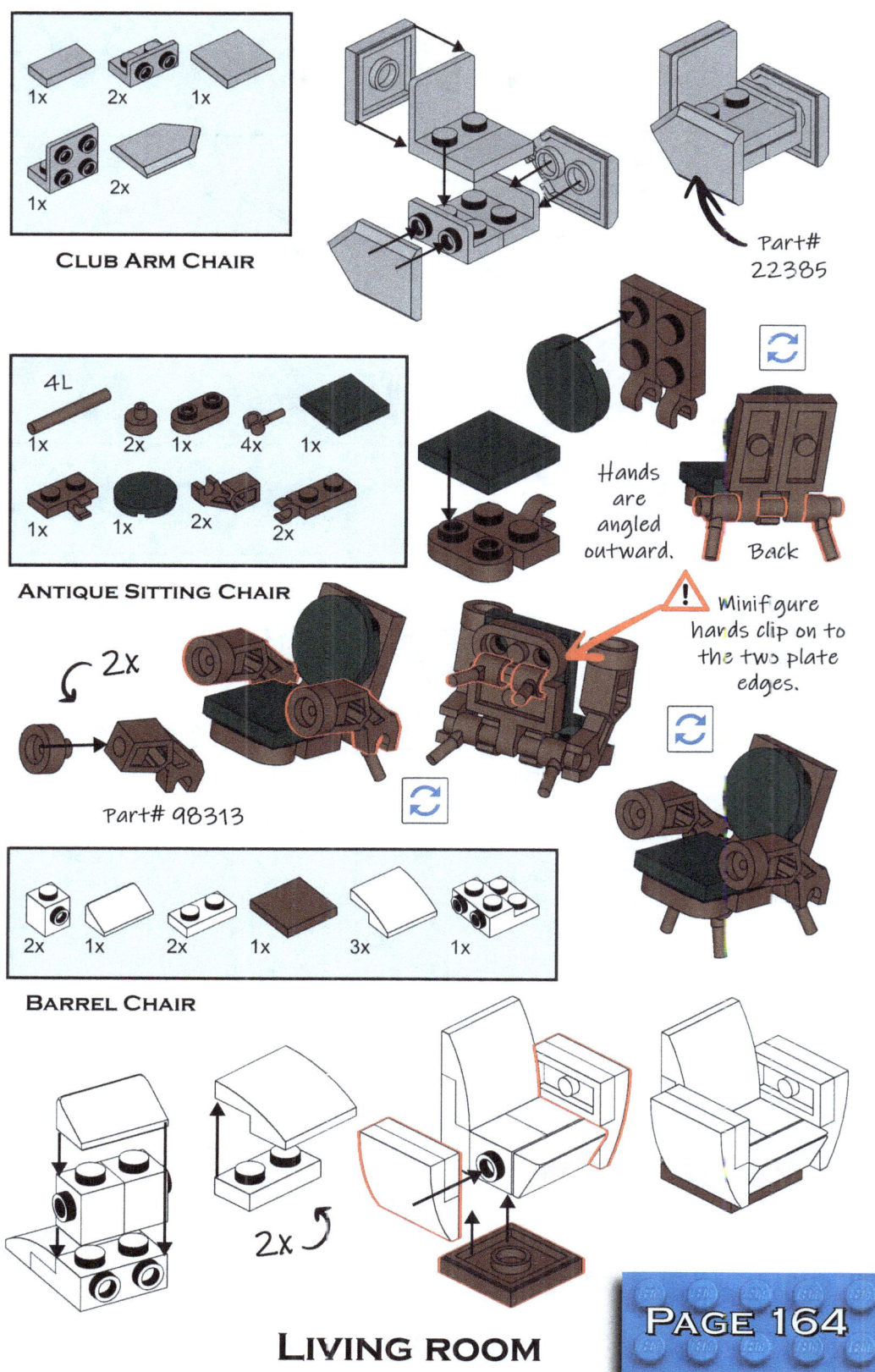

CLUB ARM CHAIR

Part# 22385

ANTIQUE SITTING CHAIR

4L

Hands are angled outward.   Back

⚠ Minifigure hands clip on to the two plate edges.

2x

Part# 98313

BARREL CHAIR

2x

LIVING ROOM

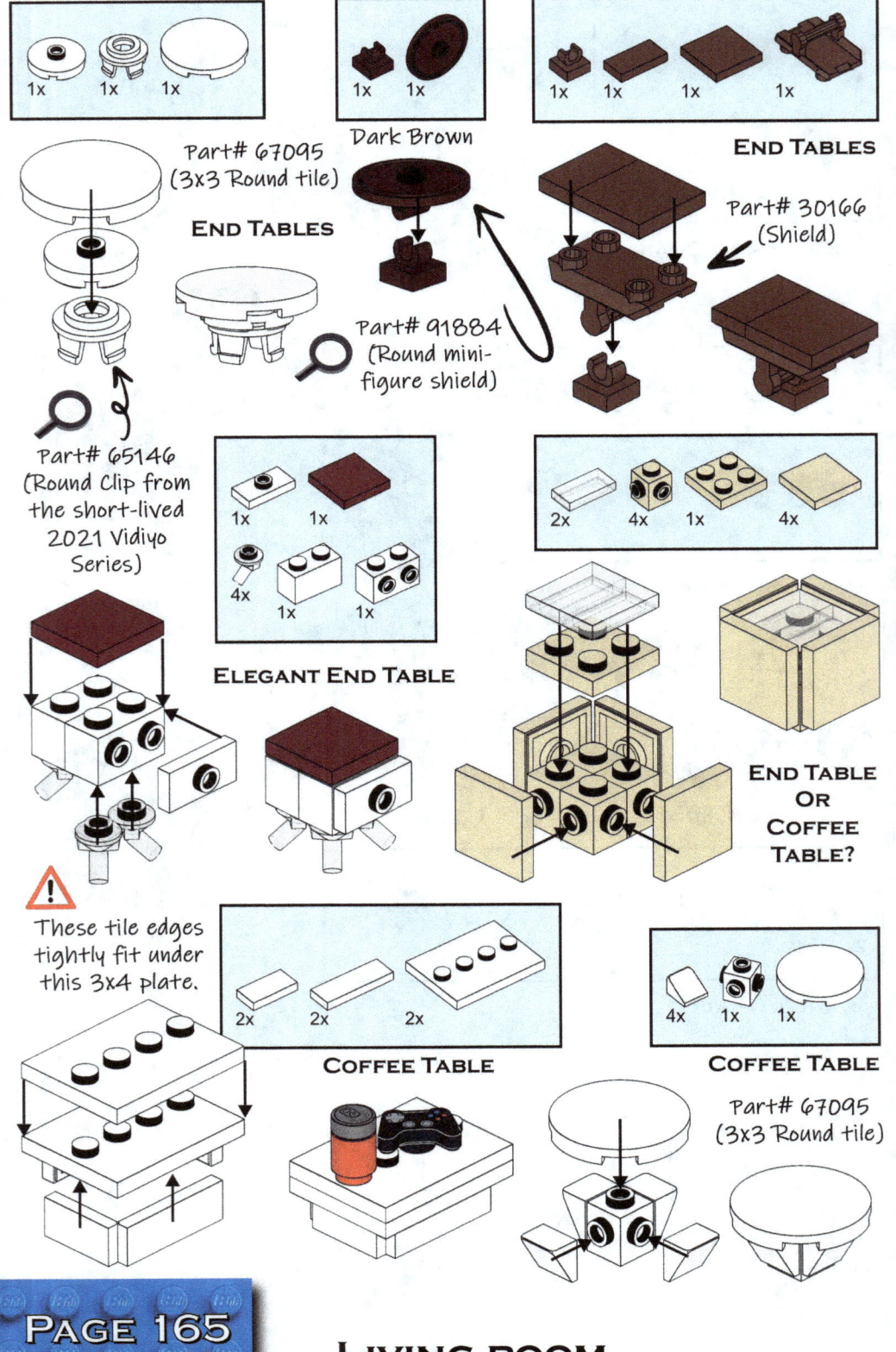

1x 1x 1x

1x 1x

Dark Brown

1x 1x 1x 1x

END TABLES

Part# 67095
(3x3 Round tile)

END TABLES

Part# 30166
(Shield)

Part# 91884
(Round mini-
figure shield)

Part# 65146
(Round Clip from
the short-lived
2021 Vidiyo
Series)

1x 1x

4x 1x 1x

2x 4x 1x 4x

ELEGANT END TABLE

**END TABLE
OR
COFFEE
TABLE?**

⚠ These tile edges
tightly fit under
this 3x4 plate.

2x 2x 2x

4x 1x 1x

COFFEE TABLE

COFFEE TABLE

Part# 67095
(3x3 Round tile)

LIVING ROOM

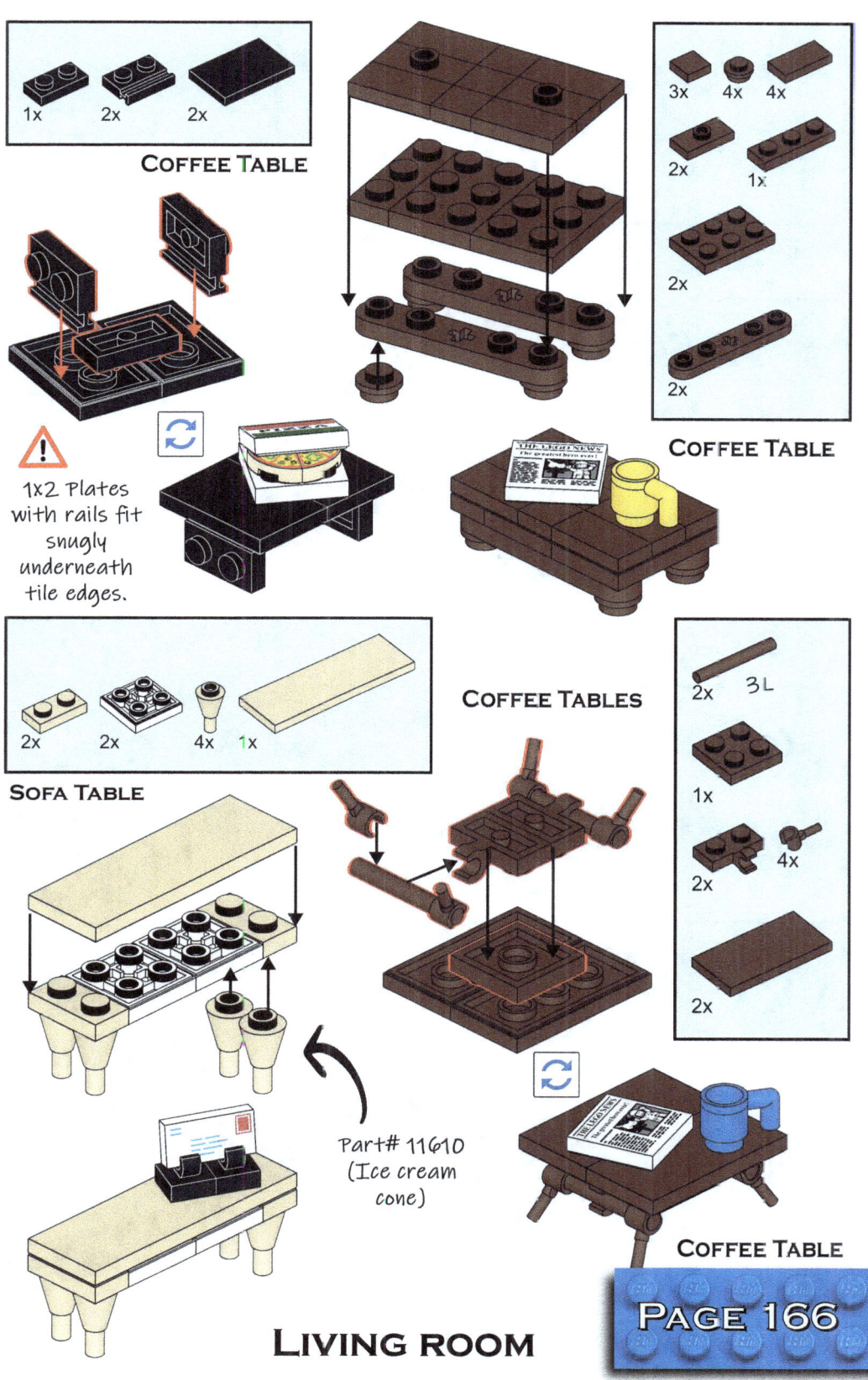

COFFEE TABLE

1x 2x 2x

3x 4x 4x

2x 1x

2x

2x

2x

COFFEE TABLE

⚠ 1x2 Plates with rails fit snugly underneath tile edges.

THE LEGO NEWS
The greatest hero ever!

COFFEE TABLES

2x 3L

1x

2x 4x

2x

SOFA TABLE

2x 2x 4x 1x

Part# 11610 (Ice cream cone)

THE LEGO NEWS

COFFEE TABLE

LIVING ROOM

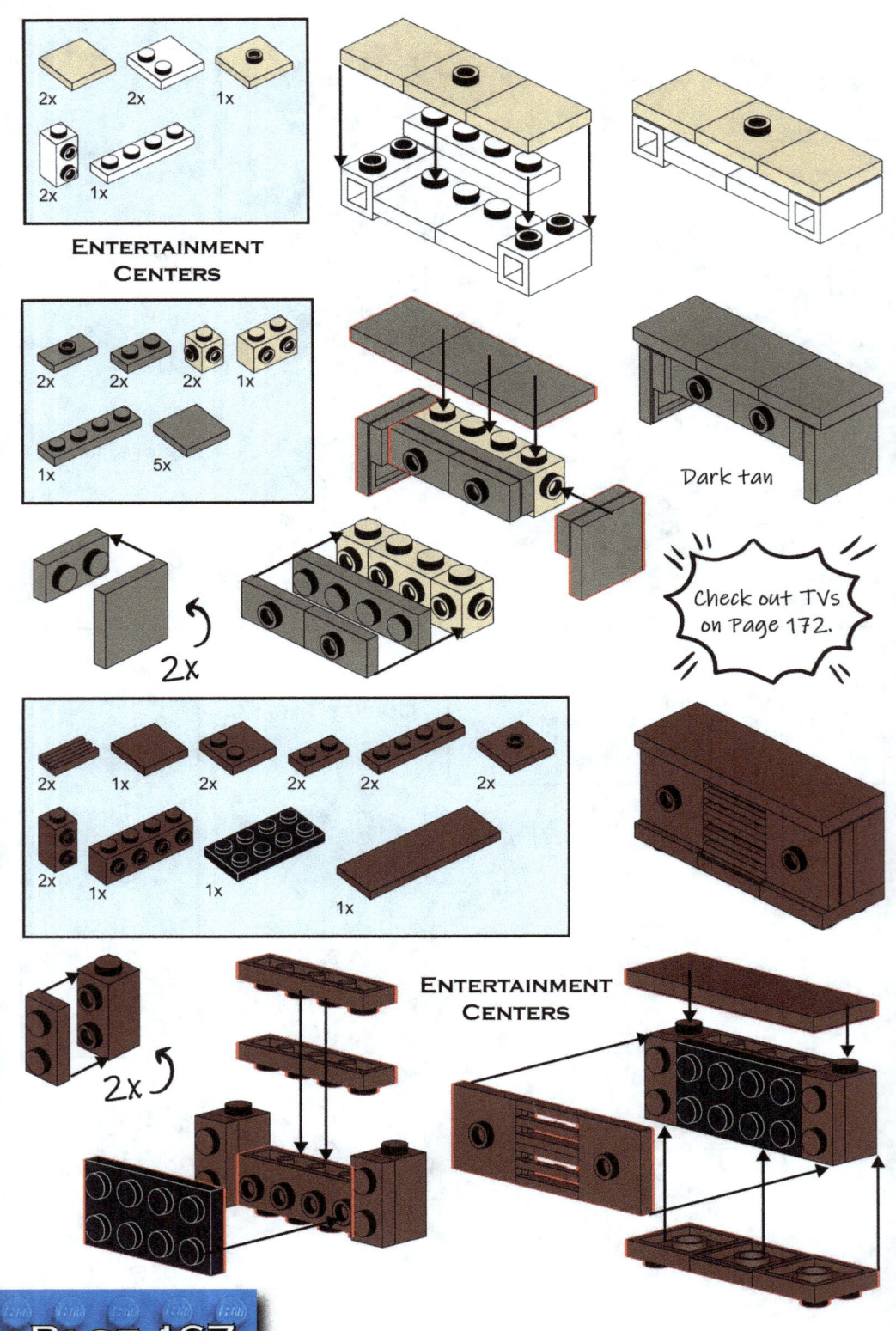

ENTERTAINMENT CENTERS

Dark tan

Check out TVs on Page 172.

ENTERTAINMENT CENTERS

LIVING ROOM

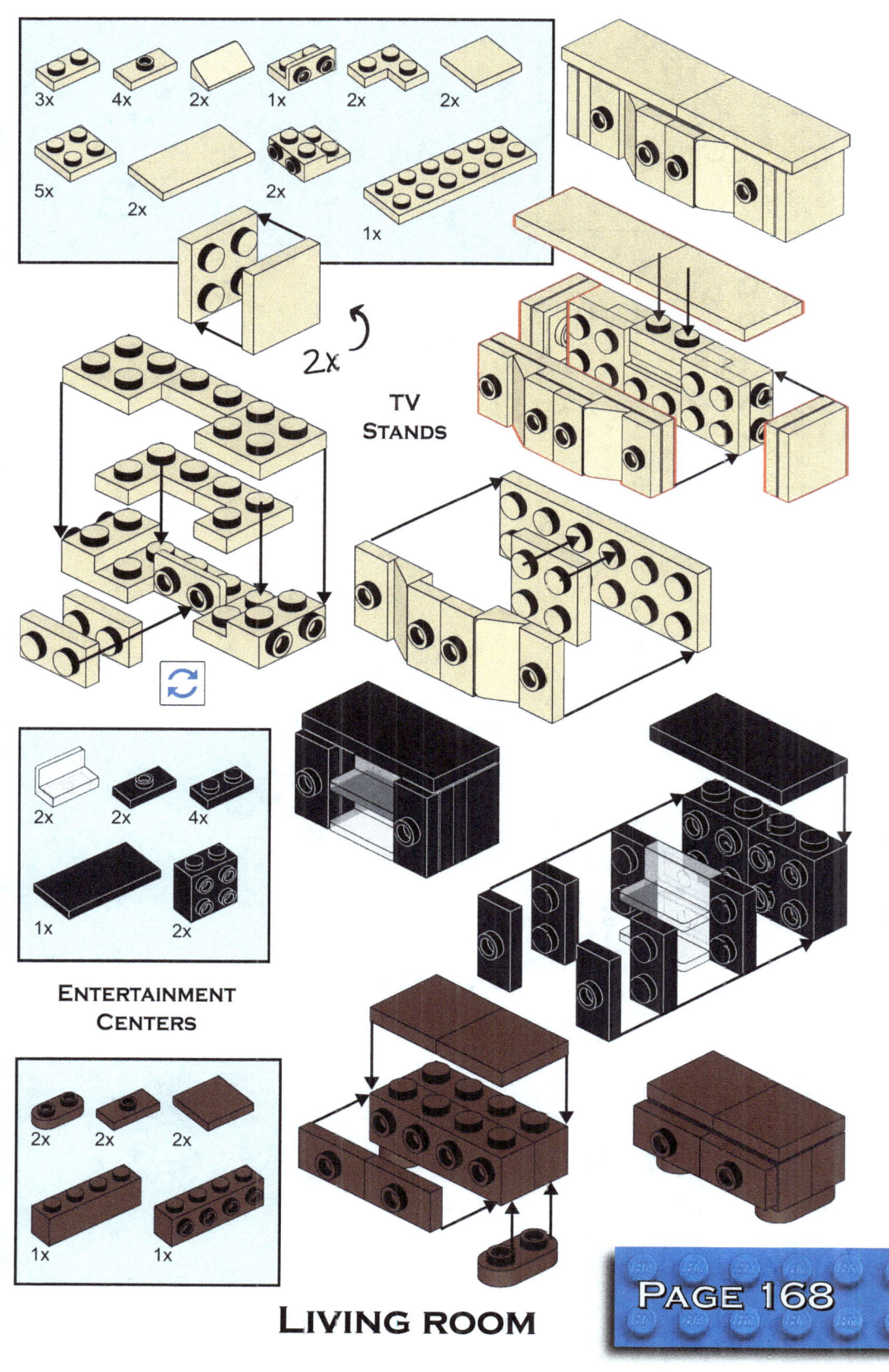

3x 4x 2x 1x 2x 2x

5x 2x 2x 1x

2x

TV STANDS

ENTERTAINMENT CENTERS

2x 2x 4x

1x 2x

2x 2x 2x

1x 1x

LIVING ROOM

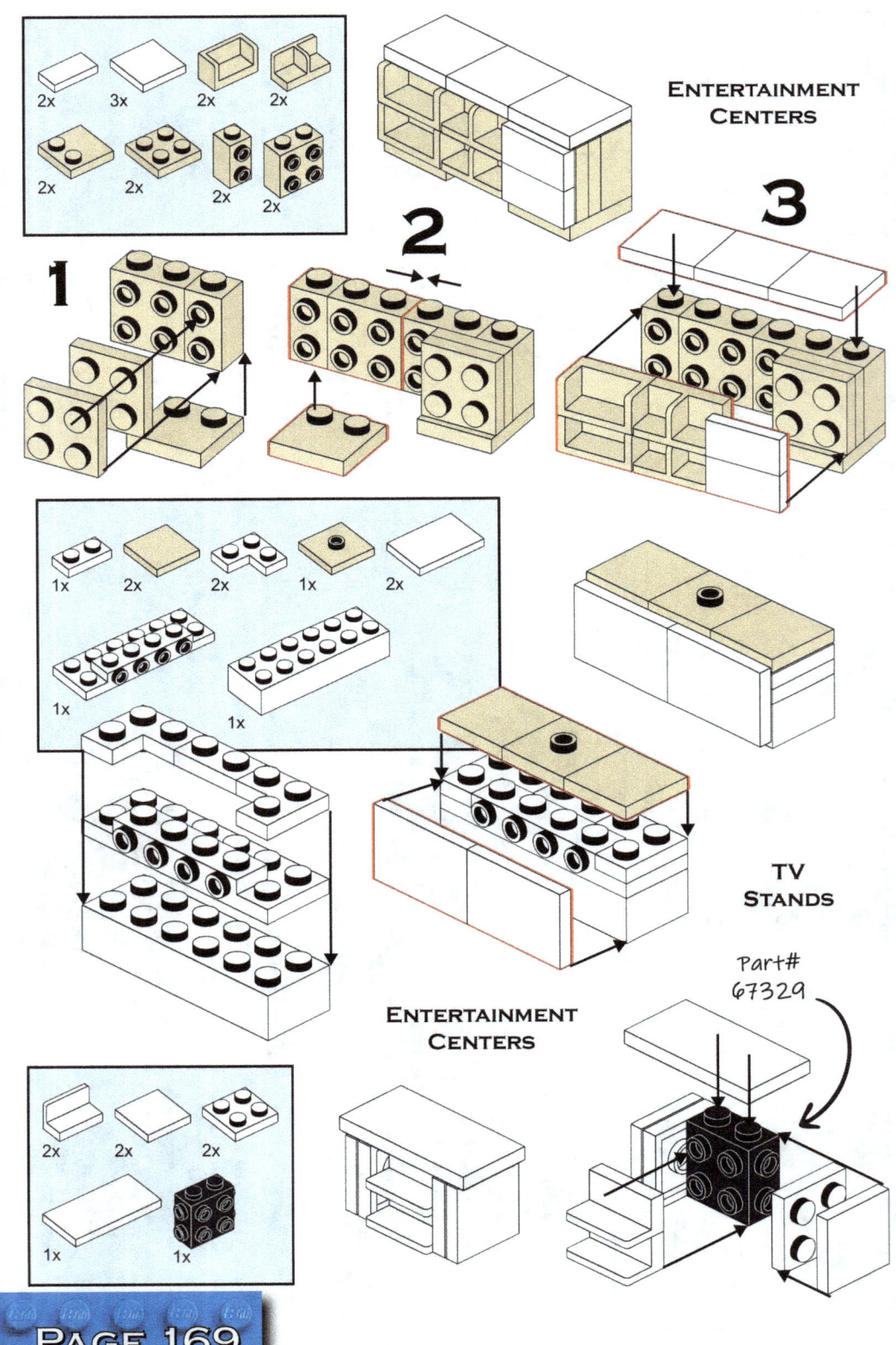

ENTERTAINMENT CENTERS

1

2

3

TV STANDS

Part# 67329

ENTERTAINMENT CENTERS

LIVING ROOM

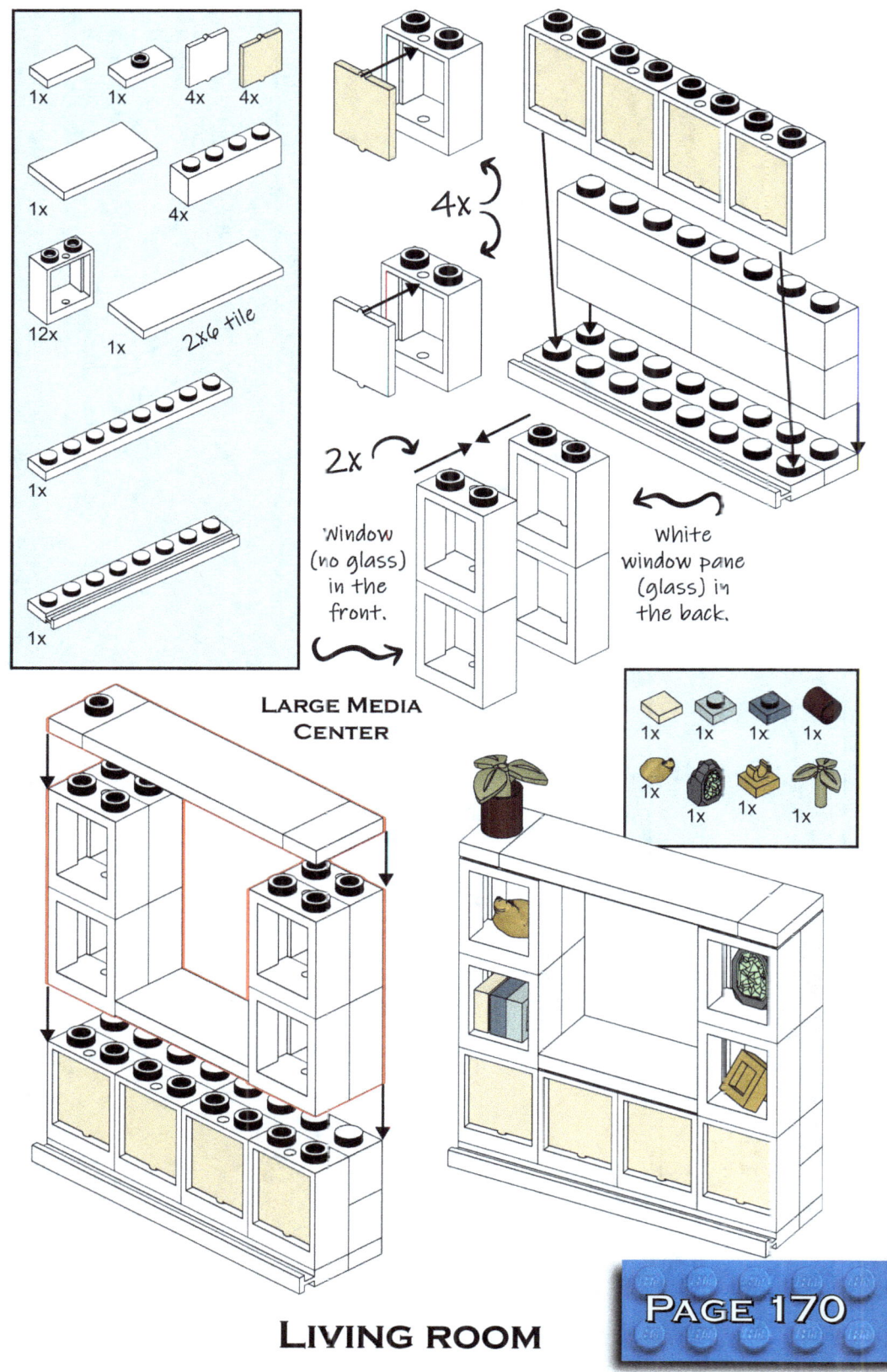

1x 1x 4x 4x

1x 4x

12x 1x 2x6 tile

1x

1x

4x

2x

Window
(no glass)
in the
front.

white
window pane
(glass) in
the back.

LARGE MEDIA CENTER

1x 1x 1x 1x

1x 1x 1x 1x

LIVING ROOM

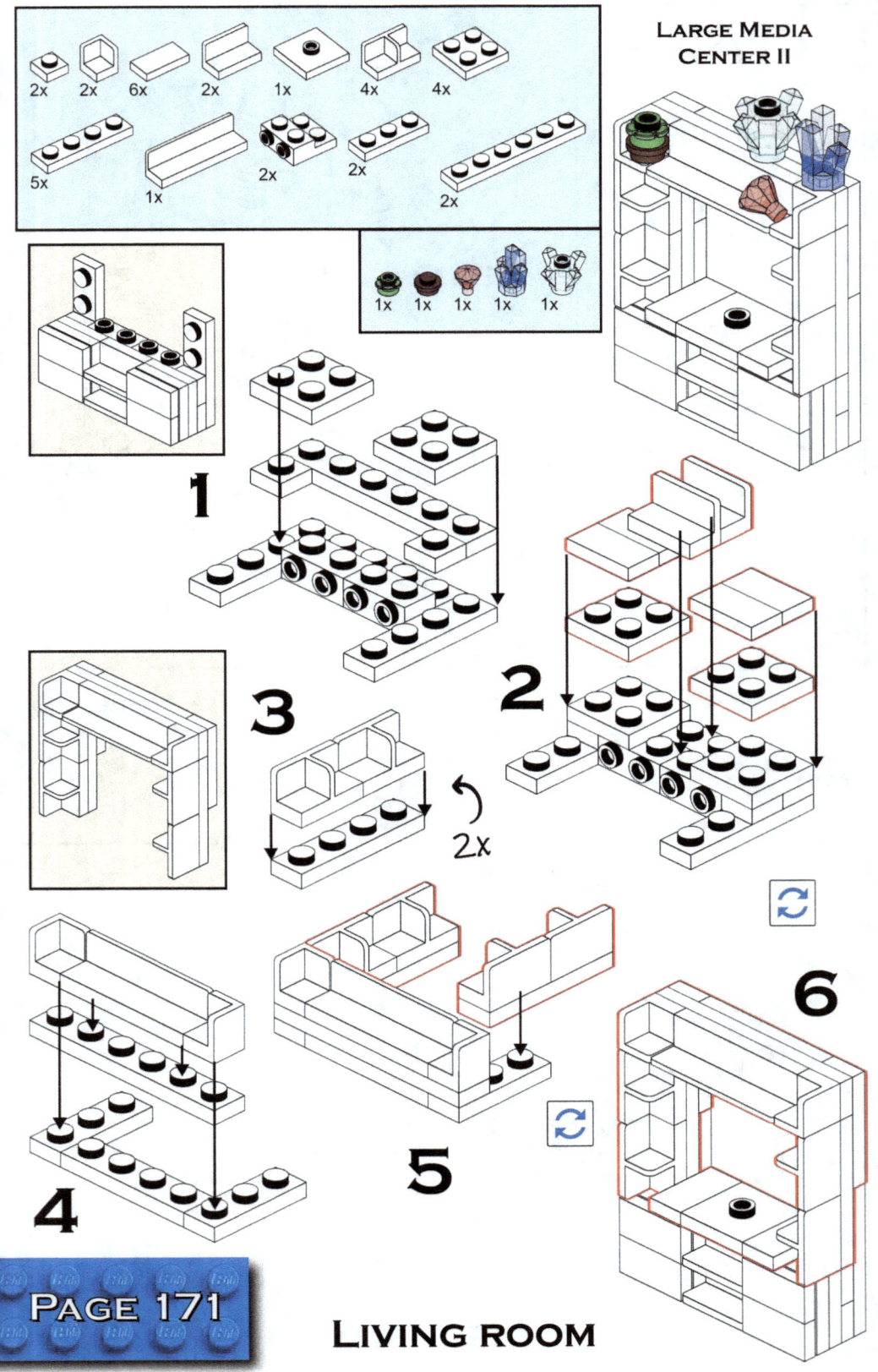

LARGE MEDIA
CENTER II

2x 2x 6x 2x 1x 4x 4x

5x 1x 2x 2x 2x

1x 1x 1x 1x 1x

1

2

3

2x

4

5

6

LIVING ROOM

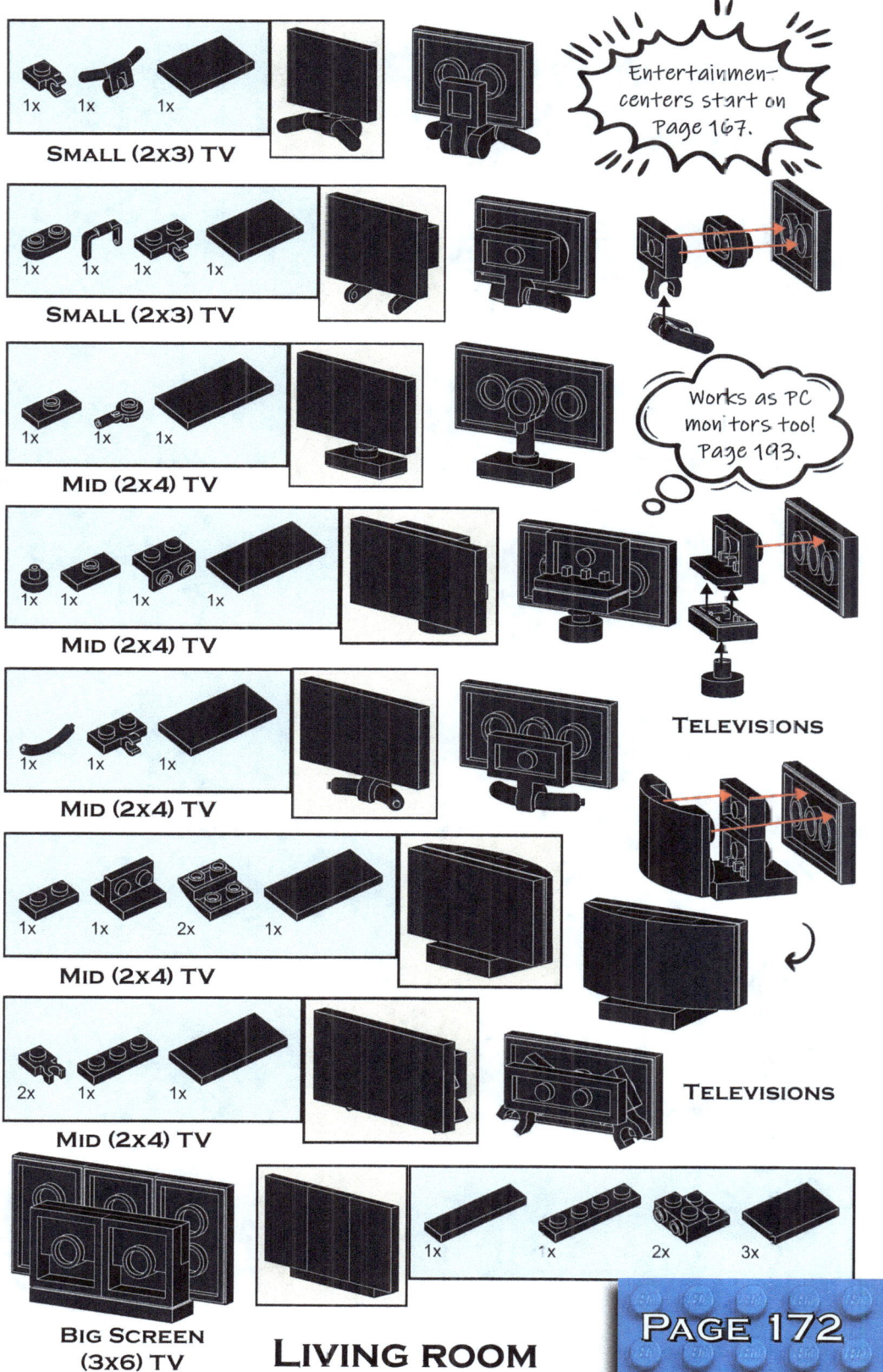

SMALL (2x3) TV
1x 1x 1x

Entertainment-centers start on Page 167.

SMALL (2x3) TV
1x 1x 1x 1x

MID (2x4) TV
1x 1x 1x

Works as PC monitors too! Page 193.

MID (2x4) TV
1x 1x 1x 1x

MID (2x4) TV
1x 1x 1x

TELEVISIONS

MID (2x4) TV
1x 1x 2x 1x

MID (2x4) TV
2x 1x 1x

TELEVISIONS

BIG SCREEN (3x6) TV
1x 1x 2x 3x

LIVING ROOM

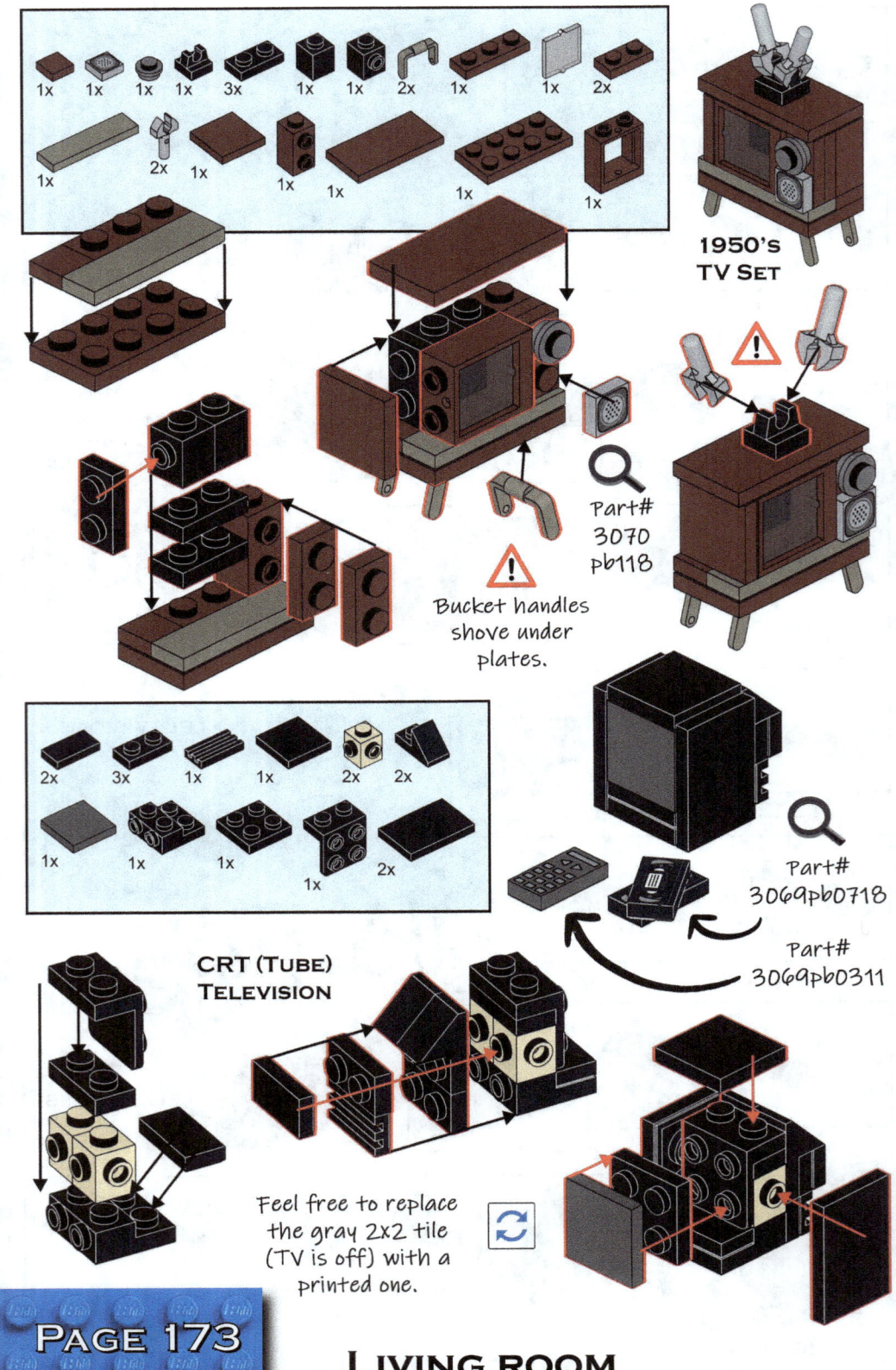

1x 1x 1x 1x 3x 1x 1x 2x 1x 1x 2x

1x 2x 1x 1x 1x 1x 1x

1950's TV Set

Part# 3070 pb118

⚠️ Bucket handles shove under plates.

2x 3x 1x 1x 2x 2x

1x 1x 1x 1x 2x

Part# 3069pb0718

Part# 3069pb0311

CRT (Tube) Television

Feel free to replace the gray 2x2 tile (TV is off) with a printed one.

LIVING ROOM

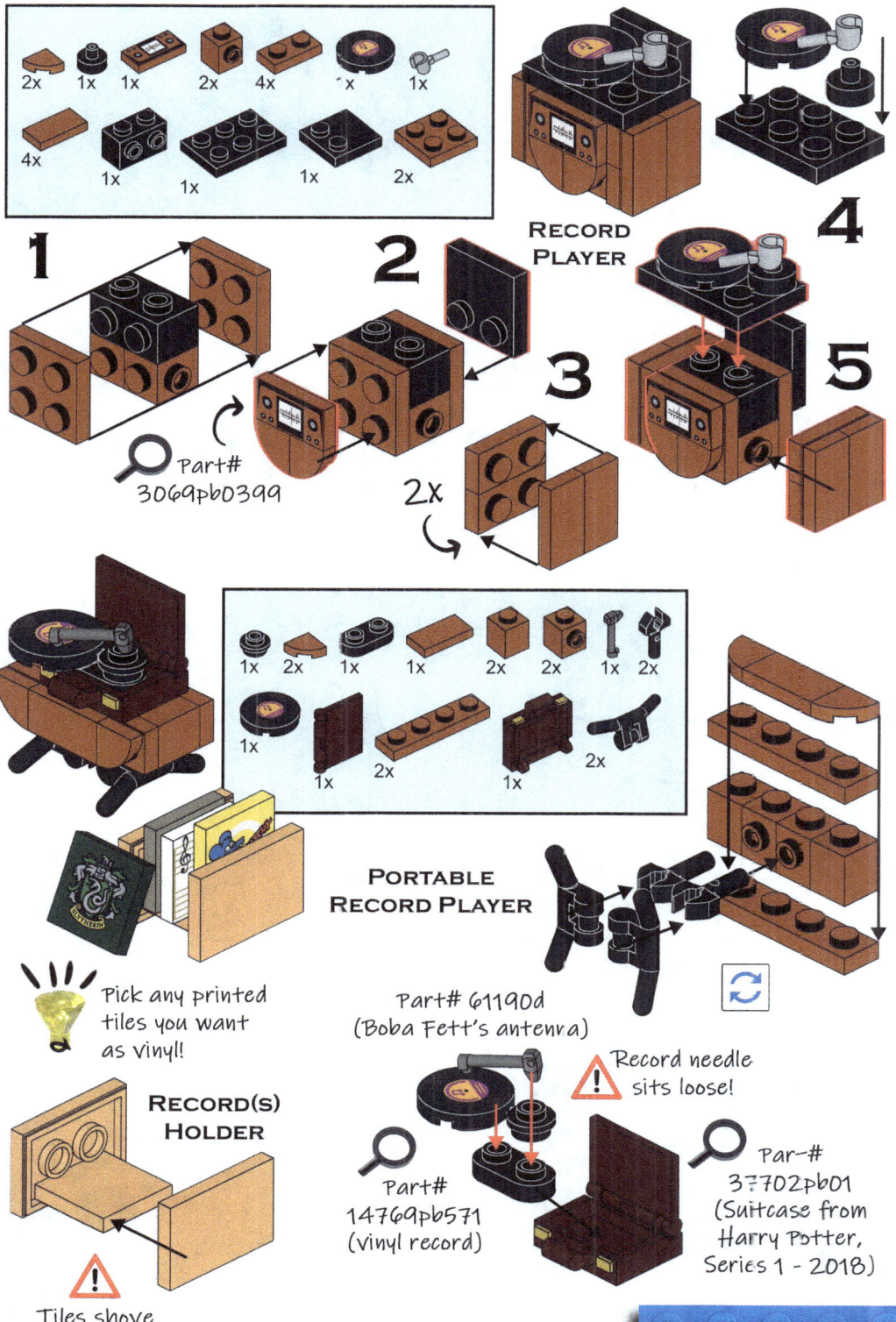

1

2

Part#
3069pb0399

RECORD PLAYER

3

2x

4

5

Pick any printed tiles you want as vinyl!

PORTABLE RECORD PLAYER

Part# 61190d
(Boba Fett's antenna)

RECORD(S) HOLDER

⚠️ Tiles shove together in the gaps.

Record needle sits loose!

Part# 14769pb571
(vinyl record)

Par-#
37702pb01
(Suitcase from Harry Potter, Series 1 - 2018)

LIVING ROOM

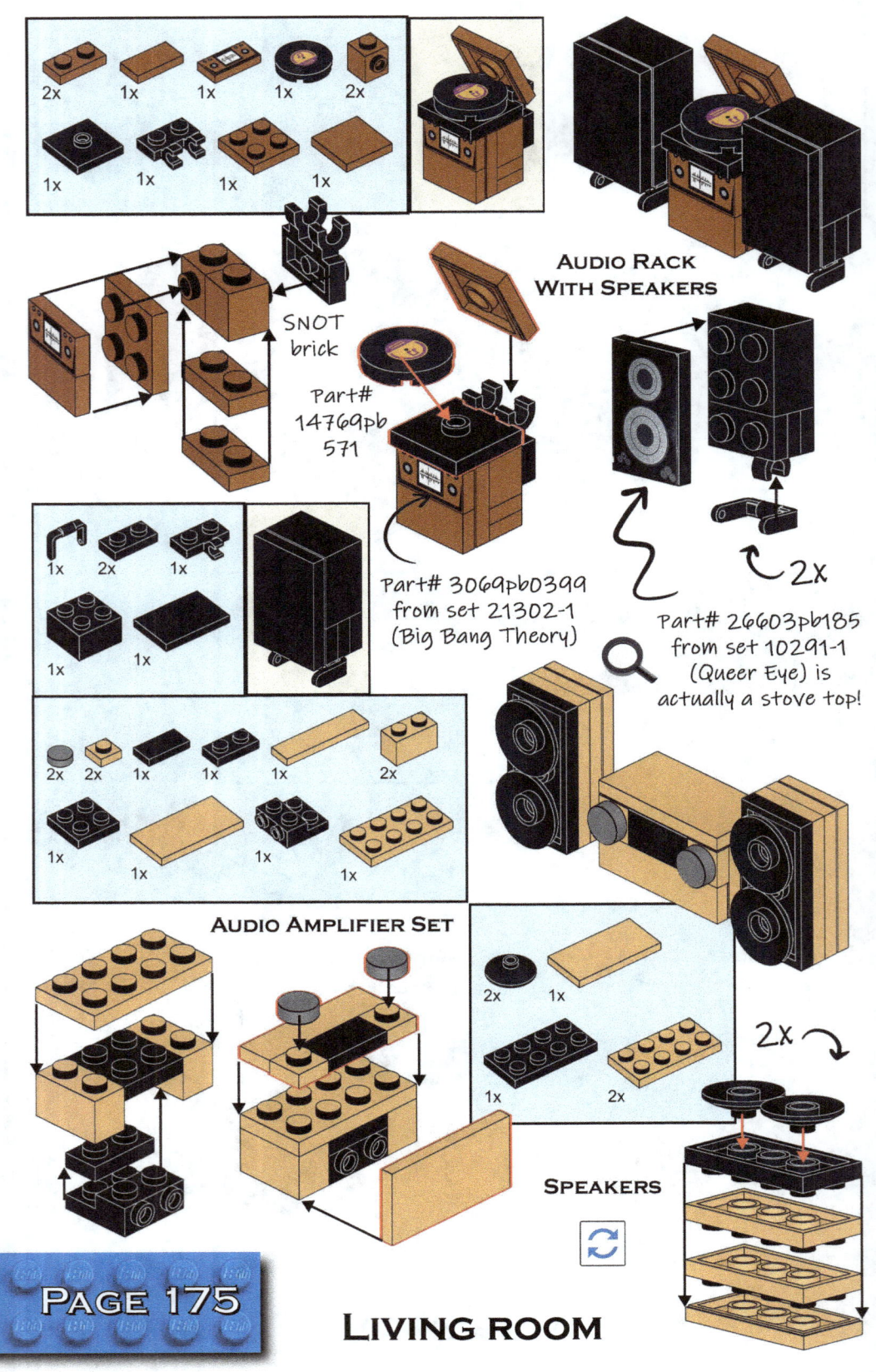

AUDIO RACK WITH SPEAKERS

SNOT brick

Part# 14769pb 571

Part# 3069pb0399 from set 21302-1 (Big Bang Theory)

Part# 26603pb185 from set 10291-1 (Queer Eye) is actually a stove top!

2x

2x

AUDIO AMPLIFIER SET

SPEAKERS

2x

LIVING ROOM

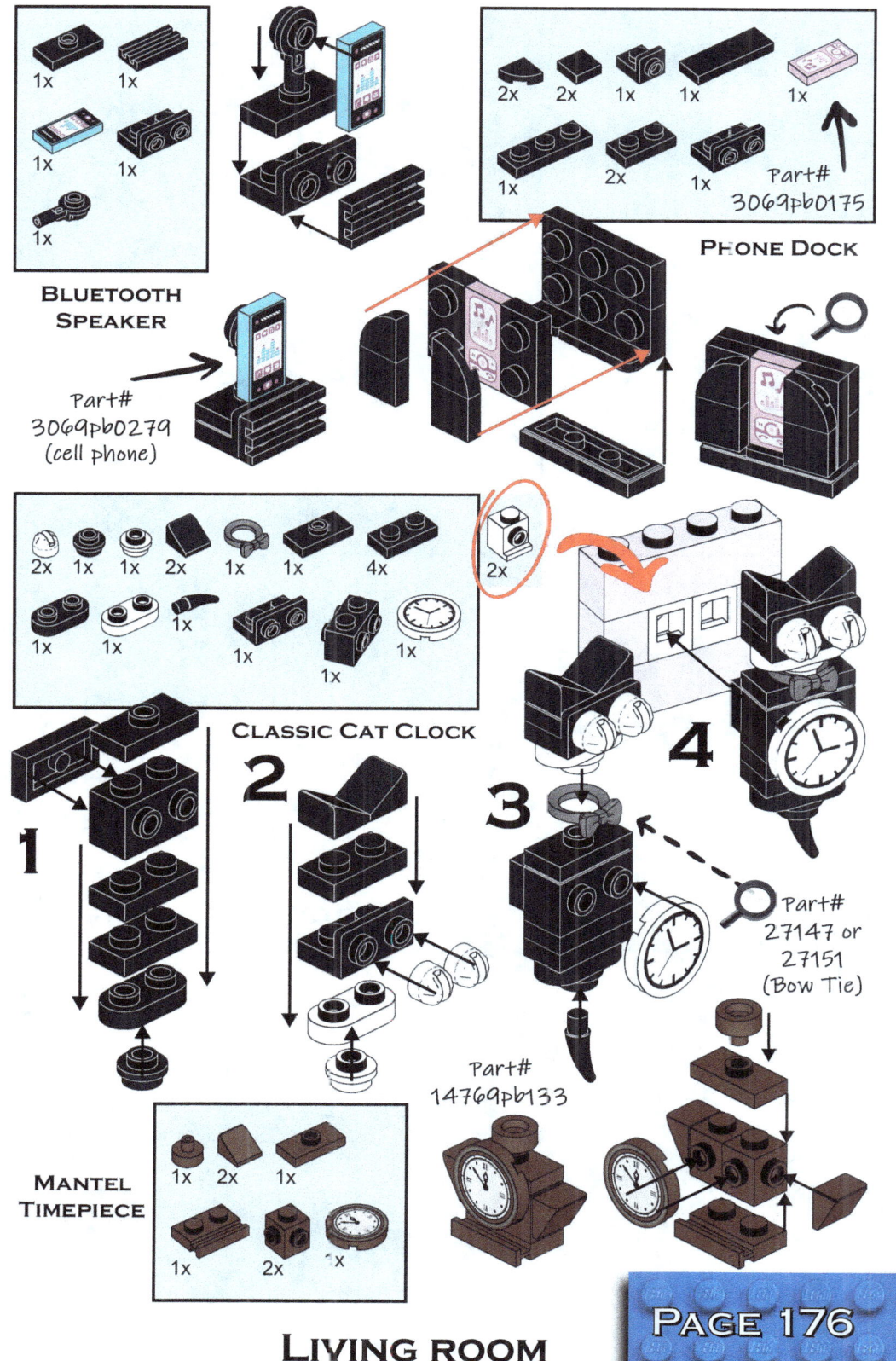

BLUETOOTH SPEAKER

1x 1x
1x 1x
1x

Part#
3069pb0279
(cell phone)

PHONE DOCK

2x 2x 1x 1x 1x
1x 2x 1x

Part#
3069pb0175

CLASSIC CAT CLOCK

2x 1x 1x 2x 1x 1x 4x
1x 1x 1x 1x 1x 1x
2x

1 2 3 4

Part#
27147 or
27151
(Bow Tie)

Part#
14769pb133

MANTEL TIMEPIECE

1x 2x 1x
1x 2x x

LIVING ROOM

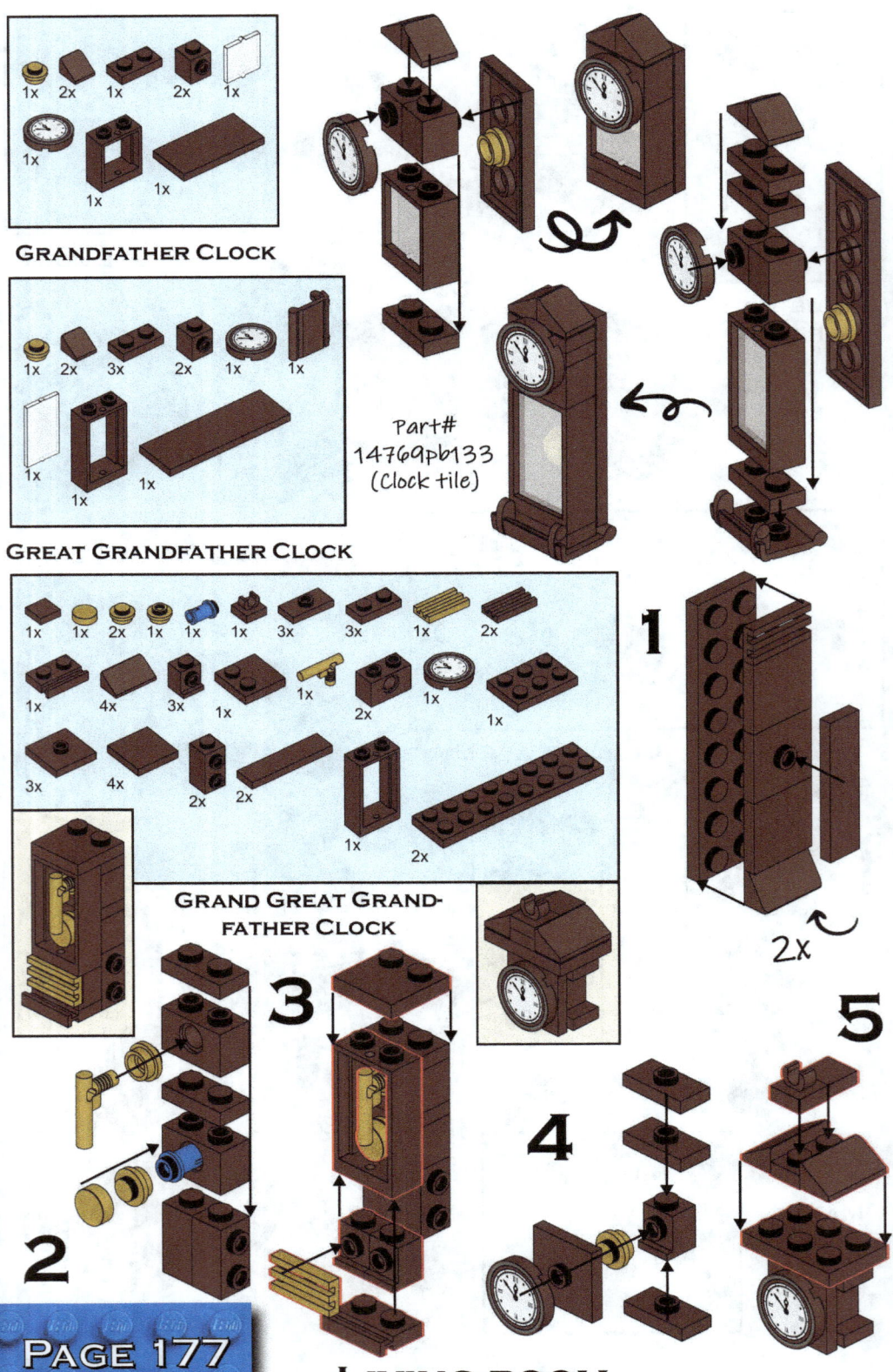

GRANDFATHER CLOCK

1x 2x 1x 2x 1x
1x
1x 1x

GREAT GRANDFATHER CLOCK

1x 2x 3x 2x 1x 1x
1x
1x 1x

Part#
14769pb133
(Clock tile)

GRAND GREAT GRAND-
FATHER CLOCK

1x 1x 2x 1x 1x 1x 3x 3x 1x 2x
1x 4x 3x 1x 1x 1x 1x
3x 4x 2x 2x
1x 2x

1

2x

2

3

4

5

LIVING ROOM

6

BIG & TALL PLANTER I

Part# 35574
(Cotton Candy)

HELMET PLANTER

Part# 30172
(Pith Helmet)

(from Flowerpot Girl Series 18)

Part# 35709

BIG & TALL PLANTER II

1x 1x 5x 7x

1x 1x

1x 1x 1x 1x

1x 1x

1x 1x 1x

1x 2x

LIVING ROOM

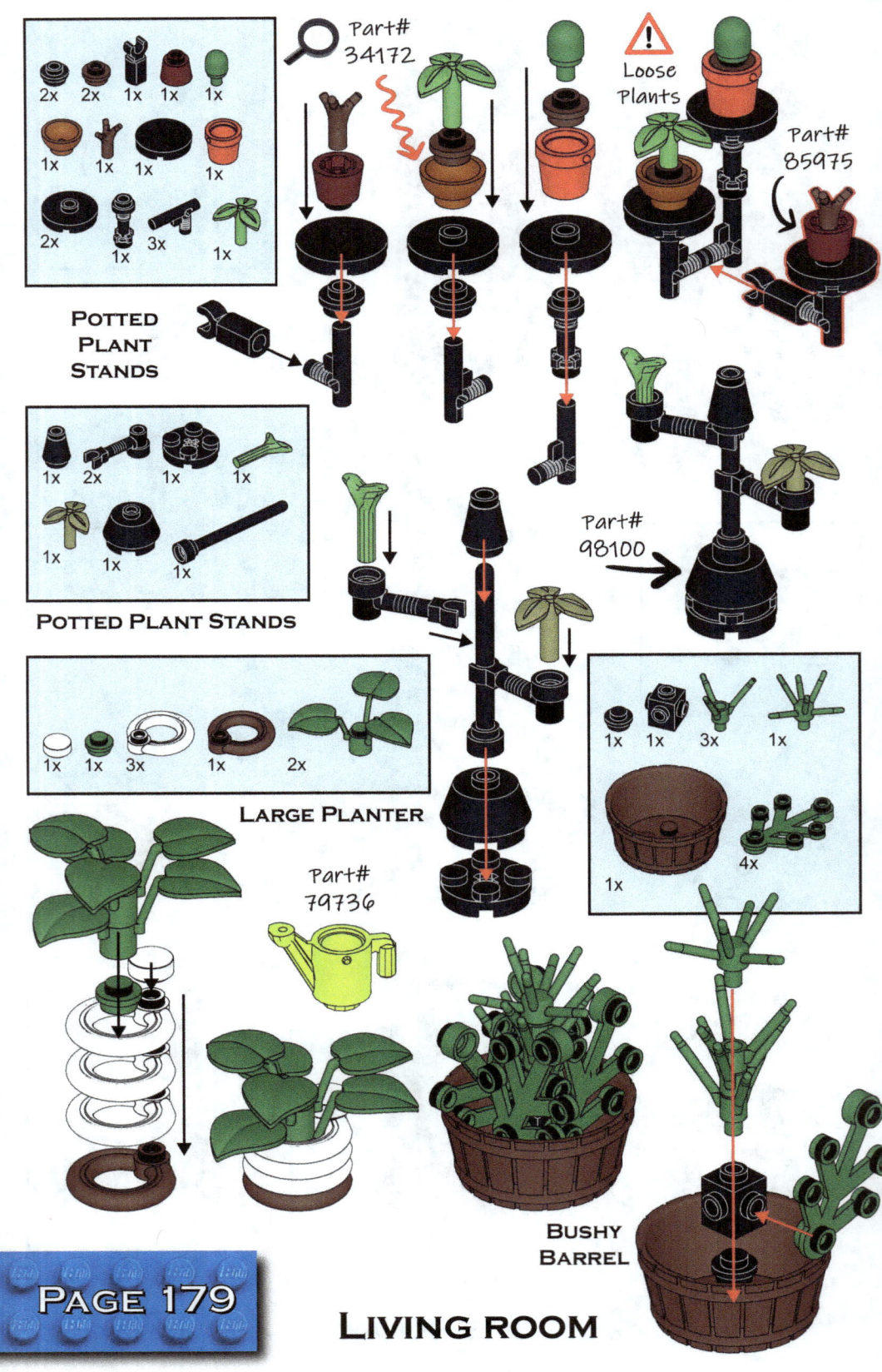

POTTED PLANT STANDS

Part# 34172

Loose Plants

Part# 85975

POTTED PLANT STANDS

Part# 98100

LARGE PLANTER

Part# 79736

BUSHY BARREL

LIVING ROOM

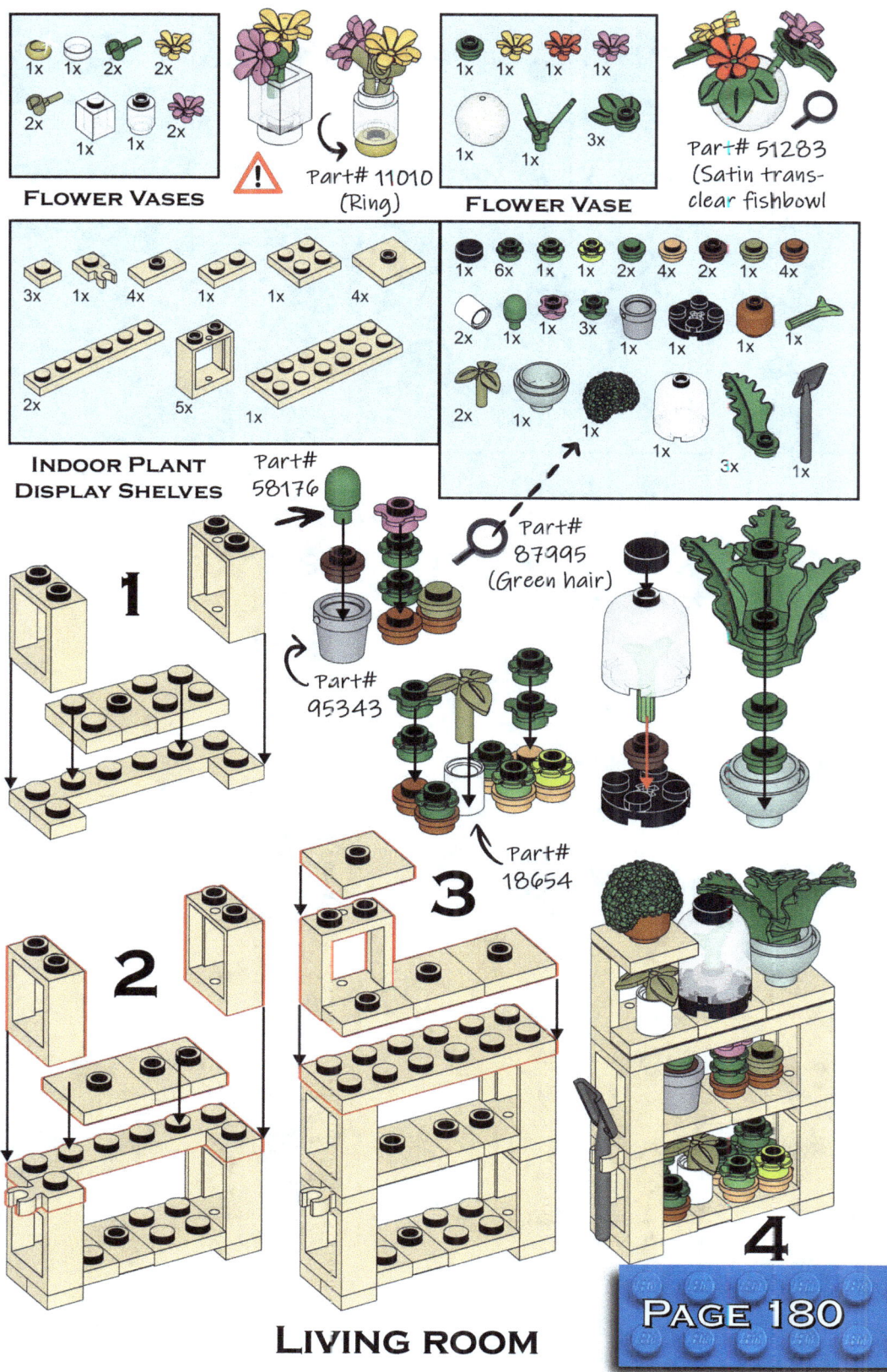

FLOWER VASES

1x 1x 2x 2x
2x 1x 1x 2x

⚠ Part# 11010 (Ring)

FLOWER VASE

1x 1x 1x 1x
1x 1x 3x

Part# 51283 (Satin trans-clear fishbowl

INDOOR PLANT DISPLAY SHELVES

3x 1x 4x 1x 1x 4x
2x 5x 1x

1x 6x 1x 1x 2x 4x 2x 1x 4x
2x 1x 1x 3x 1x 1x 1x 1x
2x 1x 1x 1x 3x 1x

Part# 58176

Part# 87995 (Green hair)

1

Part# 95343

Part# 18654

2

3

4

LIVING ROOM

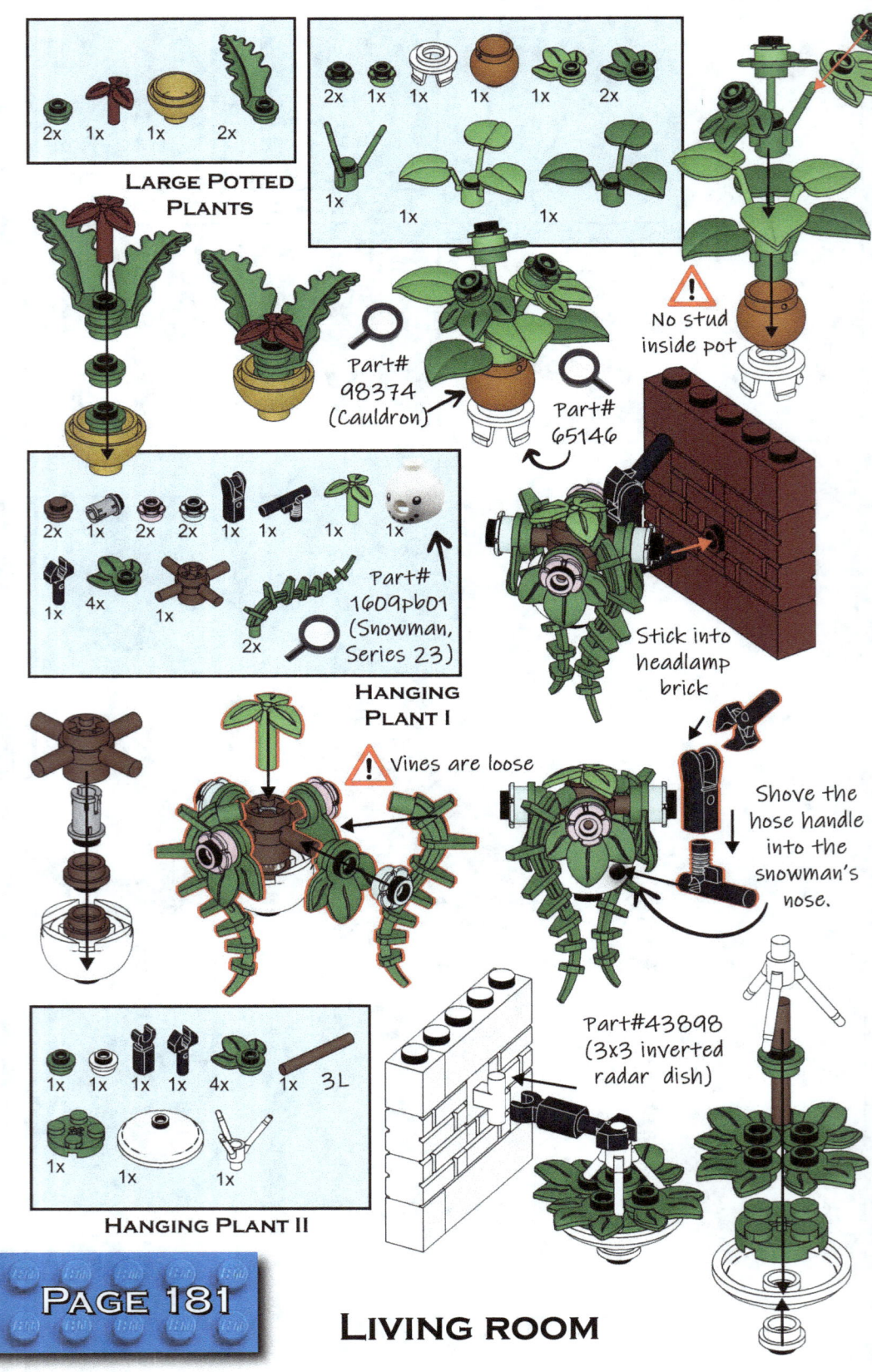

LARGE POTTED PLANTS

2x 1x 1x 2x

2x 1x 1x 1x 1x 2x

1x

1x 1x

Part# 98374 (Cauldron)

Part# 65146

⚠ No stud inside pot

HANGING PLANT I

2x 1x 2x 2x 1x 1x 1x 1x

1x 4x 1x

2x

Part# 1609pb01 (Snowman, Series 23)

Stick into headlamp brick

⚠ Vines are loose

Shove the hose handle into the snowman's nose.

HANGING PLANT II

1x 1x 1x 1x 4x 1x 3L

1x 1x 1x

Part#43898 (3x3 inverted radar dish)

LIVING ROOM

MEDIUM POTTED PLANTS

1x 1x 1x 3x 1x 1x

1x 1x 1x 1x 2x

These potted plants are built upside down for a different look!

Part# 78258

Part# 20482

2x 2x 2x

1x 1x

PLANTER BENCH

1x 1x 1x 1x 1x 1x 1x 1x 1x

1x 1x 1x 1x 1x 1x

1x

Part# 65578

⚠️ Flames sit loosely inside window frame.

2x

4x 2x 1x 2x 1x 2x

2x 1x 2x 2x

2x 1x 1x

MARBLE FIREPLACE

LIVING ROOM

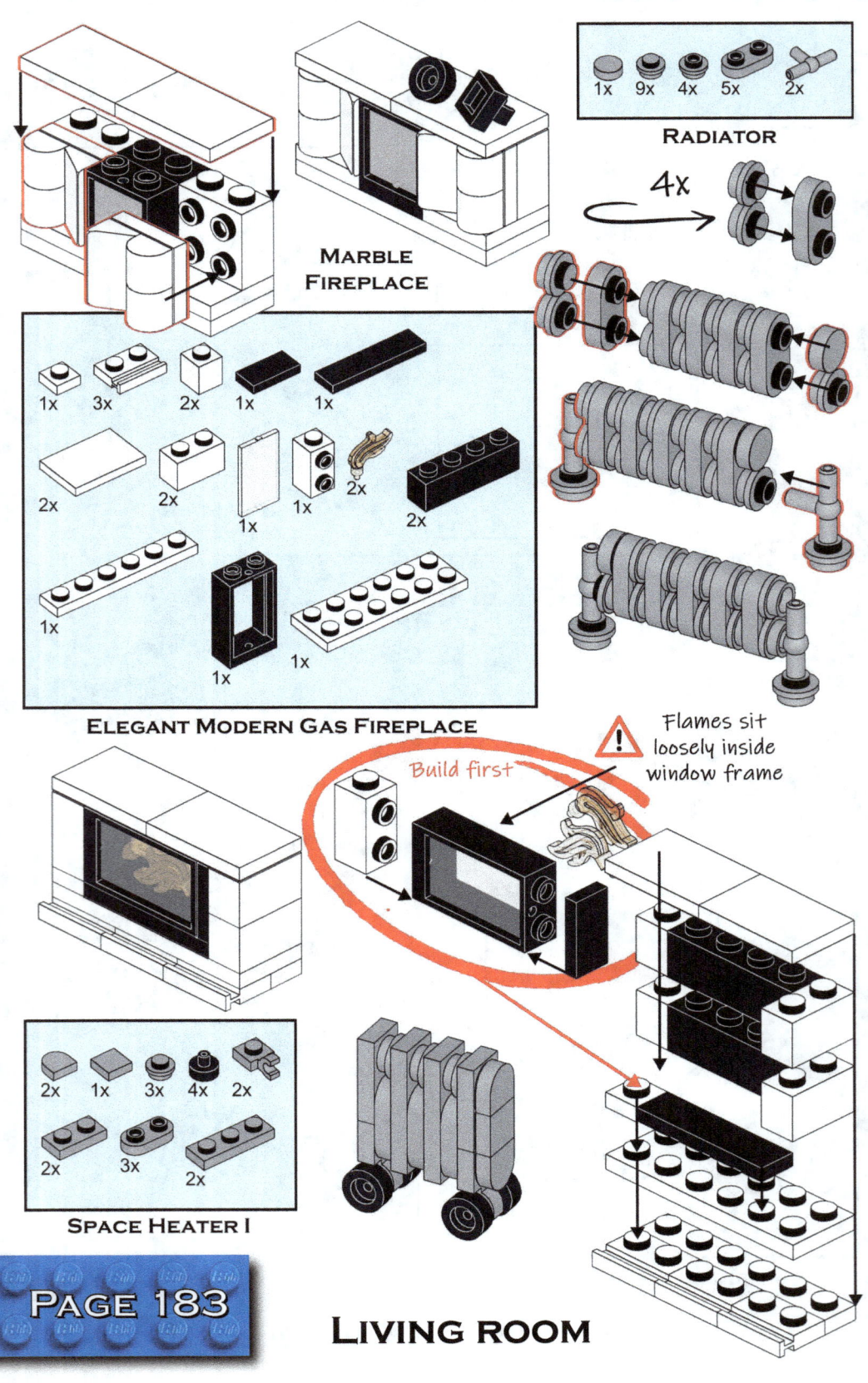

RADIATOR

4x

MARBLE
FIREPLACE

ELEGANT MODERN GAS FIREPLACE

Build first

⚠ Flames sit
loosely inside
window frame

SPACE HEATER I

LIVING ROOM

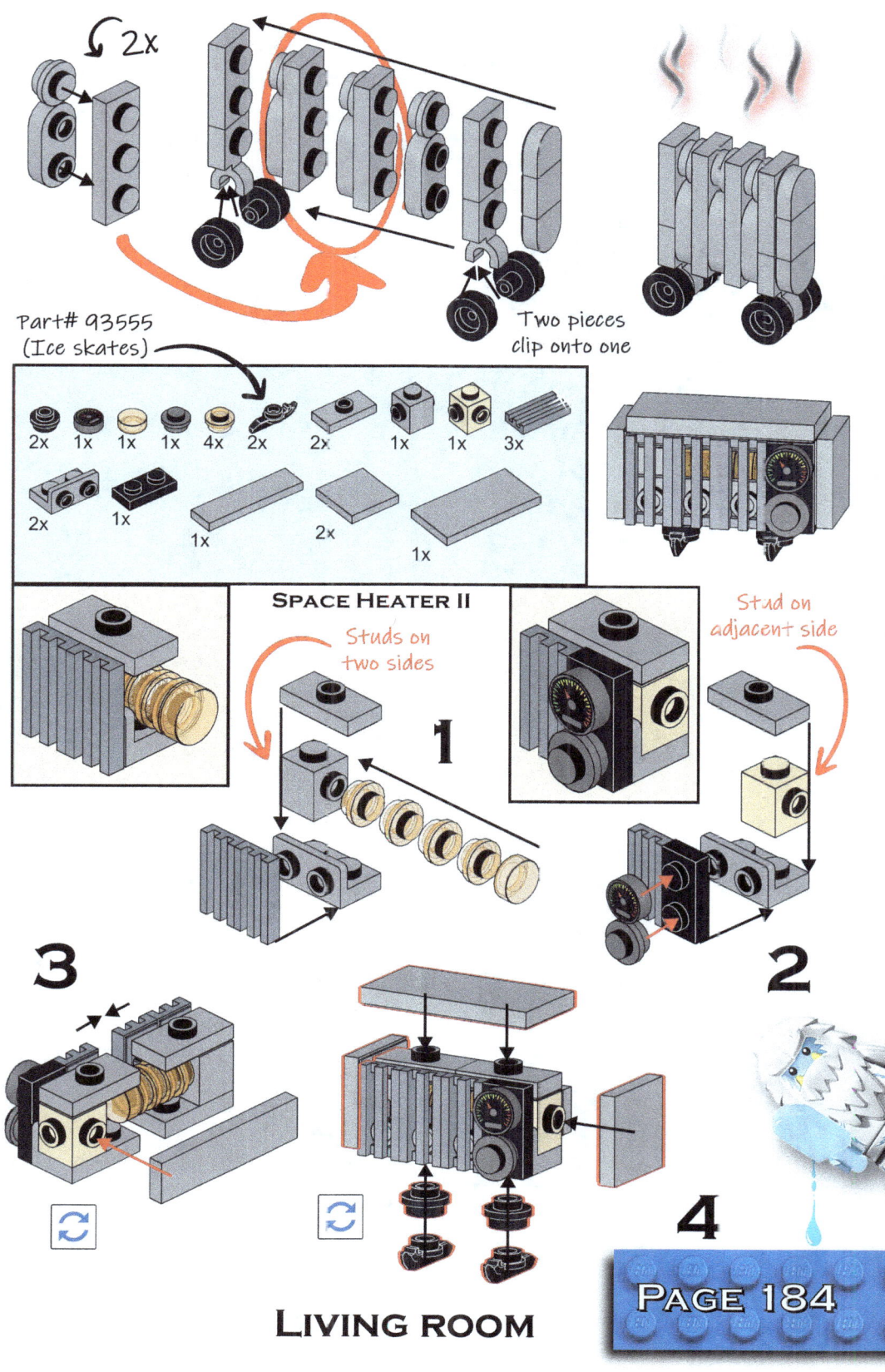

2x

Part# 93555
(Ice skates)

2x 1x 1x 1x 4x 2x 2x 1x 1x 3x

2x 1x 1x 2x 1x

Two pieces
clip onto one

SPACE HEATER II

Studs on
two sides

Stud on
adjacent side

1

2

3

4

LIVING ROOM

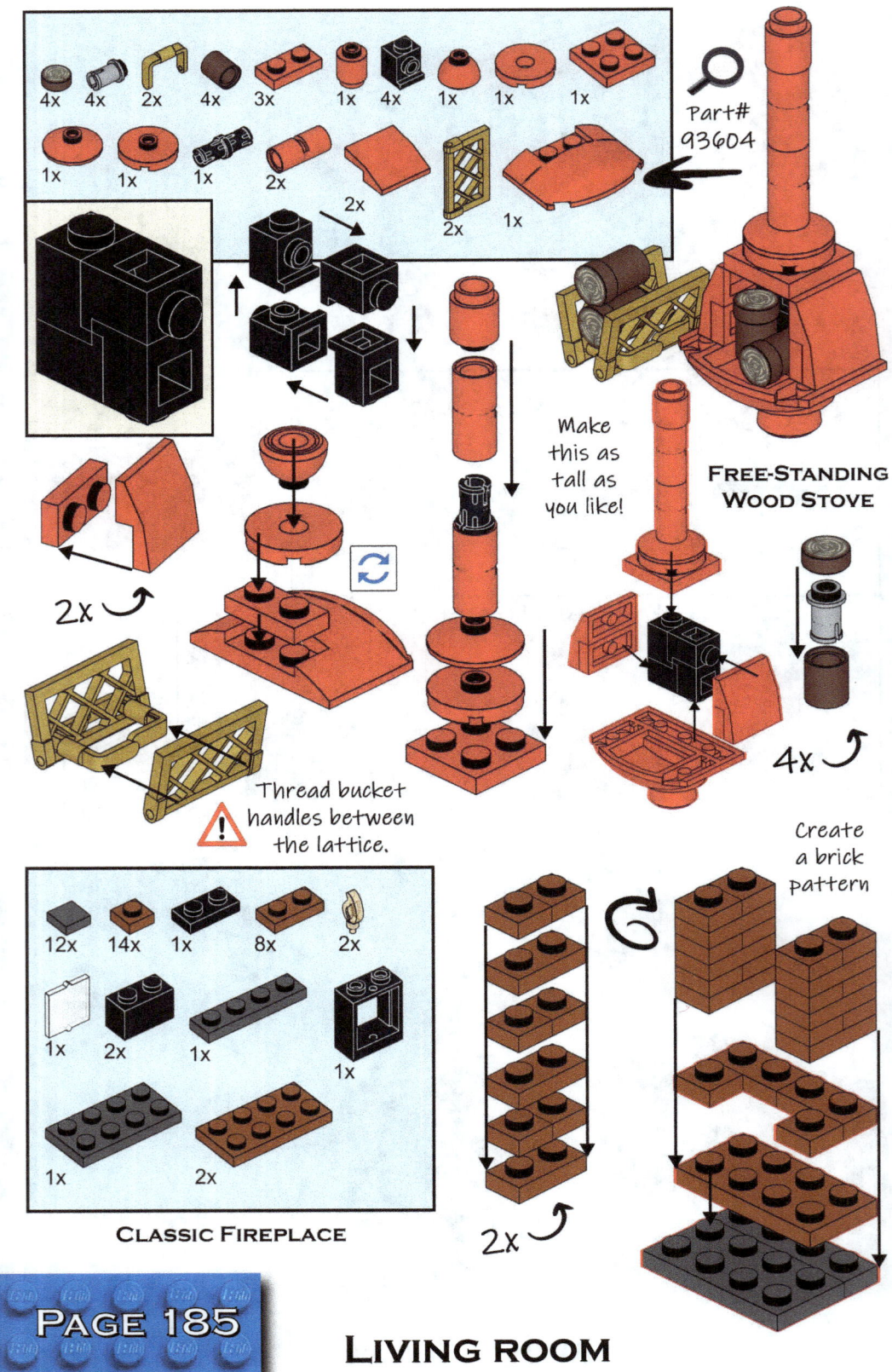

Part# 93604

Make this as tall as you like!

FREE-STANDING WOOD STOVE

2x

Thread bucket handles between the lattice.

4x

Create a brick pattern

CLASSIC FIREPLACE

2x

LIVING ROOM

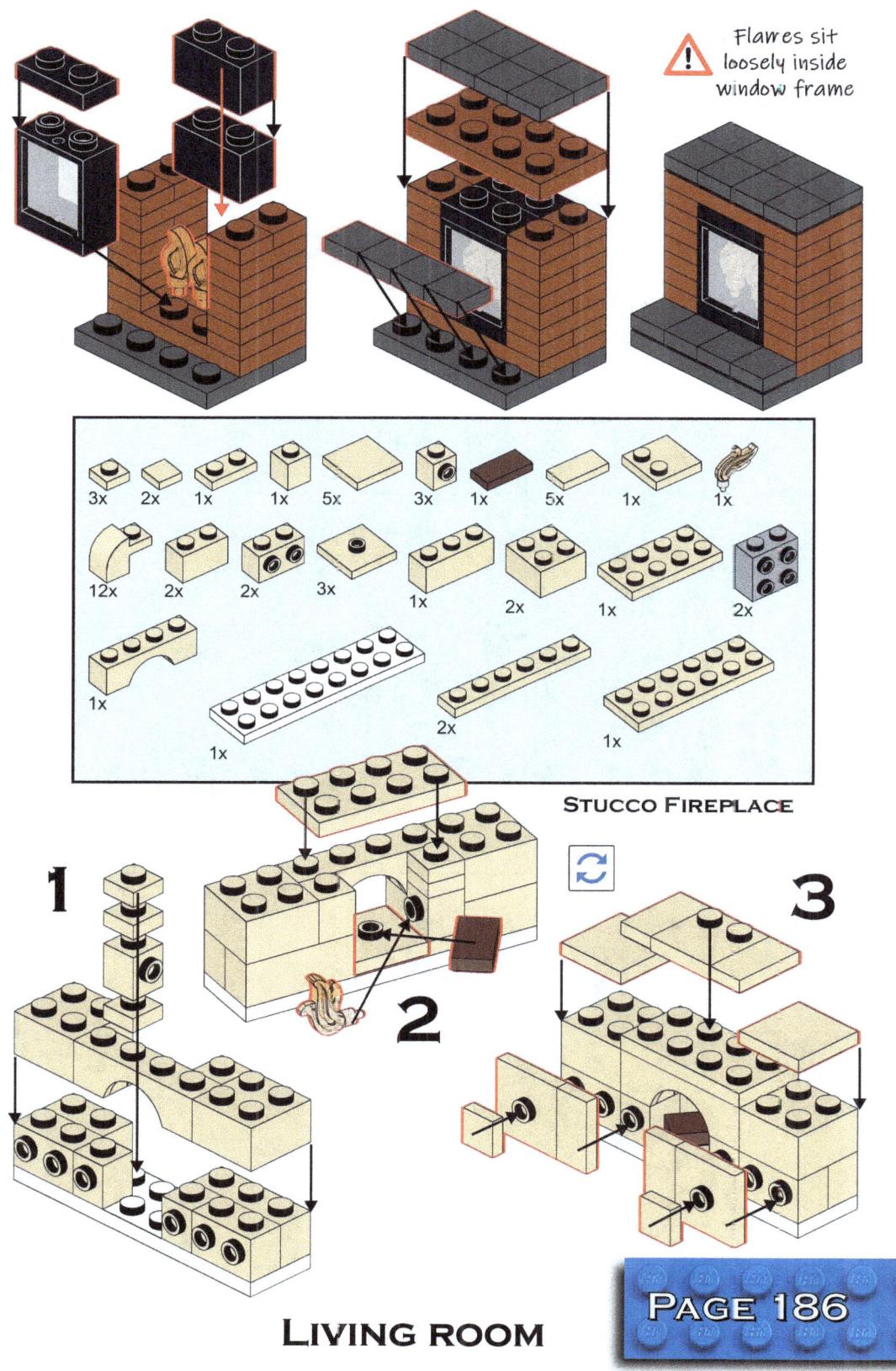

Flames sit loosely inside window frame

STUCCO FIREPLACE

1

2

3

LIVING ROOM

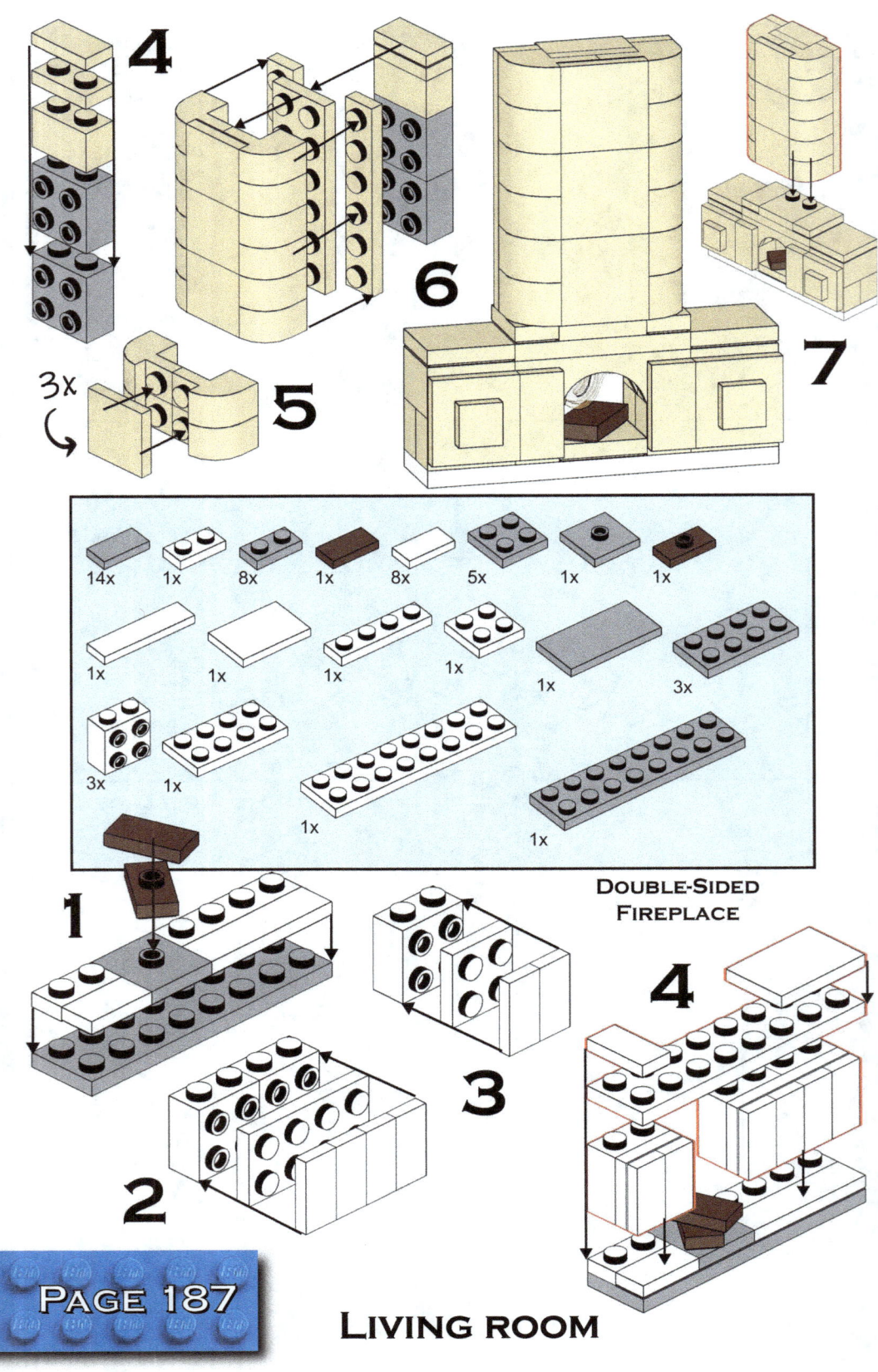

4

5 3x

6

7

DOUBLE-SIDED
FIREPLACE

14x 1x 8x 1x 8x 5x 1x 1x

1x 1x 1x 1x 1x 3x

3x 1x 1x 1x

1

2

3

4

LIVING ROOM

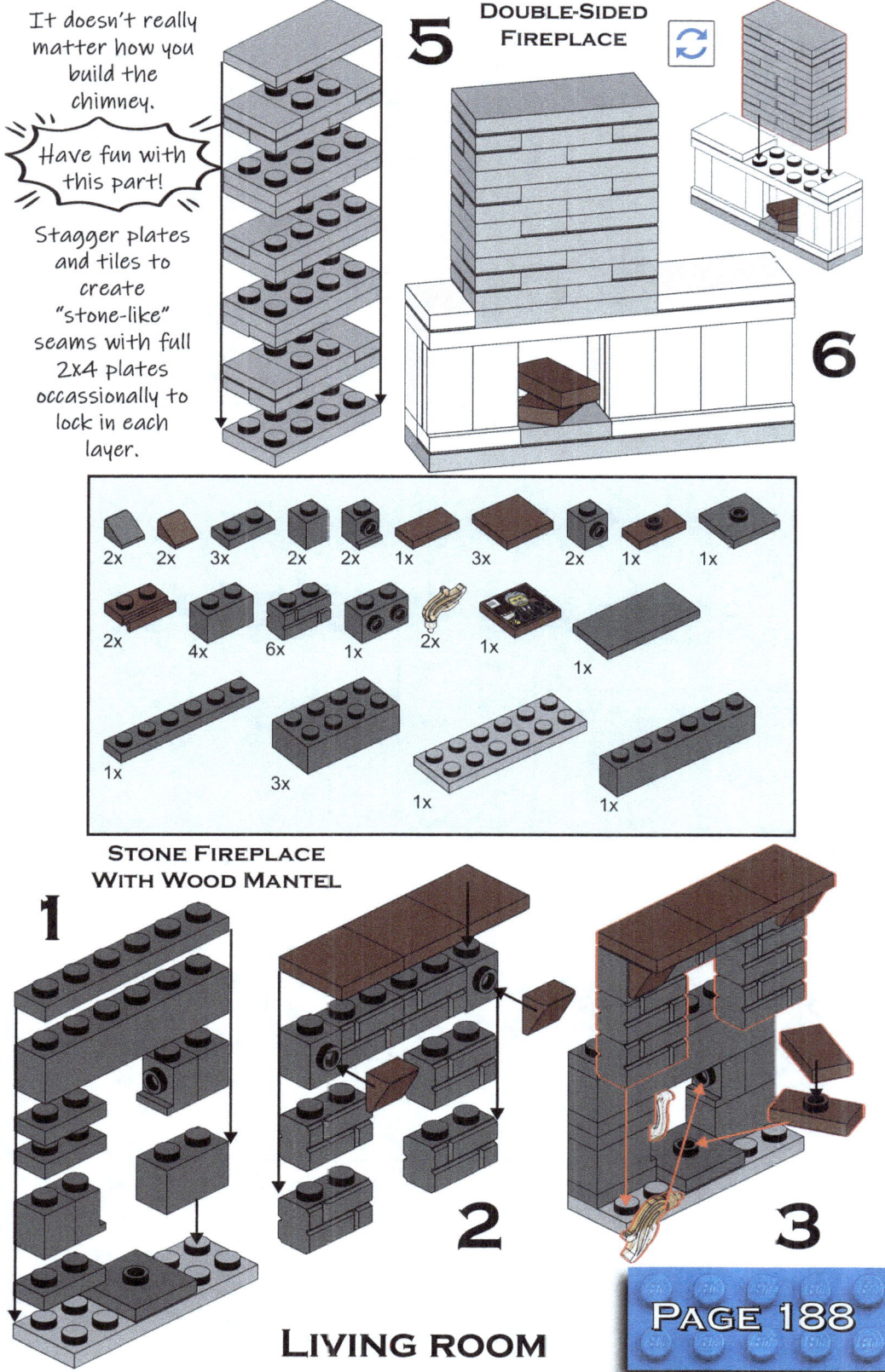

It doesn't really matter how you build the chimney.

Have fun with this part!

Stagger plates and tiles to create "stone-like" seams with full 2x4 plates occassionally to lock in each layer.

DOUBLE-SIDED FIREPLACE

5

6

2x 2x 3x 2x 2x 1x 3x 2x 1x 1x

2x 4x 6x 1x 2x 1x 1x

1x 3x 1x 1x

STONE FIREPLACE WITH WOOD MANTEL

1

2

3

LIVING ROOM

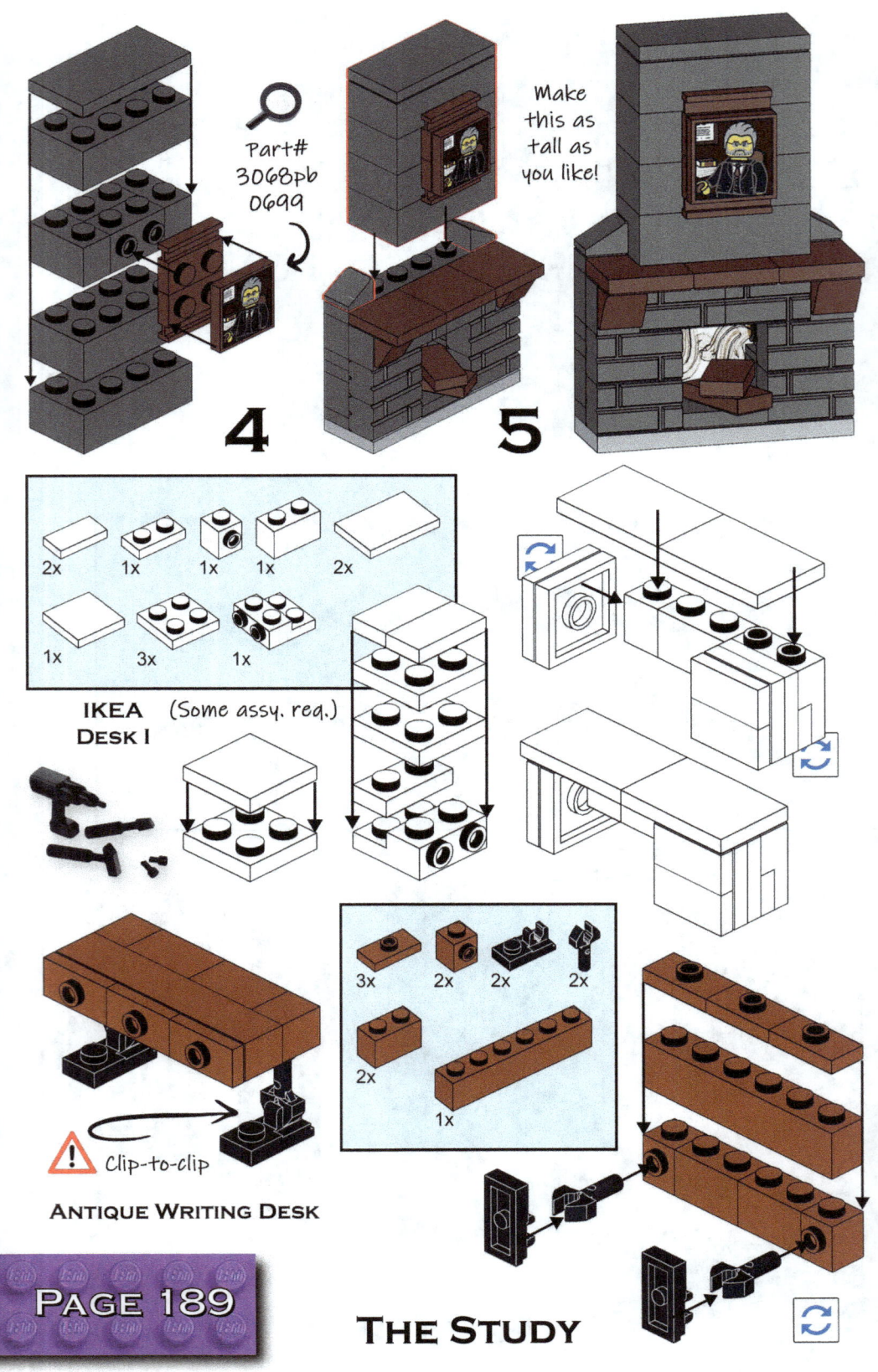

Part# 3068pb 0699

Make this as tall as you like!

4

5

IKEA DESK I   (Some assy. req.)

2x 1x 1x 1x 2x

1x 3x 1x

⚠ Clip-to-clip

ANTIQUE WRITING DESK

3x 2x 2x 2x

2x

1x

THE STUDY

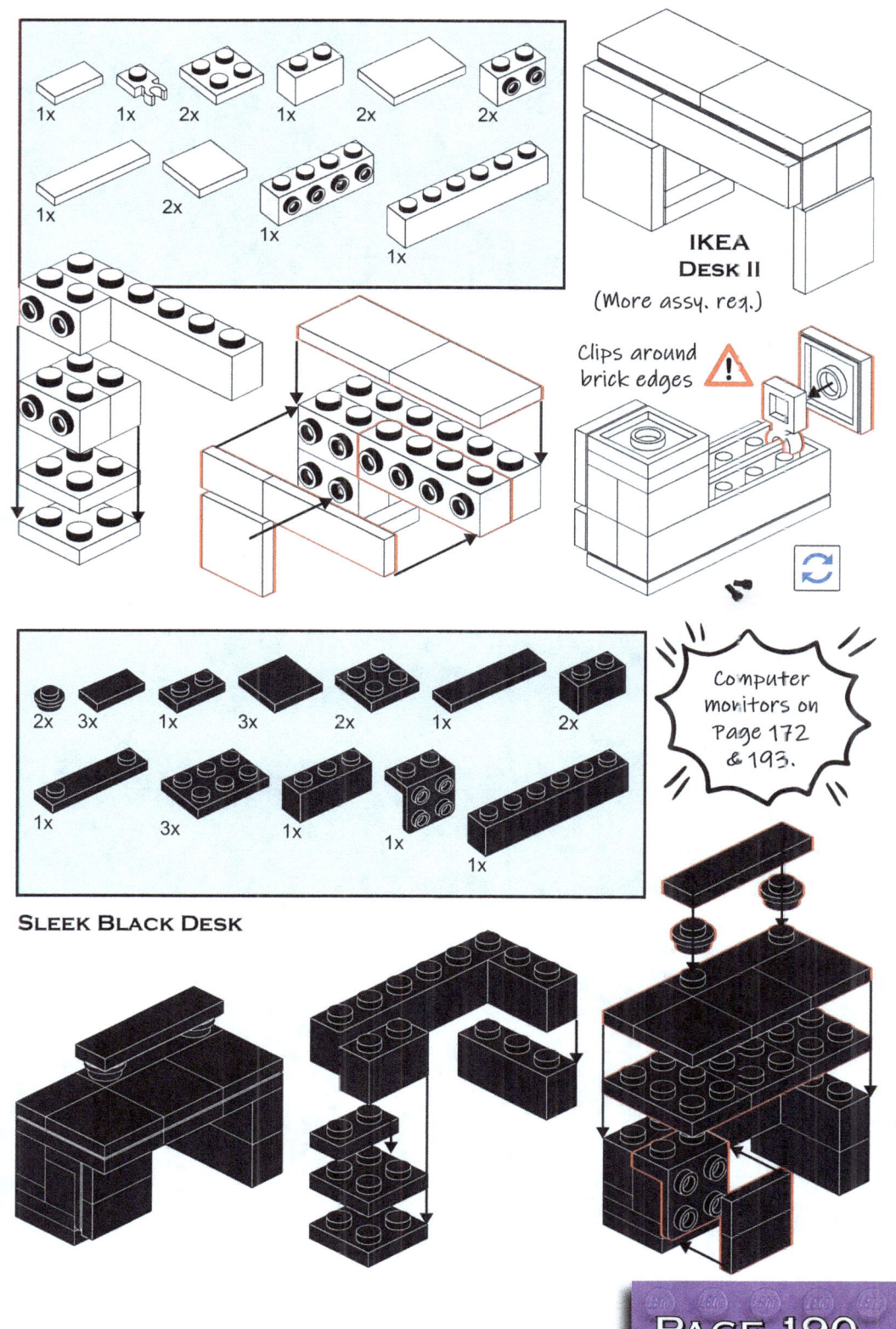

IKEA DESK II

(More assy. req.)

Clips around brick edges ⚠

Computer monitors on Page 172 & 193.

SLEEK BLACK DESK

THE STUDY

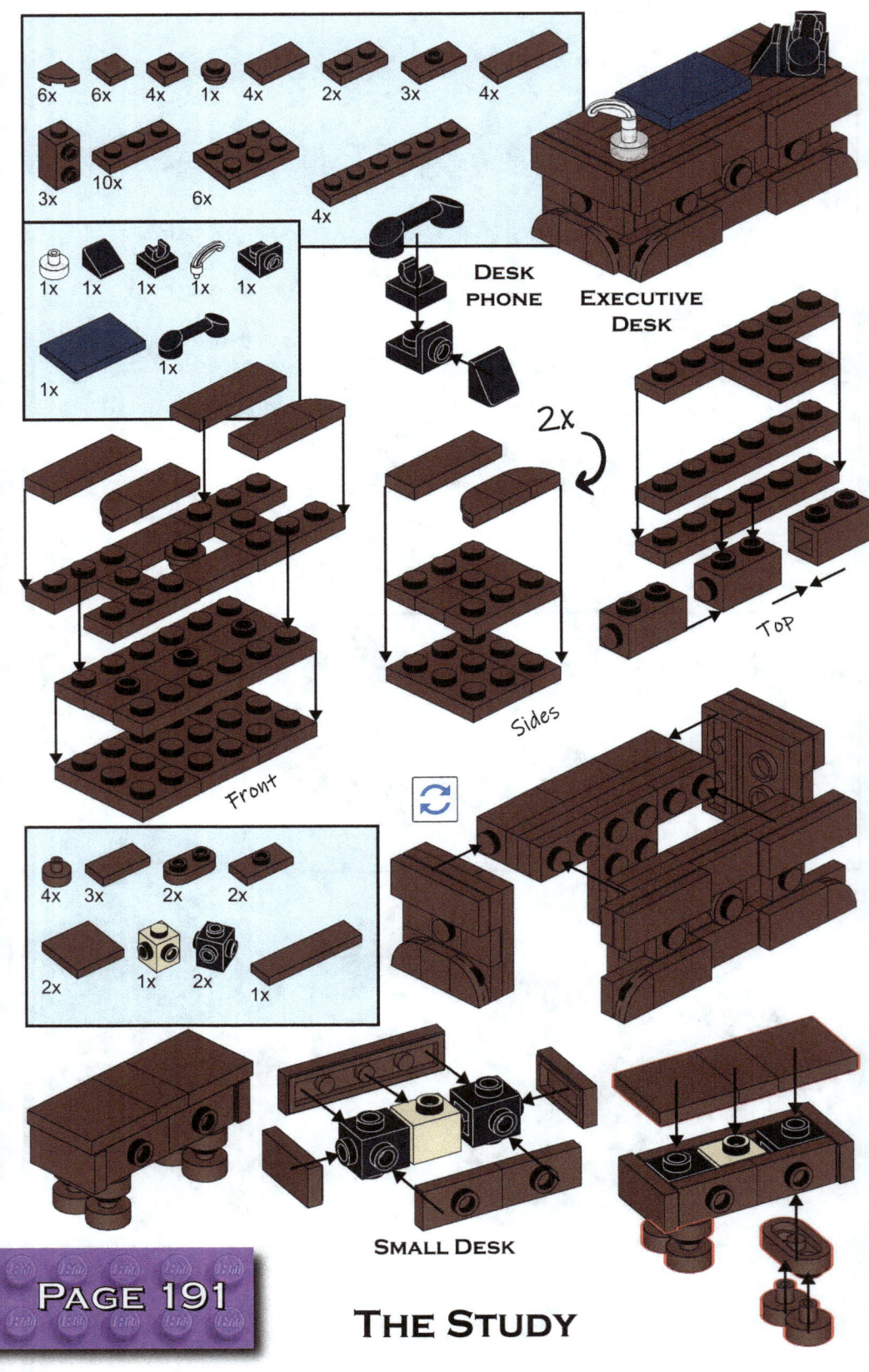

6x 6x 4x 1x 4x 2x 3x 4x

3x 10x 6x

4x

DESK PHONE

EXECUTIVE DESK

1x 1x 1x 1x 1x

1x 1x

2x

TOP

Sides

Front

4x 3x 2x 2x

2x 1x 2x 1x

SMALL DESK

THE STUDY

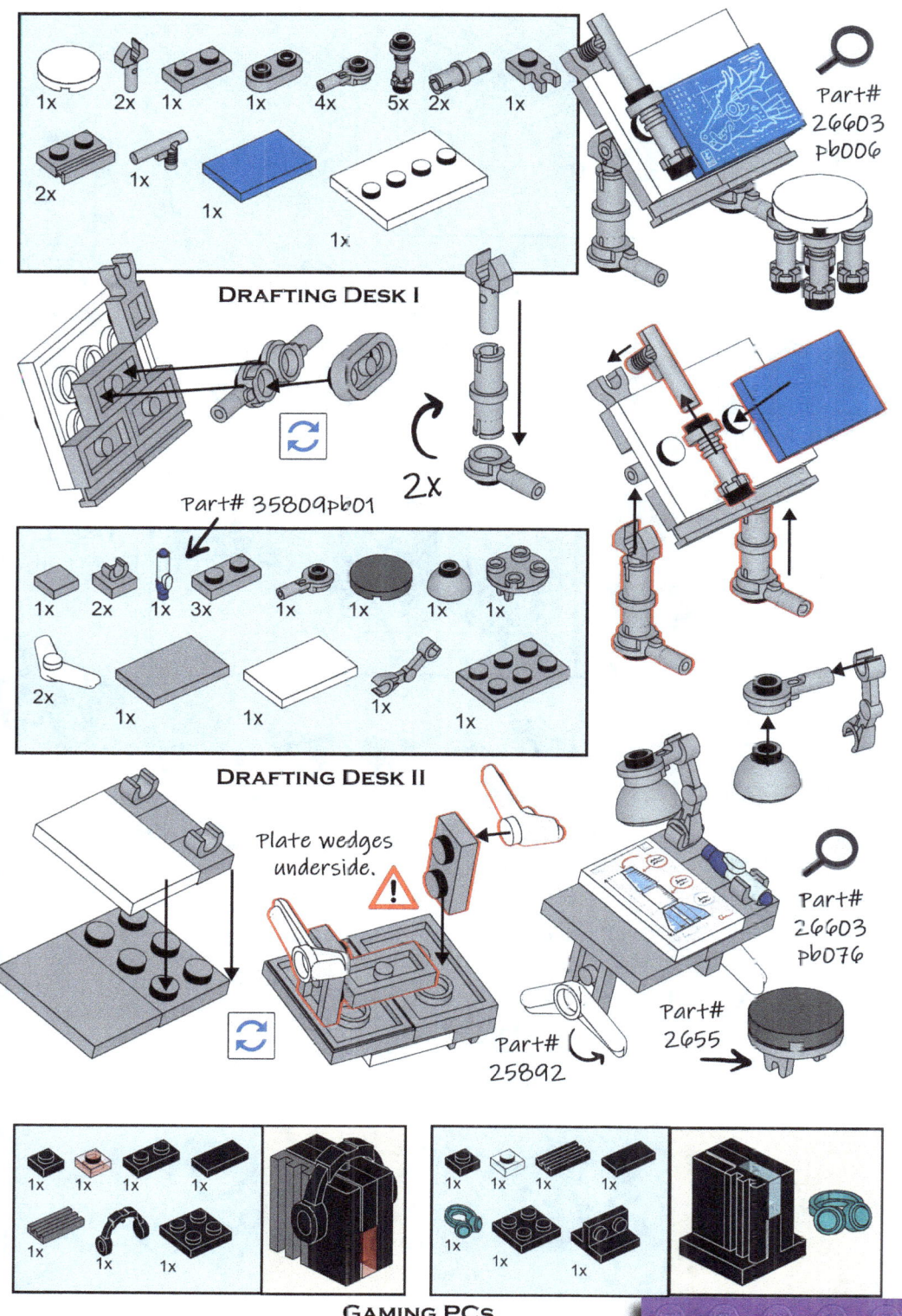

DRAFTING DESK I

Part# 26603 pb006

2x

Part# 35809pb01

DRAFTING DESK II

Plate wedges underside. ⚠

Part# 25892

Part# 26603 pb076

Part# 2655

GAMING PCs

PAGE 192

THE STUDY

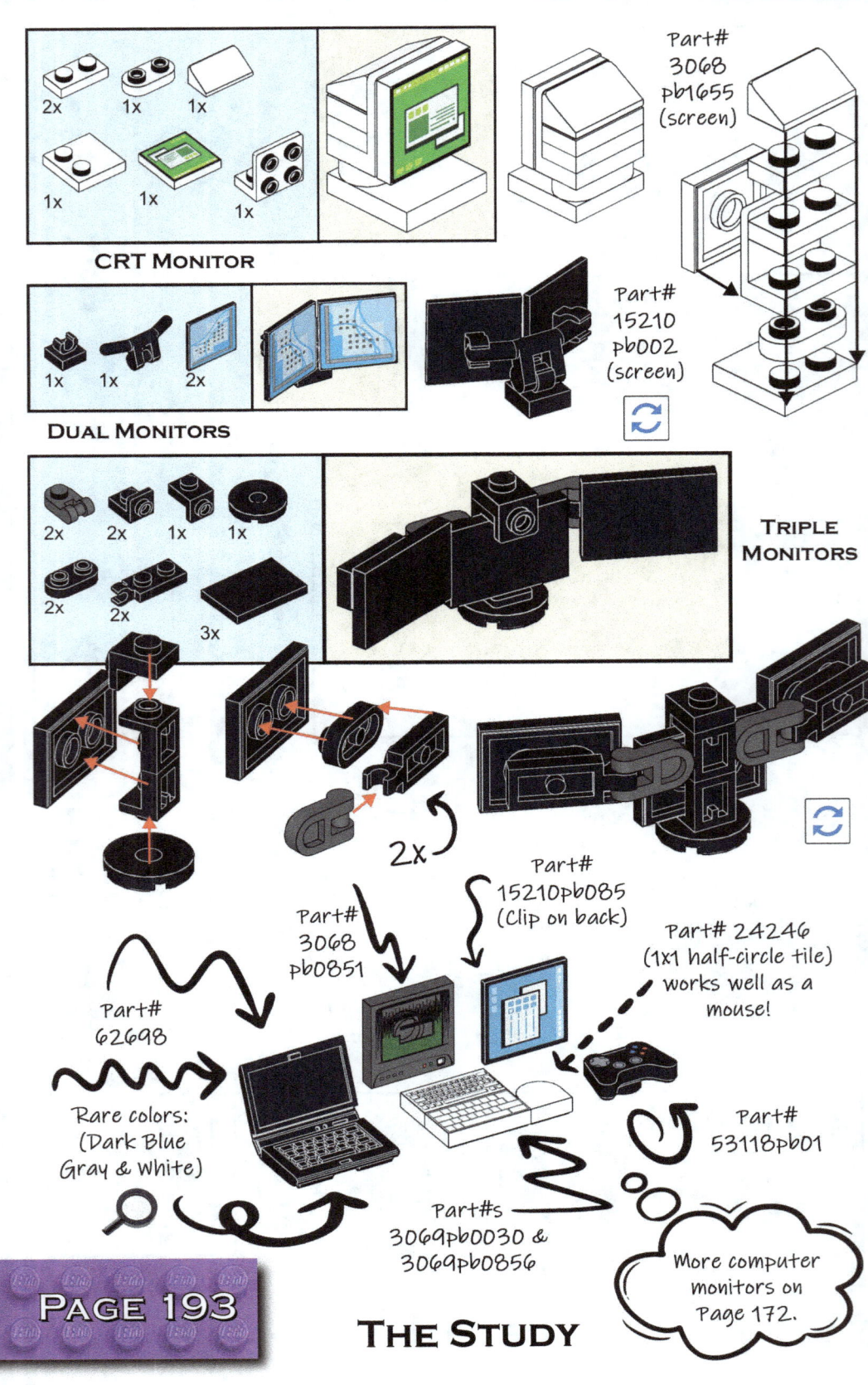

CRT MONITOR

Part#
3068
pb1655
(screen)

Part#
15210
pb002
(screen)

DUAL MONITORS

TRIPLE MONITORS

2x

Part#
15210pb085
(Clip on back)

Part# 24246
(1x1 half-circle tile)
works well as a
mouse!

Part#
3068
pb0851

Part#
62698

Rare colors:
(Dark Blue
Gray & White)

Part#
53118pb01

Part#s
3069pb0030 &
3069pb0856

More computer
monitors on
Page 172.

THE STUDY

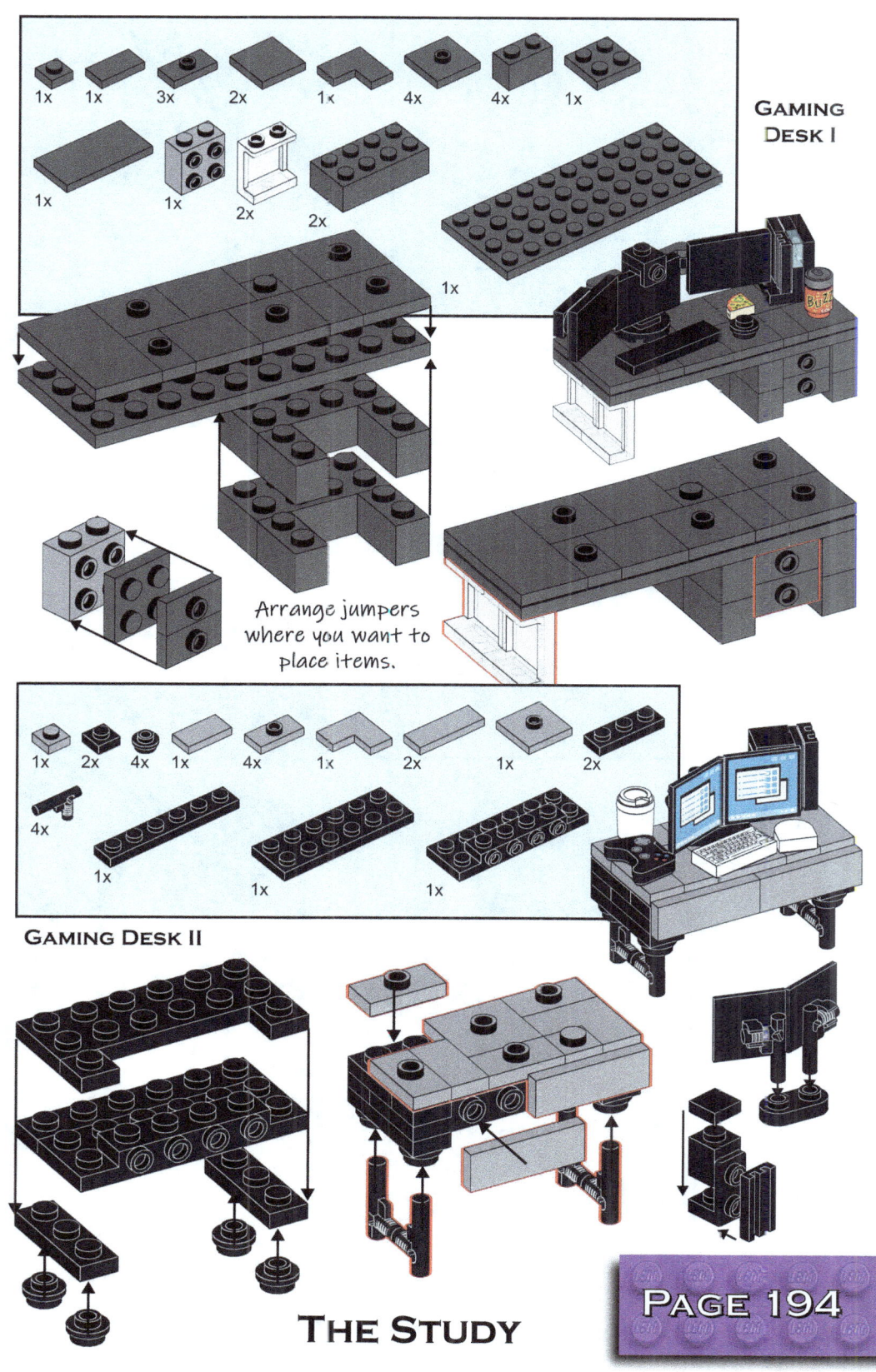

GAMING DESK I

Arrange jumpers where you want to place items.

GAMING DESK II

THE STUDY

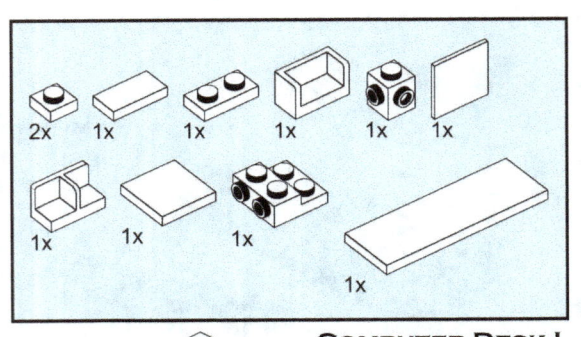

COMPUTER DESK I

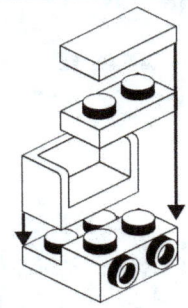
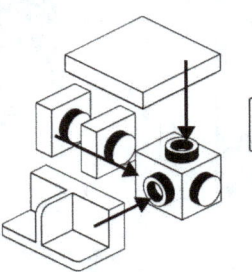
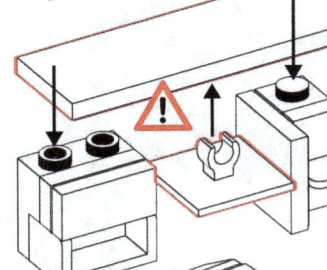

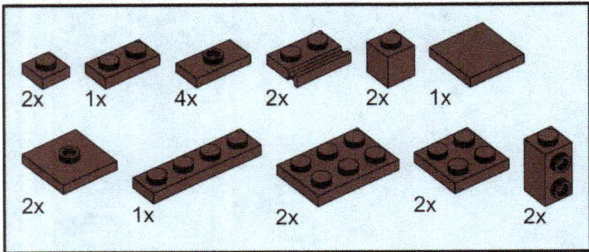

COMPUTER DESK II

These are
mirrored.

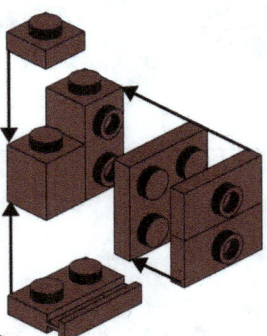

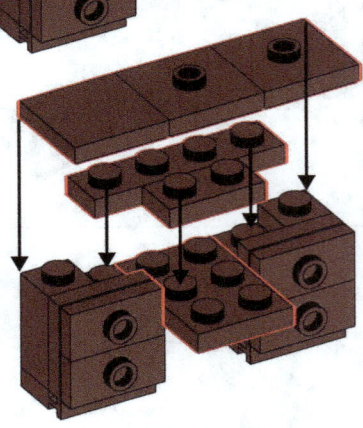

PILOT'S
CHAIR

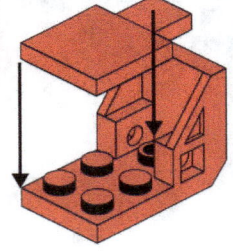
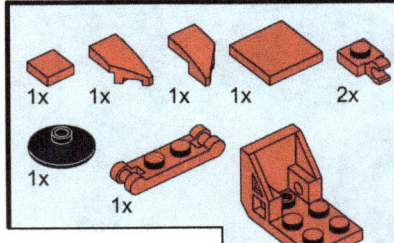

THE STUDY

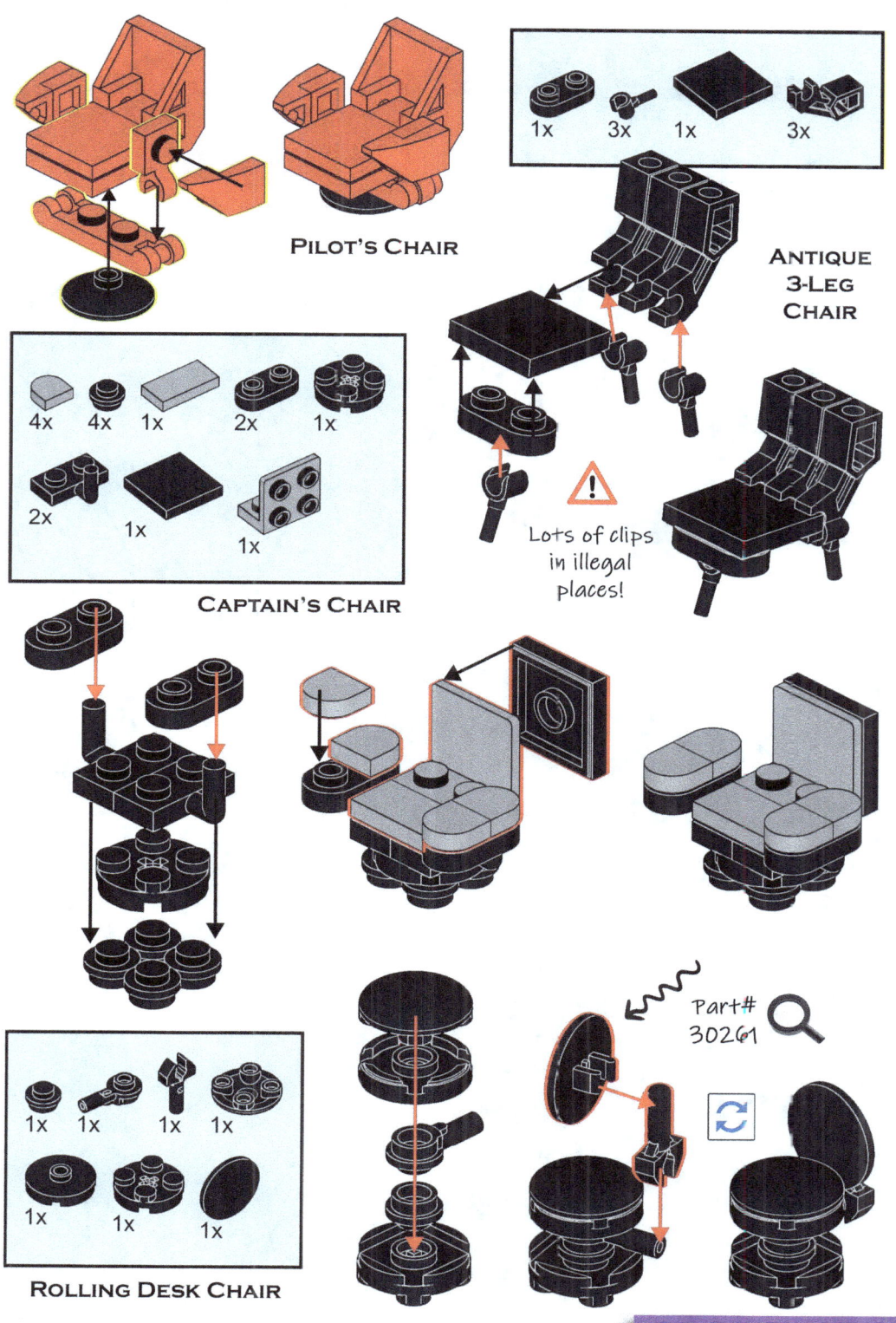

PILOT'S CHAIR

ANTIQUE 3-LEG CHAIR

1x   3x   1x   3x

⚠ Lots of clips in illegal places!

CAPTAIN'S CHAIR

4x   4x   1x   2x   1x

2x   1x   1x

Part# 30261 🔍

🔁

ROLLING DESK CHAIR

1x   1x   1x   1x

1x   1x   1x

THE STUDY

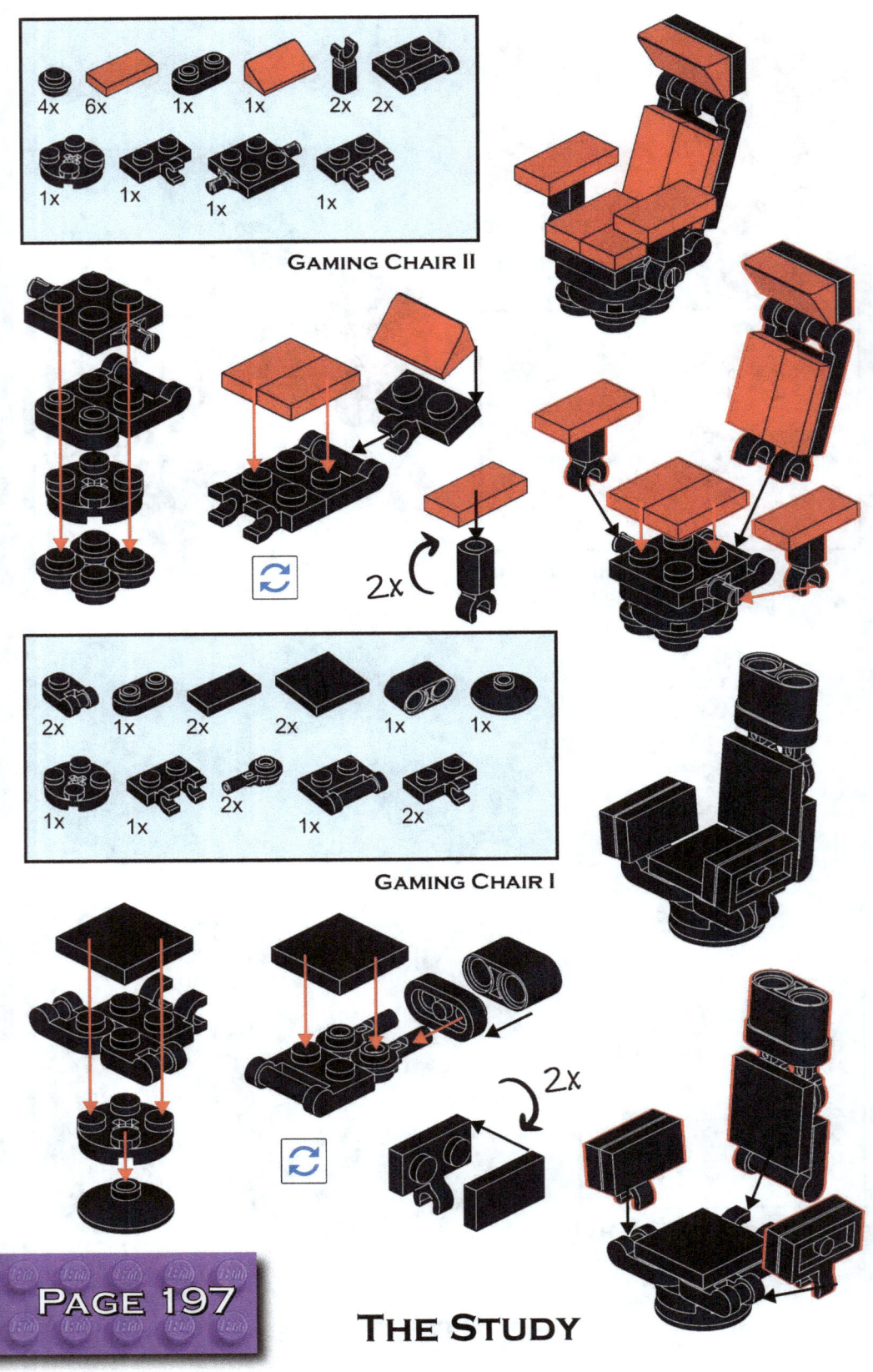

GAMING CHAIR II

2x

GAMING CHAIR I

2x

2x

THE STUDY

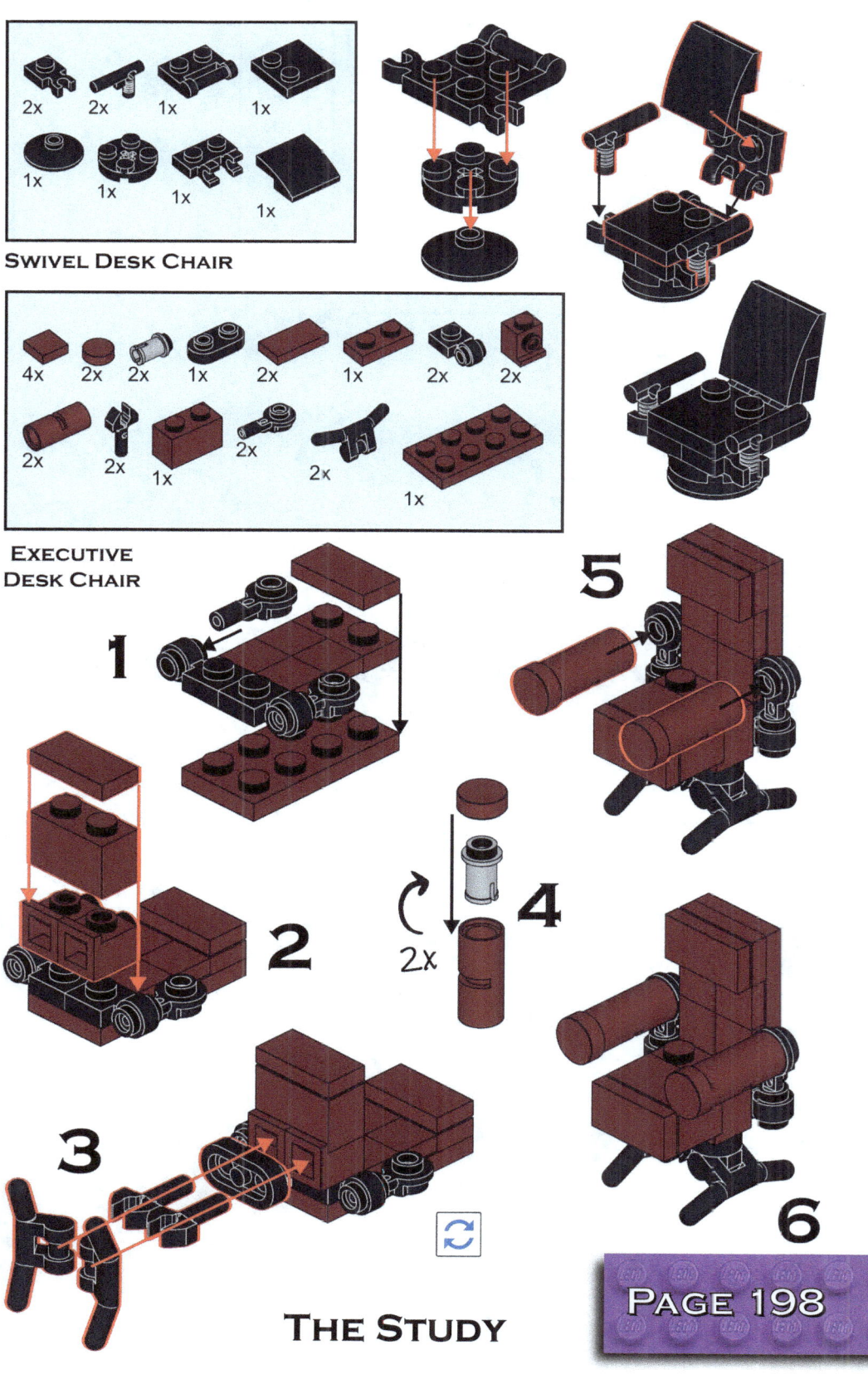

SWIVEL DESK CHAIR

EXECUTIVE DESK CHAIR

1

2

3

4 2x

5

6

THE STUDY

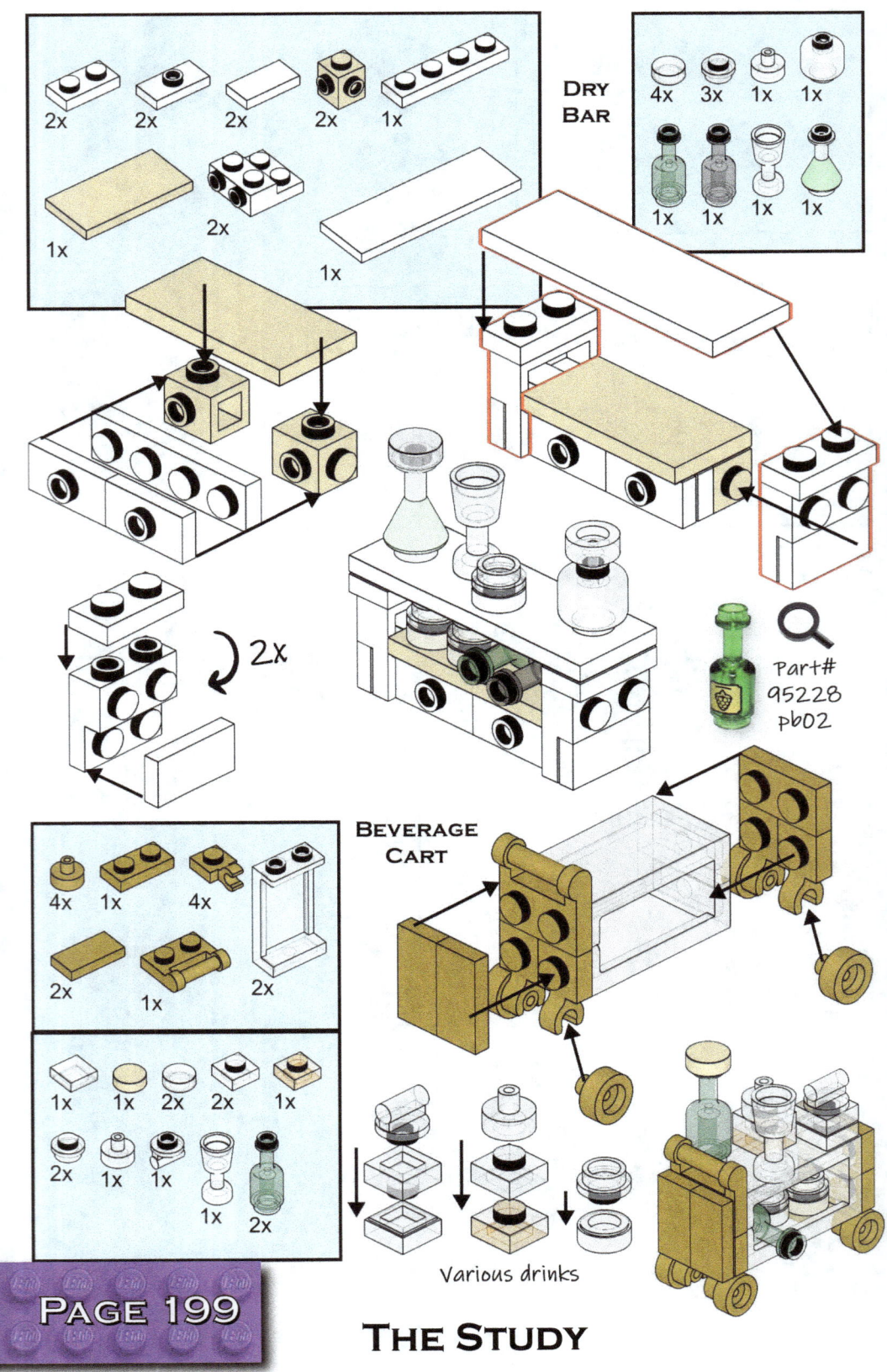

DRY BAR

4x 3x 1x 1x

1x 1x 1x 1x

2x 2x 2x 2x 1x

1x 2x

1x

1x

2x

Part#
95228
pb02

BEVERAGE CART

4x 1x 4x

2x 1x 2x

1x 1x 2x 2x 1x

2x 1x 1x

1x 2x

Various drinks

THE STUDY

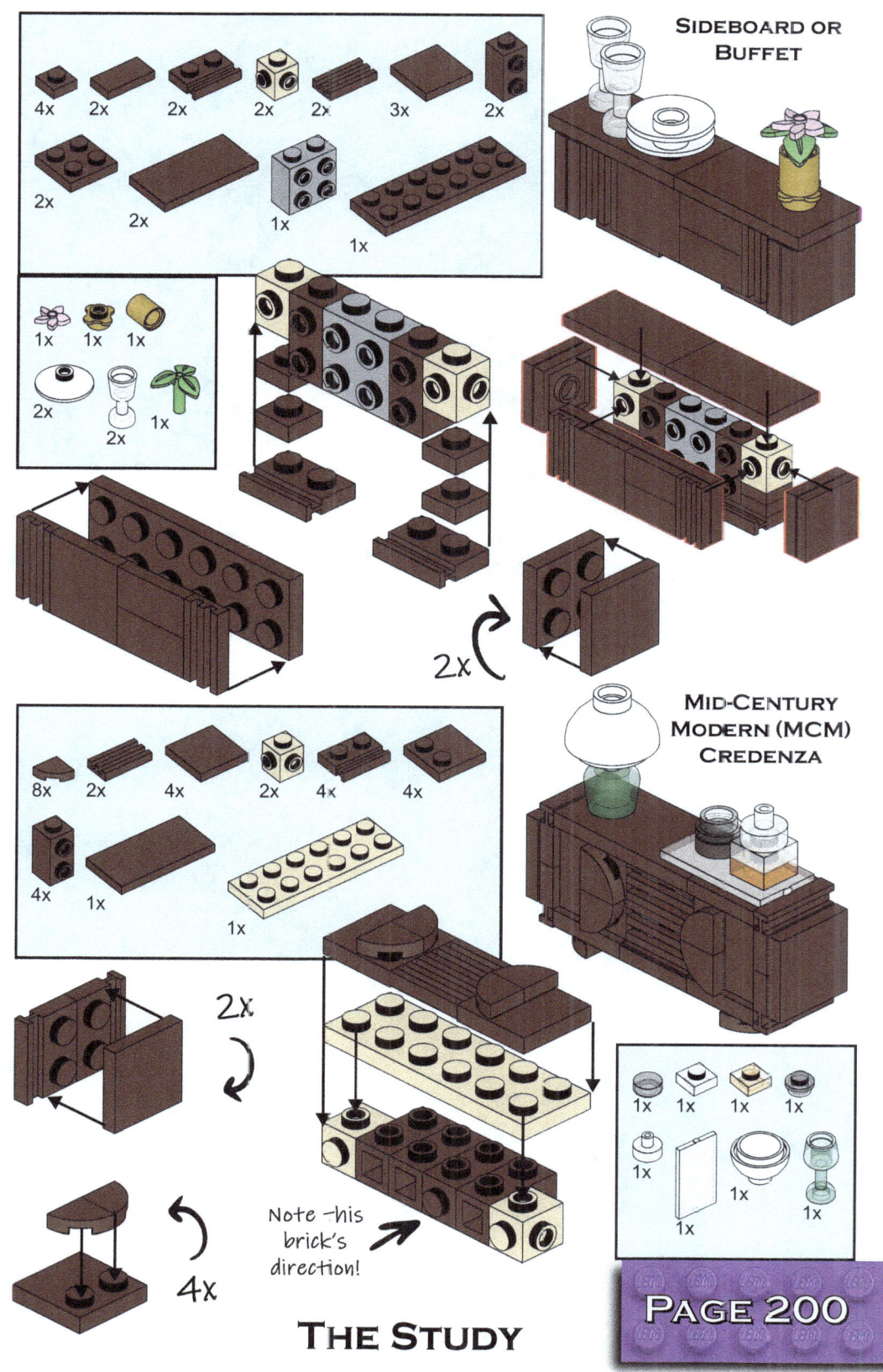

SIDEBOARD OR BUFFET

4x
2x
2x
2x
2x
3x
2x

2x
2x
1x
1x

1x 1x 1x
2x 2x 1x

2x

MID-CENTURY MODERN (MCM) CREDENZA

8x 2x 4x 2x 4x 4x

4x 1x
1x

2x

2x

Note –his brick's direction!

4x

1x 1x 1x 1x

1x
1x 1x 1x

THE STUDY

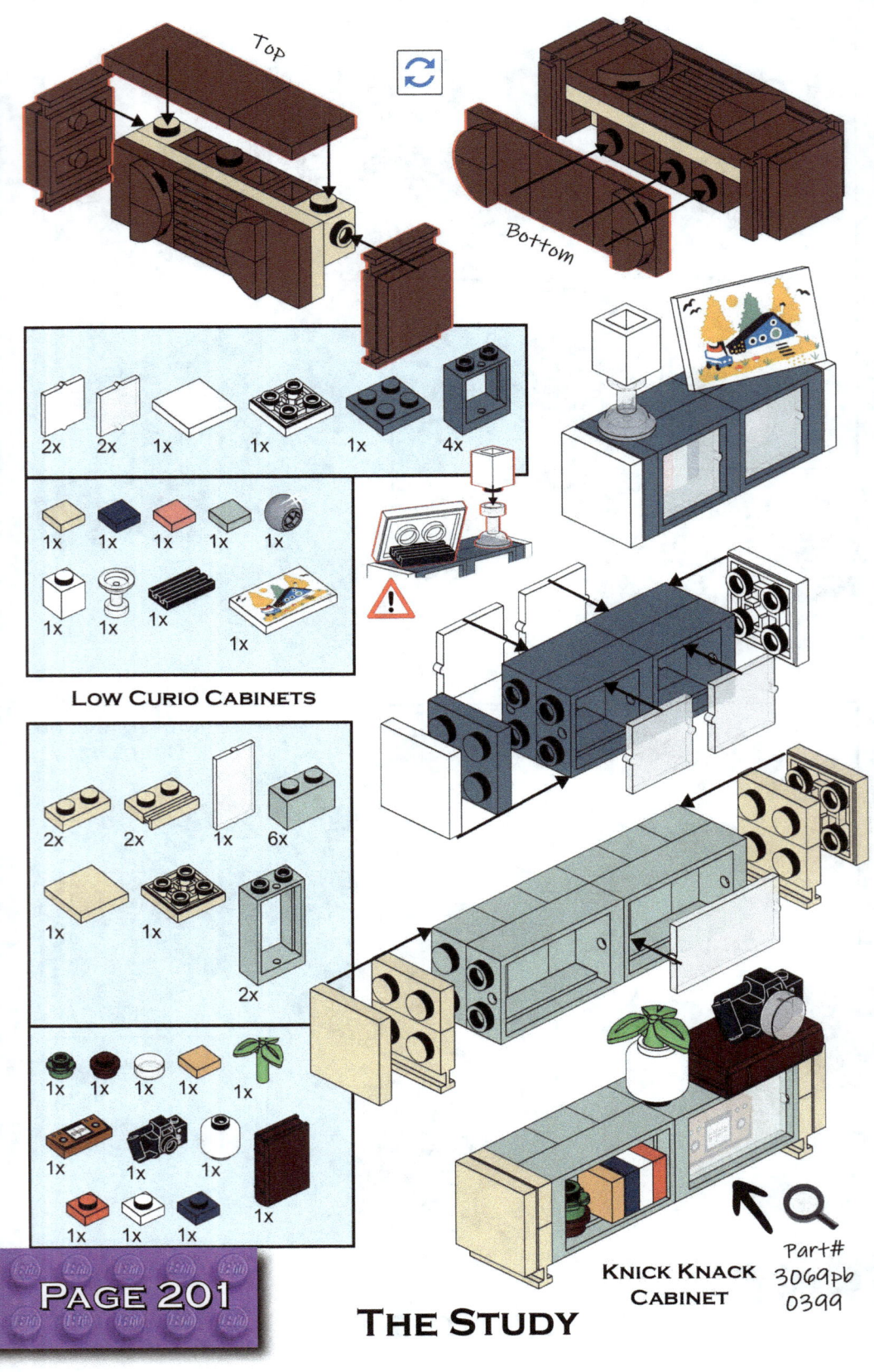

Top

Bottom

2x 2x 1x 1x 1x 4x

1x 1x 1x 1x 1x

1x 1x 1x

1x

LOW CURIO CABINETS

2x 2x 1x 6x

1x 1x

2x

1x 1x 1x 1x 1x

1x 1x 1x

1x

1x 1x 1x

KNICK KNACK CABINET

Part# 3069pb 0399

THE STUDY

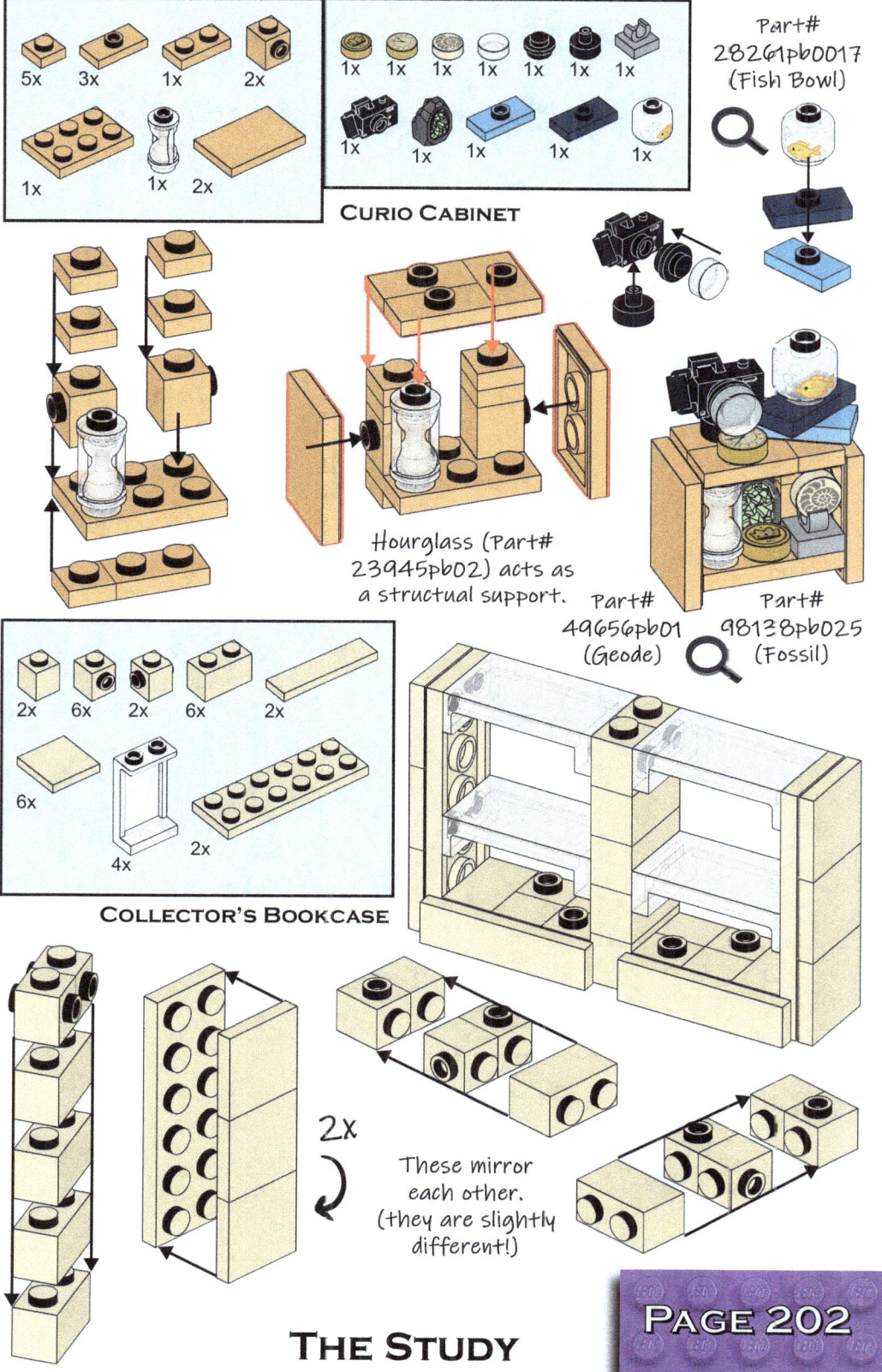

CURIO CABINET

Part#
28261pb0017
(Fish Bowl)

Hourglass (Part#
23945pb02) acts as
a structual support.

Part#
49656pb01
(Geode)

Part#
98138pb025
(Fossil)

COLLECTOR'S BOOKCASE

2x

These mirror
each other.
(they are slightly
different!)

THE STUDY

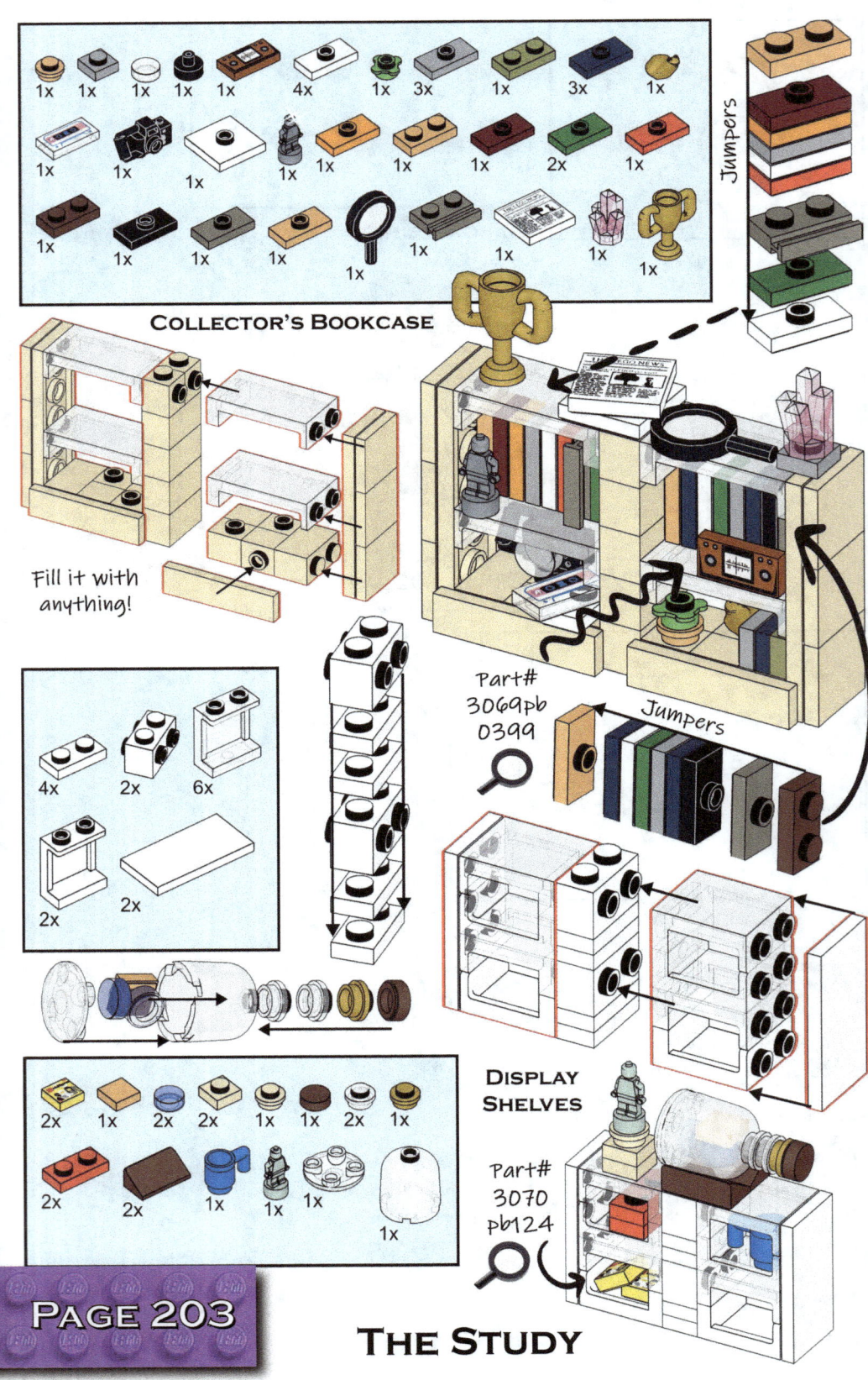

COLLECTOR'S BOOKCASE

Jumpers

1x 1x 1x 1x 1x 4x 1x 3x 1x 3x 1x

1x 1x 1x 1x 1x 1x 1x 2x 1x

1x 1x 1x 1x 1x 1x 1x 1x 1x

Fill it with anything!

4x 2x 6x

2x 2x

Part#
3069pb
0399

Jumpers

2x 1x 2x 2x 1x 1x 2x 1x

2x 2x 1x 1x 1x 1x

DISPLAY
SHELVES

Part#
3070
pb124

THE STUDY

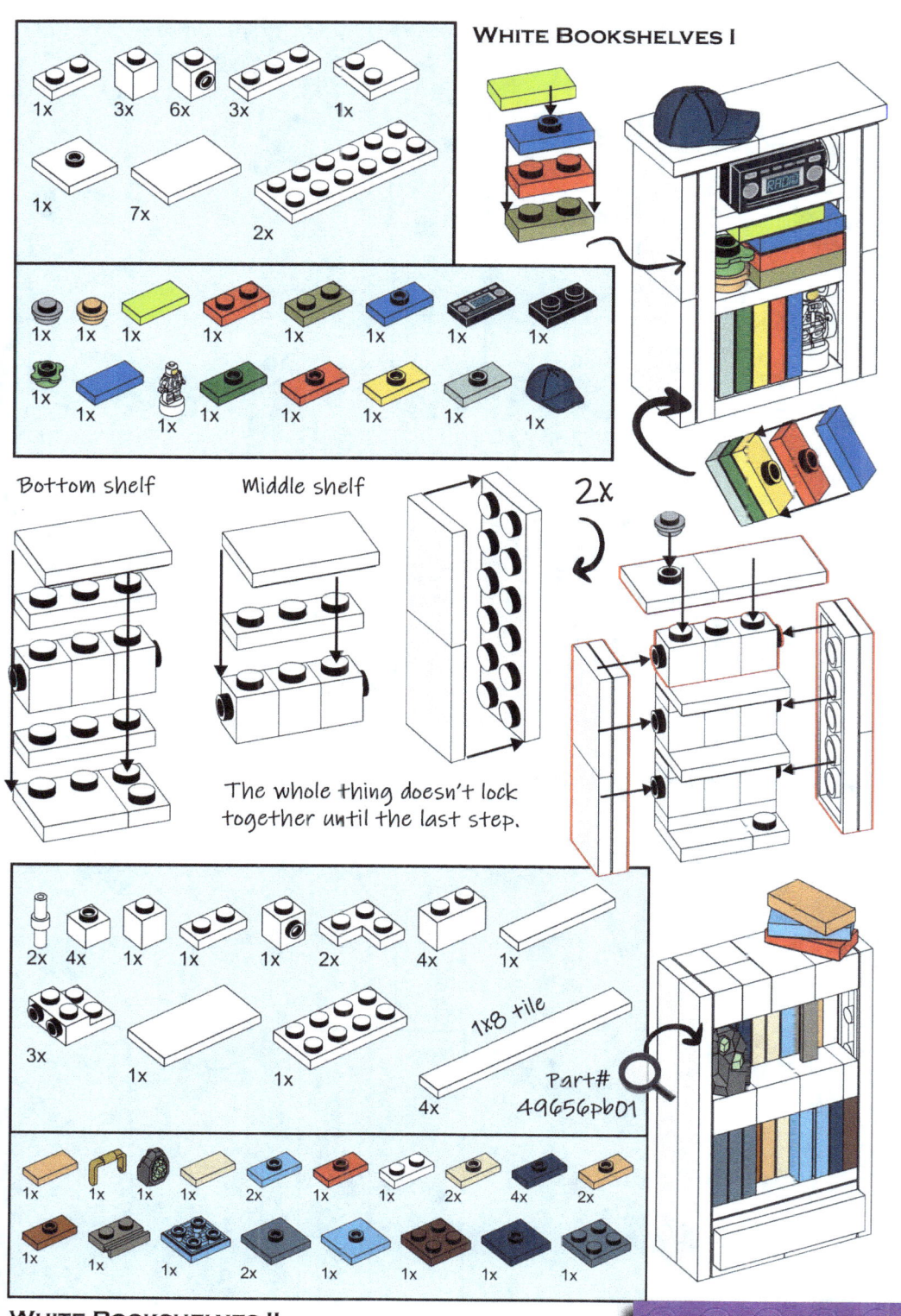

WHITE BOOKSHELVES I

1x 3x 6x 3x 1x

1x 7x 2x

1x 1x 1x 1x 1x 1x 1x 1x

1x 1x 1x 1x 1x 1x 1x 1x

Bottom shelf

Middle shelf

2x

The whole thing doesn't lock together until the last step.

2x 4x 1x 1x 1x 2x 4x 1x

3x 1x 1x

1x8 tile

Part# 49656pb01

4x

1x 1x 1x 1x 2x 1x 1x 2x 4x 2x

1x 1x 1x 2x 1x 1x 1x 1x

WHITE BOOKSHELVES II

Next Page →

THE STUDY

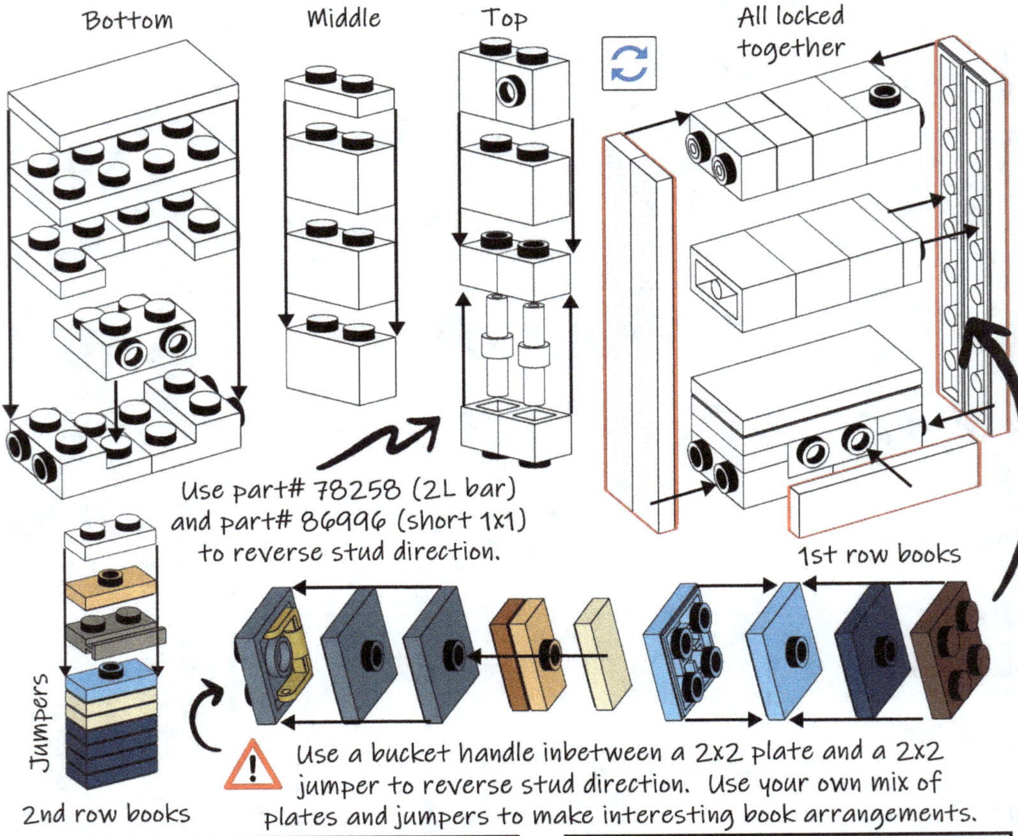

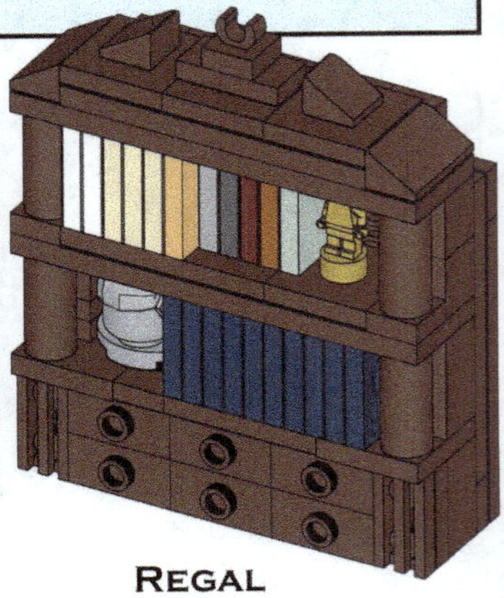

Bottom   Middle   Top   All locked
                                        together

Use part# 78258 (2L bar)
and part# 86996 (short 1x1)
to reverse stud direction.

1st row books

Jumpers

2nd row books

⚠ Use a bucket handle inbetween a 2x2 plate and a 2x2
jumper to reverse stud direction. Use your own mix of
plates and jumpers to make interesting book arrangements.

5x   2x   1x   1x   8x   2x   3x

2x   2x   4x   4x   1x

2x   4x   2x   3x

1x   1x   1x   1x   1x   1x

1x   1x   1x   1x   tile

2x   3x   1x   jumper

9x

1x

3x

2x

4x   1x

THE STUDY   REGAL
                 BOOKSHELF

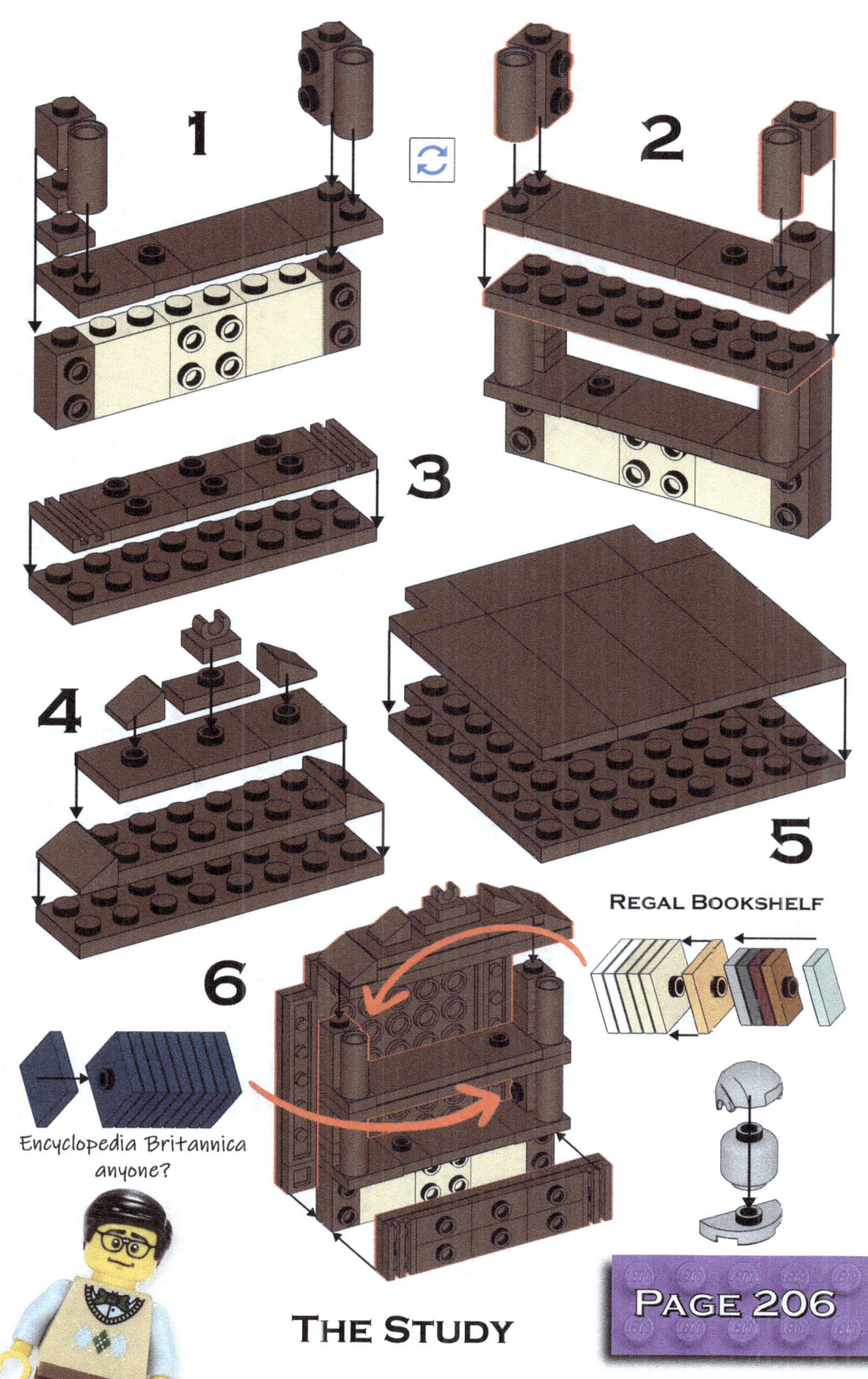

1

2

3

4

5

6

REGAL BOOKSHELF

Encyclopedia Britannica anyone?

THE STUDY

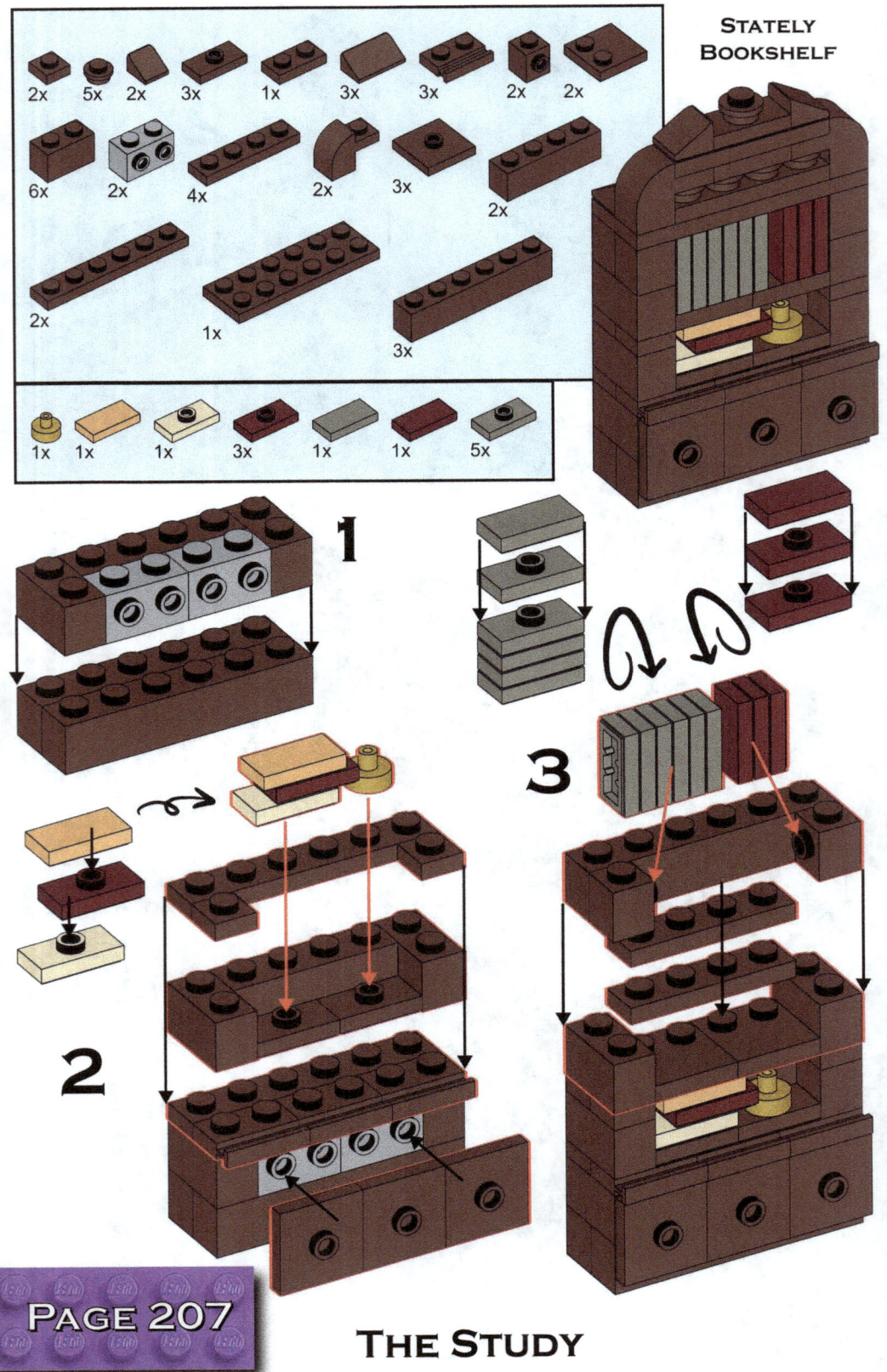

STATELY
BOOKSHELF

1

2

3

THE STUDY

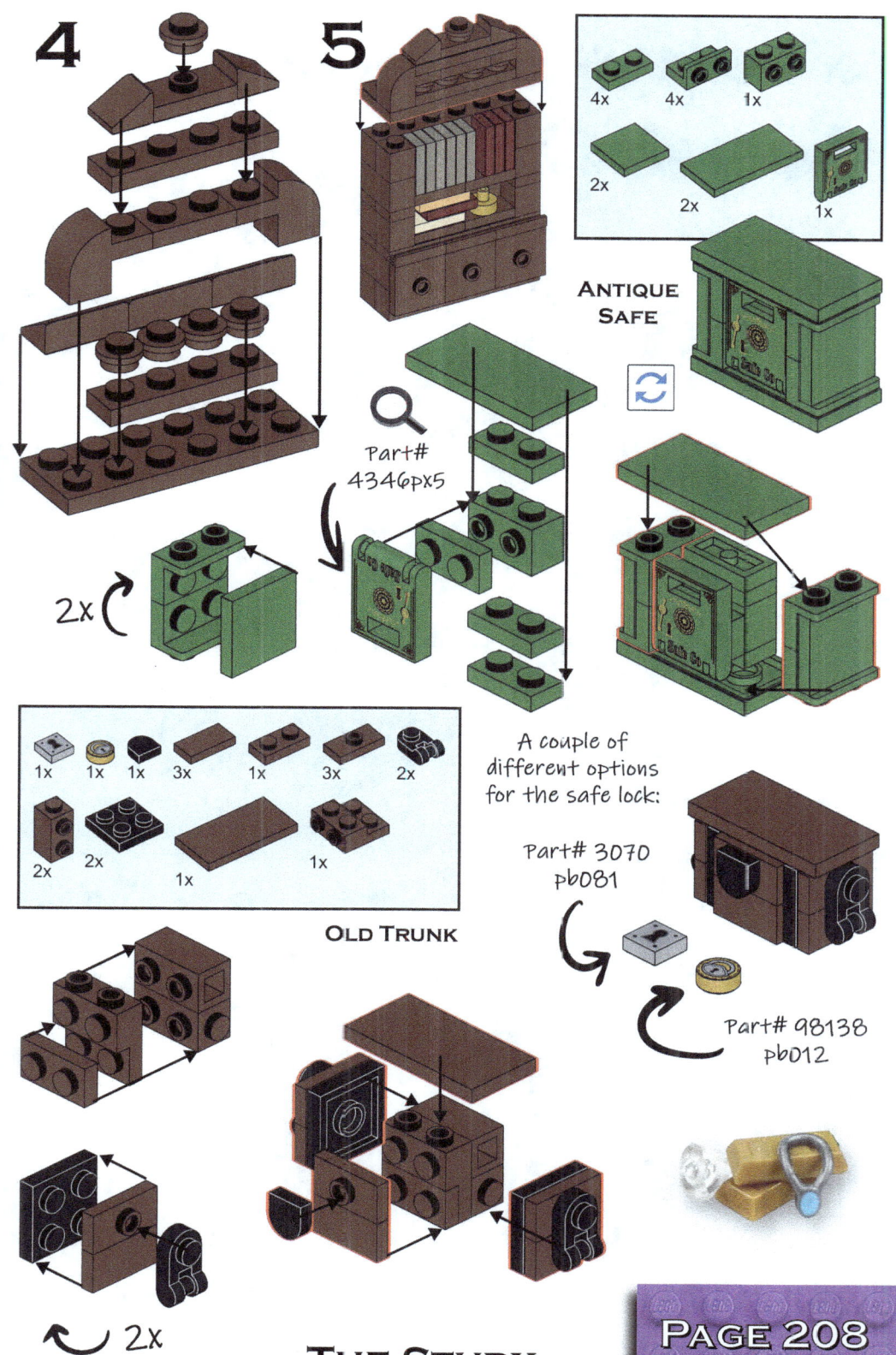

4

5

4x   4x   1x

2x   2x   1x

ANTIQUE SAFE

Part#
4346px5

2x

A couple of
different options
for the safe lock:

Part# 3070
pb081

Part# 98138
pb012

1x   1x   1x   3x   1x   3x   2x

2x   2x   1x   1x

OLD TRUNK

2x

THE STUDY

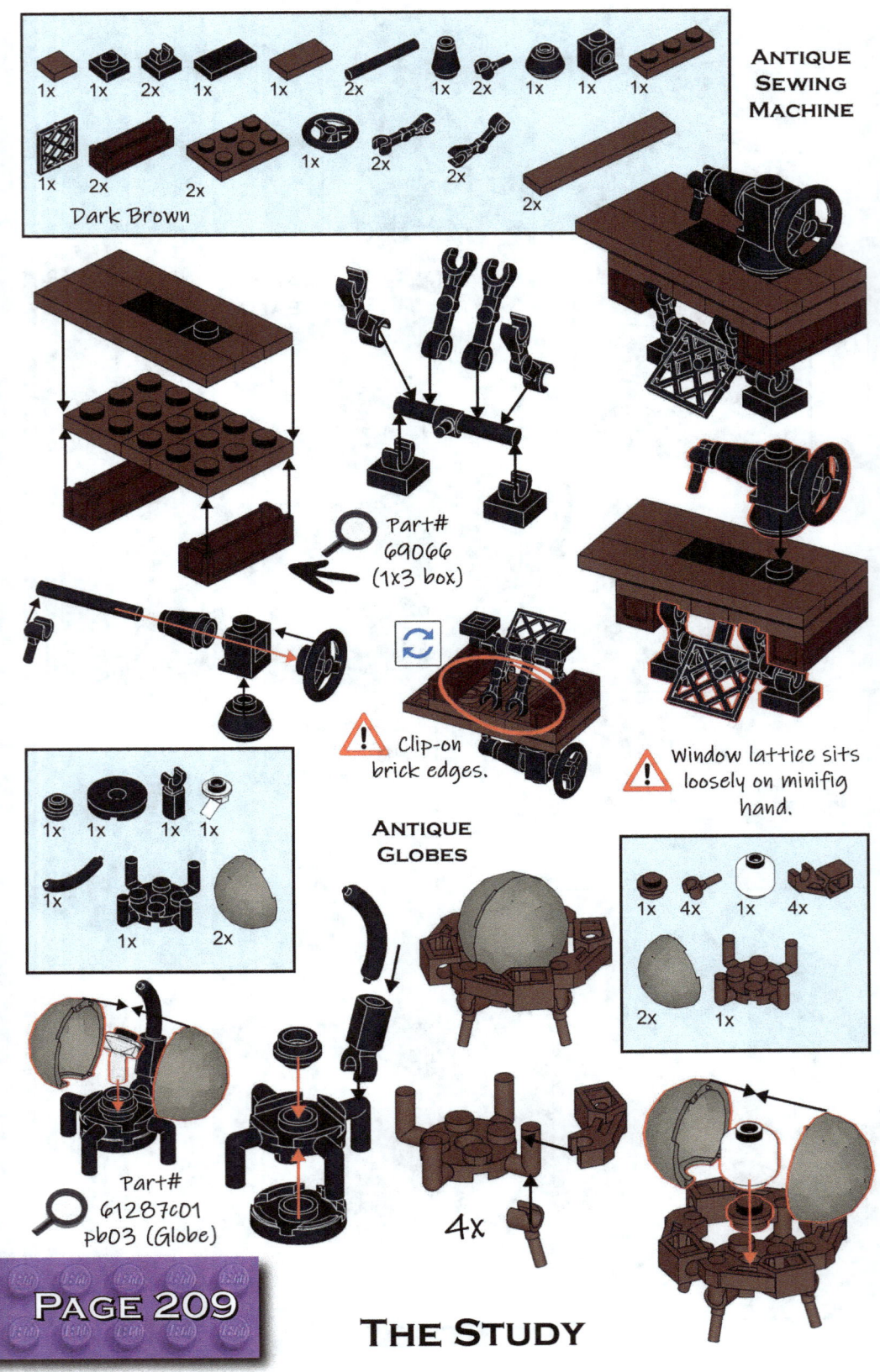

ANTIQUE
SEWING
MACHINE

1x 1x 2x 1x 1x 2x 1x 2x 1x 1x 1x

1x 2x 2x 1x 2x 2x 2x

Dark Brown

Part#
69066
(1x3 box)

Clip-on
brick edges.

Window lattice sits
loosely on minifig
hand.

ANTIQUE
GLOBES

1x 1x 1x 1x

1x

1x 2x

1x 4x 1x 4x

2x 1x

Part#
61287c01
pb03 (Globe)

4x

THE STUDY

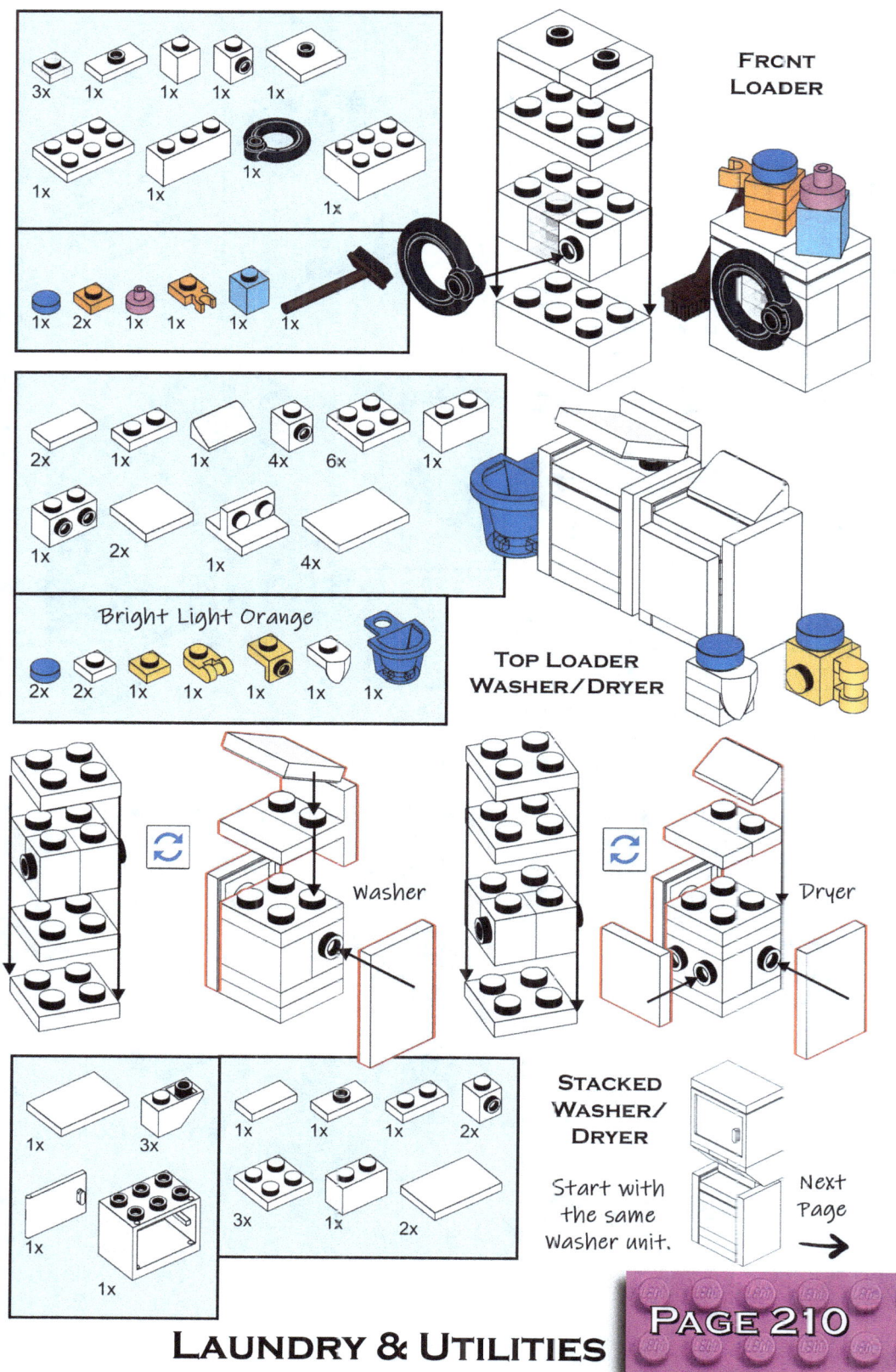

FRONT LOADER

3x 1x 1x 1x 1x

1x 1x 1x 1x

1x 2x 1x 1x 1x 1x

TOP LOADER WASHER/DRYER

2x 1x 1x 4x 6x 1x

1x 2x 1x 4x

Bright Light Orange

2x 2x 1x 1x 1x 1x 1x

Washer

Dryer

1x 3x

1x 1x 1x 2x

1x 1x 3x 1x 2x

1x

STACKED WASHER/ DRYER

Start with the same Washer unit.

Next Page →

LAUNDRY & UTILITIES

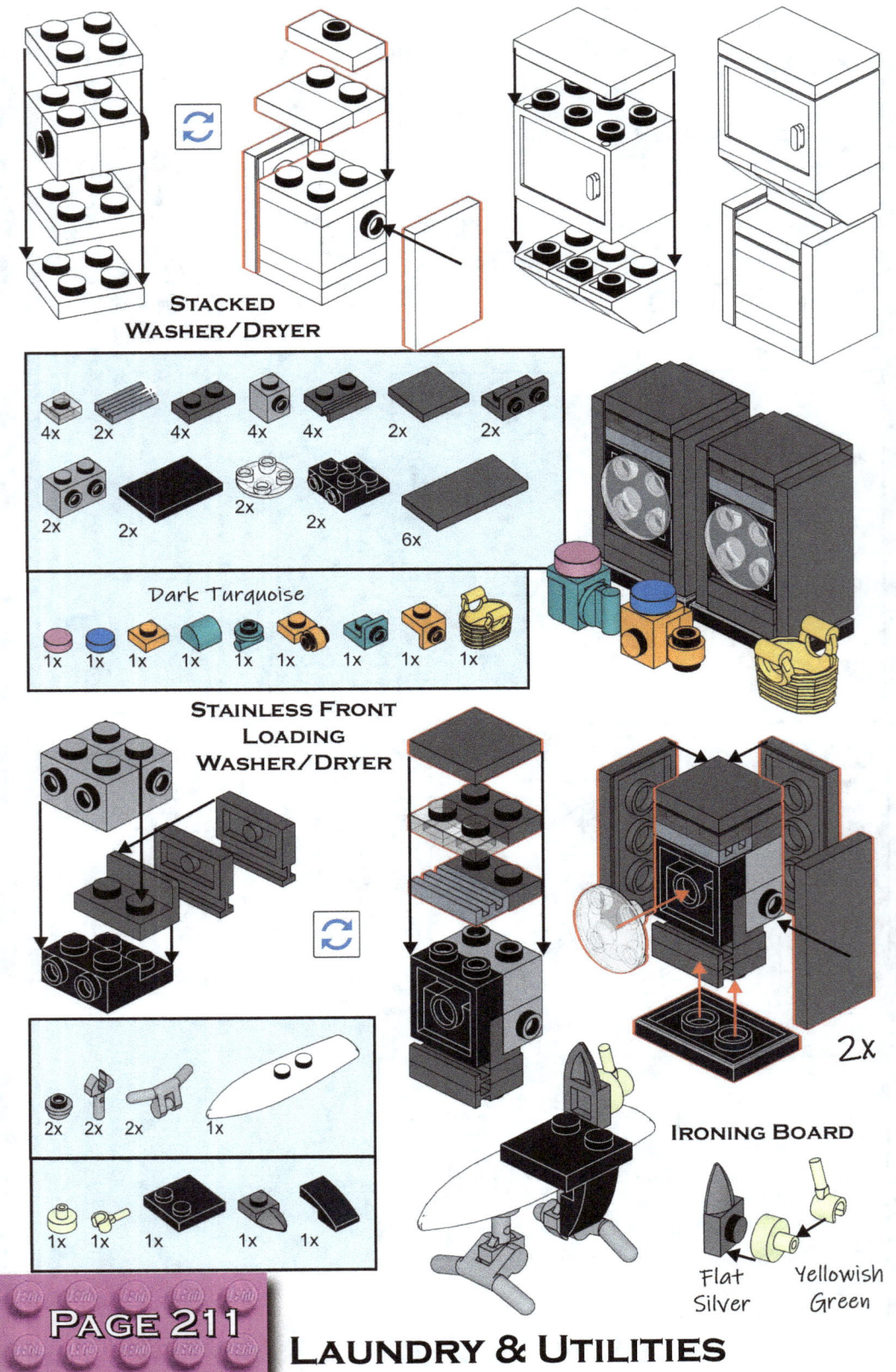

**STACKED
WASHER/DRYER**

4x 2x 4x 4x 4x 2x 2x

2x 2x 2x 2x 6x

Dark Turquoise

1x 1x 1x 1x 1x 1x 1x 1x 1x

**STAINLESS FRONT
LOADING
WASHER/DRYER**

2x 2x 2x 1x

1x 1x 1x 1x 1x

2x

IRONING BOARD

Flat   Yellowish
Silver   Green

LAUNDRY & UTILITIES

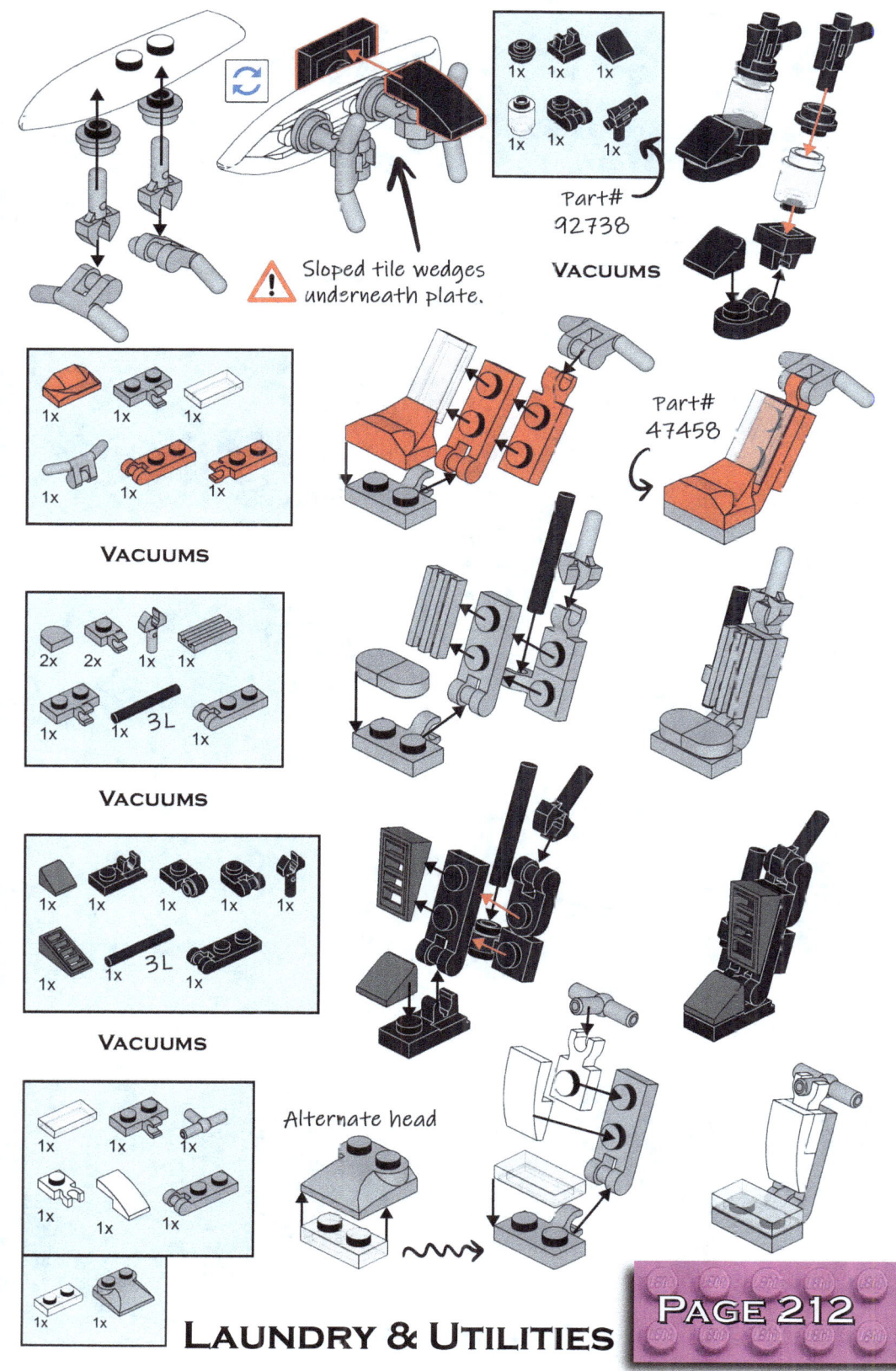

Sloped tile wedges underneath plate.

Part# 92738

VACUUMS

1x 1x 1x
1x 1x 1x

VACUUMS

Part# 47458

2x 2x 1x 1x
1x 1x 3L 1x

VACUUMS

1x 1x 1x 1x 1x
1x 1x 3L 1x

VACUUMS

1x 1x 1x
1x 1x 1x

Alternate head

1x 1x

LAUNDRY & UTILITIES

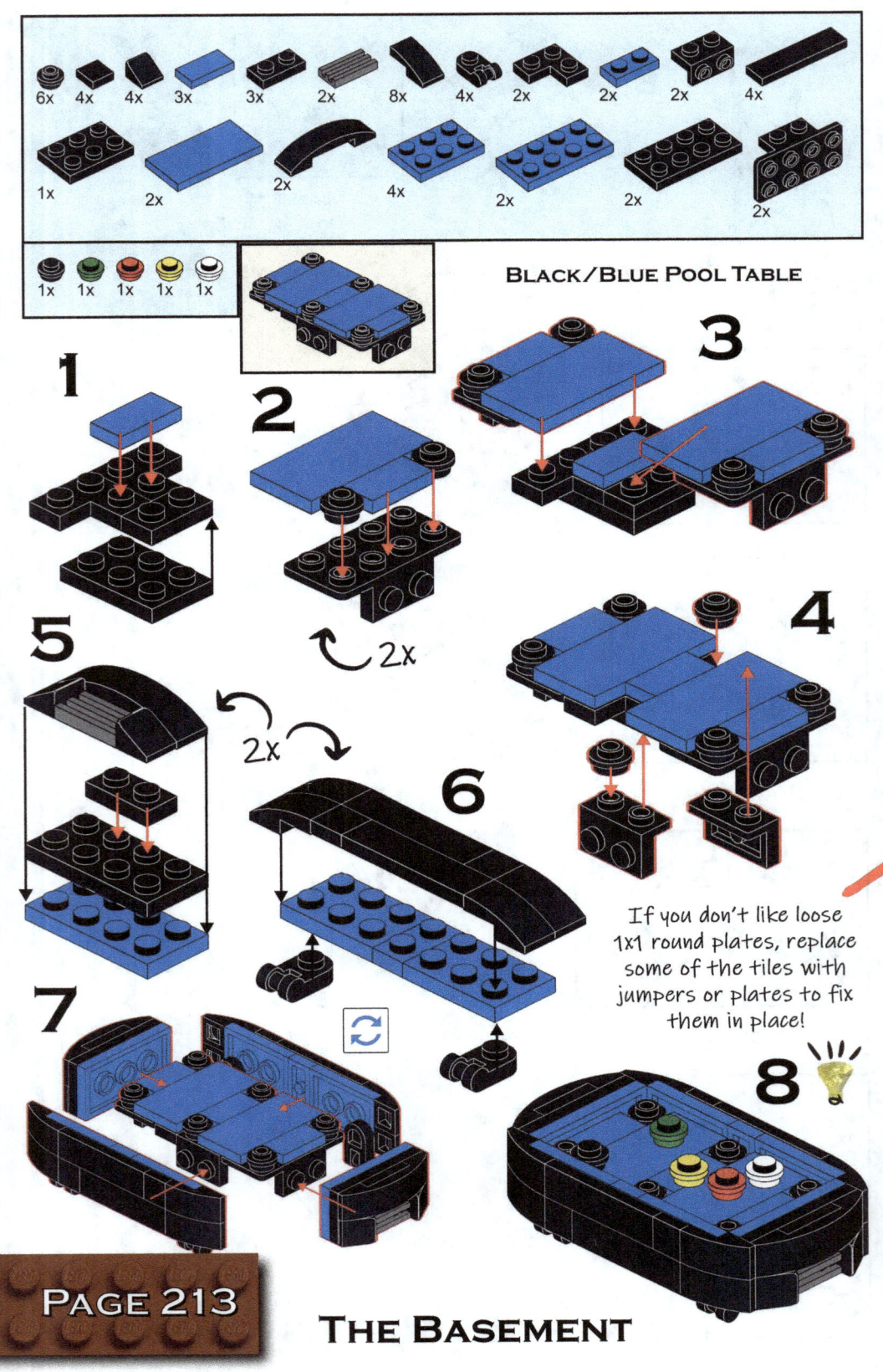

BLACK/BLUE POOL TABLE

1

2

2x

3

4

5

2x

6

7

If you don't like loose 1x1 round plates, replace some of the tiles with jumpers or plates to fix them in place!

8

THE BASEMENT

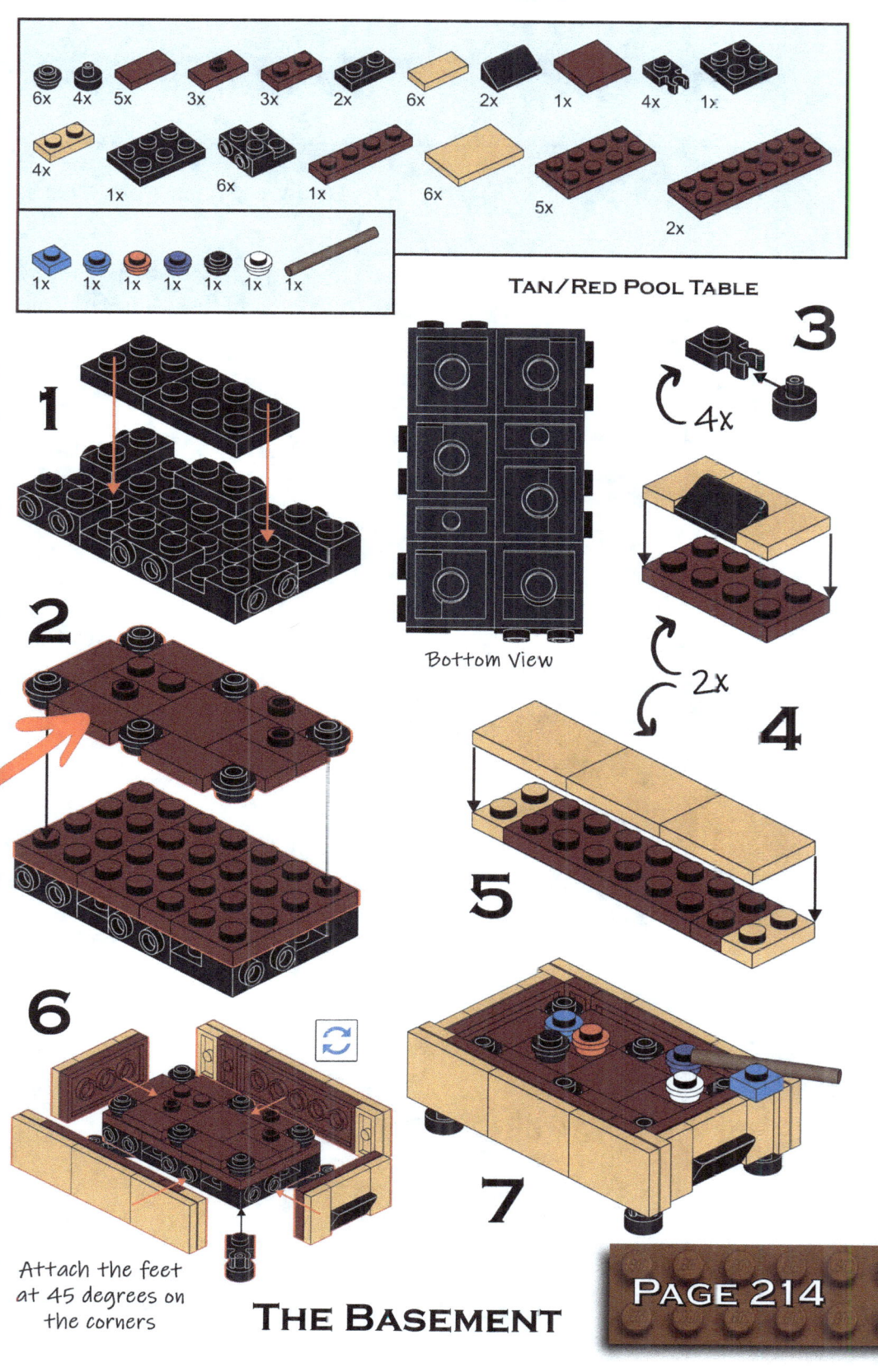

6x 4x 5x 3x 3x 2x 6x 2x 1x 4x 1x

4x 1x 6x 1x 6x 5x 2x

1x 1x 1x 1x 1x 1x 1x

TAN/RED POOL TABLE

1

2

3

4x

2x

4

5

Bottom View

6

Attach the feet at 45 degrees on the corners

7

THE BASEMENT

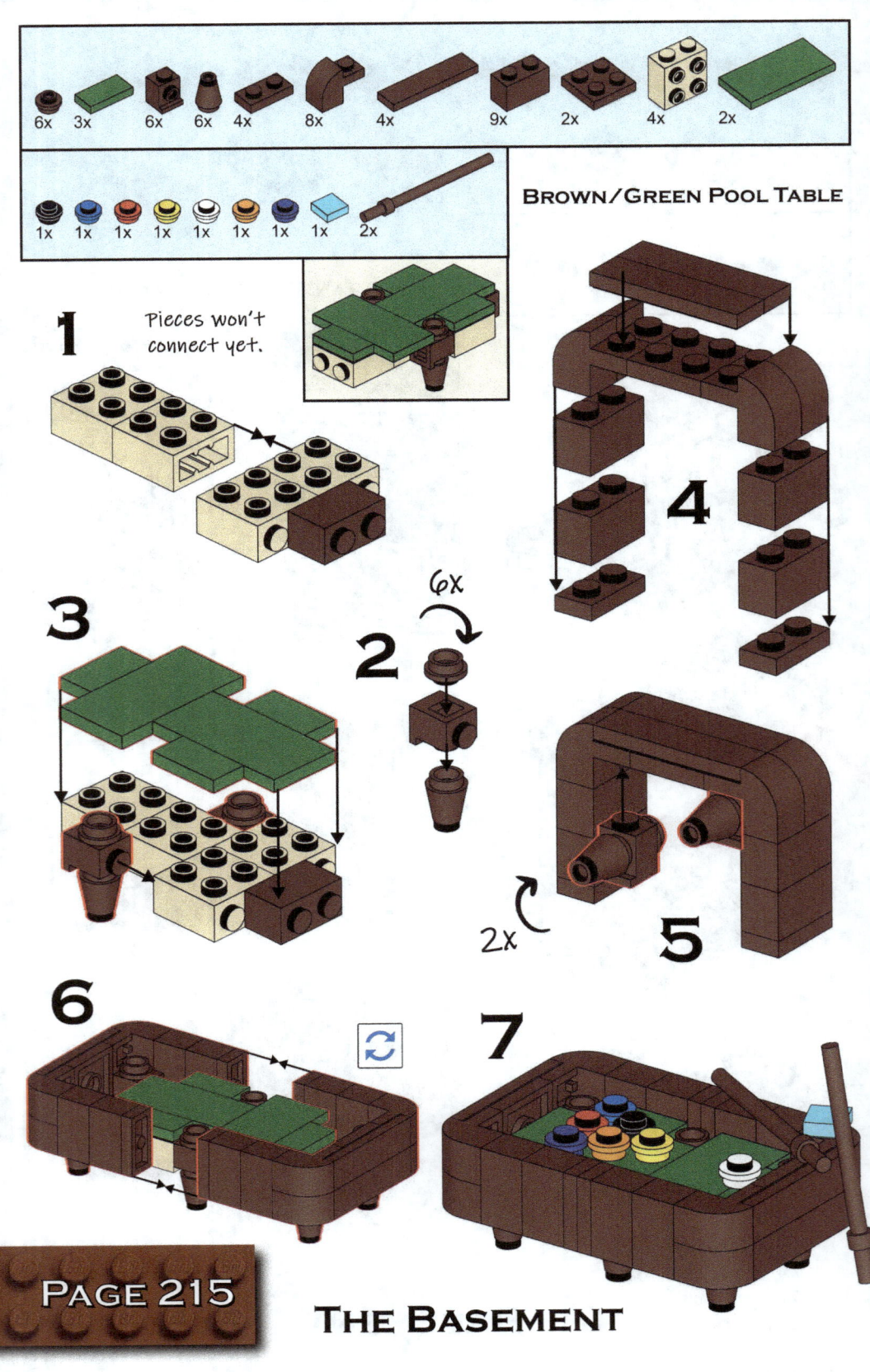

1. Pieces won't connect yet.

2. 6x

3.

4. BROWN/GREEN POOL TABLE

5. 2x

6.

7.

THE BASEMENT

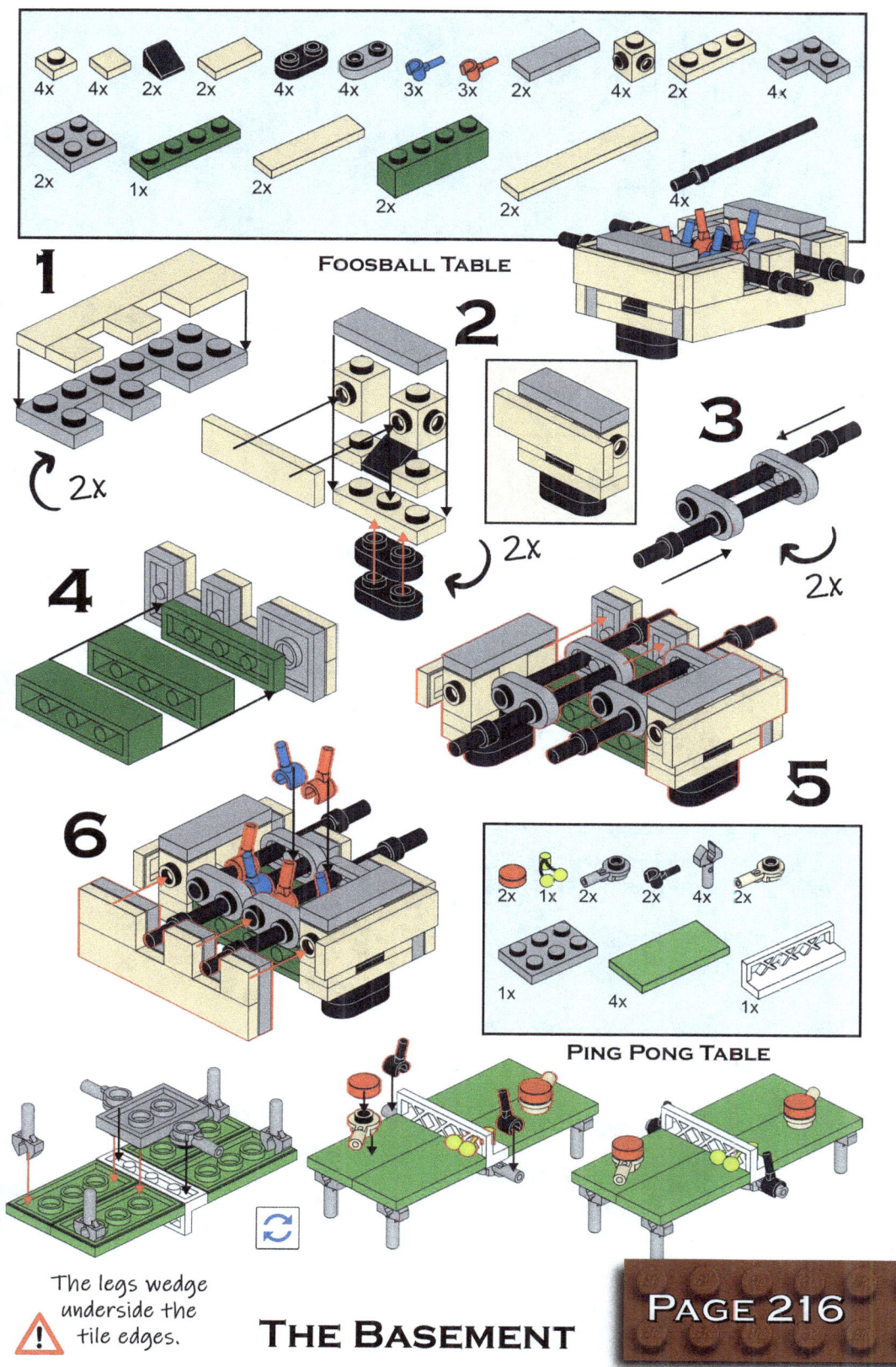

FOOSBALL TABLE

1 2x

2 2x

3 2x

4

5

6

PING PONG TABLE

The legs wedge underside the tile edges.

THE BASEMENT

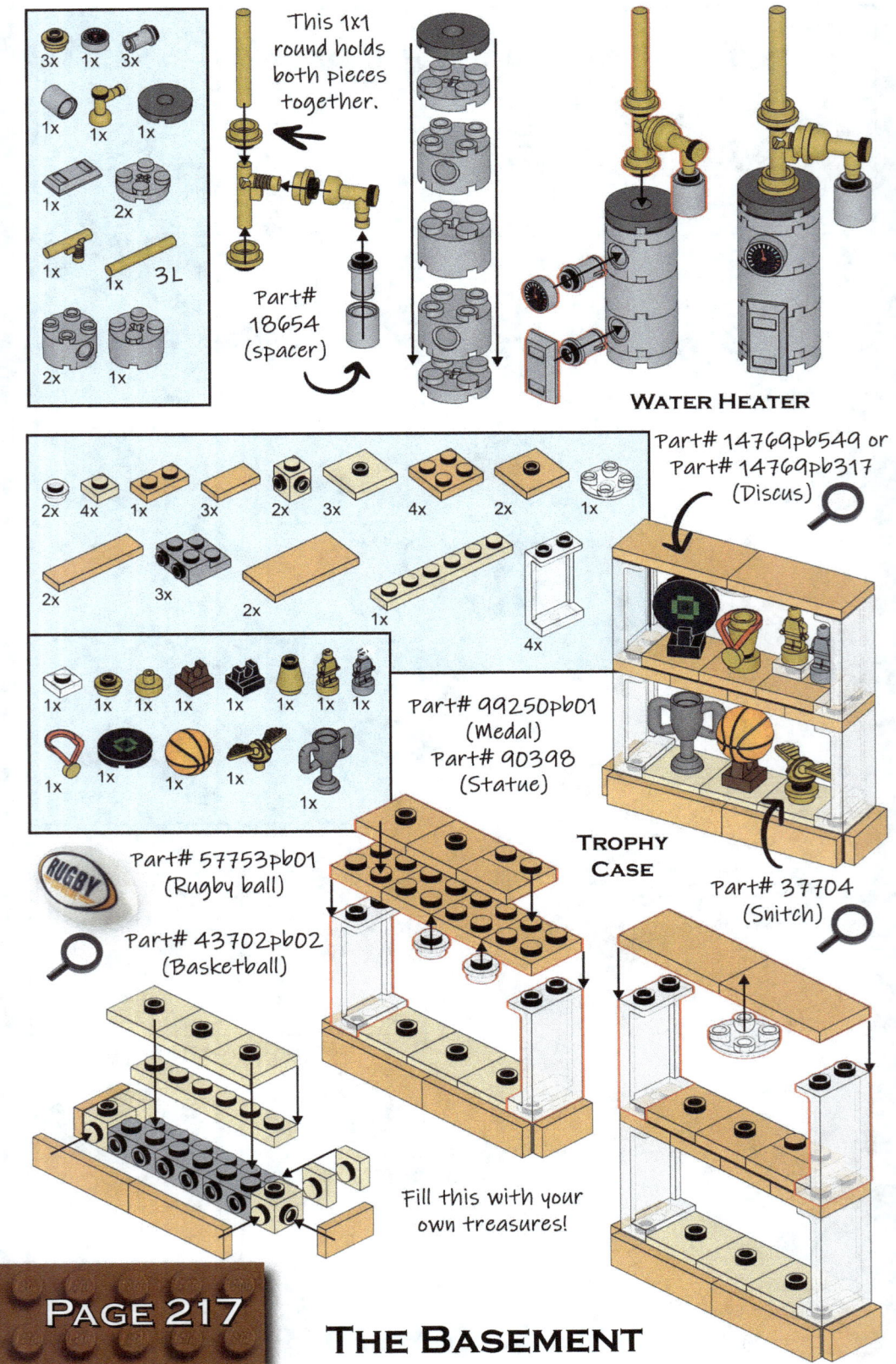

This 1x1 round holds both pieces together.

Part# 18654 (spacer)

WATER HEATER

Part# 14769pb549 or Part# 14769pb317 (Discus)

Part# 99250pb01 (Medal)
Part# 90398 (Statue)

TROPHY CASE

Part# 37704 (Snitch)

RUGBY

Part# 57753pb01 (Rugby ball)

Part# 43702pb02 (Basketball)

Fill this with your own treasures!

THE BASEMENT

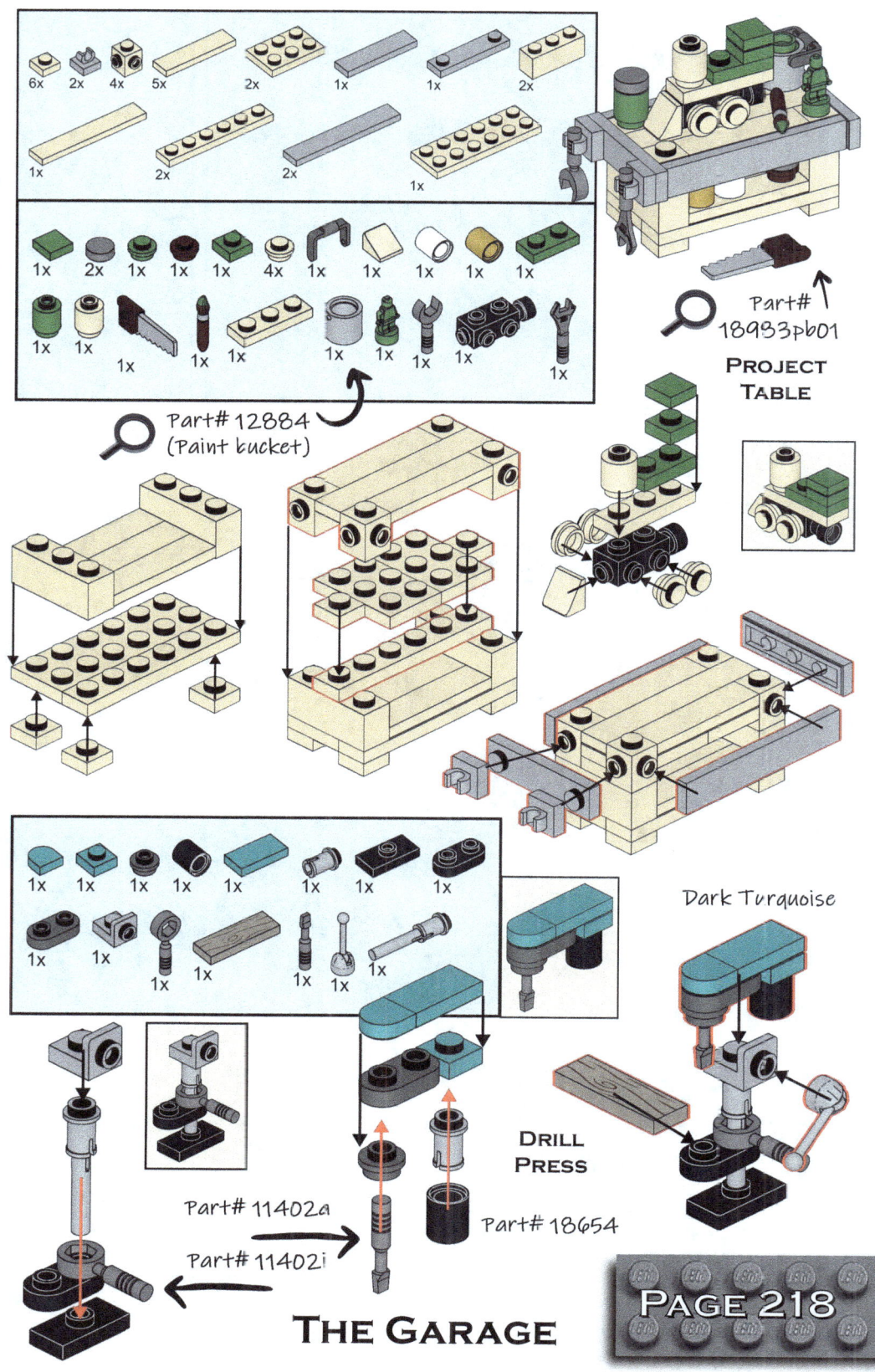

6x 2x 4x 5x 2x 1x 1x 2x

1x 2x 2x 1x

1x 2x 1x 1x 1x 4x 1x 1x 1x 1x 1x

1x 1x 1x 1x 1x 1x 1x 1x 1x

Part# 12884
(Paint bucket)

Part#
18993pb01

**PROJECT
TABLE**

1x 1x 1x 1x 1x 1x 1x 1x

1x 1x 1x 1x 1x 1x

Dark Turquoise

**DRILL
PRESS**

Part# 11402a

Part# 18654

Part# 11402i

THE GARAGE

PAGE 218

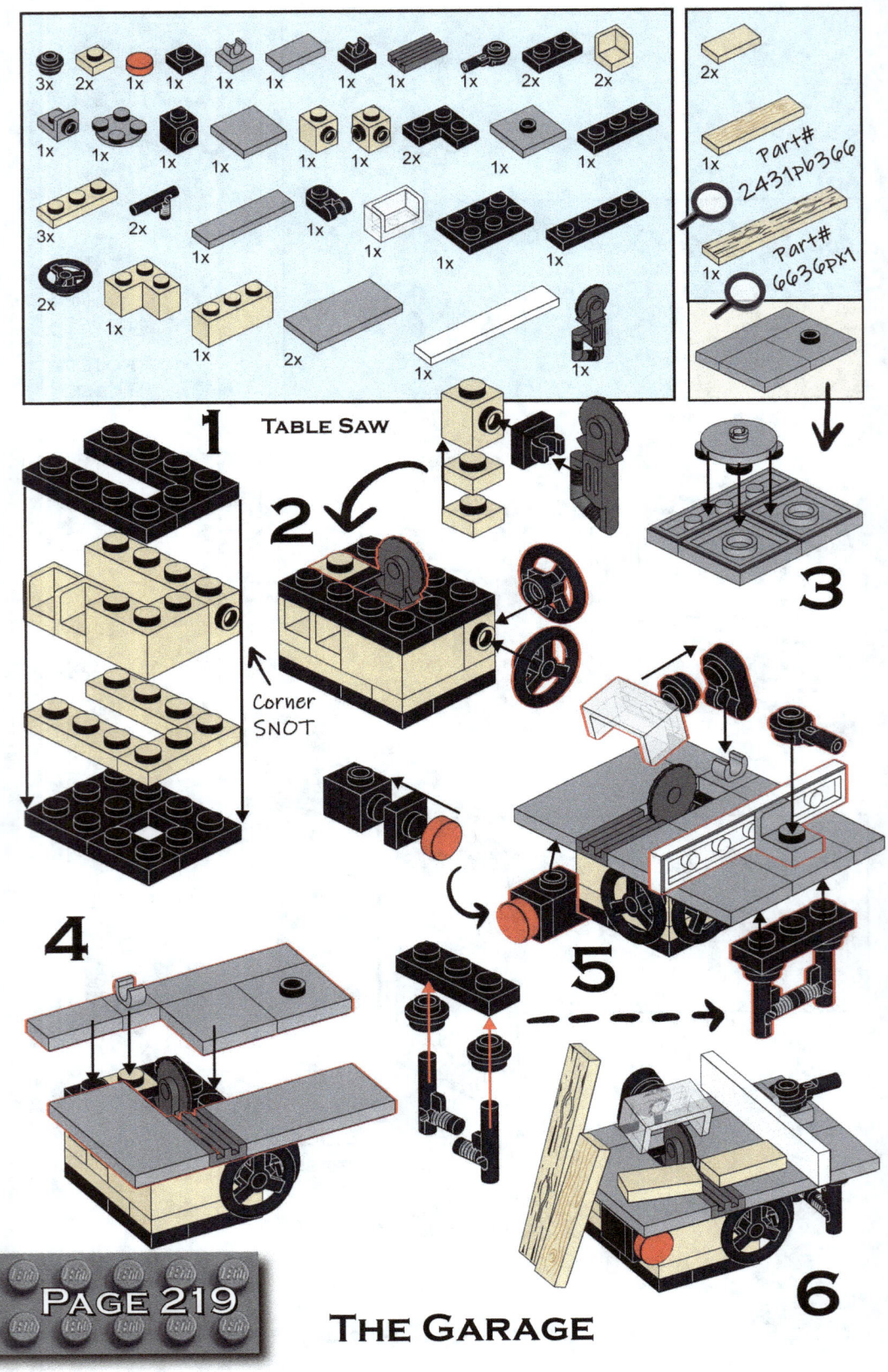

TABLE SAW

1

Corner
SNOT

2

3

4

5

6

Part# 2431pb366

Part# 6636PX1

THE GARAGE

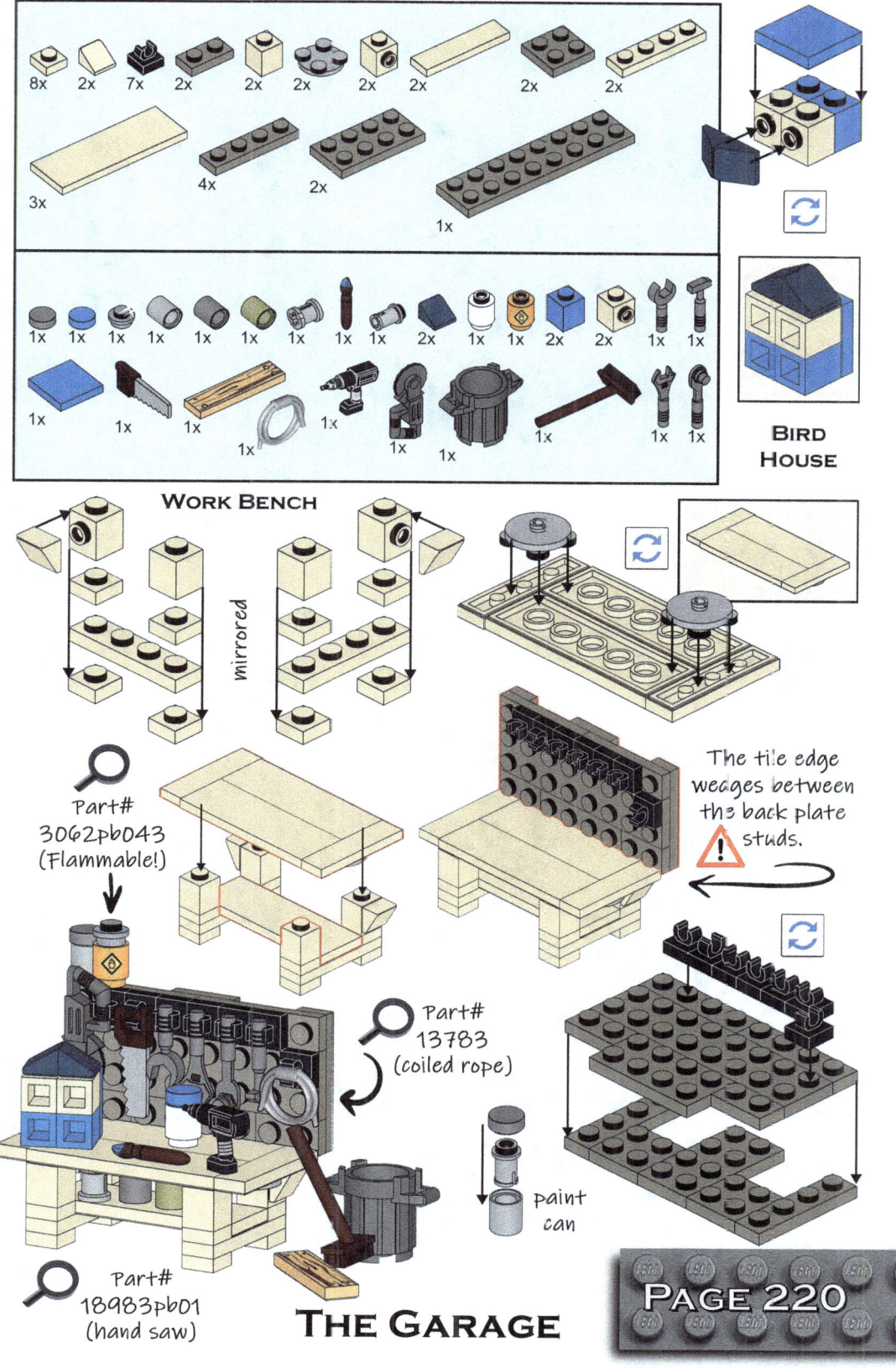

BIRD HOUSE

WORK BENCH

mirrored

Part#
3062pb043
(Flammable!)

The tile edge
wedges between
the back plate
studs.

Part#
13783
(coiled rope)

paint
can

Part#
18983pb01
(hand saw)

THE GARAGE

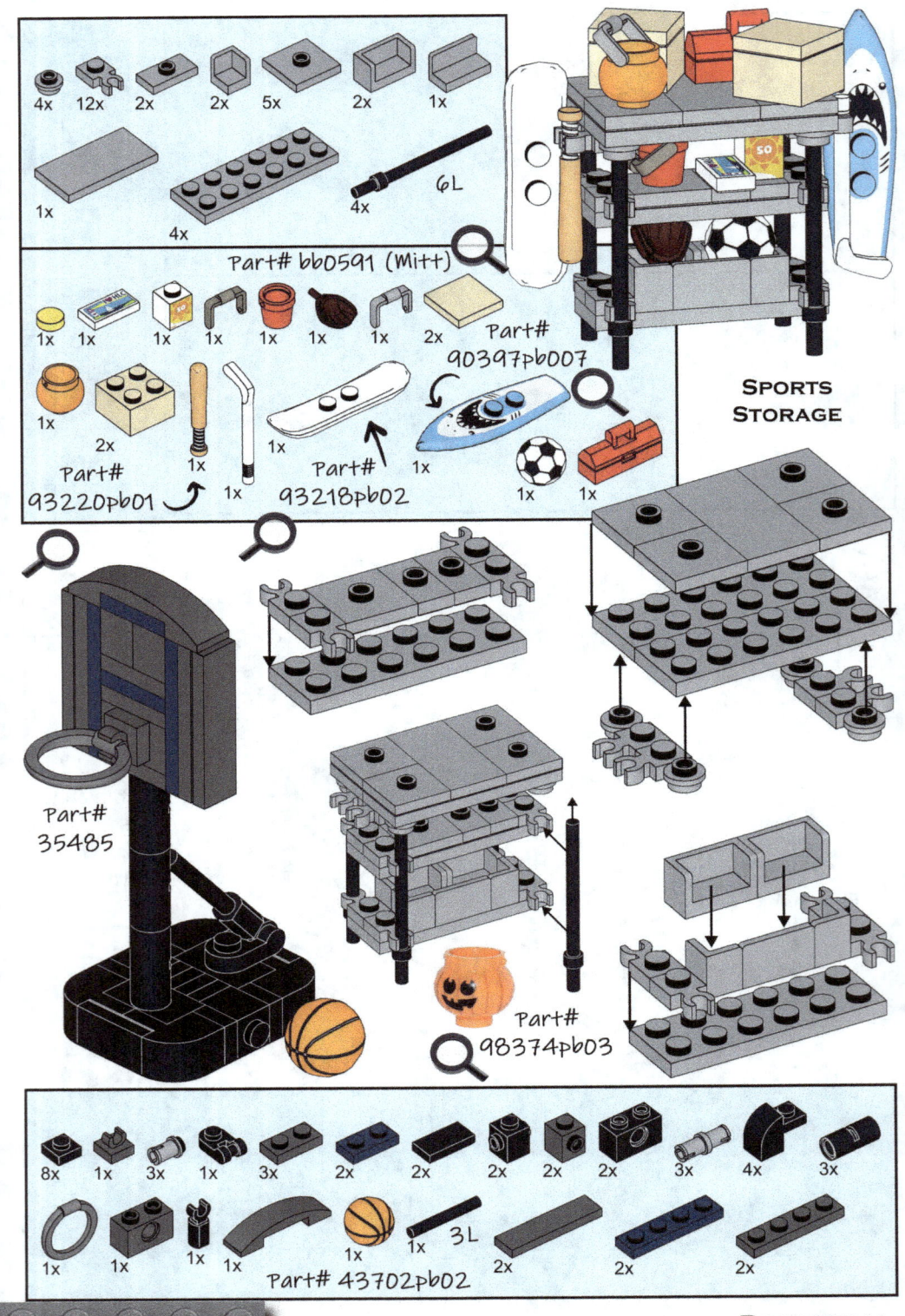

Part# bb0591 (Mitt)

Part# 90397pb007

SPORTS STORAGE

Part# 93220pb01

Part# 93218pb02

Part# 35485

Part# 98374pb03

Part# 43702pb02

6L

3L

BASKETBALL GOAL

THE GARAGE

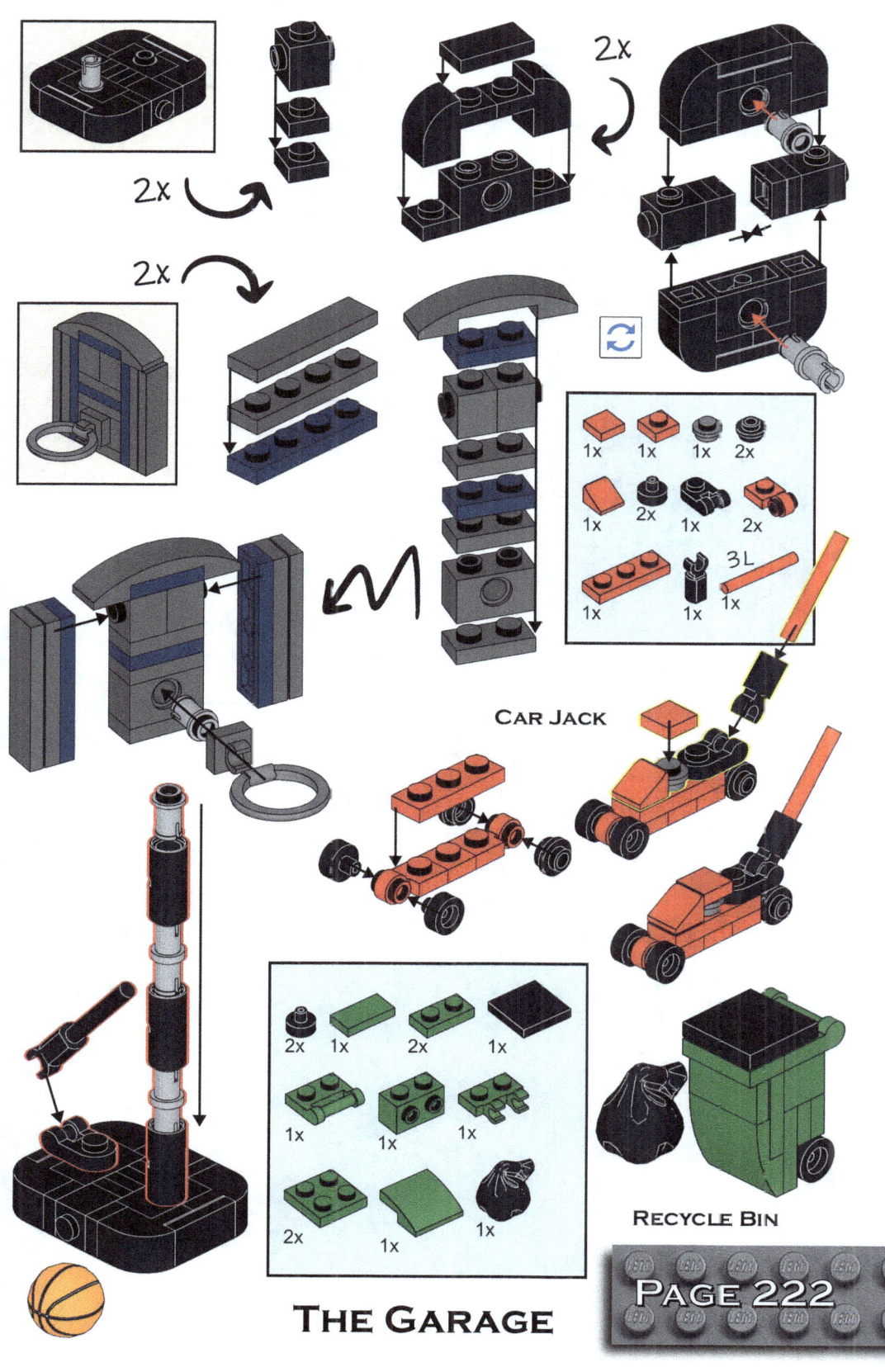

2x

2x

2x

2x

CAR JACK

3L

RECYCLE BIN

THE GARAGE

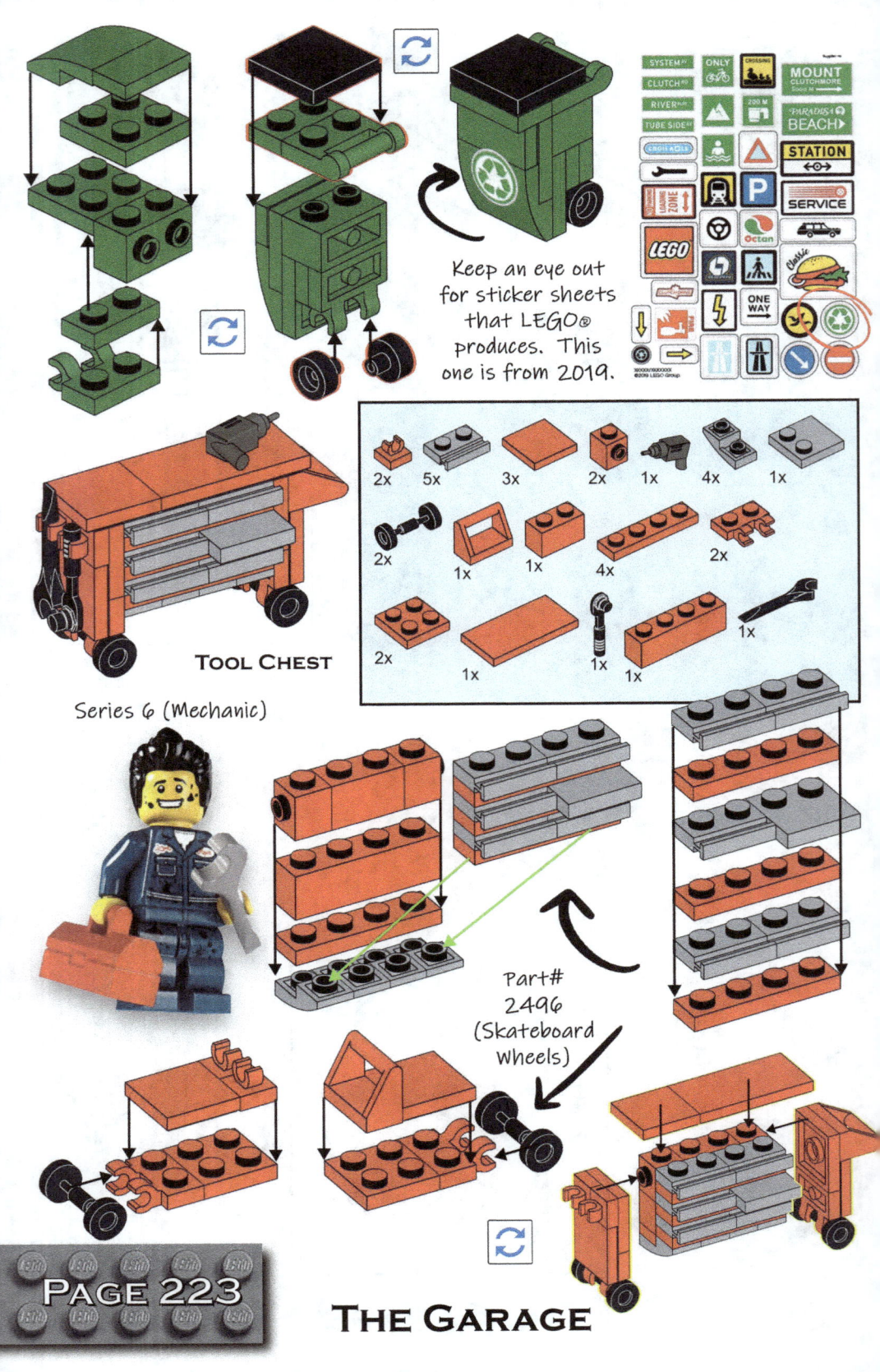

Keep an eye out for sticker sheets that LEGO® produces. This one is from 2019.

TOOL CHEST

2x 5x 3x 2x 1x 4x 1x

2x 1x 1x 4x 2x

2x 1x 1x 1x 1x

Series 6 (Mechanic)

Part# 2496 (Skateboard Wheels)

THE GARAGE

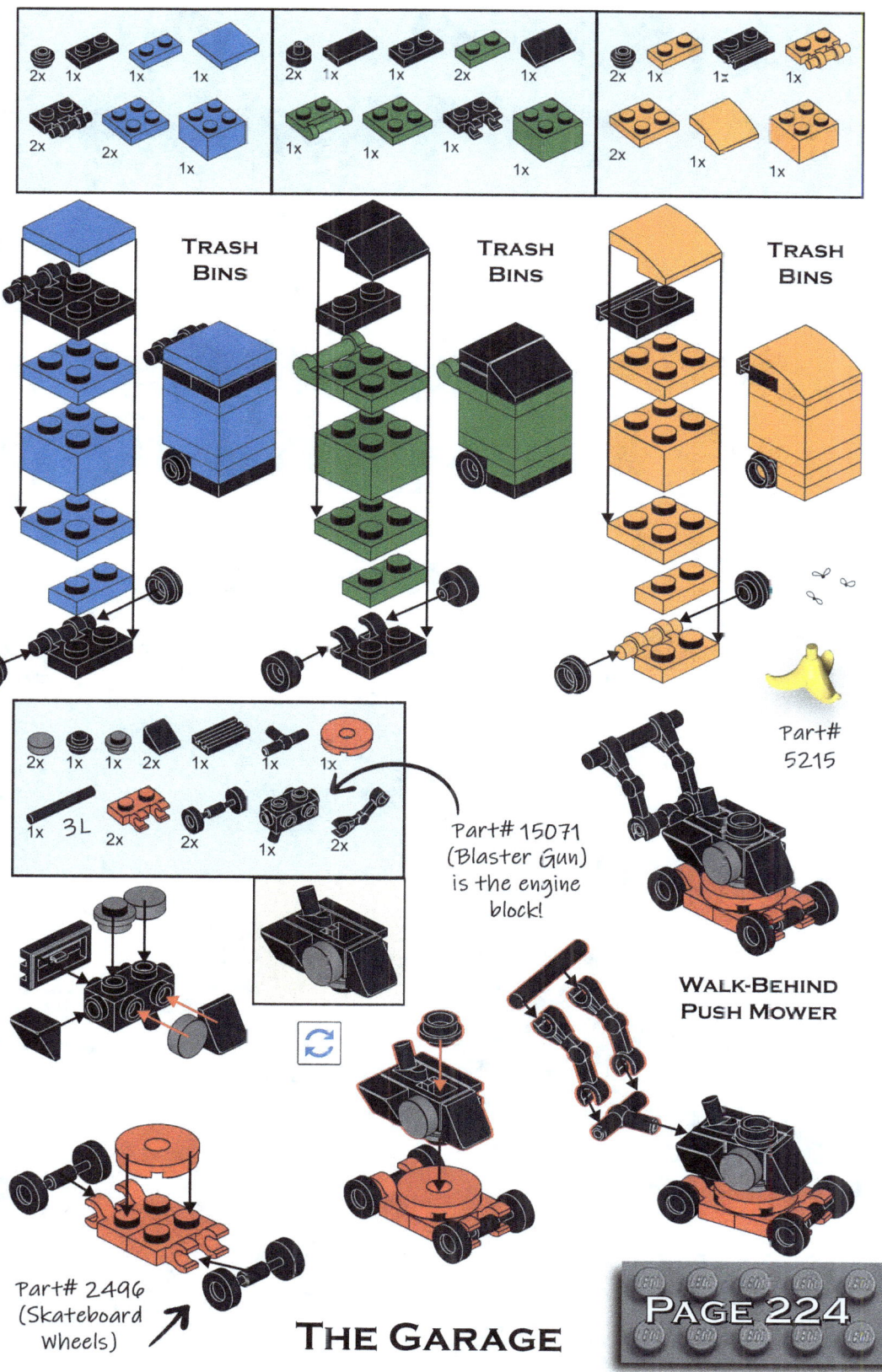

TRASH BINS

2x 1x 1x 1x
2x 2x 1x

TRASH BINS

2x 1x 1x 2x 1x
1x 1x 1x 1x

TRASH BINS

2x 1x 1x 1x
2x 1x 1x

2x 1x 1x 2x 1x 1x 1x
1x 3L 2x 2x 1x 2x

Part# 15071
(Blaster Gun)
is the engine
block!

Part#
5215

WALK-BEHIND PUSH MOWER

Part# 2496
(Skateboard
Wheels)

THE GARAGE

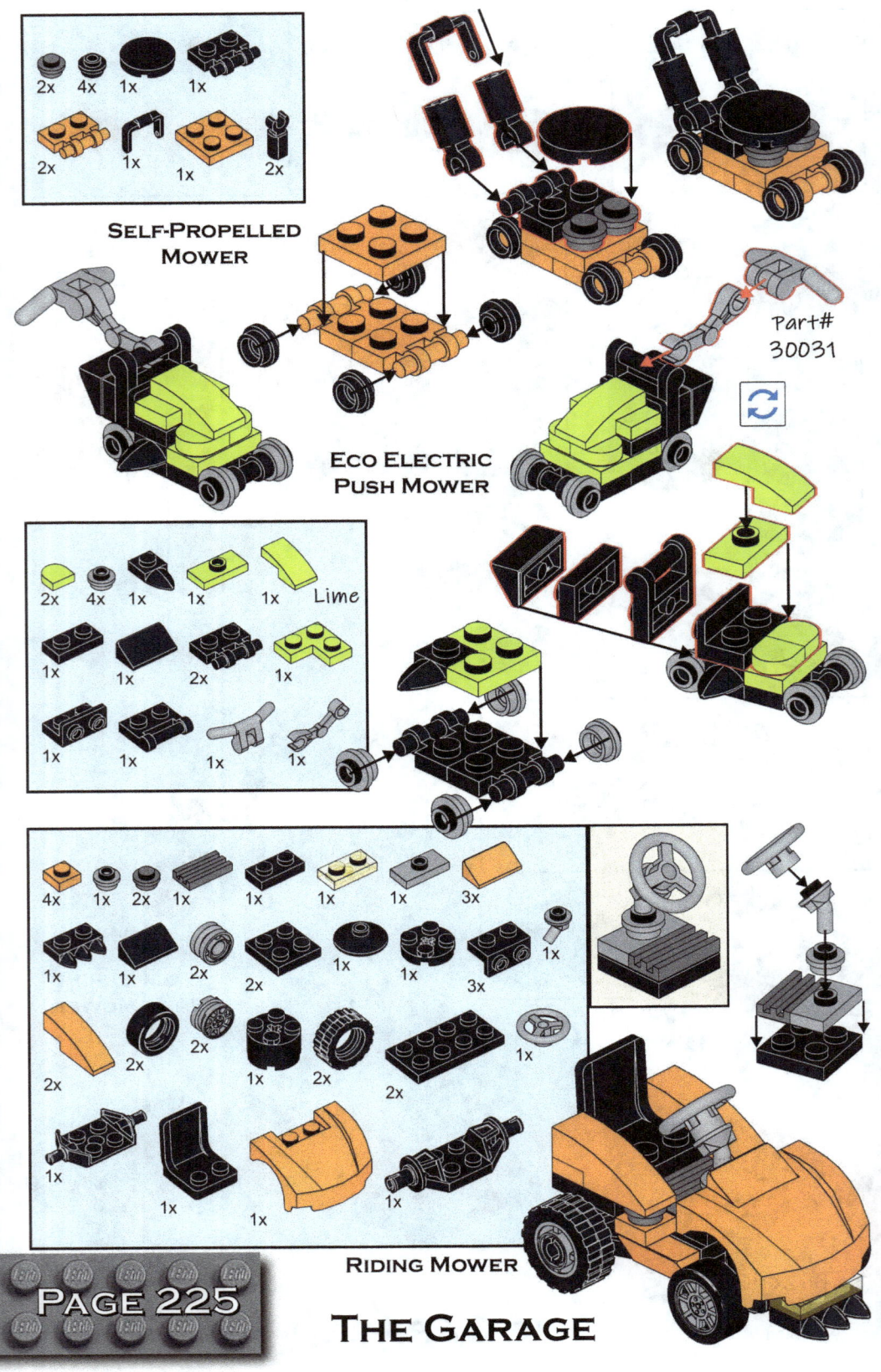

SELF-PROPELLED MOWER

ECO ELECTRIC PUSH MOWER

Lime

Part# 30031

RIDING MOWER

THE GARAGE

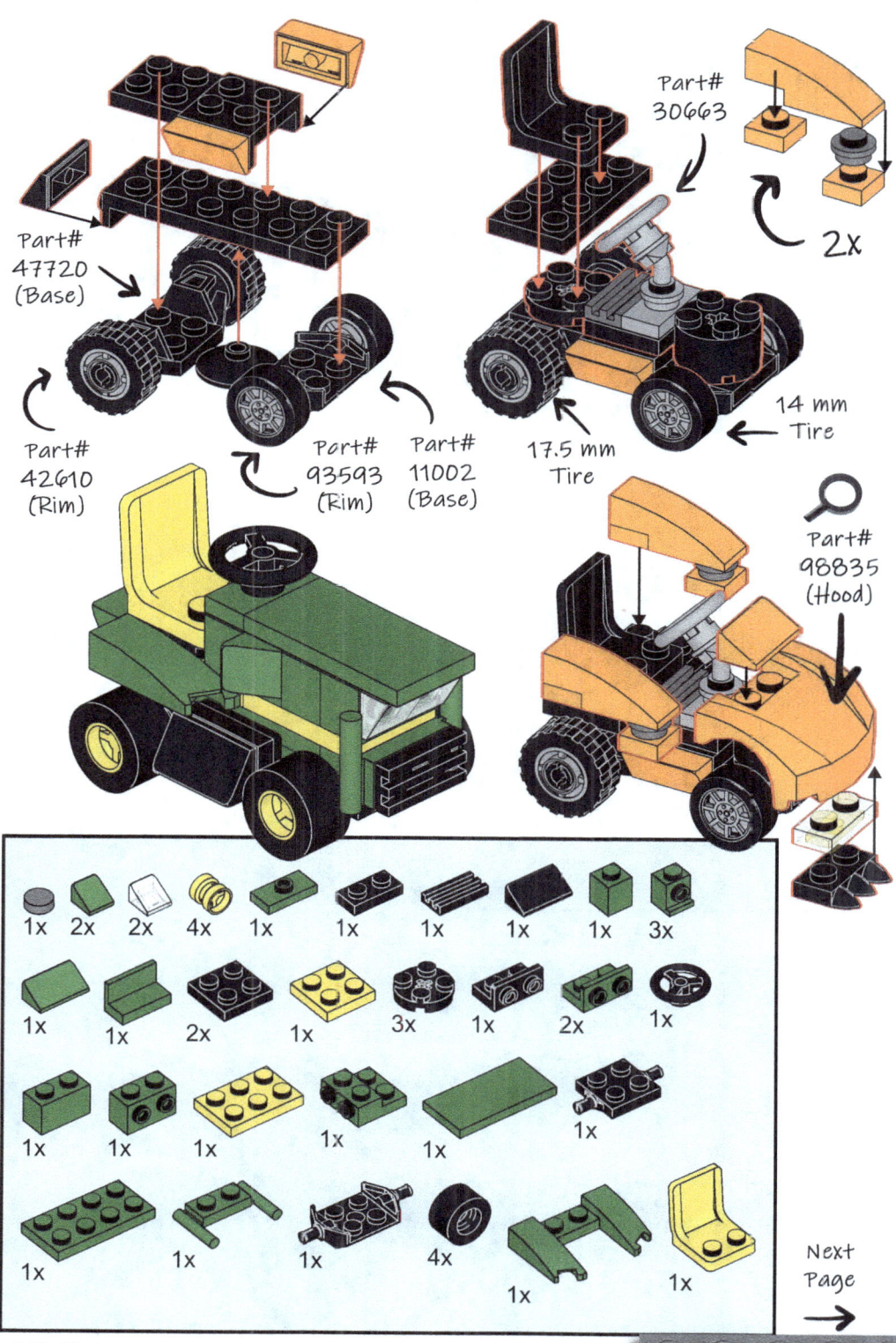

Part#
30663

2x

Part#
47720
(Base)

Part#
42610
(Rim)

Part#
93593
(Rim)

Part#
11002
(Base)

17.5 mm
Tire

14 mm
Tire

Part#
98835
(Hood)

1x   2x   2x   4x   1x   1x   1x   1x   1x   3x

1x   1x   2x   1x   3x   1x   2x   1x

1x   1x   1x   1x   1x   1x

1x   1x   1x   4x   1x   1x

Next
Page
→

J.D. HYDROSTATIC
LAWN MOWER

THE GARAGE

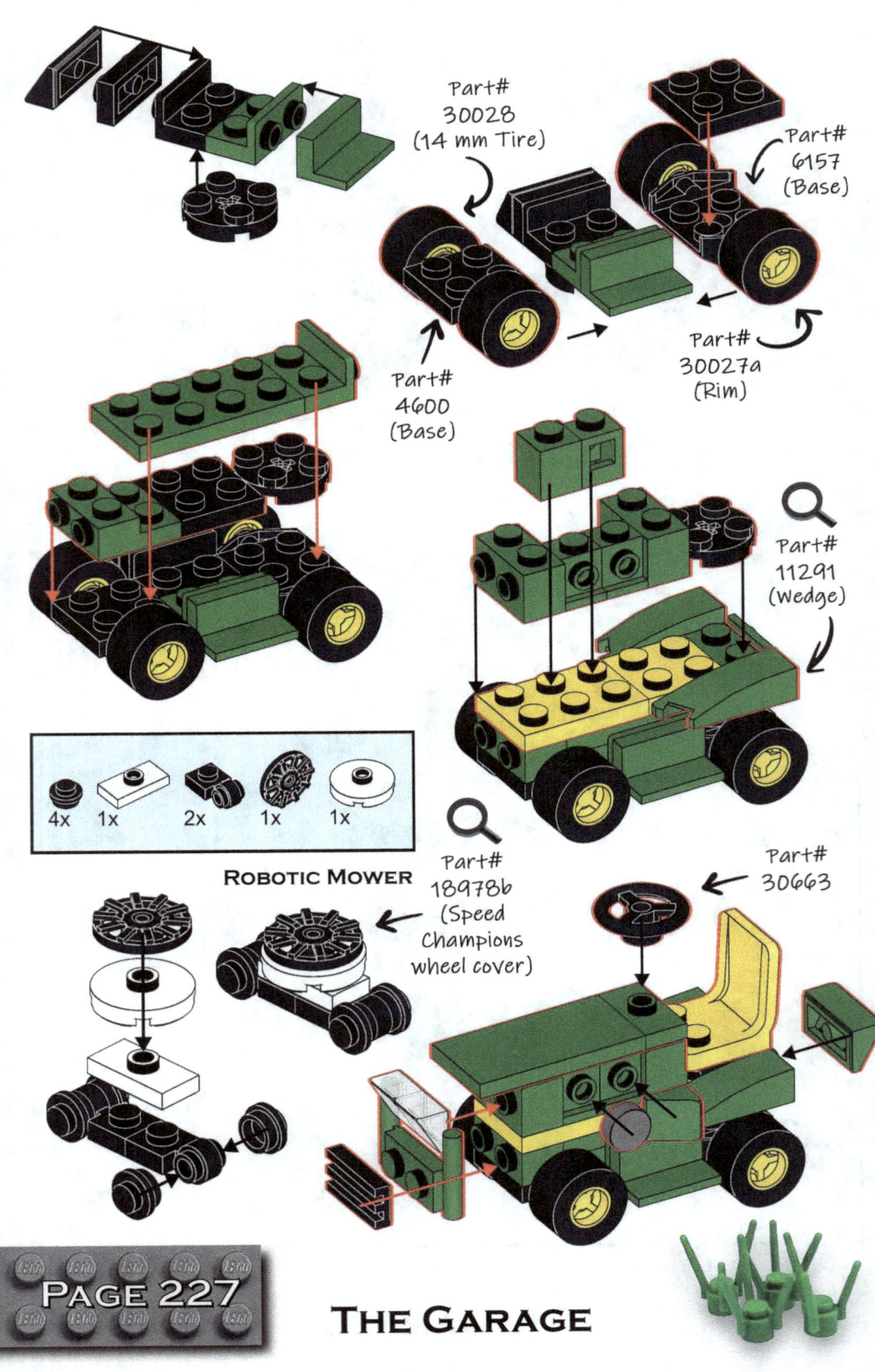

Part#
30028
(14 mm Tire)

Part#
6157
(Base)

Part#
4600
(Base)

Part#
30027a
(Rim)

Part#
11291
(wedge)

4x   1x   2x   1x   1x

ROBOTIC MOWER

Part#
18978b
(Speed
Champions
wheel cover)

Part#
30663

THE GARAGE

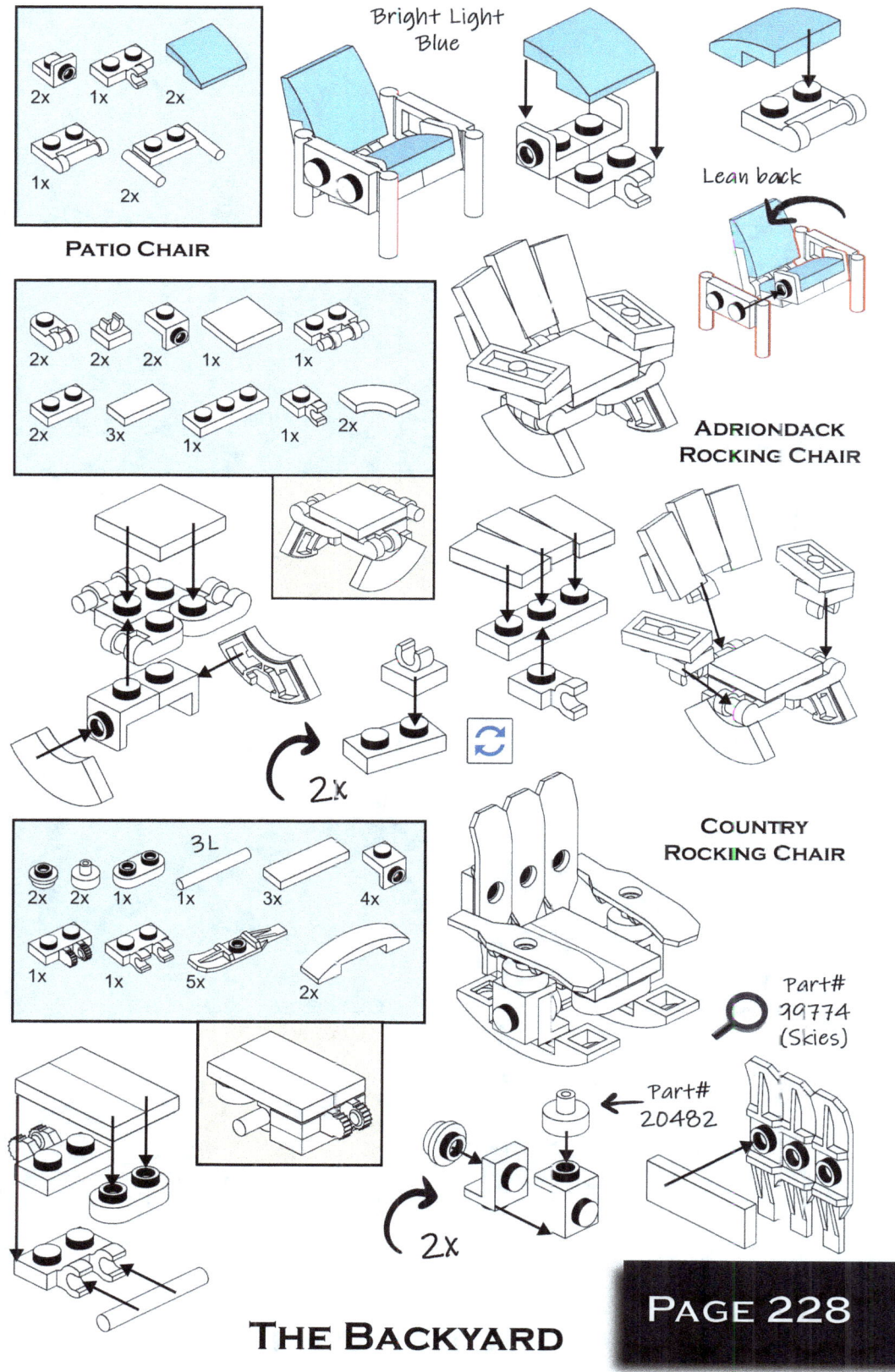

Bright Light Blue

PATIO CHAIR

Lean back

ADRIONDACK ROCKING CHAIR

2x

COUNTRY ROCKING CHAIR

3L

2x

Part#
39774
(Skies)

Part#
20482

2x

THE BACKYARD

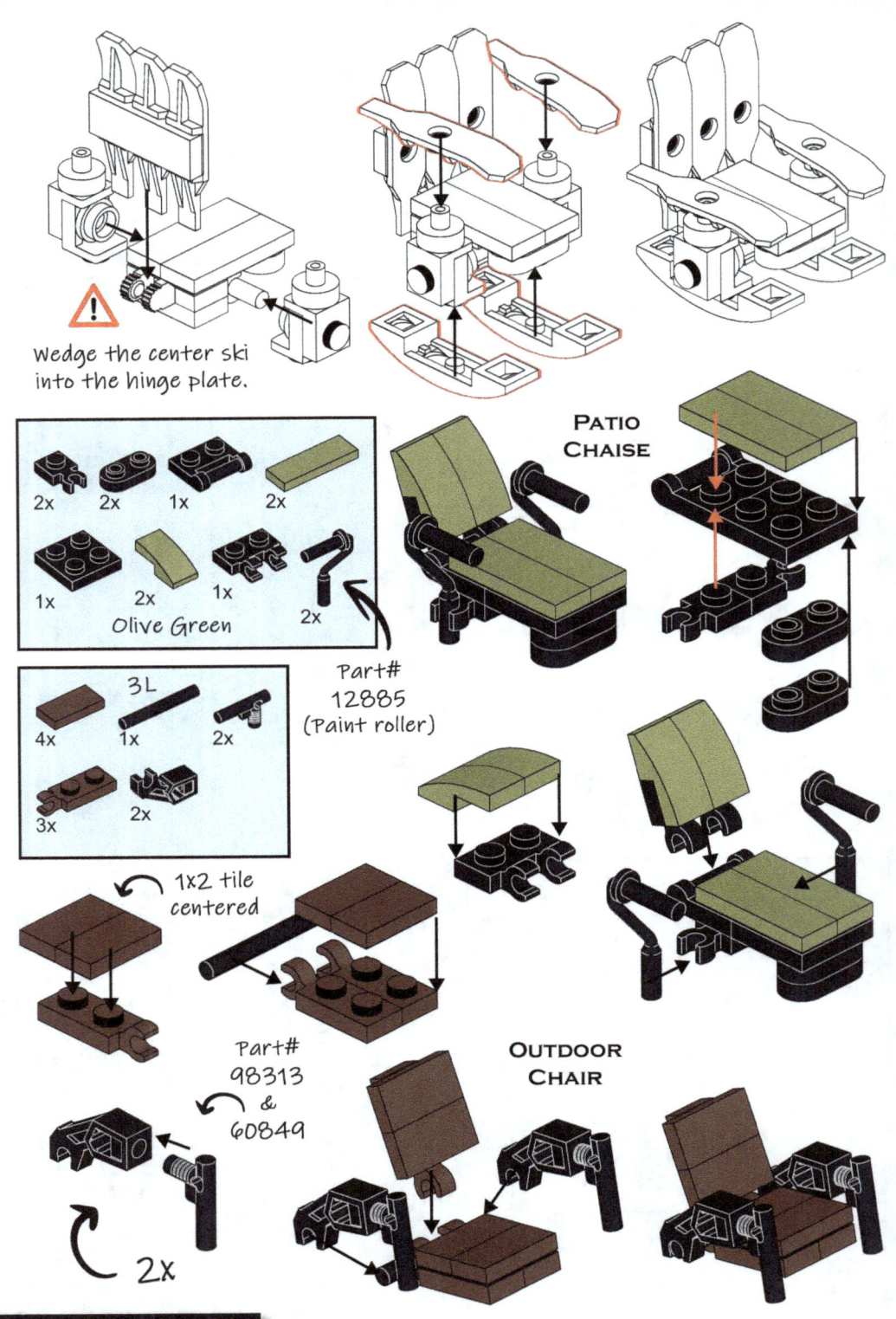

wedge the center ski into the hinge plate.

2x 2x 1x 2x

1x 2x 1x 2x
Olive Green

Part# 12885 (Paint roller)

PATIO CHAISE

3L
4x 1x 2x
3x 2x

1x2 tile centered

Part# 98313 & 60849

2x

OUTDOOR CHAIR

THE BACKYARD

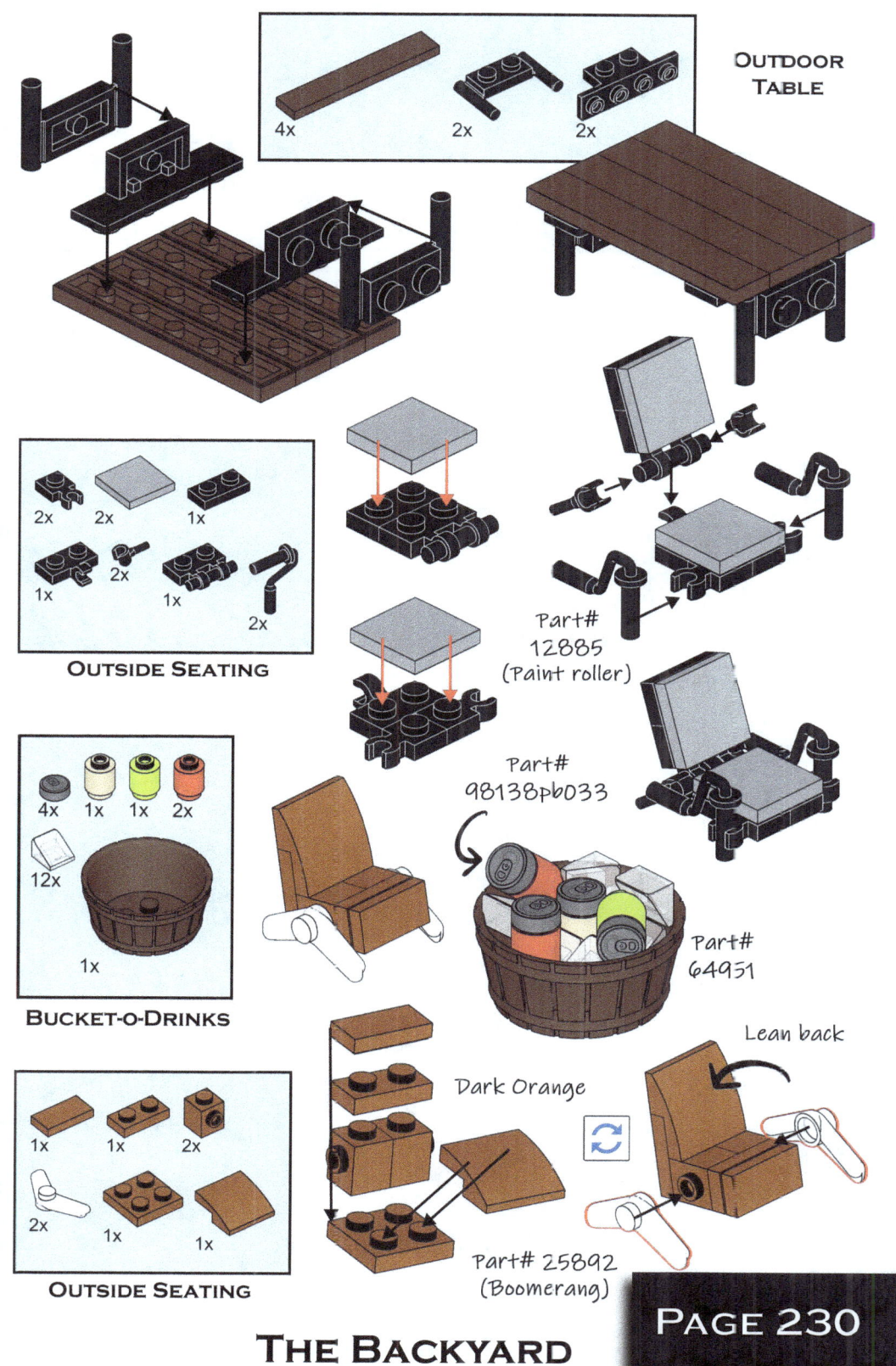

4x 2x 2x

OUTSIDE SEATING

2x 2x 1x
1x 2x 1x 2x

BUCKET-O-DRINKS

4x 1x 1x 2x
12x
1x

Part# 12885
(Paint roller)

Part# 98138pb033

Part# 64951

Dark Orange

Lean back

Part# 25892
(Boomerang)

1x 1x 2x
2x 1x 1x

OUTSIDE SEATING

PAGE 230

THE BACKYARD

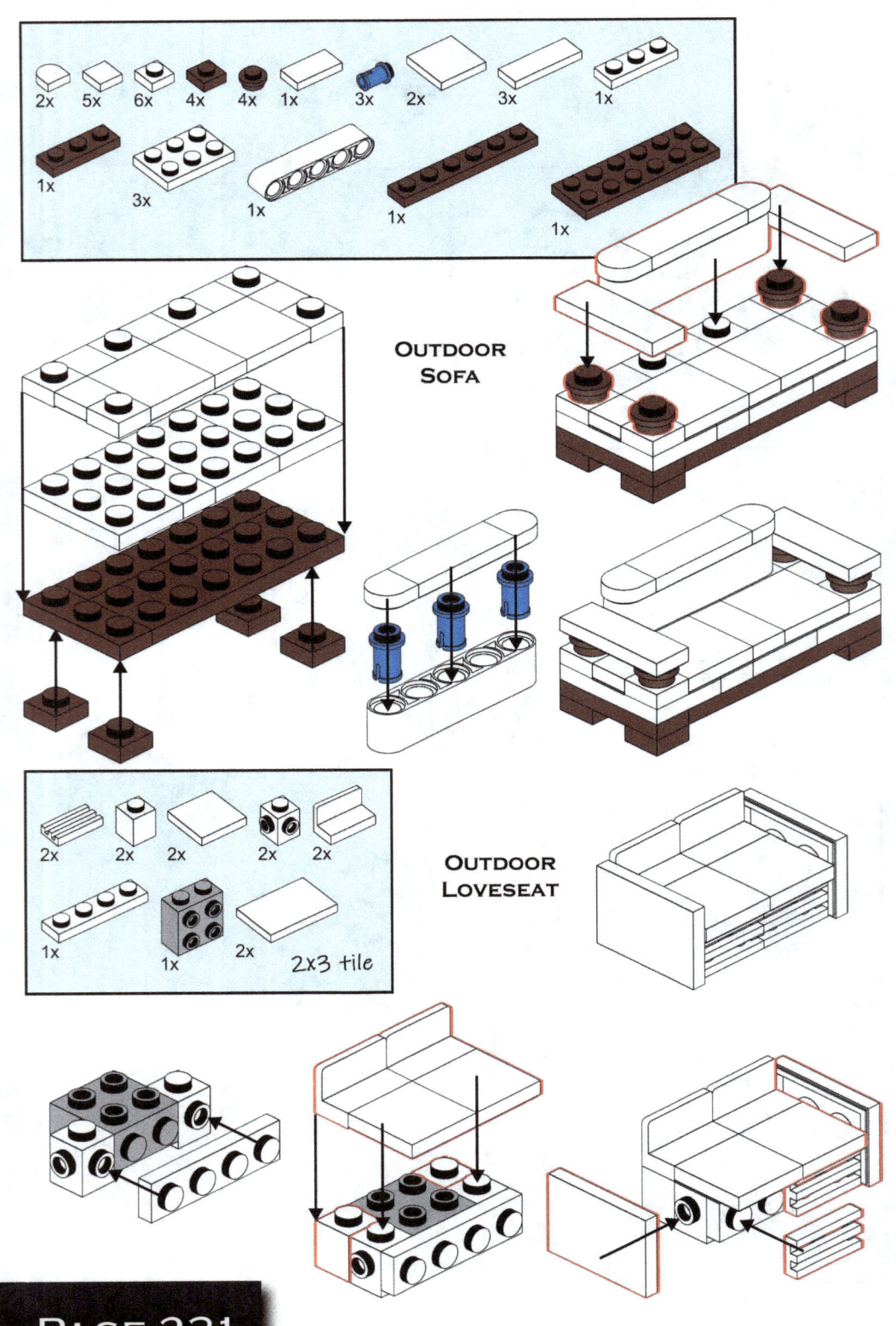

OUTDOOR
SOFA

OUTDOOR
LOVESEAT

2x3 tile

THE BACKYARD

4L

5 links

2x

PORCH SWING
WITH STAND

Seat bottom

Seat back

Part#
92690

THE BACKYARD

PAGE 232

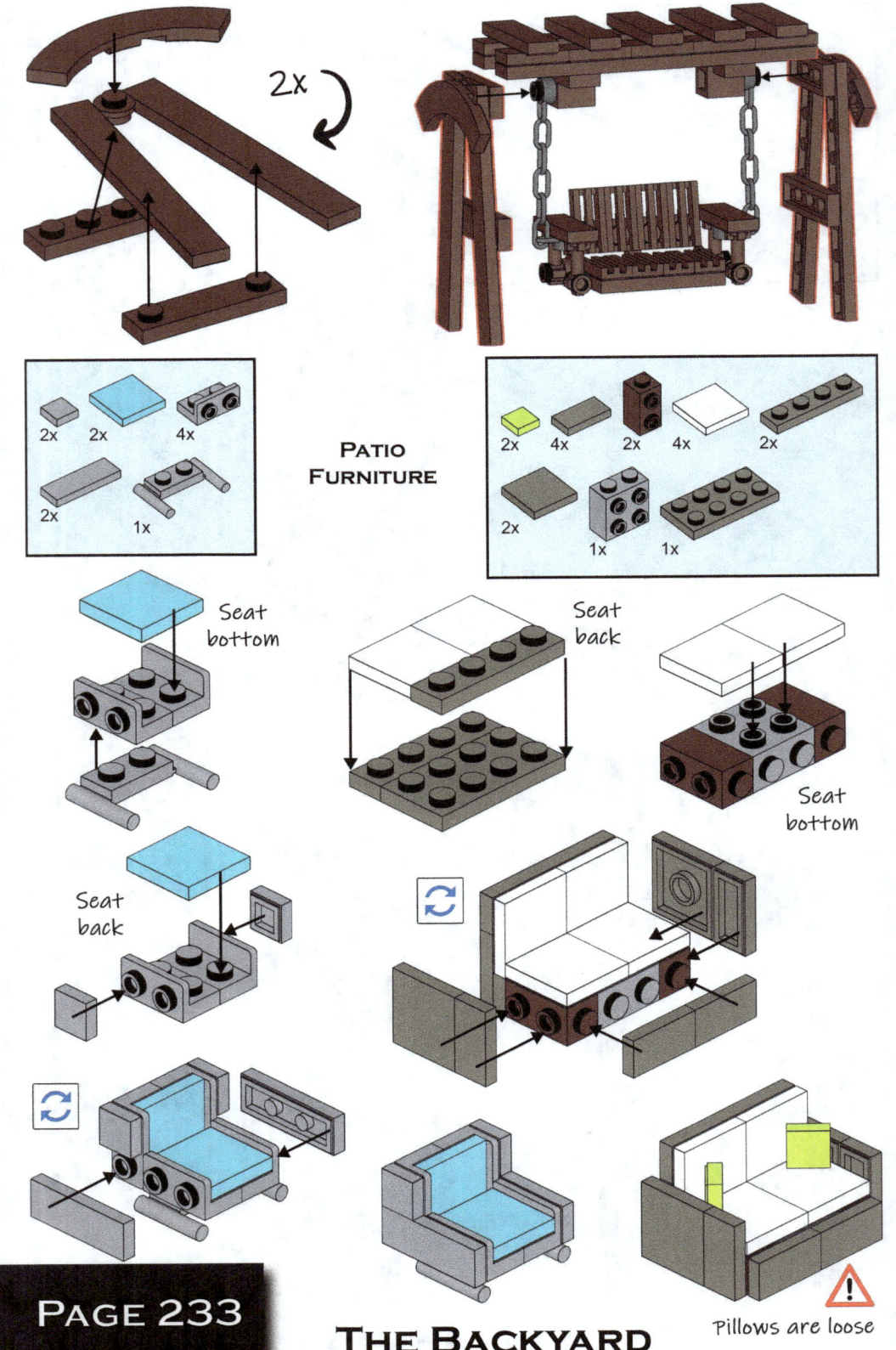

2x

PATIO
FURNITURE

2x 2x 4x

2x 1x

2x 4x 2x 4x 2x

2x 1x 1x

Seat
bottom

Seat
back

Seat
back

Seat
bottom

Seat
back

Pillows are loose

THE BACKYARD

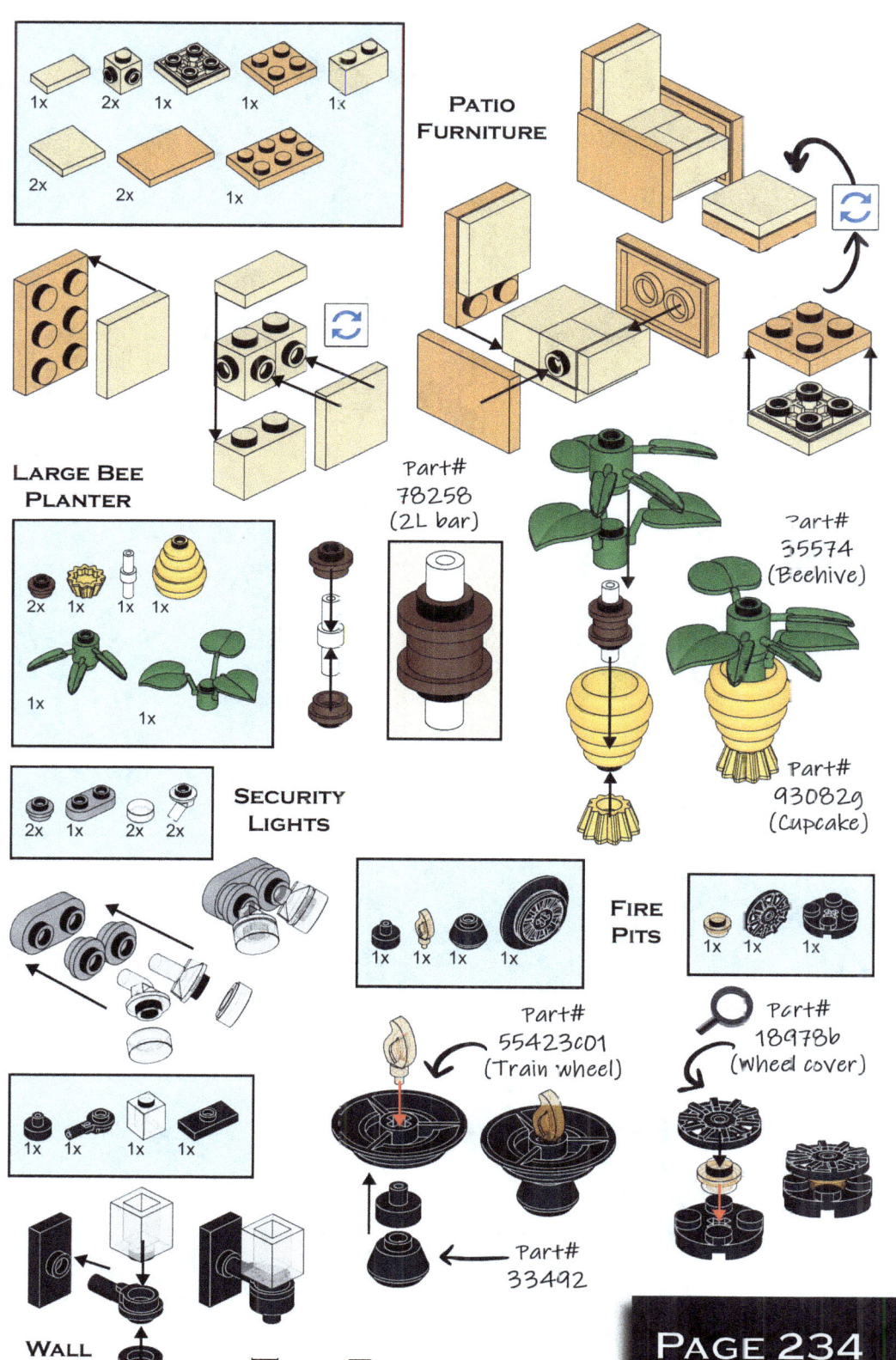

PATIO FURNITURE

1x 2x 1x 1x 1x
2x 2x 1x

LARGE BEE PLANTER

2x 1x 1x 1x
1x 1x

Part# 78258 (2L bar)

Part# 35574 (Beehive)

Part# 93082g (Cupcake)

SECURITY LIGHTS

2x 1x 2x 2x

FIRE PITS

1x 1x 1x

1x 1x 1x 1x

Part# 55423c01 (Train wheel)

Part# 18978b (Wheel cover)

1x 1x 1x 1x

Part# 33492

WALL SCONCE

THE BACKYARD

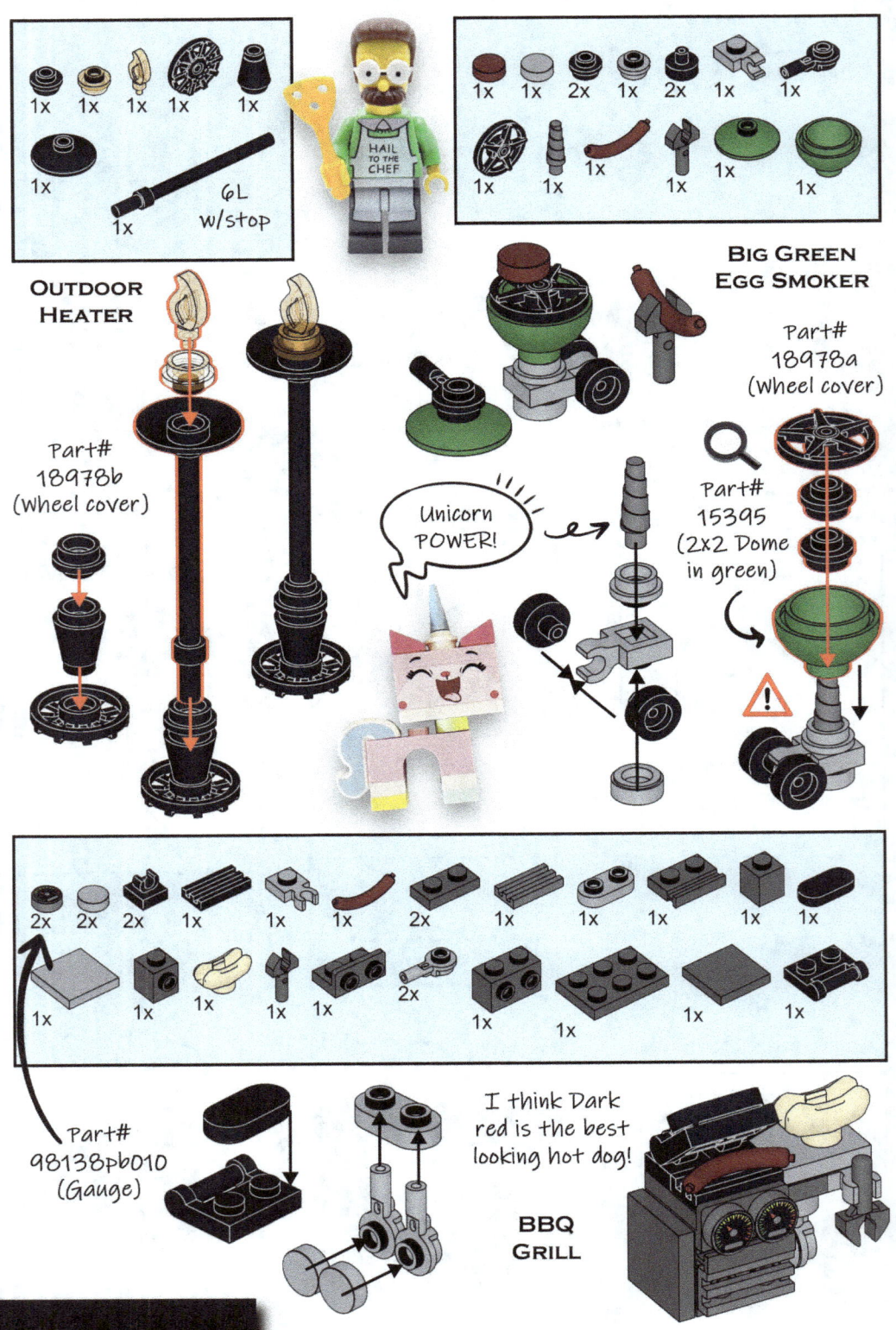

OUTDOOR HEATER

Part#
18978b
(wheel cover)

BIG GREEN EGG SMOKER

Part#
18978a
(wheel cover)

Part#
15395
(2x2 Dome
in green)

HAIL TO THE CHEF

Unicorn POWER!

6L w/stop

Part#
98138pb010
(Gauge)

I think Dark red is the best looking hot dog!

BBQ GRILL

THE BACKYARD

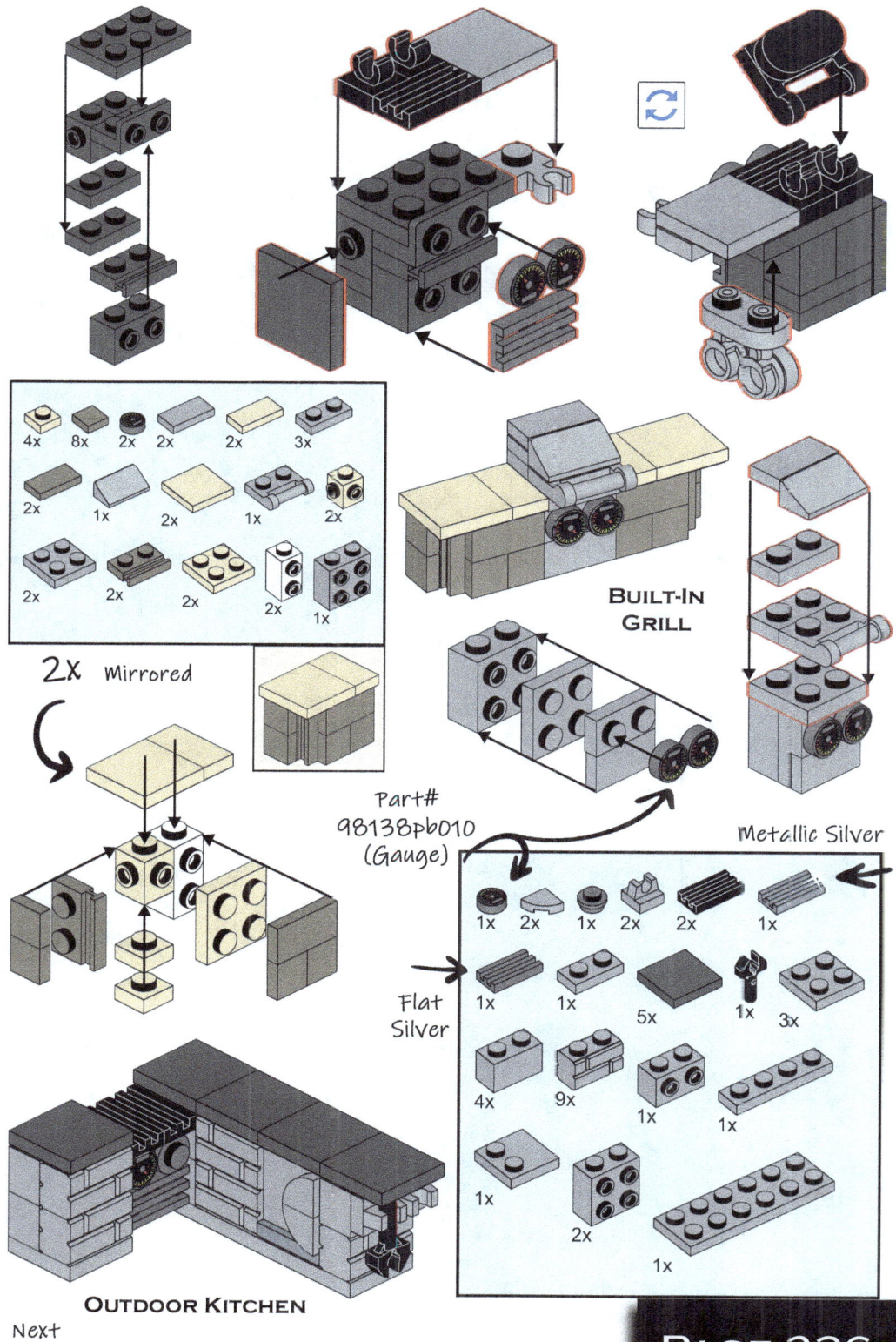

BUILT-IN GRILL

2x Mirrored

Part# 98138pb010 (Gauge)

Metallic Silver

Flat Silver

OUTDOOR KITCHEN

Next Page →

THE BACKYARD

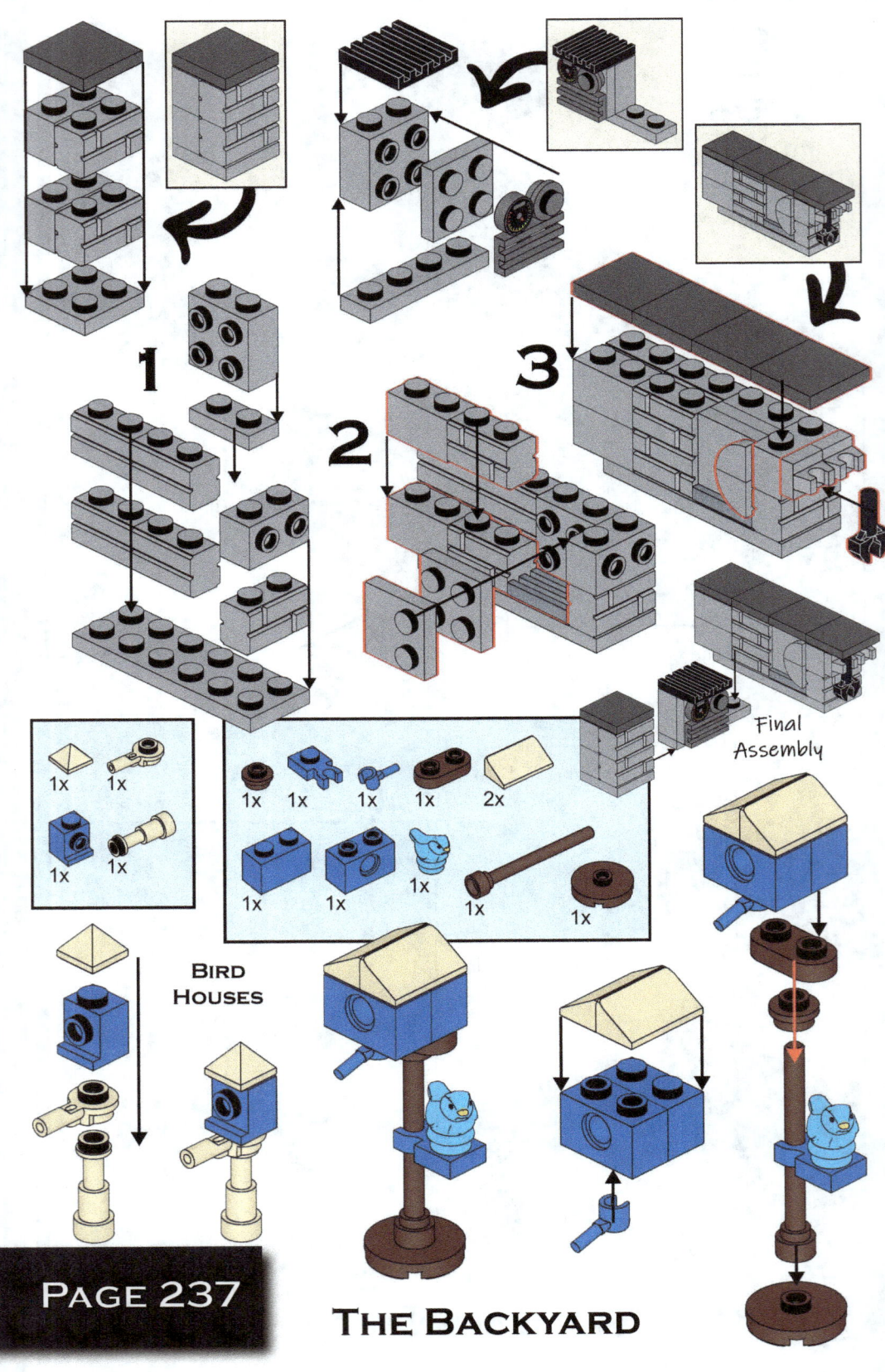

1

2

3

1x 1x

1x 1x

1x 1x 1x 1x 2x

1x 1x 1x 1x 1x

Final
Assembly

BIRD
HOUSES

THE BACKYARD

Parts list

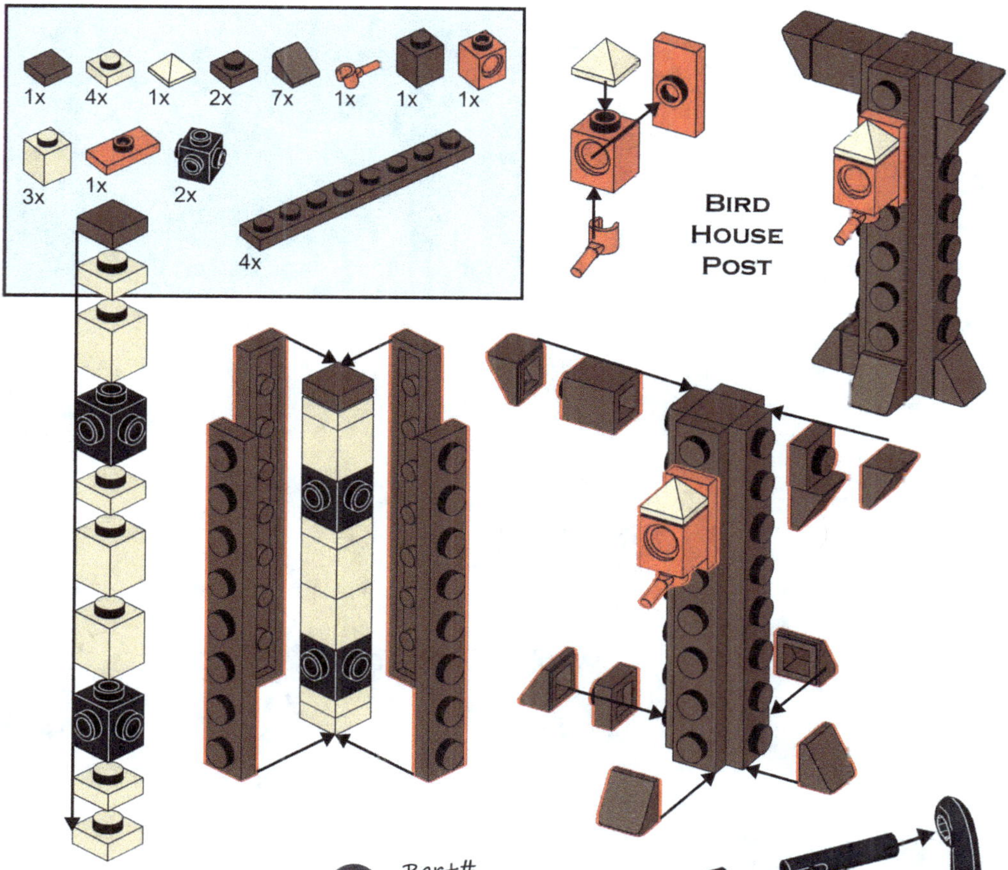

1x	4x	1x	2x	7x	1x	1x	1x

3x	1x	2x

4x

BIRD HOUSE POST

BIRD FEEDER I

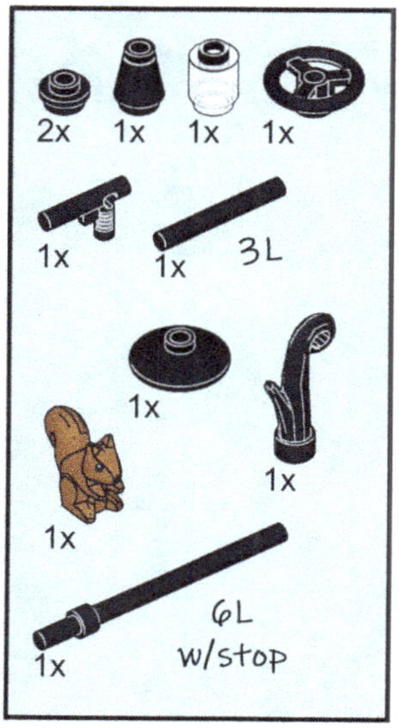

2x	1x	1x	1x

1x	1x 3L

1x

1x

1x

1x 6L w/stop

Part# 15279 (Plant stem in black)

Part# 30663 (Steering wheel)

Part# 80679pb01

THE BACKYARD

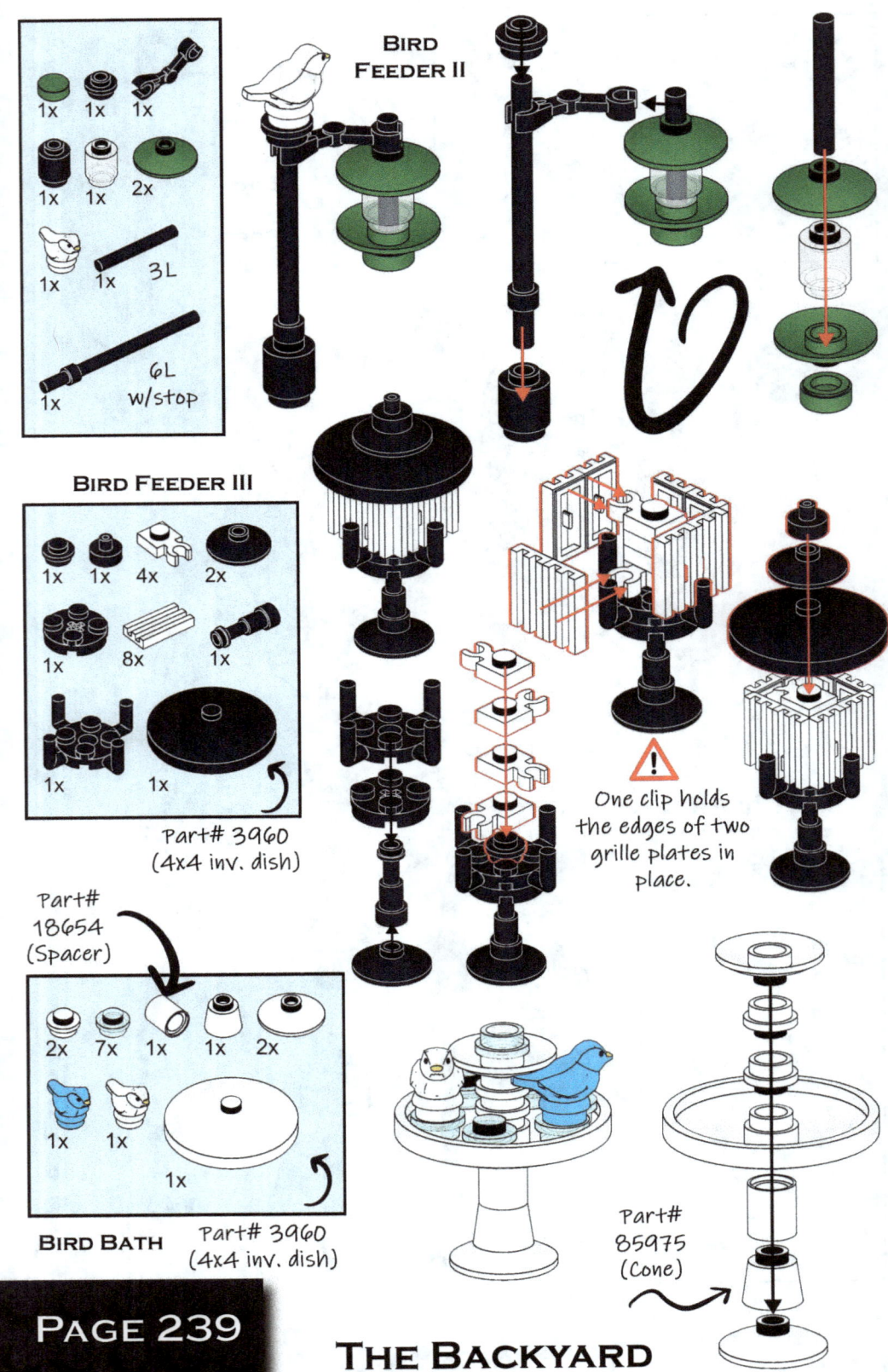

BIRD FEEDER II

1x 1x 1x
1x 1x 2x
1x 1x 3L
1x 6L w/stop

BIRD FEEDER III

1x 1x 4x 2x
1x 8x 1x
1x 1x

Part# 3960
(4x4 inv. dish)

Part# 18654 (Spacer)

⚠ One clip holds the edges of two grille plates in place.

2x 7x 1x 1x 2x
1x 1x 1x

BIRD BATH Part# 3960
(4x4 inv. dish)

Part# 85975 (Cone)

THE BACKYARD

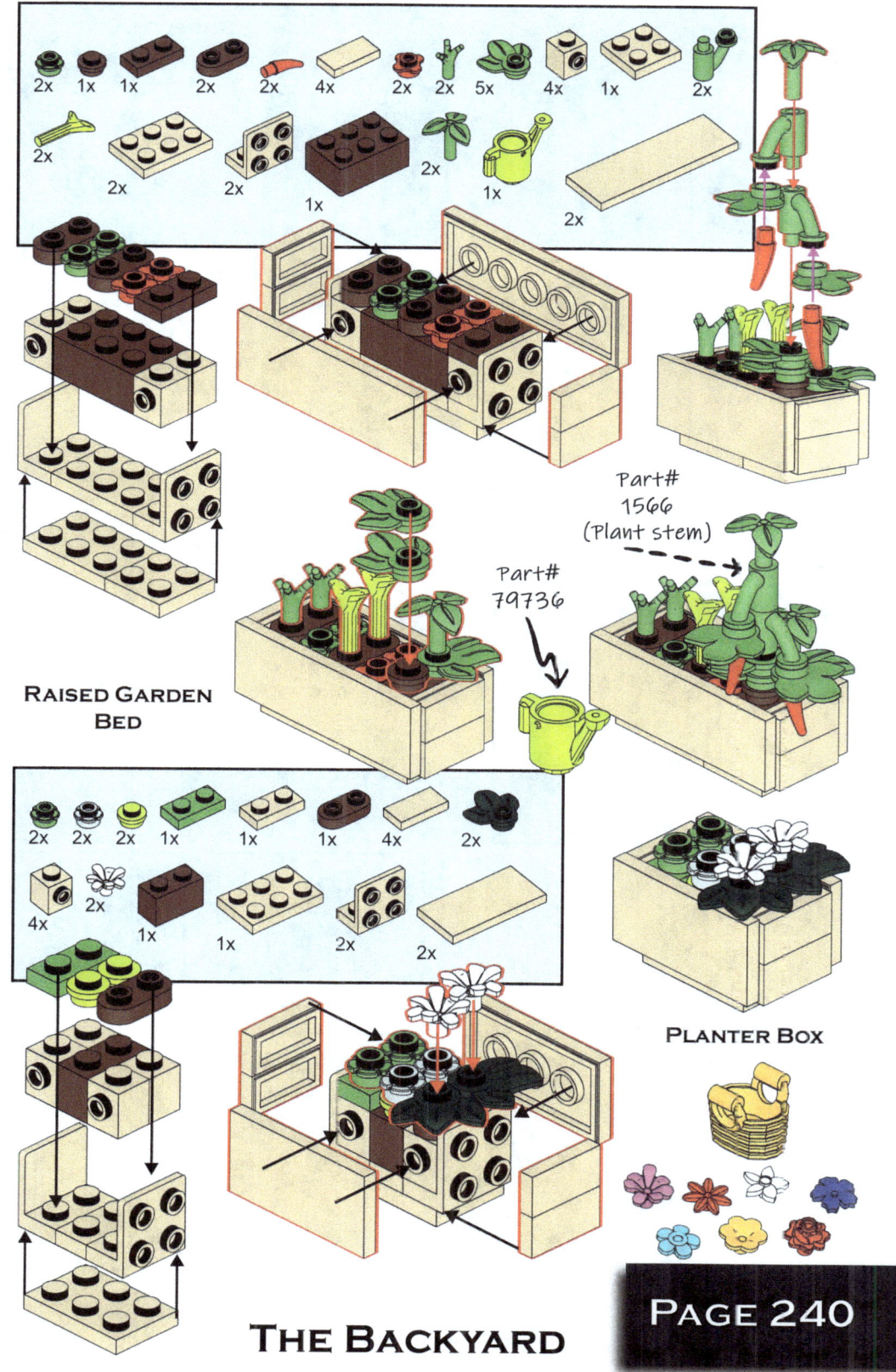

RAISED GARDEN BED

Part#
1566
(Plant stem)

Part#
79736

PLANTER BOX

THE BACKYARD

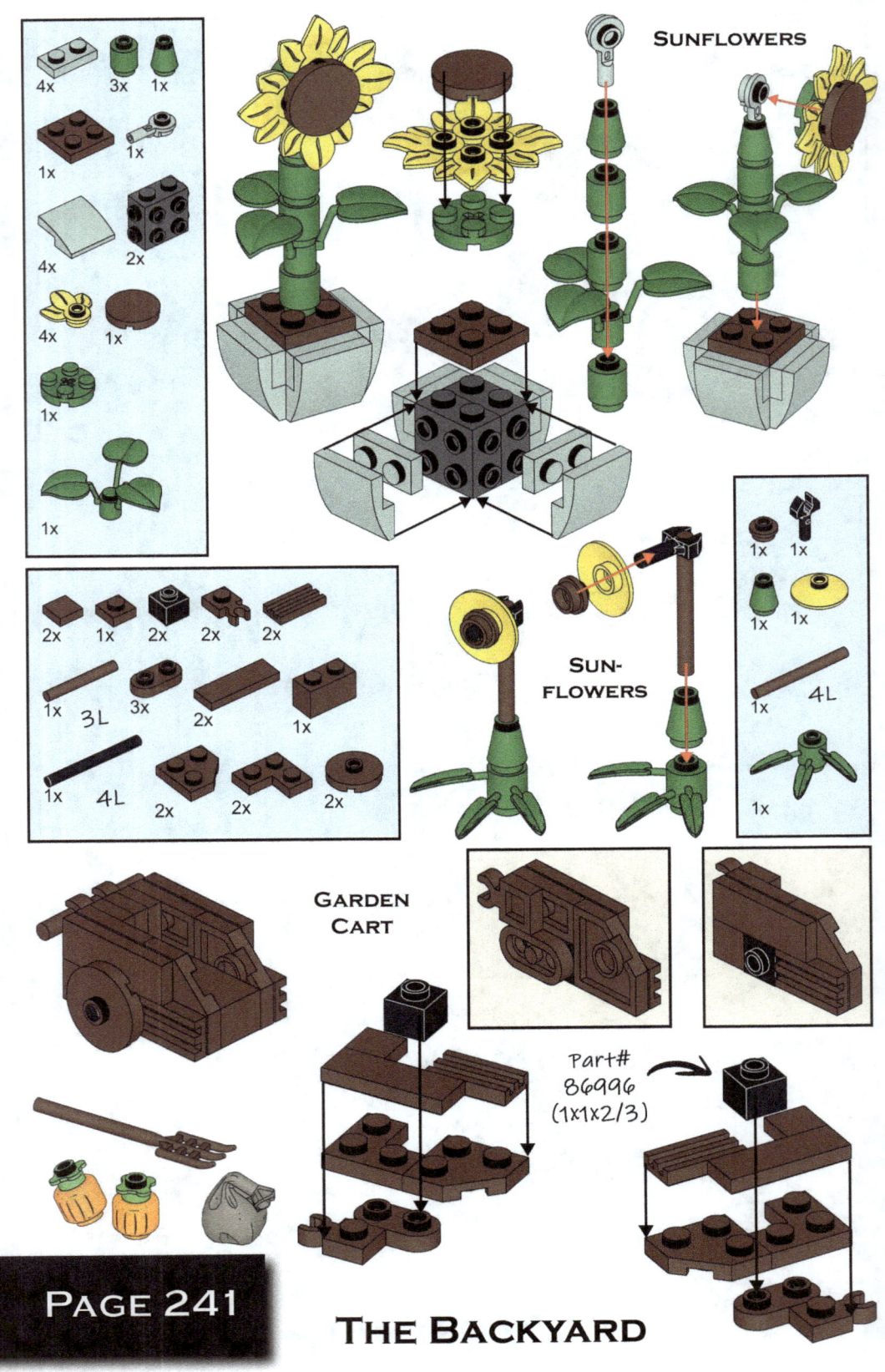

SUNFLOWERS

SUN-
FLOWERS

GARDEN
CART

Part#
86996
(1x1x2/3)

THE BACKYARD

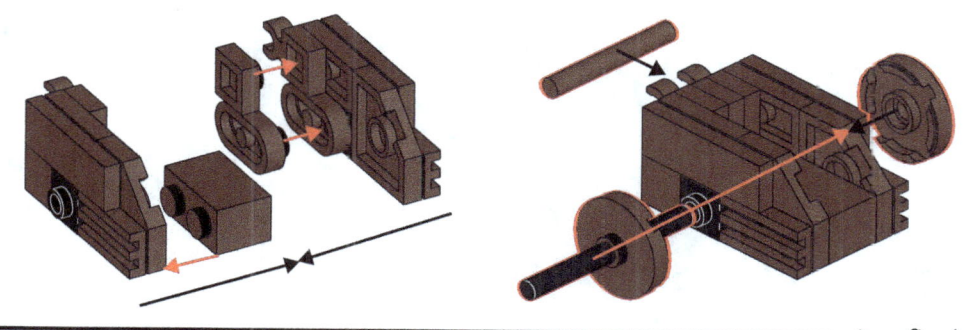

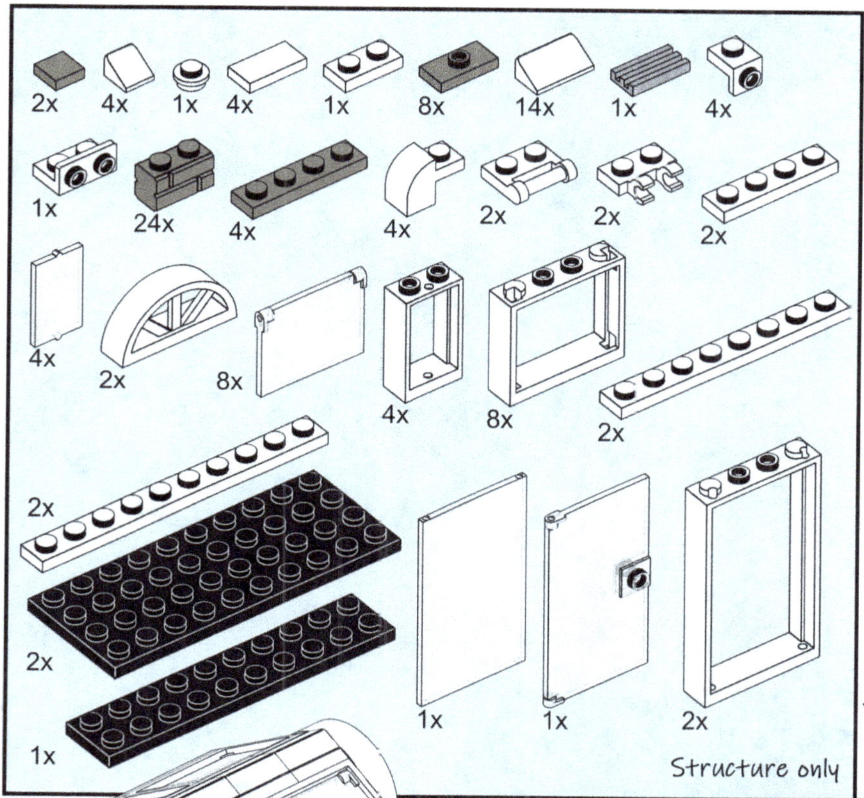

Our final build is an open, airy greenhouse.

This is the largest model in the book, but it's still very basic.

Choose to follow the parts list below or use your imagination to add plants, flowers, or veggies and make it your own!

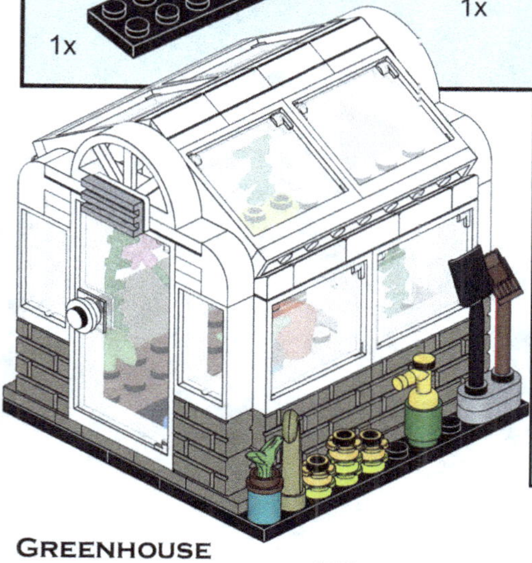

2x   4x   1x   4x   1x   8x   14x   1x   4x

1x   24x   4x   4x   2x   2x   2x

4x   2x   8x   4x   8x   2x

2x

2x

1x

1x   1x   2x

Structure only

8x   3x   5x   1x   2x   1x   1x   2x   1x   2x

3x   1x   1x   2x   2≡

1x   1x   1x   1x   3x

Decoration

GREENHOUSE

THE BACKYARD

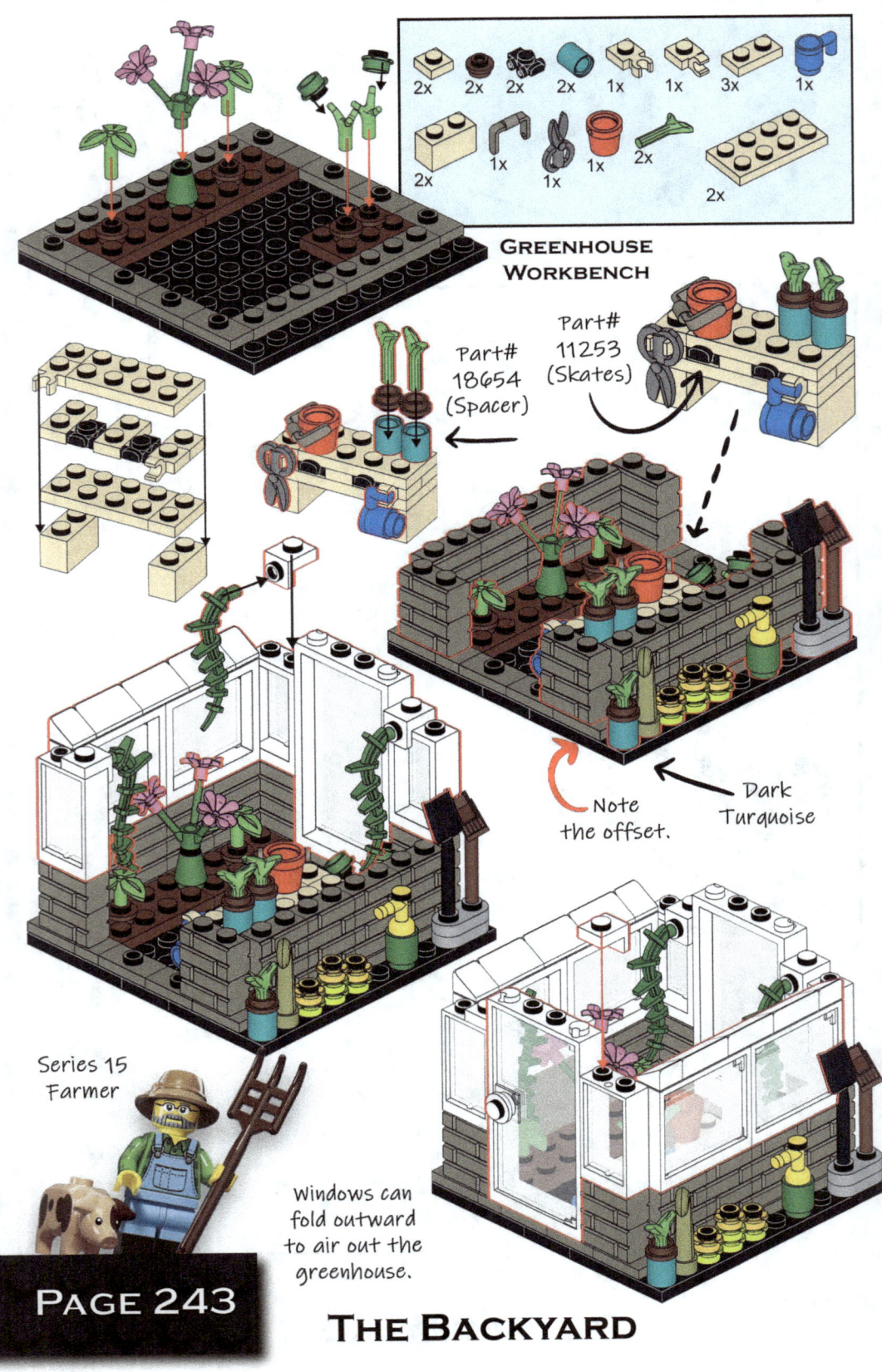

GREENHOUSE
WORKBENCH

Part#
18654
(Spacer)

Part#
11253
(Skates)

Note
the offset.

Dark
Turquoise

Series 15
Farmer

Windows can
fold outward
to air out the
greenhouse.

THE BACKYARD

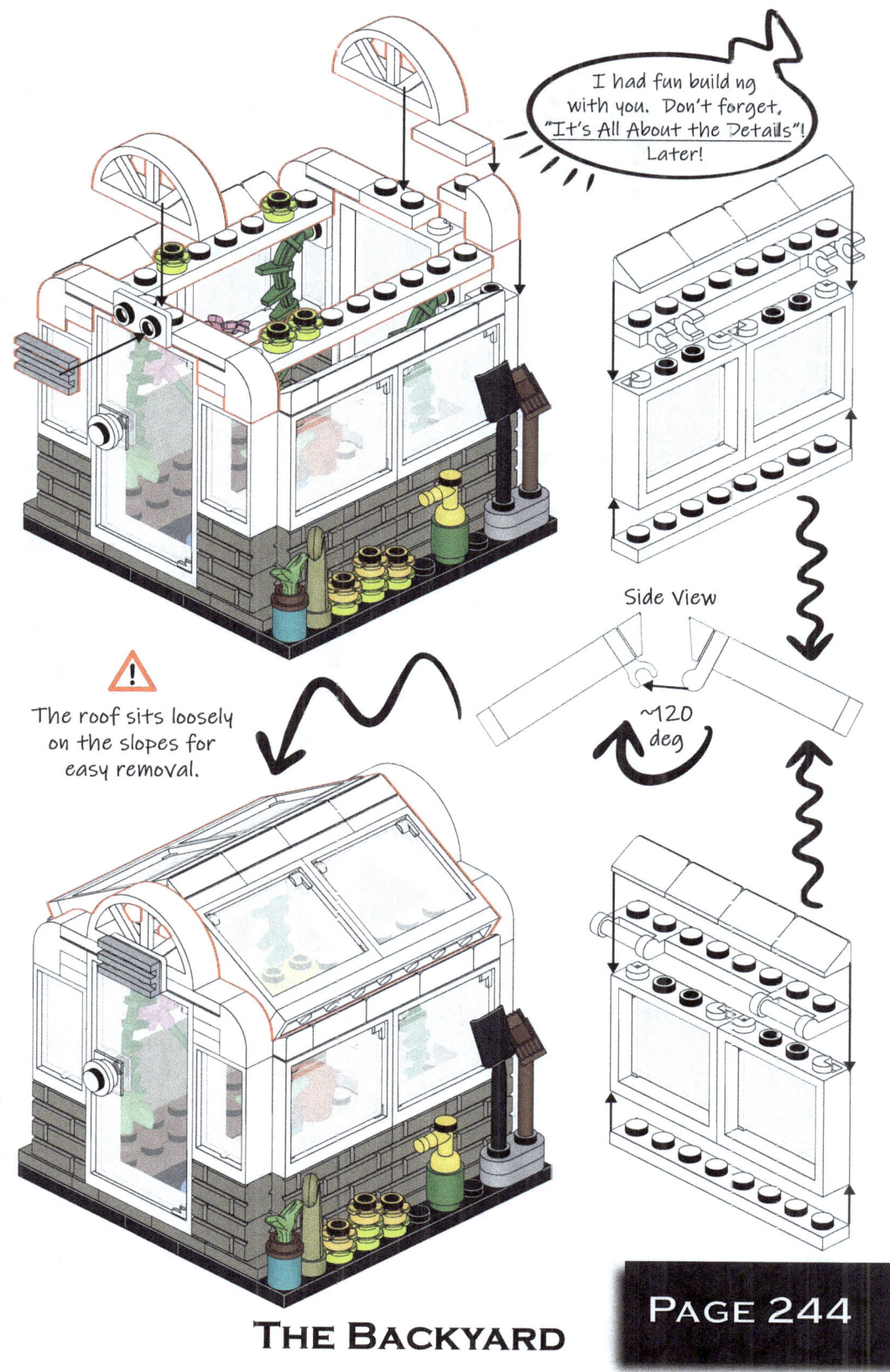

THE BACKYARD

ABOUT THE AUTHOR

Chris Schroeder

Chris is a part-time engineer and a full-time nerd! A graduate of Purdue University in Indiana, Chris has been a coder, project manager, and IT professional for over 20 years. He has also had a knack for entrepreneurship with successful DJ and eBay businesses. Chris, a true-to-heart maker and craftsman, loves creating, fixing, and tinkering with things. He has always shared a passion with good design and attention to detail.

Chris awoke from "the dark ages" in 2019 and like so many other creators following the pandemic, he started a YouTube channel which now sits neglected! After completing his MBA last year, he aimed for a new milestone - authorship and publishing. His favorite AFOL themes are City, Modulars, and Ideas. He's a little over 40, a little overweight, and has a little less hair every year on his head, but that comes with the "Dad" territory! Chris loves to work on projects, keep his mind active, and stay busy creating. He loves humor, music, and pop culture, but most of all, LEGO® and it's endless potential for artistic and self-expression!

If you're bored!

youtube.com/@Lets-Go-LEGO

About the Designers

Jesse, known online as @brickdesigned, is an AFOL from Atlanta, GA, with a lifelong passion for LEGO® and a keen eye for small details. He loves to build intricate minifigure-scale furniture, and draws inspiration from everyday objects. His favorite part of the building process is getting to experiment with different LEGO® elements and doesn't shy away from unconventional building techniques. Through sharing his creative builds, Jesse hopes to inspire fellow brick enthusiasts to see the potential in every brick. Check out www.brickdesigned.com

In 2014, Peter started making small models, which sold as fast as he could make them. The popularity of his designs made him wonder if he could scale-up and create a business. At One More Brick, they now design and sell hundreds of models, try to keep prices as low as possible, and make sure all models are strong designs with easy to use instructions. "The humble LEGO® brick has helped us through tough times and we hope it helps you too. Whatever you build, there's always room for one more brick." Check them out at www.onemorebrick.com

Coming Soon

All About the Details:
Around Town

This grueling book took over a year to create, but I am already excited about the next one. I still have plenty of designs and ideas to elevate the detail in your Modulars, Town buildings, or City themes.

The next book will expand into these areas with back alleys, fences, fire hydrants, street signs, lamps, clocks, traffic, and train crossings. City services like ATMs, bus stops, newspaper and post stands, public facilities, trash bins, rooftops, and fire escapes. Park benches, bike racks, scooters, charging stations, bushes, flower planters, trees, and fountains. What about other detailed mini-builds inside town buildings like the library, a school, the gym, an office or warehouse setting, movie theatre, arcade, the salon, hospital, baby stuff, and the pet store!

If you enjoyed this book, those ideas just excited you, and you want to see another one made, please consider supporting me with the following link:

paypal.me/LEGOSchroeder

www.ingramcontent.com/pod-product-compliance
Lightning Source LLC
Chambersburg PA
CBHW071720120626
46550CB00001B/311

* 9 7 9 8 9 9 2 7 2 3 5 0 2 *